Wrestling with God in Context

M. P. JOSEPH, PO HO HUANG, AND VICTOR HSU

FORTRESS PRESS
MINNEAPOLIS

WRESTLING WITH GOD IN CONTEXT
Revisiting the Theology and Social Vision of Shoki Coe

Copyright © 2018 Fortress Press, an imprint of 1517 Media. All rights reserved. Except for brief quotations in critical articles or reviews, no part of this book may be reproduced in any manner without prior written permission from the publisher. Email copyright@1517.media or write to Permissions, Fortress Press, PO Box 1209, Minneapolis, MN 55440-1209.

Cover image: Illustration of Shoki Coe reproduced by permission
Cover design: Laurie Ingram

Print ISBN: 978-1-5064-4580-9
eBook ISBN: 978-1-5064-4581-6

The paper used in this publication meets the minimum requirements of American National Standard for Information Sciences — Permanence of Paper for Printed Library Materials, ANSI Z329.48-1984.

Manufactured in the U.S.A.

Contents

Part VIII. Prophet from the Fourth World: Life and Legacy of Shoki Coe

Foreword

Council for World Mission believes that "churches are called to prophetic witness, to proclaim and live out the vision of Jesus Christ of fullness of life for all creation." It envisages "a different world, a world inspired by the values of love, justice, peace and compassion." A prophetic vision for a different world is what makes the church a true embodiment of love and peace. In the history of Christian faith, there have been many prophetic voices and witnesses that lived such a radical vision. However, many such voices and witnesses, particularly from the southern hemisphere, have been marginalized because of their political and geographical location. CWM is committed to remember and relive such voices. Through a series of volumes titled "Prophets from the South," it aims to give witness to prophetic voices from the Global South. This volume is a tribute to the radical and prophetic life and legacy of Shoki Coe. Coe is one of the great theologians of the twentieth century who led the way in calling for and constructing contextual theologies and mission that addressed such colonized contexts as his own beloved Taiwan.

M. P. Joseph, in his profound introduction to this volume, identifies the following four major areas in which Shoki Coe's contributions are significant: 1. Theologizing in the context of colonization; 2. Redefining Christian mission; 3. Political dimension of faith; 4. Contextualization as theological and missional methodology. Being a Taiwanese, born under the Japanese Empire, Coe experienced and encountered colonial power and aggression throughout his life. Taiwan's colonization, by the Japanese and then the Chinese, was the immediate context in which he had to define and redefine his faith. His profound and prophetic vision for a theology that is liberated from the captivity of empire challenges us even today as we remain captives to the "empire" of global forces that pool their economic, military, political, religious, and cultural powers in frightening ways. In such a context where the empire has colonized, dominated, and subjugated the weak and the vulnerable, Coe challenges the church to be daring in its prophetic witness, to be valiant in its commitment to justice, to be resolute in its quest to confront power, and to be nonconformist and deviant in the witness of its faith. In other words, contextualization is a process of reclaiming the subjectivity of the marginalized. While empire seeks to rob people of the dignity of their context and identity, Coe's powerful assertion of context as the primary locus for constructing theology and doing mission immediately makes it liberative and counterimperial. CWM recognizes this is an urgent struggle in all our contexts, and especially in Coe's home, Taiwan, which still wrestles to be free of empire. I am sure, for example, that Coe would be excited by the work of the indigenous people of the Presbyterian Church of Taiwan, who are constructing a contextual theology and mission that reflects their struggle with empire as well as PCT's commitment to the journey of justice and peace within Taiwan and the wider South East Asia context.

Coe, like all prophets, made discernment of signs of the times key to this way of doing theology. Contextualizing theology and discerning signs of the times is not about making church more culturally "relevant" but more prophetically resistant. This equips the church to come together in order to be more radical and vibrant. The mission of the church is to come together in engaging radically with the burning concerns of our context today. This is music to the ears of CWM. We assert that we are "called to partnership in Christ to mutually challenge, encourage and equip churches to share in God's mission." Contextualization as a theological methodology thus enables us to witness our faith as a radical movement of resistance to all kinds of dominance, subjugation, and violence. Identifying Christ in the midst of people's struggle thus becomes an imperative for the mission of the church for a dynamic participation with the saving activity of God in history. It also requires a political engagement with the context. This political engagement enables the church to be a movement of justice, peace, love, and compassion. It is a prophetic missionary practice that transforms unjust structures and embodies the love of God.

We place Shoki Coe within the profound history of the prophets, who interrogate the present context through their radical envisioning of the future. His writing and his witness remind us of the true direction from which God's transformation comes. It comes as a new world from the "fourth world," from the marginalized, because first and foremost Jesus's gospel is a gospel of the poor declared from the poor. Coe's embracement of the fourth world reality for doing theology and mission is a political statement that points out to a global political order that it is being overturned by the political identities of marginalized people and locations such as the Taiwanese and Taiwan. The relocation of Coe's geographical and political being as fourth world is thus a profoundly nonconformist affirmation. His prophetic interlocutions and interrogations from the "fourth" location should challenge the very perspective and rationale that the world is mapped by. Therefore, this volume is not only a tribute to such a daring prophetic voice, but also an invitation into the radical reversal of an unjust imperial global political order.

Rev. Dr. Collin Cowan
General Secretary, CWM

Acknowledgments

Prophets, as observed by Abraham Joshua Heschel, are people who speak of the future in the present tense. They refuse to conform to the prevailing order; instead, they use the vision of the future to demand a radical change in the present. They speak because they are compelled by an inexplicable force that is taken to be the summons of God.

The prophetic tradition is not a story of the past. Throughout history, prophets have raised powerful dissent informed by an ethical imperative that speaks of an "ought to be." As prophets spoke concretely in a particular time, place, and circumstance through a critical comprehension informed by an unwavering hope in the future, the recognition and validity of their pronouncements as universal truths is not of much significance.

This book is in honor of a modern-day prophet, Shoki Coe (1914–1988), who rebuked the political social order with pain to ensure subjecthood and the right to self-determination for all the marginalized. Coe's contributions to and impact on the current theological discourse span many areas, including the genres of missiology, ecclesiology, theological education, and global human rights. Particularly, the name Shoki Coe resonates with the new paradigm in theology, termed contextualization. Coe converted the term "contextualization" along with a corresponding methodology for doing theology as a conceptual space for marginalized communities around the world. The result was the overflowing of various theological articulations by communities that were historically denied their right to speak.

This book is published in the series titled "Prophets from the South" sponsored by the Council for World Mission.

This book would not have been completed without the efforts and contributions of several individuals and movements. We are immensely honored and grateful to all who have dedicated their time and research toward this volume. We extend our profound gratitude to Dr. Sudipta Singh, secretary for research, Council for World Mission. Without his untiring and constructive engagement, this book would not have come to fruition. We are also deeply indebted to Dr. Collin Cowan, general secretary of CWM, for selecting this project for the CWM series, for his encouragement, and for his gracious offer to write a fitting Foreword to this volume.

We are also grateful to Mr. Samuel Abraham for his professional and passionate assistance in preparing the manuscript. It is significant to note that the articles in this volume are by authors from diverse cultural and linguistic backgrounds, with specificity in their nuances and thought forms. Samuel's work ensured the coherent style of this volume.

We extend our gratitude to Will Bergkamp, Dr. Jesudas Athyal, and the team of editors at Fortress Press for their encouragement, invaluable guidance, and support in bringing out this volume for wider discussion.

We also thank all the eminent authors from around the globe. Their enthusiasm and support were overwhelming. A special thank you to all the authors in this volume.

The production of this volume is a public expression of our commitment and determination to journey with the poor and marginalized in their struggle for subjective right to construct new theological discourses as a response to their encounter with the living reality of God. At the same time, it is also a call to assume the legacy of a prophetic tradition, to remain restless for peace, equality, and justice, and gain courage to speak the truth.

Introduction:
Context, Discernment, and Contextualization: Theology of Shoki Coe, the Prophet from the Fourth World

M. P. JOSEPH

Prof. Dr. Shoki Coe is acknowledged globally as a great theological craftsman who supported the liberation of theological articulation from its Western doctrinal captivity. In doing so, he not only reinforced the subjectivity of the people in theological discourse but also broke the propositional boundaries used to understand the revelation of God in human history. Perhaps that stands out as his distinctive contribution. Kosuke Koyama, in his tribute to Coe, has acknowledged Coe as his spiritual father.[1] It is necessary to recall that not just Koyama but thousands of theological students and church members around the world consider Coe a guru and prophet, one who goaded them into a theological journey to find the living reality of God.

With an aim to give witness to prophetic voices from the southern hemisphere, the Council for World Mission (CWM) has been bringing out a series of volumes titled "Prophets from the South," and the current volume is the third in that series. Articles in this volume are a tribute to the life and legacy of Shoki Coe. It is often acknowledged that the use of the term "contextualization" in theological education today is Coe's contribution, even though the term has been employed with different functional meanings.[2] By giving a new perspective to the term

---

1. Kosuke Koyama, "Christ's Homelessness," *The Christian Century*, July 14–21, 1993, p. 703.

2. In 1957 the Rockefeller Foundation established a fund to promote "Contextualizing Gospel," and perhaps this was the first coinage of the term "contextualization." However, the practice of contextualizing has a long history. The development of African independent churches in the late 1800s and the "Rethinking" group in 1877 are certain early initiatives that captured the meaning of contextualization. At present, the term "contextualization" owes its

"contextualization" in theological discourse, Coe offered a new methodological structure for doing theology. Contextualizing theology, as he
emphasized, is an incarnational necessity that takes the word of God, its
practice, and the context seriously. Central to the method of contextualization is the conviction that theology is a response to the self-disclosing
initiative of the living God. That means theology is not a reiteration of
past formulas or doctrines, but a radical attempt to respond to the living
incarnation of the Divine.

Among the various contributions of Coe, four specific involvements—in theological education, redefining mission and ecumenism,
reimagining the church, and contextualization of theology—have been
hailed globally. To correspond to his life and contributions, the articles
in this volume will focus on:

(a) A brief account of the life and legacy of Shoki Coe;

(b) A critical evaluation of contextual theologies, their methodology,
engagement with the text, challenges of contextual theology for theological education, and the new epistemological assumptions proposed by
contextual methodologies;

(c) Redefining of the practice of ecumenism, ecclesiology, and mission
as proposed by Coe. The search for broadening the practice of ecumenism remains a vital concern in the present context;

(d) Evaluation of the political thought of Coe, who through various
means reiterated the need and urgency for the political witness of faith.
The articles in this section delineate the theological discourses pertaining
to the concept of self-determination for which Coe offered passionate
leadership; and

(e) Development of contextual theologies in different contexts around
the world, responding to the challenges proposed by Coe. Articles
within this section critically examine the development of theology
among the subalterns, blacks, Dalits, women, indigenous, and other
marginalized communities.

RIGHT OF THE COLONIZED FOR
THEOLOGICAL ARTICULATION

One of the profound contributions of Coe to the global theological
world was his unrelenting effort to promote the creation and develop-

origin to Shoki Coe, who was the director of the Theological Education Fund (TEF), and
Aharon Sapsezian, its associate director. To explain the policy of the Third Mandate (1970–77)
of the TEF, two pamphlets titled *Ministry in Context* and *Learning in Context* were published,
which became the reference for contextualizing theology.

ment of theological education centers in previously colonized lands. As director of the Theological Education Fund (TEF) of the World Council of Churches (WCC), Coe accepted this task as a primary vocation. His experience in rebuilding the Tainan Theological College and Seminary, Taiwan, from ruins prepared him to assist theological communities around the globe, especially in the third world, to build centers that focus on theologies relevant to and informed by the struggles of the people for their respective life contexts. By doing so, Coe and the TEF strived to offer subjecthood to the people in the third world for theological construction.

Colonized communities were mere consumers or recipients of a faith and theology of the colonizers. In the majority of cases, people were made to believe in a theology that was constructed to satisfy the political and economic ambitions of the colonizers. A colonial Christ delegitimized the god concept of the colonized lot. The God experience for local people became an alienating experience, and besides, they were made to worship a god who appeared to rationalize the victimization of the colonized people.

The subjective right of the colonized to articulate their encounters with God was not often welcomed in the theological debates of the missionary era. People's enquiry of God was not considered as anything of value. The contribution of Coe and the TEF was to negate this prevailing assumption and to encourage people in Asia, Africa, and Latin America to engage seriously with the process of articulating their encounters with the living reality of God. From being consumers of an alien product, people were guided to be creators of their own theology and urged to be always in a state of pilgrimage in search of the meaning of faith.

REDEFINITION OF MISSION

The second contribution for which Coe is remembered is his effort to redefine mission and its practice. Since the late eighteenth century, Asian Christians have expressed their reservations about the truncated concept of mission propagated and practiced by mission agencies.

There were two major concerns. First was the patronage given by the colonial establishment to mission activities. Missionaries in general considered that colonialism was part of God's providence and as a result colonial domination helped extend Christianity around the world.[3] This

3. John R. Mott, the chairperson of the 1910 World Mission Conference, Edinburgh, made the implication more lucid: "The marvellous ordering of providence during this century assisted

feeling was expressed by Commission I of the World Missionary Conference, which met at Edinburgh in 1910. The report reads:

> One of the most significant and hopeful facts with reference to world evangelization is that the vast majority of the people of the non-Christian nations and races are under the sway, either of Christian governments or of those not antagonistic to Christian missions. This should greatly facilitate the carrying out of a comprehensive campaign to make Christ known.[4]

This view proposes a deceptive understanding that God in history at times depends upon and thus offers legitimacy to the unjust political structures of domination in order to express the gift of compassion to humanity.

A wider understanding of God's revelation as contemplated by Asian theologians was the second issue of contention within the colonial missionary movement. Asian theologians maintained the view that the knowledge of God was utterly determined by the self-disclosure of God. However, this gift of revelation through self-disclosure cannot be exhausted in one cultural tradition or in one language. Besides, limiting God to one culture and one language negates the universality of the creator God. Kosuke Koyama expressed this concern through his imaginative language. He believed that there are more than 7,000 languages on this planet. If a god speaks 3,500 languages and reveals Godself in 3,500 cultural derivatives, such a god can be considered as a 50 percent god. On the contrary, if self-revelation is limited to one language and a singular cultural tradition, such a god is less than 1 percent god.[5]

Koyama's statement was only a reflection of the legacy of a long tradition that refused to accept the attempt to make the creator God a tribal construct of one language or cultural tradition. In the inaugural issue of the *International Review of Mission* (1912), Tasuku Harada of Japan observed that "it is inconceivable that anyone who has impartially studied the history of religions can fail to admit the universality of the activity of spirit of God and the consequent embodiment of a decree of faith in all religions."[6] Harada's was not a lone voice in the wilderness; this

the whole world to be open to the church." Quoted by Kenneth Scott Latourette, "Ecumenical Bearings of the Missionary Movement and the International Missionary Council," in *A History of the Ecumenical Movement: 1517–1948*, ed. Ruth Rouse and Stephen C. Neill (London: SPCK, 1967).

4. World Missionary Conference, 1910, report of Commission I, *Carrying the Gospel to All the Non-Christian World* (Edinburgh: Oliphant, Anderson & Ferrier), 6.

5. Kosuke Koyama, "How Many Languages Does God Speak?" *Cross Currents* 46, no. 2 (1996): 172.

6. *International Review of Mission* 1 (1912): 91.

view was shared by people from other nations. Christo Samaj of India, through a statement released in 1921, called upon the churches in Asia to accept the evidence of the diffused energy of the divine logos in Asian religion and philosophy. The same feeling was expressed by T. C. Chao of China as a response to the spread of neo-Barthianism in Asia after the Tambaram Mission Conference in 1938 (near Madras, India). T. C. Chao observed: "All nations with their various religions have seen God more or less clearly; although the forms in which their visions have been clothed are incomplete, insufficient and unsatisfactory. In them and in Jesus Christ, God has been revealing Himself (Herself) and the same self to (hu)mankind."[7]

Coe found his thoughts among the views of these Asian theologians who were aware that it was difficult to deny that the deep, inner stirrings of the human spirit present among the followers of Asian religions were in response to the creative activity of the Holy Spirit. They considered that the inability to believe and understand God's equal concern of redemption for people of all religions and cultures was only an expression of the blindness of the Christian mind.

Coe redefined the concept and practice of mission by incorporating the experience of people in Asia with God. He argued that wrestling with incarnational moments in specific time and place was the point of reference for the construction of mission priorities. Coe equally emphasized that the gift of incarnation was the gathering of a theological community, the ecclesia, which aimed at the total reconciliation of the creation with God and manifested the divine righteousness and love in a given context.

Mission discourse during this time was informed by the challenges of the emerging technological culture. It was often recognized that in the industrial culture, personhood was at stake. Production practices create an alienating and dehumanizing process where workers are counted along with the "soul-less" means of production. During working hours, a worker becomes a "thing" like any other tool used in production. She or he kills the personhood to convert herself or himself into a laborer, and this process leads to the alienation of a person from her or his own being. The nonpersonalization of the people of God needs to be a profound concern for mission, for the primary assertion of the biblical understanding is that personhood is central to God's being. God engages in covenantal relationship with persons. The Gospel of Mark describes the process of the [nameless, identity-less] crowd turning into people so

7. International Missionary Council Meeting at Tambaram, Madras, *The Authority of Faith*, vol. 1, 40.

as to be called children of God. Denial of personhood is against God's plan to reconcile with the entire creation. Mission, therefore, needs to address the central question of alienation of the person from their being, a process enforced by the capitalist industrial culture. This issue became a major concern in the 1970s when Coe was heading the mission debates.

FAITH NEEDS POLITICAL WITNESS

A relentless appeal to have a political witness for faith is Coe's third contribution to the theological world. Faith without political witness is a lifeless faith. The political struggle for justice, freedom, and self-determination is at the core of mission practice. If God is a God of justice, participating in the struggles to construct a just society is the only way to witness faith in God. In his *Recollections and Reflections*, Coe wrote, "I am politically involved because I am a Taiwanese" and "I am politically involved because I am a Christian." Taiwanese is the context "into which I was born, and in which I was brought up, and which has been and still is very determinative to my whole existence."[8]

He named Taiwan, his beloved nation, as the "fourth world." This was a political statement. The term "third world" was used to identify and delineate the history of brutal colonialism, plunder, and the destruction of human possibilities to lead a dignified life. Coe went further in coining the term "fourth world," in which the right of peoplehood was denied to the inhabitants of a region. The struggle for self-determination was to claim the subjective right of peoplehood. Coe converted this struggle into a theological issue. His theology marveled at the integration of the text and the context; at gospelizing the context and contextualizing the gospel. For Coe, the identity of a Christian is the text. And to be a Christian is to be a follower of Jesus with a sense of freedom. Freedom is the fundamental nature through which one can identify Jesus. And, to be Taiwanese, according to Coe, was his context. The integration of the text and the context, or the theological task, is to make realize the spirit and freedom in places where they are denied. This task drives every Taiwanese Christian to search for new and authentic forms of existence. The struggle between concrete context and specific text is the root of political involvement. Coe commented that deep down in his inner being, there was a refusal to be put in any other category and a refusal to accept the treatment that had been meted out to the people in Taiwan. Therefore, to be Taiwanese is to be political.

8. Shoki Coe, *Recollections and Reflections*, 2nd ed. (New York: Formosan Christians for Self-Determination, 1993), 234.

In the midst of massive poverty and marginalization, the political witness of faith challenges Asian theology to take sides with the poor and the marginalized in their struggles change the conditions of marginalization. The love of God incarnates in human situations to construct a relationship of love by removing the forces, be they economic, political, social, gender, or racial, that prevent people from entering into a compassionate and caring relationship with other humans and nature. Lack of political witness is to deny God from history.

TOWARD A NEW METHODOLOGY IN DOING THEOLOGY

Coe's fourth contribution was his creative engagement in offering a new methodology for doing theology. Coe is honored around the world for the effective use of the term "contextualization" to explain how one should construct relevant theologies. The concept of contextualization became prominent during the Third Mandate period of the TEF.[9] During the First Mandate period of the TEF, from 1958 to 1964, the primary focus was to encourage academic training as a means of formation of church leaders throughout the world. The Second Mandate period marked a shift in focus: a challenge to locate indigenous education models for both training church leaders and for the construction of local theologies. Coe called it a shift from a protective "greenhouse" to a tent.[10] In a greenhouse, local plants are seldom planted for the simple reason that local plants may not require such protection for their normal growth. A greenhouse, on the contrary, is to offer protection to plants that are not able to withstand the wind, the rain, the sun, and the soil of a given place. A greenhouse is meant to help the growth of plants alien to a particular environment. For theology to be relevant and responsive to the living reality of God, it should not be grown in a greenhouse, but exposed to the wind and the conditions of the local soil.

Besides, theology should be able to adapt. The church in the pre-Constantine period primarily met in caves or in tents. They pitched their tents in different places and moved to newer locations, thus preventing any possible desire to build secure places in order to settle in a place.[11] Theological education should utilize this tentmaking approach, making everyone outlove, outthink, and therefore, outlive the given hostile

9. The Theological Education Fund was launched in 1958 in Ghana, West Africa, as a program of the International Missionary Council and later the World Council of Churches.

10. Shoki Coe, "Theological Education—A Worldwide Perspective," *Theological Education* 11, no. 1 (Autumn 1974): 8.

11. During the formation ceremony of the Church of South India, a common litany was "God help us *not* to settle down."

contexts. If secular movements can do this, why not theological education of the church? Labor unions, like the socialist movements of the
1960s and the 1970s, are gaining strength around the world without
any protective greenhouses, where labor philosophy or socialist principles have been taught as revelatory principles.

The central concern behind this shift, as the TEF explained, was the
quest to move away from a predominantly church-directed approach to
a world-directed approach in mission, and by doing so, it was assumed
the people of God would be led to participate in the movement where
God embraced the entire world. God in Christ was reconciling the
world to Godself, and this gospel imperative is a call to bring radical reconciliation among people, and between people and nature. Contextualization is, therefore, related to the dialectical relationship between the
particular and the universal, with catholicity as both space and unity.

Coe acknowledged that "out of this concern for a world-directed
ministry," a rethinking of the curriculum of the Tainan Theological
College and Seminary (TTCS) with the overall concern for the gospel
of the world and the ministry needed to evolve. The world-directed
approach was subsequently explained as a movement that becomes
"God-directed" and "world-directed" by abandoning the narrow realm
of the church.

This concern for a new curriculum for the TTCS also grew out of
the fear that theological education under missionary leadership was done
under a "greenhouse" situation, without allowing it to be exposed to
wind and soil. Theological education meant urging students to read
Western classics in theology. Coe termed this approach "cathedral mentality," a thinking that there is only one pattern of theology suitable to
all people and at all times.[12] Cathedral mentality reinforces the concept
of revelation as a past event in which doctrines are constructed as regu-
latory principles. Subscribing to Coe's approach, Koyama observed that
the use of "Aristotelian pepper" in the kitchen of a northern Thailand
peasant was not a welcome approach. Koyama asked what relevance was
there for him to teach Luther in Chiang Mai, Thailand.[13]

12. Shoki Coe says, "To think that there might be one pattern suitable for all peoples and
times, is what I call the 'cathedral mentality.' God's people, as pilgrims, must be free sometimes to pitch their tents and other times to pull them up and move on; for there is no permanent abiding place between the times." In "Theological Education—A Worldwide Perspective,"
Theological Education 11, no. 1 (Autumn 1974): 9

13. Kosuke Koyama, "Aristotelian Pepper and Buddhist Salt," in *Readings in Missionary
Anthropology II*, ed. William A. Smalley (South Pasadena, CA: William Carey Library, 1978),
109–14. Also see Kosuke Koyama, *Waterbuffalo Theology* (Maryknoll, NY: Orbis, 1974), 78–88.

CONTEXTUALIZING THEOLOGY

The contextualization proposal was made at a time when indigenization was accepted as a rational mission strategy as well as an ecclesiastical practice in Asian and African countries. Recognizing the cultural and ecclesiastical pluralities of the global church, Vatican II encouraged intercultural dialogue and liturgical adaptation of the local cultures, and that initiative prodded the efforts to indigenize theological formulations. It was assumed that for effective mission, it was imperative to share the gospel in a culturally compatible format that could be meaningfully appropriated by the local people. Using the typologies of Richard Niebuhr's "Christ and culture," the inculturation model was identified as a historical process in which Christian beliefs and practices entered into another cultural worldview and transformed it from within. The primary presumption was that culture and gospel could cohabit in a mutually enriching way.

Contextualization, as explained by the TEF and Coe, differs from indigenization theology. Indigenization, as Coe explains, is derived from nature metaphors that concern the soil, or taking root in the soil.[14] Although it is important that the churches in the non-Western world, which became objects for mission activities, take their own cultural background seriously, replanting the gospel in the local soil is not the primary theological task. Soil denotes a static nature and, besides, this metaphor assumes that planting a foreign plant in static soil is a theological responsibility. D. T. Niles observed that missionaries brought the gospel in the form of a potted plant with well-defined doctrines and ecclesiastical practices. While missionary theology used imported soil and a plant from the West, indigenous theological articulations attempted to plant this tree in local soil by breaking the pot. Despite being planted in the local soil, the plant remained a foreign tree. Of course, the plant was nurtured in the local soil, but it could not become a local plant. Coe wondered why Buddhism, which was also a foreign religion, had transformed itself into a local religion, while Christianity could not.

CONTEXTUALITY AND CONTEXTUALIZATION

Contextualization, on the other hand, proposes that theology needs to be a response to the living incarnations of a living God. Theology is not

14. Shoki Coe, "Contextualizing Theology," in *Mission Trends No. 3: Third World Theologies*, ed. Gerald H. Anderson and T. F. Stransky, CSP (New York: Paulist, 1976), 20.

revelatory, but a response to revelation, what Raimon Panikkar termed an anthropo-theandric practice.

Coe makes a distinction between contextuality and contextualization. Contextuality is the critical assessment of the factors that make a context significant in the mission of God, "a missiological discernment of the signs of the times, seeing where God is at work and calling everyone to participate in it."[15] Contextuality is the reality of wrestling with God's word in such a way that the power of incarnation, which is the divine form of contextualization, can enable people to follow in God's steps to contextualize. This process involves decontextualization and recontextualization, recalling the gospel imperative of death and resurrection.

Discernment of the signs of incarnation, therefore, is the key to theologizing. And this discernment sets the theological question. As Gustavo Gutiérrez argues, if God's incarnation is the key for theological imagination, the question of the nonbeliever, as traditional theology always contended, is not a theological issue.[16] The question that becomes central for theology is, "Where is God?" With whom is God? With what social group and in which social location do we find God? This identification is an imperative for missional practice, for a dynamic participation with the saving activity of God in history.

However, the discernment of the significance of the context is possible only through an organic participation with the context. That participation is the key in constructing a critical consciousness of the presence of God. Contextualization is the response that springs from it. The discernment of what makes the context significant for God's movement of justice and compassion should be matched by an active and ongoing contextualizing theology informed by a prophetic missionary practice to transform the structures of injustice. Authentic contextuality will lead to contextualization.

Contextual theology thus is prophetic, growing out of a genuine encounter with the living reality of God in a living context informed by the gospel. Coe warns that in the absence of the gospel, the context will be like building a tower, similar to the tower of Babel, with its technological innovations, economic structures, and consolidation of political might, but which may end in self-destruction.

To remain as a prophetic witness, the discernment of the context should help gain courage to delegitimize the dominant structures of power that reify the division between the subject and the object. And this discernment also means the signaling of a willingness to live with the

15. Coe, "Contextualizing Theology," 21.
16. Gustavo Gutiérrez, *The Power of the Poor in History* (London: SCM, 1983), 57.

specifics of the living context in order to change it according to the will of God. Generalization, instead of specificity, of context is not to serve the gospel. Theology as a human discourse must begin with the empirical situation of humans as perceived from a specific standpoint of a given people. That is the reason why black theology, as James Cone observes, starts with retelling the suffering under a savage slavery to which black people were subjected. This retelling of the specific is important in their search for interpreting the meaning of God's liberative presence among the community. Gustavo Gutiérrez explains this concept of contextuality more clearly. He writes:

> Theology is done by persons who, whether they know it or not, are caught up in particular social process. Consequently, all theology is in part a reflection of this or that concrete process. Theology is nothing disembodied. On the contrary theology is an attempt to express the word of God in the language of today—in the categories of a particular time and space.[17]

The concept of contextualization assumed importance after the Uppsala Assembly of the World Council of Churches. The assembly observed that the social and economic conditions of the world were in a precarious state. After a brief period of independence, the majority of the nations in the third world were facing the danger of being recolonized. Recolonization was promoted through the financial power of multinational corporations. The Uppsala Assembly identified that to enable recolonization, the Western economic forces created a new normative, with appalling consequences, of development and modernization. These concepts were, in effect, leading to the radical displacement of the cultural ethos of communities in the third world in order to create a niche for the hegemony of a market-led consumerist culture.

Theologians proposed the concept of contextualization as a political protest against the destabilizing process of capitalist forces in their attempt to recolonize the economies in the third world. Struggles for the right to construct counternormative epistemologies, whether in the field of economics, political organization, or in the world of faith, were conceived as part of the fundamental prerequisite for the people to gain selfhood and independence.

The Uppsala Assembly also noted that the goal of mission was not to establish ecclesial communities but to establish shalom, which involved the ultimate reconciliation and unity of all creation in God. The theology of Coe and the TEF was informed by the challenges of Uppsala.

17. Gutiérrez, *The Power of the Poor in History*, 90–91.

Contextualization was in response to these challenges from the global ecumenical community.

The Third Mandate of the TEF emphasized the need to equip the churches to confront social injustices that are built into the very texture of the capitalist economic structure, besides the call to empower local communities to reverse the process of delegitimization of the cultural and social practices of poor communities around the world.

THE LEGACY OF SHOKI COE

The impact of Coe's theology in the Asian theological world is enormous. The Critical Asian Principle (CAP) adopted by theological schools in Asia in 1972 was an immediate outcome of the dialogue initiated by Coe and the TEF on contextualizing theology. Two concerns were addressed through its formulation: First, to promote an Asian orientation in theological education, and second, to seek and identify what is considered as "distinctly Asian" and use such distinctiveness as a critical principle of judgment on matters dealing with the life and mission of the Christian community, theology, and theological education. Hence, the CAP took into account the common spiritual and socioeconomic context of Southeast Asian countries as the point of reference for biblical reflection and theologizing.

The CAP proposed four principles, namely, Situational, Hermeneutical, Missiological, and Educational. Each of these principles had general objectives to help the churches in Asia to develop Asian theologies that take seriously the life of people in Asia and pursue total liberation from the epistemological foundations of the Western theological framework. It also encouraged Asian churches to be truly Asian by evolving an attitude that would seek to think Asian and act Asian in order to create space for living theologies. To be Asian, the CAP argued, was to be free from the legacy of being the religion of the colonial masters.[18]

In theological constructions, Coe's thought has greater ramifications. Following are some of the distinctive changes brought about by the theological debates he initiated.

18. Minutes of the Senate of SEAGST, Bangkok, February 1972.

PROPOSITIONAL NATURE TO INCARNATIONAL
NATURE OF REVELATION

A shift from the propositional nature of revelation to the incarnational nature of revelation is one of the cardinal changes brought about by Coe in Asian theological thinking. The propositional nature of revelation reduced God to dogmatic language, with clearly defined parameters. The church thus created the doctrine of god, the doctrine of human, and whatever else and elucidated the attributes of an unchangeable god in unmovable square boxes—what could be called a "geo-metric god," if one follows the logic offered by C. S. Song.[19] The measurable god is predictable, not a mystery, not self-disclosing as a gift that brings joy. For the political and ecclesial powers, an unpredictable mystery is a frightening proposition. God, for their security, needs to be predictable and unchanging, should be the same yesterday, today, and tomorrow. God should not have the freedom to change. The unfreedom of god is prone to manipulation by the hegemonic powers that control theological and ecclesiastical discourse. In the past, monarchic kingdoms of ancient Israel attempted to enslave god in the darkness of the temple. In the present ecclesial structures, god is enslaved in unchangeable doctrines. This "geometrization" of God, and the "God-human" encounter in history, is a simplification as well as a caricature of God. A god in defined measurements is meant to prevent people's freedom to encounter God and to articulate the immense complexity of God's loving encounter through poetic imagination.

Coe's theological affirmation asserts that incarnation is an expression of God's freedom, a gift, not a defined one-time event in the past, but an ongoing process in which the self-disclosing living God encounters the creation in time and space. Faith is the response to the living reality of God who dwells in the living history.

The search for revelation reminds us of three things:

(a) Revelation is not always a pleasant encounter that brings prosperity and comfort in life; on the contrary, it often demands one's life. Moving from a position of political and religious power, Paul became a victim of power and a martyr of faith due to revelation.

(b) Revelation is not to endorse the prevailing nuances of faith formulations, but to subvert them. Revelation has to do with the knowledge of God and ourselves that is utterly surprising and disturbing. It is an event that shakes humanity and history. Although revelation is a gift, offering

19. C. S. Song, *The Compassionate God* (Maryknoll, NY: Orbis, 1982), 25.

us a glimpse of the very heart of mystery, it radically questions the structures that prevent the word of God from germinating.

(c) Revelation in Jesus radically shakes our consciousness regarding the social location of God in history. The story of the three wise men inserted by the evangelist Matthew[20] in the birth narrative is to reiterate this radical consciousness. After reading the signs regarding the incarnation, they set themselves on a pilgrimage to meet the divine. This narrative tells us that they were products of a traditional school of theology that correlated divinity with state power, so they went to the palace to meet the divine, but their theology proved to be wrong. For them God cohabits with power. Anything different is an aberration. But the revelation of God in Jesus was in the cattle shed, wrapped in dirty cloths, and placed in the midst of cattle refuse, where normal human life is not feasible. Incarnation of God in a cattle shed was God's protest against all forms of hierarchical powers, all alienating systems that marginalized a segment of the people. Matthew's narrative reminds us that God is not in cohabitation with power, but God's presence should be located in the wretched conditions of life.

Following Jesus begins with incarnation, the process by which a person makes a conscious choice to adopt the condition of the poor and marginalized just as God did. The "crucified people" of the world are already in this incarnation, but those who do not belong to this group sociologically must "achieve this belonging by denying their social locations of power and making common cause with the crucified people by taking on their struggle and their destiny. This is not simply accomplished by visiting or working with impoverished populations but requires the taking on of their conditions and risks."

Incarnation of God in Jesus also challenges us to abandon the dualistic definitions of salvation. If it were to speak about the salvation of souls, the incarnation of Jesus in the midst of the wretched conditions of human life was only a mockery. It speaks nothing. Incarnation in the powerless form of human structures is a challenge to perceive the totality of the being of personhood.

AN EPISTEMOLOGICAL BREAK

A conscious appeal for a radical break in the epistemological foundations for doing theology is the second impact of Coe's theology. The subject of theology since the time of Constantine has been the elite, the powerful—either the monarch or the rich man. Liberal theology of the West

---

20. Matthew 2:1–12.

placed the person with the rational mind, or the "modern man," as the subject of doing theology. Dietrich Bonhoeffer formulated the penetrating question as to how we proclaim God in a world become adult, a world grown up, a world come of age. Contextual theology, on the contrary, identifies the primary theological challenge as coming not from the legatees of modernity, but from the victims of it, from the nonpersons, the ones whom the prevailing sociopolitical order fails to recognize as persons.

The description of Taiwan as the "fourth world" rings from a profound protest against a global political order that reduces a large number of people to political nonbeings. In the third world, the nonpersons are the poor, the exploited, the migrants, and the ones systematically and legally despoiled of their humanness, the ones who scarcely know that they are persons at all. These nonbeings become the interlocutors for theological thinking. Mission is to tell a nonperson that she or he is a child of God and to help her or him to experience their being in empirical terms.

Sergio Torres gives a lengthy explanation of this shift in epistemology. He explains that the traditional way of knowing considers truth as the conformity of the mind to a given object, and in such a concept truth conforms to and legitimizes the world as it now exists. The other way of knowing is the dialectical one, where the world is not seen as a static object that the human mind confronts and attempts to understand; rather, the world is the unfinished project being built.[21] This building of the world is done by accepting the subjecthood of the poor and the marginalized in society. The Dar-es-Salaam meeting of third world theologians affirms: "We reject as irrelevant an academic type of theology that is divorced from action. We are prepared for a radical break in epistemology which makes commitment the first act of theology and engages in critical reflection on the praxis of the reality of the people in the third world."[22]

An epistemological shift also alludes to the change in subjecthood in theology. Contextual theologies affirm pathos as the epistemological starting point for theology. This observation reiterates the cognitive power of the poor in appropriating the presence of God. The epistemological privilege of the marginalized is the story of the Bible. Theologies done by accepting the agency of the poor remind us that the "experience

21. Sergio Torres, "Opening Address," in *African Theology en Route*, ed. Kofi Appiah Kubi and Sergio Torres (New York: Orbis, 1983), 5.

22. "Final Statement, Ecumenical Dialogue of Third World Theologians, Dar-es-Salaam, Tanzania, August 5–12, 1976," in *The Emergent Gospel: Theology from the Developing World*, ed. Sergio Torres and Virginia Fabella (London: Geoffrey Chapman, 1978), 269.

of suffering and poverty provides an opportunity for understanding the message of the Bible." Biblical messages remain hidden to those who are on the other side of the fence of the oppressed class.

PEOPLE'S HERMENEUTICS

The third legacy is the new hermeneutical challenges that come from the agency of the people. The result is a radical shift in the purpose of appropriating the biblical message. In the traditional Christian parlance, the Bible is a fetish. And, as a fetish, its function is not to point toward the living presence of God, but to limit the god event as a past issue. As D. T. Niles observes, what we received, namely the gospel, is only one of the pointers to the truth. Traditional theology, however, put a veil around it and prevented it from growing. By presenting the Jesus event as fixed, "God Stopped." The gospel, however, offers a different perspective; incarnation in Jesus, according to the Gospel writers, was an act to break such veils and to look for the presence of God in the living conditions of the people.

Moreover, in the traditional Christian approach, the Bible is viewed as God's revelation to a sacred writer, but in doing so, it fails to comprehend the production process. It is important to recall that behind the text stands an event or dialectically interlinked events; "before it was God's word it was God's event."[23] The salvific experience of the event is interpreted not as a documentary film of the event but an exploration of "its significance as message." Later, this report or interpretation is incorporated into a tradition, which is a living interpretation bound up with praxis. And the very conflict of interpretations leads the "fixing of event-report-tradition in the form of a canon." Canonization is a "closure," a phenomenon that excludes other readings in the past traditions and closes the space for new creative readings by setting parameters for interpretations.

The Bible as it is today is the product of a long hermeneutical process. Neither revelation nor inspiration should be considered in isolation. "Rather they complement and re-create each other dialectically. The word of God is generated in the salvific event. Then the event is interpreted and enriched by the word, which takes it up and transmits it in the form of a message."[24]

---

23. J. Severino Croatto, "Biblical Hermeneutics in the Theologies of Liberation," in *Irruption of the Third World: Challenge to Theology*, ed. Virginia Fabella and Sergio Torres (Maryknoll, NY: Orbis, 1983), 151.
24. Croatto, "Biblical Hermeneutics in the Theologies of Liberation," 158.

This approach challenges the fetishization of the text, or what Aloysius Pieris termed bibliolatry, the worship of a book with all that it says.[25]

The Bible is the faith reading of paradigmatic events of salvation history, and in Jesus, it is the paradigmatic reading of an unfinished salvation history. Thus the present hermeneutical challenge is to help see the face of God as God enters into the present history of women and men to continue the salvific process. J. Severino Croatto asserts, "The process of liberation that we are experiencing today are historical facts in which faith is able to 're-cognize' the presence of God."[26]

GOD OF LOVE AND THE OMNIPOTENT GOD

A fourth affirmation that springs out of contextual theology is informed by the experience of the compassionate God in human history. The God of compassion negates the traditional attributes that doctrinal revelation speaks about. Wherever there is abundant expression of love, the exercise of power is found the least. On the contrary, wherever the demonstration of power is visibly high, expressions of love are the least. Love and power do not cohabit. Power evokes fear and not love. And God in Jesus, as the Evangelist John reiterates, is the ultimate manifestation of self-giving love. Besides, the cross demonstrates the vulnerability of power.

Incarnation in Jesus challenges us to radically shift our attempt to equate God as absolute power, or one resembling a cosmic monarch, who rules over an appallingly unjust world order. The omnipotent god is the god of empire, and the empire god legitimizes all hierarchies of power. Constructing the empire god is a deception, and contextual theologies seek a transposition from the omnipotent god to the God of love, God who was defeated on the cross by the powers of the time and accepted defeat out of agapeic love toward the defeated people. Through the experience of defeat on the cross, God in Jesus became one among the billions of people who have been defeated by the powers of money, militarism, patriarchy, and racial bigotry.

CONCLUSION

An attempt to live as a true witness to the living incarnation of God in the political context of being ruled by alien powers—being denied the

---

25. Aloysius Pieris, *The Genesis of an Asian Theology of Liberation* (Gonawala-Kelaniya, Sri Lanka: Tulana Research Centre, 2013), 29.
26. Croatto, "Biblical Hermeneutics in the Theologies of Liberation," 164.

right to speak in his mother tongue, being forced to change his name often as the powers of domination shifted from region to region, being in exile for the best part of his adult life, and in spite of these limitations becoming a light to thousands of people in their search to locate true faith—characterizes the life of Shoki Coe.

Ray Wheeler, who writes about the legacy of Shoki Coe, observed that "Coe's concern with contextualization went beyond academic exercise. His life modelled the personal cost of engaging in a contextually appropriate ministry of the word. He was passionately Taiwanese, yet his very name reflects the changing contexts of his life and is, in part, the legacy of his political context."

Shoki Coe wrote an epilogue to his unfinished work titled *Recollections and Reflections*, asking the existential question of "Who am I?"

"At first I thought I would build up my memories round the idea of recollections and reflection, but now I incline to change it to 'An Unconcluded Search for Self-Identity,' or better still, if I may dare, 'The New,' with my life and work as the very humble example! Is my life a tragic success, or a successful tragedy?"[27]

The search for identity for Shoki Coe is an attempt to claim the right to be a child of God.

---

27. Shoki Coe, *Recollections and Reflections*, ed. Boris Anderson, 2nd ed. (New York: Formosan Christians for Self Determination, 1993), 264

PART I

Shoki Coe and the Reconstruction of Theological Methodology

1.

Revisiting the Methodology of Contextual Theology in the Era of Globalization

PO HO HUANG

INTRODUCTION

In 1987, Shoki Coe was awarded an honorary doctorate in theology by the Tainan Theological College and Seminary on his return to Taiwan twenty-two years after the authorities had exiled him from his motherland for initiating the campaign "Formosans for Self-Determination" and for his commitment to the freedom and self-determination of the Taiwanese. In the citation,[1] the TTCS hailed him as a "pastor, theologian, theological educator, and a pioneer of human rights movements." These testimonials and evaluations made by the Taiwanese church capture the rich experience and profound contributions that shaped Shoki Coe.

Coe is considered the first proponent of contextual theology, one who accentuated the need for theology to be rooted in the local soil. Later, contextualization became the professed method of doing theology. His status as the director of the Theological Education Fund (TEF) of the World Council of Churches (WCC), the first person from Taiwan to serve in a global ecumenical movement, offered him the necessary space to make contextualization an ecumenical agenda around the globe.

Along with his concern for contextualization of theological discourse, Coe was deeply committed to the social witness of the gospel and offered leadership to churches in Taiwan to devote themselves to issues pertaining to the larger society. Acknowledging his abilities, the Presby-

---

1. Po Ho Huang, preface to Jonah Chang's *The Taiwanese Prophet* (Taipei: Bāng Chhun-hong, 2004), 13–14.

terian Church in Taiwan (PCT) elected him as the moderator of its Assembly for two consecutive terms, and he eloquently used that time to strengthen the unity of Taiwanese churches.

Being in exile never dampened his political determination to create a better future for Taiwan. Along with friends, Coe commenced the "Formosans for Self-Determination" campaign based on the "Public Statement on Our National Fate" issued by the PCT. Coe's thoughts and actions encompassing the political, ecclesial, and theological world were informed by the deep resentment of unfairness "毋甘願 (m-kam-goan)" meted out under the colonial regime and shaped by his experience of being in exile due to political convictions.[2]

In retrospect, the struggles to preserve selfhood under colonial despotism and exile taught him profound lessons on how to practice Christian faith and do theology in the third world. As early as 1966, he elaborated his idea of Asian theological education in a speech, "The Text and Context in Theological Education," at the inaugural meeting of the Northeast Asia Association of Theological Schools.[3] Due to his invigorating experience from Taiwan and abroad, Coe was able to make specific relationship between theological texts and their contexts and, hence, he urged the theological community to contextualize its theological thinking. Further, he also called for theological schools to shape their pedagogical structure toward "contextual theological education."

CONSTRUCTION OF THE CONTEXTUAL THEOLOGICAL METHODOLOGY

Coe's contextual theology was not based only on his introspection of politics and social experience but also on the theological implications of incarnation that he was aware of. In his article titled "Contextualization as the Way towards Reform," Coe delineated the need for "contextualizing theology":

> Contextuality—contextualization are, I believe, a missiological necessity. But are they a theological necessity? Contextualizing theology takes the concrete local context seriously. It is rooted in a concrete, particular situation. Is there, then, a danger of losing the catholicity of the gospel? To this there is a counter question: is there such a theology which is not *in loco* and thus *in vacuo?*—*a theologia sub specie aeternitatis*, as it were—a utopian theol-

---

2. Chang, *The Taiwanese Prophet*, 366–67.

3. Shoki Coe, *Contextualization as the Way towards Reform, Asian Christian Theology: Emerging Themes*, ed. Douglas J. Elwood (Philadelphia: Westminster, 1980), 48.

ogy? But the concern for the catholicity of the gospel is a legitimate one, with which contextualizing theology is deeply concerned. And contextualization, I believe, is the authentic way to that catholicity.[4]

Coe believed that catholicity was a gift and also an agenda for mission. To see it as a gift, we must ask how it was given. He observed that catholicity was molded in churches' witness of incarnation within a given time and place.[5] He continued:

> I believe, in fact, that the incarnation is the divine form of contextualization, and if this is so, the way we receive this gift is also through our following his way. That is what I mean by contextualization. As the catholicity of the gospel is given through the Word becoming flesh, so our task should be through our responsive contextualization, taking our own concrete, local contexts seriously.[6]

After the adoption of the Third Mandate by the TEF-WCC,[7] contextual theology has been accepted as the principal perspective and strategy of ecumenical theological education. Since then, theological education of churches around the world has started to implement methods to contextualize their theology. Thus, the mandate was used as a common guideline for theology and theological education for the global churches. The principles of contextualization proposed by the TEF have not only become a guideline for theological education but also stimulated local theological constructions around the globe. Gradually, contextual methods in doing theology have assumed a cardinal position in theological education.

CONTRIBUTIONS AND CRITIQUES OF CONTEXTUALIZATION METHOD

The proposal of contextualizing theology made by Coe and the TEF has marked the advent of a new paradigm shift in the history of theology since the Enlightenment. The beginning of Christian theology was informed by the life and teaching of Jesus, which was rooted in Jewish thought. The early church, along with the authors of the four Gospels and Paul, laid the foundation for the prototypes of theological thinking.

4. Coe, *Contextualization as the Way*, 53.
5. Coe, *Contextualization as the Way*, 48–55.
6. Coe, *Contextualization as the Way*, 53–54.
7. The World Council of Churches has issued three mandates for ecumenical theological education by its Theological Education Fund (TEF); they are focused on "advance," "rethink," and "reform."

On the basis of these early propositions, the Apostolic Fathers constructed what was later known as the doctrines, or the foundations of theology. Through informed dialogue with Greek philosophical thought, Tertullian, Augustine of Hippo, and Thomas Aquinas paved the way for traditions that were later identified as orthodox theology. Reformers largely reiterated the theological traditions set in motion by orthodox theologians. A shift in paradigm of these early initiatives began with the emphasis on rationalism proposed by Enlightenment thought. The Enlightenment, which was marked by an emphasis on scientific method, raised profound questions on the method and content of orthodox theology. Liberal Christianity, also known as liberal theology, was formed and advanced as a sequel to Enlightenment rationality. Friedrich Daniel Ernst Schleiermacher, regarded as an early leader in liberal Christianity, shaped Christian theology as a rational form of knowledge, coherently integrating scientism and rational thinking proposed by modernity. The advent of liberal theology marked the first paradigm shift in theology. However, though the inception of liberal theology is considered a foundation-shaking event in the theological tradition, the proponents of its Enlightenment paradigm shared the same historical and cultural context of the previous traditions of theological thinking, that is, within the political and cultural milieu of Europe, influenced by Jewish, Greek, and Roman traditions. Although its impacts were overwhelming, the nature of challenges was different from that of the contextualization principle.

The emergence of contextual theology, the third paradigm in theological thinking, coincided with the irruption of the third world on the Christian map. A large number of people who were outside so-called Christendom found meaning in Christianity. Indicating a shift of the pendulum in Christian geography, Coe from Asia and Desmond Tutu from South Africa assumed responsibilities as the director and deputy director respectively of the TEF. This appointment was historic as it demonstrated the fact that third world Christians could play a pivotal role in the global ecumenical movement. As the former colonies gained independence, one of the challenges that the Christians there faced was to revisit their identities. Obviously, the legacy of the colonial missionary movement was placed under serious critical scrutiny. The emergence of contextual theology inherited those critical evaluations of the colonial past and strived to break free from those legacies. In other words, while the first paradigm shift initiated by the Enlightenment remained in the same geographic location and cultural environment of the previous epoch, the second paradigm shift resulted in a shift of geographic location. While the locus of the first paradigm shift was the adaptation of theological thoughts in the changing civilizational framework of a given cultural context, the second paradigm shift attempted to locate and affirm the importance of people's culture in doing Christian theology. Besides, it also represented the struggles of Christians in the third world for their identities.

The development of contextual theology was greatly influenced by different regional histories and cultures that were shaped by the life and mission of the various churches and individual Christians in the third world. When Coe coined the term "contextualization," he was reflecting and acknowledging the unique contributions of third world Christians, but at the same time proposing that theology should be constructed as a reflection of the praxis in the local context. Japanese theologian Kosuke Koyama, a contemporary of Coe, engaged in a similar theological articulation after encountering the peasants in northern Thailand. In his monumental work *Waterbuffalo Theology* (1974), he argued that theology must listen to the people and it must be easy to understand.[8] While appreciating Koyama's theological approach in connection with indigenous experiences and contexts, Coe suggested that one should not be satisfied with the act of taking root in the soil. On the contrary, local theological practice must transform from "indigenization" into "contextualization," since indigenization tended to be past-oriented and focused on static cognition. For Coe, contextualization was a dynamic concept, constantly looking for new breakthroughs and bringing forth the renewal of cultures. Therefore, other than recognizing the direction of the efforts of indigenization, he mentioned that more emphasis should be placed on the dynamic and future orientation of theology.[9] Immediately after he introduced the idea of contextualization, he stated that this theological process was a continual process of contextualizing through decontextualization and recontextualization.[10]

Notwithstanding the fact that contextualization theology had led to a wide range of influence and made outstanding contributions to the world, it was not without challenges and questions. As mentioned earlier, the defense made by Coe about the catholicity and universality of contextualization is one of the good examples. Even to date, there are critics of contextualization theology reproving it as a narrow "local theology without universal value and lack of Catholicity."

Choan-Seng Song's proposition was an example of the various

---

8. Kosuke Koyama, *Waterbuffalo Theology* (London: SCM, 1974), vii.

9. Shoki Coe, *Contextualizing Theology, Mission Trends No. 3, Third World Theologies*, ed. Gerald H. Anderson and Thomas F. Stransky, CSP (New York: Paulist, 1974), 19.

10. Coe, *Contextualizing Theology*, 24.

critiques of Coe's contextualization theology. Song's comments were based on his critical reflection on H. Richard Niebuhr's book *Christ and Culture*, which proposed five models of relationship between Christ and culture. He rightly pointed out that Niebuhr perceived Christ and culture as two different entities, and suggested that Christ was distinguished from culture. On the contrary, Song insisted that Christ and people were one, and the gospel and culture were inseparable.[11] This issue of the gospel and culture was a common struggle within the ecumenical space during the 1980s and the 1990s; the change in perspective became evident between the WCC's Vancouver Assembly in 1983 and the Canberra Assembly in 1991. The theme of the Vancouver Assembly was "Gospel and Cultures." After seven or eight years of studies by the member churches of the WCC, the theme was changed to "Gospel in Diverse Cultures" at its Canberra Assembly. This revision of theological propositions may not have attracted much attention from the member churches and all Christians. However, a discerning mind could sense the serious theological struggles behind them and their profound theological implications. If the gospel and culture are not two separate entities, then the methodology of contextualization requires a thorough discussion.

As Song insisted, the gospel and culture are inseparable, and he thus proposed the theme "Doing Theology with Asian Resources" as the key objective of the Programme for Theology and Cultures in Asia (PTCA), of which he was serving as dean. This theological movement could represent the next paradigm shift brought about by contextual theology in the theological history of the third world. It was one of the most radical and revolutionary theological proposals. Although this theological movement led by the PTCA also focused on doing contextual theology, it tried to avoid using the term "contextualization." Hence, there is a fundamental difference between contextual theologies and contextualization theologies. The revolutionary changes brought about by this theological movement in Asia also broke the dichotomy between the terms "Christian" and "gentile." It affirmed that the so-called gentile cultures were also created by God. Strictly speaking, there is no such differentiation in God's creation. With the redefinition of Christian identity in Asia, Christian theologies have struggled to take off their colonialist colors and are gradually mending their gaps with people's life experiences so that they can serve to shape a relevant Asian Christian identity and to witness a vital gospel message in Asia.

11. C. S. Song, "Theology That Tells People's Passion Stories," unpublished paper, 2002.

THE CHANGING CONTEXT AND THE CHALLENGES OF CHRISTIAN THEOLOGY

Notwithstanding some critiques and the reformulation of the contextualization principle, Coe provided a penetrating insight with his observation of the variability of the context and his proposal that theology need to be dynamic and future-oriented. It is almost half a century since the Third Mandate of the WCC (1972) was issued by the TEF, and it is time to evaluate its significance. Fifty years may seem too little time to bring about an influence in the history of the church, which has more than two thousand years of history. In the past fifty years the world has witnessed rapid changes thanks to the development of science and technology. It is estimated that the accumulated knowledge of humankind in the past century can be equated with the sum of the accumulated knowledge in all of past history, and in the past decade alone it has surpassed the accumulated knowledge of the past ninety years.[12] That is, there have been immeasurable transformations and advancements in the situation of the international community and human life in the past two or three decades. If the idea of contextualization advocated by Coe is a constant and ongoing process of decontextualization and recontextualization, then the identification and insight of the context of every new era, as well as the constant renewal and reconstruction of theology, are unavoidable tasks for Christians and the church. Theological update and reconstruction must not only be limited to the content and amendment of figures but also include the changes in the scope and methodology of theology, or even the reconstruction of them all over again.

Due to the rapid development of high-tech systems and information technology as well as the strong integration of economic liberalization in the twenty-first century, political, economic, and cultural fields have been rapidly moving toward globalization. The collapse of traditional social structures and the large population flow resulted in the diversity of society. Postmodernist thought patterns emerged as the Enlightenment-inspired rational social structure was unable to respond appropriately to the advancement of new situations. Meanwhile, with the critical thinking brought about by postcolonialism, the present society experienced a characteristic estrangement. While globalization effectively and rapidly integrated both economic and cultural fields globally with new technologies of transportation and communications, a large segment of the populace remained marginalized. Even though the idea of the global

---

12. Daisy L. Hung, "Reading makes you climb up to the shoulders of the giants"; see-https://tinyurl.com/yb5orktf.

village brought convenience to daily life to a certain extent, it was essentially a movement of monopolization and exclusion.

From an economic perspective, globalization is derived from the ideology and principle of neoliberalism and a free market economy, which functions according to the capitalist mechanism of market operation. Through the World Trade Organization (WTO), the International Monetary Fund (IMF), the World Bank (WB), and other international financial and trade organizations, economic and trade activities of different countries are vigorously integrated into this global economic system. The main task of the WTO is to force its member states to eliminate tariff barriers so as not to impede open markets, which make it easier for the movement of international capital and investments and its accessibility. The rule of law established for international trade by the WTO weakened the sovereignty of states, particularly those weaker and developing countries. In order to remain competitive in the global economic system, the governments determined to sacrifice the most disadvantaged people while at the same time actively developing their advantageous industries. In other words, it was the law of the jungle, an expression of "survival of the strongest." Thanks to technology, there are almost no boundaries among the capital, production, and consumer markets. Investors, entrepreneurs, and consumers are invisible from the scene. They move like migratory birds here and there as long as it is profitable. Only labor and lands that are limited by nationality and geography have become the target of exploitation. And the extent of economic exploitation has been worse compared with the time before globalization. Capitalists who own business and exploit people hide behind computer screens or stock charts, leaving no evidence of or concern for the exploited labor. This shows why even as the gap between the rich and poor keeps widening and there is no sign of any slowdown in oppression and exploitation, contextual theologies that blossomed out of the third world in the 1960s to react to exploitations and oppression have withered and even gradually begun to disappear. As the new oppressors are hard to identify, and the initial cause is missing, the liberating economic-oriented contextual theology has become powerless and cannot be justified.

From a cultural point of view, many people in the past were optimistic about globalization and believed that the establishment of a global village would shorten the distance between people and give rise to the opportunity of achieving diversity and harmony in an ideal world. In fact, people gradually realized that the development of technology and the internet has effectively brought the world closer together after the rapid globalization process of the past three decades. Nevertheless, it is undeniable that only wealthy people have been able to enjoy the fruits of technology. There are even more people who have become only objects of consumption. They are assessed but do not have the capability to assess, and thus they are marginalized. Even   people who are able to enjoy the technological advances are being controlled by the supremacy of technology and capital. For instance, the controversy over the abolition of nuclear energy is often monopolized by so-called experts. The people most affected by an incident are often humiliated and made fun of as the ignorant masses. They are not entitled to their opinion even when it comes to choices concerning their health and safety. The so-called experts and intellectuals spread their views via the internet. With the intervention of capital, power, and technology, the internet has become a platform that misleads and confuses people instead of increasing their chances to search, know, and make decisions. The law of the jungle of the internet is obvious from events of the past ten years. Initially, Chinese web pages were in Traditional Chinese (used in Taiwan), but now the number of the websites using Simplified Chinese (largely used by mainland Chinese) have grown exponentially. In other words, cultural globalization has been not as positive as many people thought—the expectation that it would lead humankind to a multicultural, pluralistic, and interconnected world. Lacking vigilance and critical thinking, it is used as a tool by hegemonies to brainwash, deceive, or mislead the people.

Changes in these contexts are unprecedented and magnificent. Do Christian missionaries see through its nature and impact? Does Christian theology address the challenges and threats posed by this new context to humankind? Are Christian missionaries going to reconstruct contextual theology appropriately, as Coe envisioned the concepts of "decontextualization" and "recontextualization," to serve prophetically and bring hope for the sufferers?

TO DISMANTLE THE TOWER OF BABEL AND RECONSTRUCT THE HOUSEHOLD OF GOD

The consequences of globalization in today's society are not only expansion of oppressive structures, the widening gap between the rich and the poor, and the further speeding up of hegemony and centralization of global economy and culture. Following globalization, the market dominated by consumers and the principle of supply and demand have been coercively controlled by suppliers with the help of international enterprises and capital operations. Through the elimination of small enterprises, and mergers and acquisitions, international corporations have gradually monopolized the market. They promote their products through a lot of advertisements. In order to achieve sales, the market, which is no longer concerned about people's needs, constantly stimulates people's desires. The marketplace has become an engine that incites desires, piques people's vanity, and stimulates competition, which in turn leads to uncontrolled abuse of resources and destruction of the environment. Consequently, the implication of globalization is not just a change in the social structure. It entails a negative and serious impact on spiritual formation. People become more vulnerable to vanity, and are competitive and uncompassionate, which are signs of the deterioration of hearts and souls. How can we expect that prophetic voices be raised and acknowledged when minds and souls, including the spiritual life of the oppressed and the poor, are corrupted by the ideology of the market?

The reason that globalization can be so influential and is able to make such an overwhelming impact is because it has stolen the secret power of God, that is, the mystery of creation. It has made good use of the organic concept of creation and is trying to replace the kingdom of God with the tower of Babel. It has proposed that the ideologies of neoliberalism and free market economy are the best ways for human salvation. It is thus that economists encourage more spending and consumption when the economy is confronted with a tremendous setback. These solutions, in fact, add to the exploitation of the environment and damage the ecosystem. By showing a misleading and distorted image of the kingdom of God, globalization poses challenges and threats to the Christian faith. It also provides false redemptive ways and life values. In the context of globalization, what Christian theologies confront is not simply an unjust society or unfair economic structure, race and gender antagonism, dictatorship or colonial rule, but a false religion that regards capital as divine, a false theology that treats the market as the Redeemer, and a false kingdom of God that considers money and material as the promise. This is the new tower of Babel constructed by human intelligence in the twenty-first century, which has shown that humanity is trying to compete with God. The numerous contextual theologies embodied in various areas during the past decades are now incapable of demolishing the huge tower of Babel. The new context requires a new theological thought and tactic.

Since globalization has created a false kingdom of God, our theology must be devoted to the theology of the "household of God" to resist this unreal promise. The only way to debunk the illusion of globalization that pretends to be the redeemer of this era is to declare the truth of the kingdom of God and build the world as the household of God. We must explore the theology of the household of God from God's creation. The ancient Greek word "oikos" refers to the household, and is closely related to the *oikologia, oikonormos*, and *oikoumene* that we are most concerned about today. In other words, talking about the theology of God's home, we must deal with topics such as "ecological justice," "economic justice," and "social justice." These subjects involve several paradigm shifts of theological concepts, strategies, and methodologies:

1. The nucleus of theology should be changed. It should not be focused on anthropocentrism but on the holistic character of God's creation. Christian theology has been anthropocentric since early times, as traditional theology focused on human salvation. The anthropocentric Christian theology has not been challenged for the past two thousand years. It was Lynn Townsend White, an American ecologist, who first pointed out that traditional Christianity was an accomplice in ecological destruction because of the biased interpretation of the Genesis story of creation. This narrative leads to the development of an anthropocentric Christian theology. His critics articulated Christian environmental concerns and the possible interpretation of the creation stories.[13] However, those articulations were limited as they failed to gain insight into the anthropocentric nature of Christian theology.

    Environmental concerns cannot be addressed by the traditional concept of environmental protection, which has as its main concern human well-being in the face of massive destruction propelled by the current state of the global market. A holistic development of ecological justice or ecosystems should not, theologically speaking, be considered as a subordinate issue under human development or its threats. The theology developed by the early churches focused on Christology, because the challenge then was to engage with the emerging religious community. Thus they were engrossed in Christological explanations rather than on the reality of creation. As a result, Christian theology failed to pay enough attention to the holistic nature of creation.[14] However, this does not mean

13. See Po Ho Huang, "Embracing the Household of God: A Paradigm Shift from Anthropocentric Tradition to Creation Responsibility in Doing Theology," chapter 1 in *An Anthropocentric Salvation to the Redemption of God's Creation—A Proposal Towards a Paradigm Shift of Theology* (Kolkata, India: PTCA, Sceptre, 2014), 1–17.

14. The early church, though, has people like Marcion and the Gnostics who questioned the

that theological issues concerning creation are either insignificant or negligible. On the contrary, from the point of God's creation or from the theology of God's household, humanity is but one part of God's creation, and we are not authorized to dominate over other creatures. Therefore, in the face of today's climate change and ecological disasters, we should rethink the coexistence of human beings and nature, humbly shape a theology based upon the holistic character of the household of God, and cease to continue the discourses of traditional anthropocentric theology. In this manner we can be reconciled fully with the divine creation in the face of the current global ecological catastrophe.

2. The distribution and management of human resources should assume importance in the field of economics. It should not be directed to encourage unbridled exploitation of nature in order to ensure economic growth for human pleasure. In other words, the cardinal spirit of the household of God emphasizes justice and sharing, rather than focusing on developing a prosperous and competitive economy or society. The matter of economic justice is a sensitive issue in times of globalization because it involves not only issues concerning the social system, but also human spirituality. It is impossible to achieve a just, harmonious, and joyous household without a spirituality of compassion and sharing. A theological critique of globalization cannot be reduced to issues of economic systems or structural mechanisms but has to be more notably on matters pertaining to human nature and has to be spiritually informed by the values of compassion and sharing.

3. Ecumenism not only refers to the achievements in uniting different churches and Christian denominations, it is also closely related to matters concerning hegemony or inequality in all aspects such as race, gender, class, ethnic group, culture, war, and peace. Consequently, ecumenism is also a matter of justice and the essence of the gospel. It is an important proposition of theology.

---

adequacy of the doctrine of Creation. They were soon excluded by the church fathers and condemned for heresy. The doctrine of Creation thus is included in church dogmas. The main concern of the early church was the role of Jesus, and thus Christology became the central topic of its discourses and has been ever since. See Po Ho Huang, "Embracing the Household of God."

CONCLUSION

Issues of justice relating to the environment, economy, and human social relations are three indispensable pillars of God's household. And justice is an essential characteristic of the sovereignty of God. Facing the challenges and threats of globalization, Christian theology must be humble in the face of nature, the divine creation, by sharing resources to proclaim the promise of the true kingdom of God. That is, it should shift the nature of power from domination to that of humble service. This must be the Christian way to dismantle the tower of Babel in the globalized era. Probably the only and best way for us to remember Shoki Coe's contributions is by making our theology innovative following his assertions of "decontextualization" and "recontextualization" in Taiwan's new context and by ensuring our active participation in the theological discourse of the global communities.

2.

Contextualization as Reception of the World: Shoki Coe and the Transformation of Theology

DALE IRVIN

In 1973 Shoki Coe[1] published an article titled "In Search of Renewal in Theological Education" in the US journal *Theological Education.* It turned out to be one of the most influential Christian theological works of the century.[2] The article was on the accomplishments of the Theological Education Fund (TEF), an organization that had been established by the International Missionary Council in 1958 in Ghana with $2 million from John D. Rockefeller Jr., matched by another $2 million from nine US mission boards. Coe had come on the staff of the TEF in 1965 and by 1973 was serving as its director. The purpose of the TEF was to support theological education in Asia, Africa, and Latin America.[3] Coe's 1973 article explained the way in which the mandate of the TEF was changing.

> Through the pressure of the revolutionary context, manifesting itself in the resurgence of non-Christian religions, the renascence of ancient cultures, rapid social change, and the emergence of new ideologies, we were forced

1. The name Shoki Coe is the Anglicized form of the Japanese version of his original name, Ng Chiong Hui in the Pe̍h-ōe-jī script of Taiwan, and Hwang Chang Hui in Mandarin. See Po Ho Huang, "Ng Chiong Hui (Shoki Coe, Hwang Chang Hui)," in *A Dictionary of Asian Christianity*, ed. Scott W. Sunquist (Grand Rapids: Eerdmans, 2001), 601; and Jonah Chang, *Shoki Coe: An Ecumenical Life in Context* (Geneva: WCC, 2012).

2. Shoki Coe, "In Search of Renewal in Theological Education," *Theological Education* 9, no. 4 (Summer 1973): 233–43.

3. See Charles W. Ranson, "The Theological Education Fund," *International Review of Mission* 47, no. 188 (October 1958): 432–38.

to rethink the text [of the gospel] which had been interpreted in the different contexts and different times in the West, and to come to a new understanding of the ministry which would lead to the younger churches ceasing
to be the object of missions, and becoming the subject in mission, participating in the *Missio Dei* in and for the world.[4]

In the second half of the article, Coe sought to introduce a new theological method that the TEF was seeking to implement to arrive at this new
understanding. For the better part of the previous century, discussions
on the production of new theologies in Asia, Africa, and Latin America,
that is to say, outside the dominant North Atlantic world of the "West,"
had been advanced mostly under the language of indigenization. The
problem, Coe argued, was that "indigenous, indigeneity, and indigenization all derive from a nature metaphor, that is, of the soil, or taking
root in the soil."[5] The model was little more than that of a plant that was
native to one place in the world being transplanted to another. It was the
same plant, just in a new location. Eventually one might expect to see
slight changes take place over generations of new plants that grew from
it (if indeed the plant lasted that long in the new soil), but the nature
and character of the plant, or of the church and its theology, remained
essentially the same. Coe did not use this terminology, but in effect he
was saying that under this model, Christianity in Asia, Africa, and Latin
America was destined to remain an invasive species.

It was a static model. Coe wrote, "Indigenization tends to be used in
the sense of responding to the Gospel in terms of traditional culture.
Therefore, it is in danger of being past-oriented."[6] Theological education and the broader project of theology in general required a more
dynamic model, he argued. They needed a method that would foster a
deeper assessment of the emerging social, political, and cultural situations
that churches were encountering in various parts of the world, one that
would foster change and be open to the future.[7] Coe announced that
they were calling this new process "contextualization." It began with
"missiological discernment of the signs of the times, seeing where God is
at work and calling us to participate in it,"[8] he wrote. He called this first
step "contextuality." Such discernment in turn led to new insights and
theological formulations that would "contextualize" the faith. The result
was both a process and an outcome that he called "contextualization."

Coe's essay was not the first to introduce the notion of context into the

4. Coe, "In Search of Renewal," 236.
5. Coe, "In Search of Renewal," 240.
6. Coe, "In Search of Renewal," 240.
7. Coe, "In Search of Renewal," 240–41.
8. Coe, "In Search of Renewal," 241.

wider theological lexicon of his day. Paul L. Lehmann, for instance, had published almost a decade earlier a highly influential book titled *Ethics in a Christian Context*.[9] Lehmann's work sought to provide a clearer basis for a relational ethic that was an alternative to the older absolutist ethics of Protestant and Roman Catholic traditions without succumbing to relativism.[10] God, he argued, was bringing about a new humanity in the world. Men and women were to be relating to one another in light of this new humanity. The context of this new humanity for Lehmann, however, remained steadfastly the *koinonia*, or Christian faith community. "God's activity in the world" remained decisively ecclesiocentric for Lehmann.[11] It was a dynamic concept of faith at work, but a dynamic that was happening entirely within the framework of the existing church.

For Coe, the operative word for contextualization was "renewal." But it was renewal not coming from within the church. Rather, for Coe, the church itself was being called to be renewed in Asia, Africa, and Latin America by what was happening outside of it. Renewal in theological education and in theology will come from outside the church, by participating more fully in the social, political, cultural, and religious life of the people who are not Christians among whom it lives. Coe argued that this would also result in a deeper and more authentic form of "the catholicity of the gospel" that did not entail repetition of what had been said in the past but would encounter God afresh in the diverse locations in which Christians now lived. Theologians in Asia, Africa, and Latin America had permission to set aside those trans-potted theological plants that had been brought in from overseas and engage in a fresh encounter with "the Word which became flesh and dwelt among us at a particular time and place." This was because, Coe argued, "the incarnation is the divine form of contextualization." God was in effect speaking outside the church, in the world, calling for the church to respond. Regarding such responses, Coe wrote:

> Ours can only be in following in His steps as an ongoing process of the pilgrim people. But in doing so we can accept our relativity with hope and even with joy, as we see in our faithful responses the sign of the divine contextualization unfolding its purpose for the liberation and salvation of mankind.[12]

9. New York: Harper & Row, 1963; citations here are from the reprinted edition (Louisville: Westminster John Knox, 2006).

10. Lehmann, *Ethics in a Christian Context*, 143.

11. Lehmann, *Ethics in a Christian Context*, 144.

12. Coe, "In Search of Renewal," 243.

The word took hold. Over the next several decades, the language of contextualization and resulting contextual theologies blossomed in ways Coe could not have imagined.[13] Roman Catholic theologies tended to use the term "inculturation" as it had already achieved a degree of currency among Catholic theologians, but the meaning has been the same.[14] One major exception among Roman Catholic authors is Stephen B. Bevans, SVD. In 1992, Bevans published a groundbreaking text titled *Models of Contextual Theology*. The book was a major contribution to the overall methodological understanding of contextual theologies and contextualization.[15] Bevans offered six different models of contextual theology that he found at work in various theologians. Along with Coe, Bevans argued that all of them to one degree or another accepted the world outside the church as being in some sense authoritative for theology alongside the authority of scripture and tradition that are passed on within the church. Bevans argued, "Theology that is contextual realizes that culture, history, contemporary thought forms, and so forth are to be considered, along with scripture and tradition, as valid sources for theological expression."[16] Several pages later he adds:

> If the ordinary things of life are so transparent of God's presence, one can speak of culture, human experience, and events in history—of contexts—as truly sacramental and so revelatory. Culture, human experience, and history,

13. The bibliography for contextual theology and contextualization now stretches for pages, but for a random sampling see J. Deotis Roberts Sr., "Contextual Theology: Liberation and Indigenization," *The Christian Century*, January 28, 1976, 64–68; Rosemary Radford Ruether, "Re-Contextualizing Theology," *Theology Today* 43, no. 1 (1986): 22–27; Justin Ukpong, "What Is Contextualization?" *Neue Zeitschrift für Missionswissenschaft* 43 (1987): 161–68; Hans Waldenfels, *Kontextuelle Fundamentaltheologie* (Paderborn: Schöningh, 1985); "Kontextuelle Theologie," *Lexikon missionstheologischer Grundbegriffe* (Berlin: Dietrich Reimer, 1987), 224–30; David J. Hesselgrave and Edward Rommen, *Contextualization: Meanings, Methods, and Models* (Grand Rapids: Baker, 1989); Volker Küster, *Theologie im Kontext: Zugleich ein Versuch über die Minjung-Theologie* (Nettetal: Steyler, 1995); Oscar Carlos, ed., *Teología evangélica para el contexto latinoamericano: Ensayos en honor al Dr. Emilio A. Núñez* (Buenos Aires: Ediciones Kairós, 2004); Sharon E. Heaney, *Contextual Theology for Latin America: Liberation Themes in Evangelical Perspective* (Eugene, OR: Wipf & Stock, 2008); Angie Pears, *Doing Contextual Theology* (New York: Routledge, 2009); and Paul Duane Matheny, *Contextual Theology: The Drama of Our Times* (Eugene, OR: Wipf & Stock, 2011).

14. See Diego Irarrázaval, *Inculturation: New Dawn of the Church in Latin America* (Maryknoll, NY: Orbis, 2000); Laurenti Magesa, *Anatomy of Inculturation: Transforming the Church in Africa* (Maryknoll, NY: Orbis, 2004); and Ikechukwu Anthony Kanu, "Inculturation and the Christian Faith in Africa," *International Journal of Humanities and Social Science* 2, no. 17 (September 2012): 236–44.

15. Maryknoll, NY: Orbis, 1992; Revised and Expanded Edition, 2002.

16. Bevans, *Models of Contextual Theology*, 4. See also Stephen B. Bevans, SVD, *An Introduction to Theology in Global Perspective* (Maryknoll, NY: Orbis, 2009), 18–26.

if we are true to a real dynamic in Christianity's self-understanding, must be "unpacked" of its sacredness.[17]

For Bevans, God speaks to the church not only from within the horizons of its scriptures and traditions. God speaks to the church from outside of it, through culture, other religions, events in social and political life, and the lives of ordinary human beings. This is because the horizons of God's ultimate salvation are not those of the church, but of the world. Along with Roger Schroeder, he wrote provocatively, "*One of the most important things Christians need to know about the church is that the church is not of ultimate importance.*"[18] For the church to learn about God, it must be engaged in dialogue with the world beyond its own boundaries.[19]

Bevans grounded this argument that God is not only inside the church in the work of the Spirit, who is by definition God "inside out." The 1998 article where he worked out this insight was titled "God Inside Out: Toward a Missionary Theology of the Holy Spirit."[20] He acknowledged borrowing the phrase "Inside Out" from Johannes C. Hoekendijk's 1964 publication, *The Church Inside Out*.[21] Like Hoekendijk, Bevans took the church to be radically "eccentric" in the original meaning of having the center on the outside (*ekkentros* in Greek). The church met God not just within itself, but out in the world where God also was to be found.

Hoekendijk had worked out these themes in ecclesiological terms several decades earlier. For several years during the 1960s he had been on a study project sponsored by the Department on Studies in Evangelism of the World Council of Churches on "The Missionary Structures of the Local Congregation." The final report from that study, published in 1967 and titled *The Church for Others—The Church for the World: A Quest for Structures for Missionary Congregations*, argued among other things that the proper perspective for understanding the missionary structure of the local congregation was to perceive the direction being "God-world-church" rather than the more traditional perspective of "God-church-world." God was working on the church from the outside, from the world. One of the members of the study group was Letty M. Russell, who would go on to become a major voice in feminist theology. Rus-

17. Bevans, *Models of Contextual Theology*, 13
18. Stephen B. Bevans, SVD, and Roger P. Schroeder, SVD, *Constants in Context: A Theology of Mission for Today* (Maryknoll, NY: Orbis, 2004), 7.
19. Bevans, *An Introduction to Theology in Global Perspective*, 5.
20. Stephen B. Bevans, SVD, "God Inside Out: Toward a Missionary Theology of the Holy Spirit," *International Bulletin of Missionary Research* 22, no. 3 (1998): 103.
21. Johannes C. Hoekendijk, *The Church Inside Out* (Philadelphia: Westminster, 1964).

sell noted that by the early 1970s in her own theological work she had shifted her theological terminology from that of "mission" to "liberation." She did so, she notes, to make clearer the implications of her earlier work in mission theology. "I think of God's Mission or action in the world as equivalent to God's liberating action or liberation," she wrote.[22] The shift in her thinking from "God-church-world" to "God-world-church" resulted in a shift from an *ecclesiocentric* to a *theocentric* and an *oikocentric* perspective.[23]

Hoekendijk emphasized the world, but always in the form of its eschatological realization, the kingdom of God. He had offered earlier in his 1948 dissertation a somewhat different ordering of "Kingdom-Spirit-community-history"[24] that made this emphasis clearer. For Hoekendijk, the kingdom of God encompassed the widest horizons of the world, the *oikoumenē*, and the fullness of history through which God acted upon the church. The church in this schema was called to serve the ends of the kingdom by being "an instrument of God's redemptive action in this world."[25] The church is not a permanent structure. It is neither the starting point nor the ending point of God's redemptive work in the world, argued Hoekendijk. Instead, the church is called to participate in God's wider redemptive work that takes place beyond the walls of the church. To this end he argued:

> The church has no fixed place at all in this context, it *happens* insofar as it actually proclaims the Kingdom to the world. The church has no other existence than *in actu Christi*, that is, *in actu Apostoli*. Consequently it cannot be firmly established but will always remain the paroikia, a temporary settlement which can never become a permanent home.[26]

Hoekendijk did not waver from a strong conviction that it was the power of the gospel of Jesus Christ, who was raised by the Spirit, that transformed the world. But he argued that the living Christ could not be confined to the institutional structures of the church or passed along solely through its traditions and teachings. The church is being sent out into a world where Christ is already at work. This does not negate the church's apostolic mission, its "sending," but it does entail a more complex understanding of sending that also entails receiving. This was not

22. Letty M. Russell, *Church in the Round: Feminist Interpretation of the Church* (Louisville: Westminster John Knox, 1993), 90.

23. Russell, *Church in the Round*, 88–89.

24. John G. Flett, *Apostolicity: The Ecumenical Question in World Christian Perspective* (Downers Grove, IL: IVP Academic, 2016), 203n63.

25. Hoekendijk, *The Church Inside Out*, 24–25.

26. Hoekendijk, *The Church Inside Out*, 42.

always as clear in Hoekendijk. The opposition he saw was between the church being settled and the church being sent. It was the settled church, the territorial church, the church that was comfortable within its institutional walls, the church that was turned inward upon itself, that he strenuously opposed. Yet without some degree of being settled, there is no sending. One cannot be simply sent without there being a place, however impermanent, from which the sending takes place. On the other hand, every sending is a way of being settled.[27] In Coe's terms, contextuality results in contextualization.

I am prepared to argue here that Hoekendijk was incorrect in his pairing of "sent" and "settled." Instead the pairing ought to have been "sent" and "received," or "received" and "sent." I find this pairing in one of the earliest Christian documents to refer to the apostolic office outside the pages of the New Testament, in the letter known as 1 Clement.[28] 1 Clement 42:1 says that the apostles received their orders in the message of the gospel before they could communicate this message to others. The term that the author uses is an aorist passive plural verb form of *euangelizō*, or "evangelized"—literally, "good newsed."[29] The apostles were evangelized by receiving the good news from Jesus Christ, who, Clement continues, was "sent out" from God. The pairing is not sent and settled here; it is sent and received, received and sent. Reception is as much a part of the apostolic mission and the structure of the church as sending or being sent.

This is an insight that William G. Rusch has offered the wider ecumenical movement in recent decades in his book *Ecumenical Reception: Its Challenge and Opportunity*. Rusch's argument is that reception of another, reception into one's own self or one's own community of another self or another community, is constitutive of the very nature of the church. This is so because it is constitutive of the Trinitarian nature of God and is specifically associated by Rusch with the work of

27. As Elaine Padilla and Peter C. Phan show in their three-volume series, migration is itself a kind of settledness, a new normative condition that characterizes our established institutions in every way. See Elaine Padilla and Peter C. Phan, eds., *Contemporary Issues of Migration and Theology* (New York: Palgrave Macmillan, 2013); *Theology of Migration in the Abrahamic Religions* (New York: Palgrave Macmillan, 2014); and *Migration and Church in World Christianity* (New York: Palgrave Macmillan, 2016).

28. "First Epistle of Clement to the Corinthians," in *Ante-Nicene Fathers: The Writings of the Fathers Down to A.D. 325, volume 1: The Apostolic Fathers, Justin Martyr, and Irenaeus*, ed. Alexander Roberts and James Donaldson (Grand Rapids: Eerdmans, 1954; original 1885), 5–21.

29. I thank my colleague at New York Theological Seminary, Jerry Reisig, who teaches Greek, for this particular whimsical translation.

the Spirit in constituting the church.[30] Ecumenical reception for Rusch is one recent form of "a lively, ongoing process in the life of the Church" through the ages.[31] He in effect turns the apostolic process around, focusing not on the sending but on the receiving.

Of course, for something to be received, something must be sent. Sending and receiving, receiving and sending, mutually constitute one another as processes. One can also easily identify parties in the relationship as being primarily or predominantly associated with one or the other action. Mission studies often speak of sending and receiving churches, or sending and receiving communities, in mission work. What Rusch adds to this observation is the insight that in the theological process of sending and receiving, both parties are changed. He argues:

> A result of this process [of reception] is a real change in both the sender and the receiver. It is more than merely an increase in knowledge; some real consequences occur for both parties. Receiver and sender should, by the acceptance or *reception*, enjoy a new relationship with one another.[32]

In other words, authentic reception means that the sender must receive and the receiver must also send. Theologically, sending and receiving are always far more complex than a simple formulation of the relationship might make it appear to be.

Rusch argues that reception lies at the very heart of ecclesial identity. It is a eucharistic practice in fact. In early Christian life, he notes,

> There was an awareness that *reception* is a spiritual process that takes place in Eucharistic communities, and in fact makes Eucharistic sharing a reality. The ultimate standard for this sharing is the gospel itself, transmitted since the apostles, which involves all members of communities and is an ongoing process.[33]

Sharing (*koinōeō*) and communion (*koinonia*), in other words, entail receiving (*paralambanō, dechomai*). By locating this reception at the heart of the eucharistic experience and linking it with the transmitting (or sending) of the gospel, Rusch locates both sending and receiving at the very heart of the Eucharist. In the Eucharist the Trinitarian God is both sending and receiving.[34] Sending, in other words, does not just happen

---

30. William G. Rusch, *Ecumenical Reception: Its Challenge and Opportunity* (Grand Rapids: Eerdmans, 2007), 7.

31. Rusch, *Ecumenical Reception*, 135.

32. Rusch, *Ecumenical Reception*, 2, emphasis original.

33. Rusch, *Ecumenical Reception*, 22–23, emphasis original.

34. Jeremy D. Wilkins, "Why Are There Two Divine Missions? The Development of a Tra-

at the end of the mass. It already happens in the midst of it, as part of the act of reception.

Reception was central to the inner life of the church through its first centuries, according to Rusch. It was the openness churches had to the teachings of their own leaders as well as to the teachings of others outside their own local communities. But changes in the Latin West after the sixth century led to a loss of classical reception, Rusch argues. Reception in the West eventually became reduced to a legal process and legal categories. This reduction of reception to its legal components was accompanied by a rise in the hierarchical nature of the church with one party teaching and the other party learning, one part of the church active and the other part of the church passive.[35] A recovery of the more dynamic understanding of reception in the life of the church in the West began in the sixteenth century in both Protestant and Roman Catholic branches of the Reformation, Rusch notes, and became accelerated in the twentieth century in the ecumenical movement.

The basic meaning of reception for Rusch is taking into one's life something that one has not produced.[36] For the most part he understands this "something" to be produced by another party within the church or by another ecclesial community. Reception entails a particular church receiving the decisions of a council, for instance, or one particular ecclesial community receiving into its own life teachings or practices that have been produced by another. It is not hard to see that this characterizes the very nature of Christian life and the handing on of tradition from generation to generation. Each generation must receive the gospel from another, a previous one, and make the gospel its own (thereby introducing changes) before it can hand it over to those who come after.[37] What is often not so clearly seen, at least by those who are immediately involved in this process, is the manner in which changes are introduced and the gospel becomes different than itself, or diversified. Differences and diversity in turn at times led to separation.

Ecumenical reception has been particularly associated with those separated churches being willing to move toward acknowledging one another as Christian to some degree at least, each receiving the other back into its own life to some degree or receiving ideas that emerged from dialogues and consultations between and among representatives of

dition in Augustine, Aquinas, and Lonergan," *Irish Theological Quarterly* 77, no. 1 (2012): 39, notes: "Augustine understood the Trinity to be an order of giving and receiving."

35. Rusch, *Ecumenical Reception*, 24.

36. Rusch, *Ecumenical Reception*, 39.

37. See Dale T. Irvin, *Christian Histories, Christian Traditioning: Rendering Accounts* (Maryknoll, NY: Orbis, 1989), 17–33.

various communions. Rusch at one point acknowledges briefly the parallel this process has with the process of contextualization or inculturation.[38] While he does not linger here to work out the implications, it is nevertheless an important insight that needs to be lifted up. Rather than seeing the process of contextualization as only being a one-way activity of translating the Bible or the teachings of the church into another language or cultural setting, it emphasizes the manner in which cultural values, practices, and ideas from locations outside the church (*extra ecclesia*) must be received into a church in order for that church to continue to be faithful to the living Christ.

Much of our work in mission studies over the past century has emphasized mission as sending. The task of missions has too often been reduced to simply translating the message of the gospel into a language or cultural setting in which it had not previously been expressed. Contextualization, as Coe understood it, entails more than this. It entails the reception of language, values, practices, and ideas within a particular communion or church. Reception is a process at the heart of ecclesiology, but following Bevans and Hoekendijk, it is one that locates the heart outside, in the world. This is why mission can never be a one-way street. Every church that seeks to send must also be a church that is willing to receive. Any sending that is not simultaneously an act of receiving, an openness to reception, is not the sending of the gospel; and any act of reception that is not also in some sense an act of sending is not yet fully reception of the gospel.

The great failure of the modern missionary movement that arose in the West has been the tendency to view mission as a one-way street. Churches in the West too often supported sending of ministerial agents ("missionaries") to other parts of the world, expecting persons in those other parts of the world to receive the gospel from the West, without expecting churches of the West to simultaneously be receiving. Of course, reception was going on all the time over the past five hundred years. Churches of the West have absorbed enormous amounts of knowledge, history, and practices from other cultures of the world. Missing from this situation has been a more active realization that churches of the West had to receive as well as send, that when it comes to the gospel, there is no sending that is not also receiving and no receiving without sending. The apostolic character of the church requires one to receive if one is to send. A church that fails to receive from other cultures is not yet fully apostolic.

A danger in our contemporary discussion of "reverse missions" is that

---

38. Rusch, *Ecumenical Reception*, 5, 81.

we continue to conceptualize missions as one-way traffic, or as a movement in one direction only. I have to emphasize here that mission is indeed an outward movement of sending, but it always also entails the inward movement of reception of the other if it is to be truly Christian. Applied to the current discussion of "reverse missions," one sees that the notion that Africans, Asians, and the First Nation peoples of the Americas missionizing the West is a recent phenomenon ignores much that has happened over the past five hundred years of Christian history. Furthermore, the notion that mission can only be intentional, as when a church sends an agent specifically to evangelize in a particular community, or that agents of Christian faith serving migrant communities in the West do not count as "missionaries," hampers our ability to see what is going on in the contextualization process today in world Christianity. Afe Adogame and Shobana Shankar, in their recent edited collection, *Religion on the Move! New Dynamics of Religious Expansion in a Globalizing World*, have provided a far more dynamic and multidirectional understanding of mission that captures aspects not only of the sending, but the receiving as well.[39] Their work was prefigured by Hoekendijk, who wrote in *The Church Inside Out*, "All of us have landed in the diaspora."[40]

I conclude by returning to that passage from 1 Clement that I noted above in relation to the notion of apostolic receiving and sending. My colleague in New York Theological Seminary, Jerry Reisig, points out that in 1 Clement 42:1 where the apostles were themselves said to be evangelized, the writer uses the dative *ēmin* ("for us") to locate the gospel in a particular place where one stands. In the text of 1 Clement 42:1 the term is associated with the apostles. They were evangelized "for us." But Reisig notes that Greek is quite economical, so that a word used in one clause need not be duplicated in the next, even if its meaning is repeated. He reads the sentence to say that the apostles were evangelized for us, but that God also sent Jesus for us. The term *ēmin*, "for us," has the effect here of placing the reader as the recipient of the original message, the message of Jesus himself. He goes on:

God sent Jesus to a place that is the center, but which moves out spatially and temporally in concentric circles. The farther one moves out in performance for us ημιν [*ēmin*] the closer one moves to the space of the cross.

39. Afe Adogame and Shobana Shankar, *Religion on the Move! New Dynamics of Religious Expansion in a Globalizing World* (Leiden: Brill, 2012).
40. Hoekendijk, *The Church Inside Out*, 79.

The means to carry this place forward and re-perform the cross space is the "good news."[41]

The movement from God to Christ to the apostles is simultaneously a movement of dispersion, a scattering, to those in a different time and place. The *ēmin* ("for us") makes this always also an act of first-time reception. The space in which this reception takes place is always changing, always new. Reception of the message is never without historical form. Another way of saying this is that the message is always incarnate. The God who is for us is the God who is encountered incarnationally in the flesh, in history, in the world. The mission of God that is for us is a mission that is first for the world. But this means that it also entails God taking the world into the divine self, which is what happened in the incarnation. "We never have to do with God except in some secular, worldly form, a form that disguises God—for example, the human language of Scripture and the church," writes Joseph L. Mangina.[42] Reading, discerning, perceiving, and receiving the signs of the times, especially in the spaces of the cross in the world around us, and rethinking the text of the gospel through these lenses is more than an option for churches of the world today, Shoki Coe would tell us if he were with us still. "Each period, each generation, each body of believers may and in some sense must formulate a theology for itself," argues Leonard Lovett.[43] "Our goal is to do away with injustice, to create spaces for justice to flourish, so the unfolding of the kin-dom of God can become a reality in our lives, in our society," adds Ada María Isasi-Díaz.[44] Contextualizing theology, ministry, faith, and practice is as much a mandate for us now as it was for Coe and his generation.

41. Personal email from Dr. Jerry Reisig dated July 6, 2014.

42. Joseph L. Mangina, *Karl Barth: Theologian of Christian Witness* (Louisville: Westminster John Knox, 2004), 36. He attributes this idea to Karl Barth, who wrote in *Church Dogmatics* I/1, ed. G. W. Bromiley and T. F. Torrance (Edinburgh: T&T Clark, 1969), 165, "We do not have the Word of God otherwise than in the mystery of its secularity."

43. Leonard Lovett, "Aspects of the Spiritual Legacy of the Church of God in Christ: Ecumenical Implications," in *Black Witness to the Apostolic Faith*, ed. David T. Shannon and Gayraud S. Wilmore (Grand Rapids: Eerdmans, 1985), 43.

44. Ada María Isasi-Díaz, "Un poquito de justicia—a Little Bit of Justice: A Mujerista Account of Justice," in *Hispanic/Latino Theology: Challenge and Promise*, ed. Ada María Isasi-Díaz and Fernando F. Segovia (Minneapolis: Fortress Press, 1996), 326.

3.

Epistemological Decolonization of Theology
(Translated by Néstor Medina)

ENRIQUE DUSSEL

The theme of "epistemological decolonization" originated from a group of Latin American and Latino (these last in the United States of America) philosophers, sociologists, historians, and social scientists. It is an elaboration of a problematic that began because of critical positions such as postcolonialism (in cultural studies), subaltern studies (among Indian historians), and postmodernism (mainly in Europe and the USA). It is also a further development of those who articulated the *theory of dependence* (during the decade of the 1960s), the critique of centralized capitalism (in relation to its periphery), theology of liberation, the theme of race and gender (from feminist movements), as well as from the originary peoples (as in the case of the Aztecs, Mayas, Incas, etc.). It is structured around what has been called "coloniality of power" (which was proposed by Anibal Quijano, a Peruvian sociologist)[1] and "transmodernity"[2] (which stemmed from the horizon of liberation theology that a number of us Latin American and Latino philosophers practice).[3] From this complex thematic structure emerges the "epistemological decolonization" that finds its roots in the thought of José Carlos Mariátegui

1. See A. Quijano, "Coloniality of Power, Eurocentrism and Social Classification," in *Coloniality at Large*, ed. M. Boraña, E. Dussel, and C. A. Járegui (Durham, NC: Duke University Press, 2010), 181–223; "Coloniality and Modernity/Rationality," in *Globalization and the Decolonial Option*, ed. W. Mignolo and E. Escobar (London: Routledge, 2010), 22–32.

2. See the electronic publication www.Transmodernity.com (especially Linda Alcoff's contribution).

3. See E. Dussel, E. Mendieta, and C. Bohórquez, *El Pensamiento Filosófico Latinoamericano, del Caribe y Latino (1300–2000)* (Mexico City: Siglo XXI, 2010).

(Peruvian), Frantz Fanon (from Martinique), and Immanuel Wallerstein (with his theory of the *World-System*).

In this article, I wish to describe within theology this new theoretical rupture in the horizon of the sciences (therefore epistemological). I follow the tradition of the theology of liberation without repeating what has already been said but taking a new step forward as the theology of liberation of the 1960s did not have an explicit clarity on the matter.

MESSIANIC CHRISTIANITY

To speak of messianic Christianity is a tautology: it is to repeat twice the same thing. "Christianity" comes from "Christ," which in Greek means messiah (*khristós*) and his followers are messianic (*khristianoí*). In fact, the early messianic community[4] was a proselytizing Jewish sect open to the *goim* (Hebrew: the non-Jewish); from this experience of "openness," in Barnabas and Paulo of Tarso, it expanded rapidly among the poor, the oppressed, the slaves, and other majority groups in the Hellenic-Roman Empire. The other Jewish sect was structured around the Law in the synagogues, since the diaspora was inaugurated by the Babylonian exile, and proselytized less and was able to preserve its customs without incorporating the *goim*. They were merchants for life, dedicated to commerce in the interstices of the reigning empires (Babylonian, Hellenic, Roman, Byzantine, the Muslim Caliphates, Persia, medieval feudal Latino-Germanic, Russian Czarists, up to modern Europe and the United States of America in the present). Because of the persecution by Emperor Titus, the Judaism of the temple or priestly order disappeared forever. The *messianic* sect constituted by the (Christian) church opposed the Hellenic-Roman Empire from the beginning, denying it the pretention to be called empire, the necessary mediation between the sacred and the divine. The emperor, "Son of God" and "Supreme Pontiff" (*bridge* between human beings and the gods), was deprived of such dignity by the (Christian) *messianic* church. In this way, the *messianic* church secularized the Roman Empire; at least it arrogated to itself the union or mediation of God with history,[5] whose presence springs from the poorest and the humiliated, and critically confronted the empire, desacralizing and secularizing it.

The *messianic* church (read "Christian") became the majority of the population in certain regions, above all in the east of the empire, in

4. In other words, "Christianity."
5. See the book by G. Agamben, *Il Regno e la Gloria. Per una Genealogía Teológica dell'e Economía e del Governo* (Vicenza: Edizione Neri Pozza, 2007).

today's Turkey, for example. In his internal strife to defeat all of the competing Caesars after the death of Diocletian, Constantine negotiated with the *messianic* church and proposed it the freedom of cult in exchange for not opposing the empire, thus supporting his candidacy. It is in this way that the son of Saint Elena became an emperor.

The *messianics* (read "Christians") went from being persecuted to being accepted, tolerated, and soon after became the hegemony of the empire.

CHRISTENDOM

At the turn of the fourth century, imperceptibly and slowly, without many taking consciousness of what happened, the inversion from *messianism* into triumphant Christianity was produced. The *messianics* (in a similar sense as given by Walter Benjamin and Emmanuel Levinas) ceased to be critical of the empire and became its supporters, its members, and, in time, its defenders. The Messiah crucified by the soldiers of the Roman Empire was now acclaimed as the *Christ*, the *Christ* who had lost Isaiah's image of the "suffering servant" in order to be *Pantokrator*: the all-powerful of the Byzantine basilicas. Christ was now the name of the God who founded the empire, in whose name the Roman armies confronted slaves, the Germanics, the barbarians, the rebellious farmers, and the slaves who pretended to be free. It is the "God of the armies" to whom Joshua claimed to clean up the "promised land" of the Canaanites and that pushed the destruction of Jericho. It was now a God of the oppressors: it was an idol. The God of Israel had been transformed into Baal, into Moloch.

Søren Kierkegaard and Marx critiqued the God of Hegel because it was the God of Christendom. Christendom (*Cristiandad, Christlichkeit, Chretienté*) is not the same as *messianic* Christianity (*cristianismo, Christendum, Christianisme*);[6] it is its inversion, the *first* inversion.

From the fourth century to the beginning of the seventeenth century, Christendom fetishistically replaced the philosophical and theological foundations of the Hellenistic-Roman Empire. The ancient pagan temples were destroyed, the royal market places were transformed into temples (basilicas), the philosophical school at Athens was closed, and Christendom became the new hegemonic culture. I say *culture*, and not

6. See Karl Löwith, *Von Hegel zu Nietzsche*, II (Stuttgart: Kohlhammer, 1964), chap. 5, 350. It is impossible to understand the critique of religion in S. Kierkegaard and K. Marx without regard to this inversion of Christianity. Both writers put things in their place, even from the point of *Messianic* (authentic) Christianity.

just *religion*. If it would have been only religion, it would have survived the Greco-Roman culture. But it was not like that. A complex hybrid Greco-Roman and Semite-Christian culture was produced. The earlier *messianism* became a religion that structurally gave birth to a *new* culture, which was the fruit of the transformation of the *ancient* Greco-Roman and Christian culture.

For example, in the Mediterranean and adjacent towns, the "birth of the sun" was celebrated on the shortest day of the year, December 21. Irish people near Dublin still have an ancestral Neolithic temple that has a tunnel through which the sunlight goes only one day a year, illuminating a polished stone at the very end of the tunnel. That day is only December 21. The *messianics* incorporated that pagan ritual because of the increasing numbers of proselytes in their communities celebrating the "birthday of the sun of justice": Jesus (Christmas day). It is a celebration that did not exist in the *messianic* community (of suspect fetishistic inspiration, founded on the astronomic year). As time went by, it became a central moment of the liturgical year of Christendom; from the year 1000 CE Germanic elements were added (as was the case with the Christmas tree). Many elements of the Greco-Roman culture and religious rites were subsumed by the cult of Christendom. The Greco-Roman culture had been evangelized; its symbols, cults, and rituals had been adopted and transformed as components of the *new* culture. This culture continued to move up toward the Germanic north, crossing the Rhine and the Danube and into the strange lands of the Latin Empire. With the Holy Roman Germanic Empire centered near Trier, and with the papal crowning of the Frankish Charlemagne as emperor, a state founded on the sacredness of the Christian church, Christendom, was realized. The Patriarch of the Latin Church (the Papa) consecrated emperors (he was a Caesar-like pope). Imagine the bewilderment that it would have caused to a *messianic* Christian to see the "successor" of the crucified Messiah, the Pope, crown the Roman emperor. The *inversion* was complete; the "*messianic* principle" had been confused with the principle of a religion that had negotiated being the very justification for a sacralized state (the Holy Roman Empire). This was particularly the case in the Byzantine Empire, where the emperor *de facto* governed the church;[7] when the church criticized the empire—as in the case of John Chrysostom—she was punished (by expelling from Constantinople this

---

7. This is what would happen centuries later in the Anglo-Saxon Christianity of the United Kingdom or the Lutheran countries of Northern Europe, which Thomas Hobbes would justify theologically in his work *El Leviatán* (FCE, Tercera Parte: México City, 1998), 305–498, on "Of a Christian State" (the modern fetishization of politics).

patriarch, who was dubbed a rebel). It was a "Caesar-like papacy." It is clear that there were always great saints and prophets who critiqued this state of affairs, but they were always the minority more or less persecuted (by the state or the church).

That is how the history of a wrongly called Middle Ages was developed. It was the age when Latino-Germanic Christendom (which pretended to be the *City of God* but was only the *earthly city*) was cornered, besieged, surrounded by the wall built by the Islamic civilization since 623, when the expansion of the Muslim religion began. From the seventh century to the end of the fifteenth century (exactly until 1492), the Latino-Germanic religion had been isolated from the Asian-African-Mediterranean system. As for the Eastern side of Christendom at Byzantium, which had expanded among the Slavs, it began losing ground and power because of the advance of Islam and the Ottoman Empire, and which culminated in the fall of Constantinople in 1453. Latin Christendom was more underdeveloped and insignificant than ever. The Islamic world from Córdoba and Fez (Andalusia and Morocco) to Fatimid Egypt, Baghdad as reference of the ancient system, Afghanistan, the Indian Moguls, the kingdoms of Indonesia around Malacca and present in Mindanao in the Philippines, crossing by the Samarkand deserts of the Silk Road toward China,[8] was the connection and the "center of the *ancient* world" (*ancient* for Adam Smith[9]). Latino-Germanic Europe was only a peripheral world, isolated, feudal, in its own "dark age" (which contrasted with the "age of enlightenment," the "lights" of the Islamic classical world—urban, Aristotelian/scientific, and mercantile).

METROPOLITAN CHRISTENDOM AND
COLONIAL CHRISTENDOM

Suddenly, and without previous preparation, the Latino-Germanic Christendom of the periphery and underdeveloped began an expansion that would situate it in global geopolitics through *a profound transformation that has not yet been captured*. To take cognizance of this new fact is exactly the objective of this article, a matter of which Christendom has not become aware after five centuries. It is not a small matter, and blindness to it is noticeable in the face of its evident global existence! Often, the most evident and obvious becomes the most hidden, confus-

8. A China that in the eighteenth century would begin the Industrial Revolution before England. See Kenneth Pomeranz, *The Great Divergence: China, Europe, and the Making of the Modern World Economy* (Oxford: Princeton University Press, 2000).

9. Giovanni Arrighi, *Adam Smith in Beijing* (London: Verso, 2007).

ing, and unknown. It is that which people hold as the quotidian healthy common sense that nobody puts into question. We must then put into question the quotidian evidence, which we must know how to assume, critique, and invert (to invert many inversions that were done without the awareness of it, that is, *unintentionally*, but no less responsible and grave, because we are talking about a structural sin that compounded and worsened for the last five centuries—from 1492 to date, upon the foundation of the previous nine centuries, from 623 to 1492).

In point of fact, Latino-Germanic Christendom (not *messianic* Christianity) was surrounded by the Muslim world. With the Crusades, it attempted the false adventure of the recovery of the Holy Sepulcher (that space was essential geopolitically, for the commerce of the Italian mercantile cities, to rebuild the economic connection with Asia, the center of the global markets at that time) to *open* a route through the Muslim wall, but this was rejected by the strength of the Islamic kingdoms. Christendom was left as cornered as it was before. Meanwhile, Portugal, *finis terris* of the West (of Europe) sought to *open* itself to Asian commerce by way of occupying ports and the coasts of western Africa (the eastern Atlantic).

It would be Spain, nevertheless, which after the expulsion of the last Muslim from Europe (from Granada in January 1492) attempted to get to China (the center of the markets of the known world) by way of the West. Christopher Columbus discovered the Atlantic and arrived at some lost islands in the ocean via the West, which were thought to be China, according to the Henricus Martellus[10] maps of 1489. (These maps were among other representations of China that arrived in Venice at the turn of the fifteenth century. They were later known in Portugal and in Freiburg, which allowed Martin Waldseemüller in 1506 to create the cartography of South America in a world map, as a fourth peninsula of China and as part of America in the south.) The opening made by Europe toward the Atlantic (first by Spain and Portugal, and subsequently by Holland and other European nations) was the beginning of the new age. (*The modern age was the death of the Mediterranean and the birth of the Atlantic.*) Europe unhinges and opens itself to the "wide world" through the new geopolitical center of sailing ships and commerce: tropical Atlantic (in the regions dominated by Spain in connection with the Hispanic Caribbean in the sixteenth century[11]).

10. See this problem in my work, *The Invention of the Americas: Eclipse of the Other and the Myth of Modernity* (New York: Continuum, 1995), 142. Like all my works, it can be downloaded from www.enriquedussel.com.

11. It is not so strange then that modern theology and philosophy (before Luther and

Without becoming aware, Latino-Germanic Christendom, by way of the Atlantic at the south of Europe (Spain and Portugal before anyone else), begins to build that new world: the *New World* (Hispanic America but not the Anglo Saxon one that would emerge in the seventeenth century) that would be Latin America in the first place, a matter to which the present Eurocentric social sciences (in northern Europe and the United States of America) do not recognize. These series of events situated Latino Europe (Spanish and Portuguese) as *metropolis of the colonial world* that was organized at the end of the fifteenth century (1492), before Northern Europe would wake up from its medieval sleep (Anglo Saxon, Germanic, Slav in the seventeenth century). That is to say, a new disastrous determination is produced in the nature of Christendom (which was already a destructive *inversion* of early *messianic* Christianity). Besides being *Christendom* (the *first* inversion), it would be now a *central* and *imperial* Christendom, dominating the oppressed colonies in the name of the gospel of the Crucified One (*second* inversion). It crucified the indigenous in the name of the one who was crucified.[12] It is for this reason that a Chilean indigenous person, painting the crucifixion, put in the place of Christ (or the *poor Messiah* as the Peruvian Inca chronicler Guamán Poma de Ayala would call him) an Indian, and in the place of the (Roman) soldiers who crucified him Spanish soldiers from Iberian Christendom. The indigenous painter *inverted* the *inversion*; he placed on its feet what had been put on its head twice. If the just was crucified, he had to be an Indian (because they were just and were not oppressing anyone). If the soldiers who crucified Christ were part of the oppressive empire that murdered the just, it had to be the Spanish soldiers of Christendom—which was now metropolitan, central, and the oppressor of *colonies* (as analogically Israel was during the Roman Empire) and which killed indigenous peoples in the name of a metropolitan, distant, Roman Christendom. To think theologically from the oppressed *colonial* subjectivity, and having *critical* consciousness that this "being colonial"[13] is in fact the theme of this reflection, is already an act of adopting the perspective of an *epistemological decolonizing of theology*. And it is already the transcendental presupposition that conditions the possibility of *all* theological reflection.

Descartes) began in the Caribbean. On this beginning of theology and modern philosophy, see my work, *Der Gegendiskurs der Moderne. Koelner Vorlesungen* (Berlin: Turia-Kant, 2013).

12. See Franz Hinkelammert, *The Ideological Weapons of Death* (Maryknoll, NY: Orbis, 1986).

13. M. Heidegger would say: "being-colonial-in-the-world" (*in-der-Welt-kolonial-Sein*).

Bartolomé de las Casas,[14] a *messianic* prophet at the beginning of modernity, began his struggle in 1514 in Sancti Espíritu (Cuba); the *first anti-discourse of all of modernity* (three years before Machiavelli would write *The Prince* and Luther would affix his theses at Wittenberg) criticizes the injustice in oppressing indigenous peoples as a result of the Papal Bulls in which the pope gave the Spanish emperor the responsibility to "Christianize the Indians." Bartolomé demonstrates that the pope had no power to grant the indigenous to the king of Spain because he had no rights over them. In the same fashion, the king of Spain had no rights over the members of a state who were not his subjects, and who enjoyed autonomy and power based on their own institutions. At the beginning of the colonial structures (which after Spain and Portugal were continued by Holland, France, England, Denmark, and so forth, and today by the United States of America), Bartolomé showed that this coloniality is a structural sin because the European Christians (Latino-Germanic Christendom) had no right to organize a *colonial* world. Nevertheless, during the controversy at Valladolid in the 1550, Ginés de Sepúlveda justified the need and convenience of European dominion over the peoples of the South, non-Christians, barbarians, immature children, who, by being conquered, gained participation in Christianity, that is, in the Mediterranean-European civilization.

The worse thing is not that European Christianity elevated itself as the paragon of human culture as such (an unjustifiable pretention), of being the civilization with the right to dominate other peoples and cultures (as was expressed later singlehandedly by the Eurocentric European–North American colonialism that we have studied in multiple works[15]). Rather, it created from the beginning a world of domination that contradictorily was a *colonial* Latino Christendom. It baptized allegedly free barbarians and sovereigns to make them submissive Christians, dominated the colonials of a Christian empire (thus imperial Christendom versus colonized Christendom). I say it is a greater scandal to be part of an imperial Christendom because *colonial* Christendom, not the one from Spain, for example, but the one in Mexico or Brazil, was formed with people indoctrinated by the Christendom of the *center* and the Eurocentric. They would have to admit to being *Christians* at a secondary level and not just second-class colonial *citizens*. To be "*second class* Christians" (of

---

14. See this problem in my work *Politics of Liberation: A Critical World History* (London: SCM, 2011), 182.

15. See E. Dussel, "Encuentros, Métodos Evangelizatorios y Conflictos," in *Introducción General a la Historia de la Iglesia en América Latina*, t. I/1 de *Historia General de la Iglesia en América Latina* (Salamanca: Sígueme, 1983), 336.

course not like the early *messianic* Christians of the Latino-Germanic Christendom that had inverted *messianic* Christianity) is to admit to reproducing passively and becoming a disciple of a religion, a political structure, and a confused culture, because of the Latino-European *inversion* of Christendom. Colonial Christians are *second-class children of God*.

We have stated that Christmas was the subsuming of a Greco-Roman religious celebration—it was not *messianic* Christianity or Semitic, the result of a valid transculturation that *messianic* Christianity carried out creatively in the face of the Mediterranean culture. Now, when the conquistadors and evangelizers arrived in the Incan Empire, they observed that on June 21 in the great temple of the sun in Cuzco, the Incas celebrated the *Inti Raimi*, the "birth of the Sun." All the fires in all the homes across the empire were extinguished. Early in the morning at the great temple, the rays of the birthing sun were captured, which hit a series of golden mirrors and lit up the cotton wick; it was the "sacred fire" produced by the sun itself. The Inca emperor distributed the "sacred fire" in all the provinces, villages, and homes, and fire would light up every family in the empire once again. The Sun God was its physical/real origin. Beautiful celebration of Christmas! But no; Quechua and Aymara had to abandon everything: their calendar, feasts, and symbols. Irrationally they had to adopt the liturgy of Mediterranean Christendom of the northern hemisphere.[16] This *imposition*, even liturgical, over the southern hemisphere was interpreted as the "universalization" of Christendom in the entire world. It was the pretention of one particular religion, the modern European culture, to elevate itself by violence using weapons to a spurious and fetishized universality. The resurgence of the cultures of the south (Amerindians, Bantu, Islamic, from the Southeast or the Far East) demands the rethinking of the destructive modern utopia, built upon the pretention of the *abstract* universality of Latino-Germanic Christendom, which oppressed all the peoples of the colonial South.

---

16. I remember in my childhood in Argentina that in March or April we celebrated Easter, the feast of the resurrection of life. However, it took place in the autumn, when the leaves fell from the trees and nature was dressed in the sadness of the next winter. It was a sad Easter, which in the Northern Hemisphere was celebrated in the spring. In the same way in September, when life appeared after the harsh winter in the South, there was no celebration of life, but bland Sundays of Pentecost. A liturgical disaster! A ritual imposition of a fossilized Christianity of the North was forced on the South. The time will come in the Southern Hemisphere to change the liturgical year by six months in order to restore its meaning as among the Aymara, Quechua, and Mapuche, celebrating Eucharist in the South with potatoes and chicha (and not bread and wine as in the North).

EPISTEMOLOGICAL DECOLONIZATION

The modernity (which begins as we indicated in 1492) of a scientifically peripheral world in the so-called Middle Ages (because its philosophy,[17] mathematics, astronomy, etc., originated in the Islamic and Chinese worlds, from the South and the East) after three centuries (the humanist and mercantile epoch hegemonized at the beginning by Spain and subsequently by Holland and England) placed itself as the center of the *World-System* (as I. Wallerstein calls it). Only with the Industrial Revolution and after the Chinese crisis (which begins the indicated revolution) did the Enlightenment claim that its culture was the only one with the possibilities to encompass the horizons of human universality as such. The German Romantics, as Walter Benjamin helps us see, claimed to be the historic culmination of humanity. Hegel is the best example of this Eurocentrism. For the professor at Berlin, history ran from the East (the primitive) to the West (the culmination of the process) and Christianity (read Romantic-Germanic Christendom) was the full realization of all religions; Europe was the full emergence of civilization: "England understood that it had to be the missionary of civilization for the whole world."[18] European culture and civilization as such (in the face of the barbarians from the other cultures) were one and the same thing.

The four phenomena of *modernity, Eurocentrism, colonialism,* and *capitalism* are aspects of the same simultaneous contemporary processes and determinations: they emerged and developed at the same time (they will also come to an end at the same time). The classical *theoretical* expression of this complex historical reality is the Enlightenment (la *ilustración, Aufklärung, le Siècle des Lumières)*. Horkheimer and Adorno did a first critique of the Enlightenment,[19] but because they were not able to over-

17. The path followed by philosophical renewal is a good example. Aristotle was rediscovered by Islamic thought through the influence of Byzantine Christians, and Al Kindi already practiced the thought of the Stagirite in the ninth century. From there he passed to Samarkand, Buchara, and other cities, arriving in Cordoba in the eleventh century, and through translators from Toledo to Paris in the thirteenth century. Aristotelianism was anticipated in the Arab world in comparison to Paris by four centuries. Since the ninth century, Baghdad had been the center of the study of mathematics (even the numerals are Arabic), of astronomy, and of other empirical sciences, which also came from China to Italy, along with the great technological discoveries (which have been taken in the West as inventions of Leonardo da Vinci, being that he simply copied drawings of books printed on paper in China in 1313 and that came to the hands of Pope Eugene IV, and from there to many publications of the Renaissance). See Dussel, *Politics of Liberation,* vol. 1 (London: SCM, 2011).

18. G. W. F. Hegel, *Vorlesungen über die Philosophie der Geschichte,* IV, 3, 3, in *Werke,* vol. 12 (Frankfurt: Suhrkamp, 1970), 538.

19. See Max Horkheimer and Theodor Adorno, *Dialektik der Aufklärung* (Frankfurt: S. Fischer, 1969).

come their Eurocentrism, their critique was metropolitan, centered on a Europe as yet undiscovered as the center of the world-system. It was therefore a Eurocentric critique; that is to say, they still did not notice the racist Eurocentrism in the entire discourse of the Enlightenment. It was not an "epistemologically decolonizing" critique; they did not notice the colonial attitudes of modernity. It still moved in a horizon of the center. That attitude was the "hubris of point zero"[20] shared by the great majority of intellectuals, even by those of European–North American critical thought up to the present.

If there was a "linguistic turn" that discovered the importance of language in philosophy and the social sciences (as the one produced by the "Vienna Circle"), and if there was a "pragmatic turn" as proposed by Karl-Otto Apel, now we wish to talk about an epistemological "decolonizing turn." The latter consists of *taking critical consciousness of the postcolonial world of Eurocentrism* as the place of expression of the discourse (*locus enuntiationis*) *habitus*, which was generalized by the thinker, the scientist, and the philosopher. Such Eurocentrism permeates profoundly the subjectivity of the theoretician and the objectivity of the theories (and human and social sciences); it is practically impossible to be liberated from the limitations that are accepted by all unanimously, by all the scientific communities, the theories, the research projects that practically impede overcoming its narrow and deforming limits.

Frequently I take world history as an example, which is like a theoretical horizon of the social sciences. I ask: How many of you have studied world history in a different periodization than the one proposed: Early Age, Middle Age, and Modern Age? I have never found someone who tells me that in their school, institute, or university they received a history of the world with a different periodization. No one remembers that this hypothesis of periodization is not more than two centuries old; that Novalis wrote that "we" (the romantics) invented the concept of antiquity;[21] and with that they *invented* the feudal Middle Age as a period of universal history (if we overcome Eurocentrism, such periodization is only valid for the European Latino-Germanic culture, only a small

20. In the Renaissance, painters first traced the horizon and filed all the objects they would paint to one point. That "zero point" would be, inadvertently, the very eye of the painter, but as his negative. That spot does not appear in the painting, but the whole picture is orchestrated from that vanishing point, not seen as the eye of the painter, although in reality it is omnipresent in the work. It is the absence of the *cogito ego* of all *cogitatum*. The *cogitatum*, of course, is the colonial being.

21. See "Der Begriff der Kunstkritik in der deutschen Romantik," in W. Benjamin, *Abhandlugen: Gesammelte Schriften*, vol. I/1 (Frankfurt: Suhrkamp, 1974), 116: "Erst jetzt fängt es wie der *Antike*; sie ist eigentlich *nicht gegeben*—sie ist nicht vorhanden—sondern sie soll von uns [Novalis and the romantics] erste *hervorgebracht* werden."

part of humanity), and modernity would not be the cultural fruit of an *exclusive* creation of Europe (that began in the Renaissance, continued in the Protestant Reformation, and the French Enlightenment and English Parliament, leaving to the side the sixteenth century; that is to say: Spain, Portugal, the Atlantic, and Latin America), but it was the manipulation of the centrality of the *world-system* that owed much knowledge to the colonized cultures; knowledge that never recognized where it came from.

But Eurocentrism not only deforms all of history to prove the centrality of Europe "since ever," as Max Weber did. Rather, with the Enlightenment it split Europe in two. "Southern" Europe, which *was* important in its origins (but ceased to be in the eighteenth century, such as Greece, Rome, Spain, and Portugal), and "the heart of Europe," "Northern" Europe, which as Hegel explains, includes Germany, Denmark, France, and England. That Northern Europe, which was industrial, capitalist, and mainly Protestant Christendom, was the most Eurocentric and metropolitan, because it developed an industrial capitalism, imperial (mainly with England) and in the present, globalized (with the US).

The social sciences (even psychoanalysis and Marxism) do not put into question the universality of the methods and objectives of the social sciences as they are presented in Europe. The other cultures that have been falling behind since the sixteenth century would develop in the future by imitating the sciences of Europe. This false "developmental fallacy" (the belief in the necessarily linear character of history, in the Europe that walks at the front of the necessary process, is left today uncovered because the processes of the colonial countries do not necessarily follow the processes followed by Europe, as in the case with Russia, India, Brazil, or especially China) is presupposed by all the actual social sciences.

If we ask ourselves as a form of synthesis, how did the *epistemological decolonizing turn* begin? There is no better description than Eduardo Mendieta's, which resonates with my own description at the beginning of this article:

> The *decolonial turn of* the project of *decolonizing the social sciences* and within it epistemology, is a theoretical paradigm that emerged from the productive convergence and synthesis of at *least* five different theoretical/philosophical strands: Dusselian liberation philosophy, grounded in a Levinasian-Schellingian phenomenology that is married to a post-Eurocentric, post-Hellenophilic, post-pax Americana hermeneutics with planetary reach; Wallersteinian world systems theory refracted through the lens of the Atlantic slave trade; the Quijano post-Eurocentric, post-occidentalist cri-

tique of the *coloniality of power*; and the Fanonian phenomenological critique of the racial geography and corporeality of occidental reason; as has
been elaborated eloquently by Lewis Gordon and Nelson Maldonado-
Torres; and last but not least, Mignolian border gnosis and Nepantlism.
Each of these currents is nourished by a formidable and extensive bibliography—veritable libraries.[22]

In fact, at the end of the decade of the 1960s emerged liberation philosophy, which inquired if it was possible to do philosophy in underdeveloped and peripheral countries. Note that the center-periphery issue was
the original presupposition of such question. And it concluded that "the
philosophy that knows how to think this reality, this actual world reality, not from the perspective of the center, from the cultural, rational,
phalocratic, political, economic or military powers, but beyond the border itself of the actual central world, *from the periphery*. This philosophy
will not be ideological. The reality of this philosophy is the whole earth
and for it, the wretched of the earth are (they are not non-being) also
reality."[23]

Meanwhile, Wallerstein put a historical framing to Dependency Theory in his best work in 1974,[24] which contextualized dependency within
the world market (I have dealt with the concept of dependence in my
1988 work, which was translated into English in 2001[25]). Above we have
already suggested the contributions by Franz Fanon.

In addition, it must be observed that the originality of the proposal
by Walter Mignolo[26] started with the linguistic and semiotic disciplines
and underwent an evolution that allowed him to ask about the unwritten

22. E. Mendieta, "The Ethics of (Not) Knowing: Take Care of Ethics and Knowledge Will
Come of Its Own Accord," in *Decolonizing Epistemologies: Latina/o Theology and Philosophy*,
ed. M. Isasi-Díaz and E. Mendieta (New York: Fordham University Press, 2012), 261. On a
non-Eurocentric ethic, see my work, *Ethics of Liberation* (Durham, NC: Duke University Press,
2013).

23. Enrique Dussel, *Filosofía de la Liberación* (Mexico City: Edicol, México, 1977) (translated
into English, German, Italian, and Portuguese). The hypotheses were generated in 1969, years
before the works of Edward Said and J. F. Lyotard. By using the category "center" (the metropolitan) and "periphery" (the colonial) the epistemological decolonization process would begin.

24. Immanuel Wallerstein, *The Modern World-System: Capitalist Agriculture and the Origins of
the European World-Economy in the Sixteenth Century* (New York: Academic Press, 1976). Two
other volumes on the seventeenth and eighteenth centuries would follow. It is true that Wallerstein still did not know the importance of China that André Gunder Frank would begin to
indicate with his important work *ReORIENT: Global Economy in the Asia Age* (Berkeley: University of California Press, 1998).

25. Enrique Dussel, *Towards an Unknown Marx: A Commentary on the Manuscripts of 1861–63*
(London: Routledge, 2001). See especially chap. 13: "The Manuscripts of 1861–63 and the
Concept of Dependency" (204–34).

26. See W. Mignolo, *De la Hermenéutica y la Semiosis Colonial al Pensar Descolonial* (Quito:
Ediciones del Abya-Yala, 2011).

accounts of the originary cultures of the Americas. He felt compelled to create a categorical framing where "colonial difference" began to take a central place. Its theoretical development clarified the category of the "place of enunciation" of discourse, that once it assumed the entire problematic of "understanding" (*Verstehen*) and explaining (*Erklären*), culminated with the discovery of the *colonial place* from which a semiosis that is not necessarily written is enunciated, and which is fulfilled in the colonial statements. A *pluritopocal* hermeneutics allows us to unravel the universe of meaning that makes sense only by adopting a colonial spectator-participant perspective; its import is fundamental in defining the actual epistemological decolonizing position.

We cannot expand on the contributions on the "decolonial turn" by other participants in the movement, such as Santiago Castro-Gómez, María Lugones, Nelson Maldonado, Linda Alcoff, Eduardo Mendieta, Lewis Gordon, and many others.

EPISTEMOLOGICAL DECOLONIZATION OF THEOLOGY

The theology of metropolitan (and colonizing) Latino-Germanic Christendom is perhaps the fifth essence, the spine of Eurocentrism (even more so than philosophy itself, although there is much dispute about who occupies the worst place in this ideology). Presenting the theologies of (non-*messianic*) Christianity as the religion par excellence makes it difficult for the members of Christendom to grant other religions their own *pretension to universal truth*.[27] In a dogmatic position, theology is presented as being the only one that can be true, the universal. Revelation and choice are confused; the choice is confused *as responsibility* and the revelation is confused *as privilege*, as property, as disqualification of the claim to truth by other religions. Also, cultural, economic, or military domination is confused as having universal validity (because the others cannot defend themselves given the abysmal asymmetrical position they have).

Even the great theologians of the twentieth century, such as Henri de Lubac, Karl Rahner, Yves Congar, and Jürgen Moltmann, were, *and could not-not be*, Eurocentric. They creatively renewed European theologies but were unable to situate their subjectivity (even their corporality) within the "colonial space," in the world of the colonized *other*. For its

27. One can take seriously the "pretension to universal validity" at the time in which one honestly tries to prove, on one's part, their own claim to universal validity. That knowing to leave a time of respect for the Other is necessary as a condition for the possibility of honest interreligious and intertheological dialogue.

part, Vatican II "fixed" or resolved the distance of the church with the Enlightenment through an intra-European ecumenism, but not with the colonial world.[28] F. Eboussi Boulaga, in his ontological description of the African colonial being,[29] described the tearing of such divided colonial subjectivity as follows: One part African (thanks to its languages, traditions, and references to ancestral community, the "ethical-mythical nucleus" as Paul Ricoeur would say), and one part, attempting the impossible, which is to imitate the European colonizer imposed by the received formation in education, and the exigencies made by the academy. The objective of the colonized is "to persuade, to draw attention to the one who still is their master so that it recognizes."[30]

Thus, the best European theology was taught to the Latin American, African, and Asian students who filled the classrooms of the European universities. These institutions formed them in such a way that, as J.-P. Sartre would describe it, when their teacher proclaimed from Europe "Parthenon," in a lost corner of the South someone would repeat as in an echo: "enon." It meant a "brainwashing" (which in the sixteenth century was called the method of the "tabula rasa"). The students from the South were transformed into Eurocentric intellectuals; later, returning to their cultural spaces of origin, they found themselves in a colonized world, alienated from their own culture, and from their own popular religious imaginary. Many times, the students would attempt titanically to uproot their disciples from their own culture of the South and graft them onto the European culture (which was their own). Other times, when they resisted and criticized Eurocentrism, they confronted failure and hostility in their own church, when they opposed its Europeanization (the church was completely Europeanized by the bishops who were formed in specialized Roman colleges, in which the universality of the church was identical to being a modernized European). And even at other times, impatient with the received formation, they attempted to return to their ancestral customs but without the required formation; they were lost in an endless labyrinth without an exit. Only in very few instances, which was the road taken by Latin American liberation theology, did a community of theologians assume collectively the responsibility of thinking *with their own heads* and created a new theology that was not colonized. In order to do that, it had to draw from the critical social sciences

28. That is why we became aware that the Medellín Conference was concerned with the issue of a peripheral culture, such as Latin America, absent from the Second Vatican Council.

29. F. Eboussi Boulaga, *La crise du Muntu. Authenticité Africaine et Philosophie* (Paris: Présence africaine, 1977).

30. Boulaga, *La crise du Muntu*, 7. This is the danger of the "struggle for recognition" on the horizon of a Eurocentric position proposed by A. Honneth.

that Eurocentric theology had never used (as Marxism, psychoanalysis, a non-Eurocentric history, etc.). But this new theology was persecuted, not so much for its content but because of its attempt to think *from outside of Europe* and *against the modern, capitalist, metropolitan, Eurocentric, male chauvinist, racist Europe* that had confounded its own *particularity* with a claim to *universality*. Eurocentric theology, and the equally Eurocentric and metropolitan structures of Latino-Germanic Christendom and of the church, could not afford the critique of a decolonized theological thinking. And if Latin American liberation theology had a special perception concerning the issues of poverty, then, African theology had a special aspect of importance concerning ancestral communitarian culture, and Asian theology, facing greater difficulties, was not understood at all in Rome. For example, the Sri Lankan Tissa Balasuriya, friend and companion of the first hours of EATWOT (Ecumenical Association of Third World Theologians, which was founded in 1976 in Dar-es-Salaam), was condemned for wondering[31] if there was more than one incarnation of the Word (a theological problem that demands a specific treatment, and which cannot be avoided in the ecumenical dialogue among the existing world religions). The question alone is already condemnable in a Eurocentric theology.

The *epistemological decolonization of theology* is a fact that began during the second half of the twentieth century, but which will last the entire twenty-first century. It would seem as if the Euro–North American churches have dropped the ball on this matter, organizing great questions and allowing new and better answers for future theology. It is hard for theologians of the center to overcome the narrow horizons of a culture that, despite its great development, shows gigantic flaws in responding to ecological concerns, respect for the reality of the universe, life, and cultural alterity. It is hard for theologians of the center to be open to Oriental "patience," the liturgical vitality of African rhythm, and to developing the sensibilities for the oppressed and humiliated in Latin America.

The epistemological decolonization of theology begins by situating ourselves in a *new space* from which, as *locus enuntiationis* and original hermeneutic, it will be necessary to redo theology as a whole. In the transmodern age that comes (beyond modernity and capitalism) will be equally necessary a trans-theology beyond the Latino-Germanic Christendom, Eurocentric and metropolitan, that ignored the colonial world,

---

31. I insist: the very act of "questioning" was already a problem, because he did not answer the question but rather problematized it in light of the demands of Asian interreligious dialogue. For a Eurocentric Christian the question itself stands as shocking, whereas in Asia it is obligatory.

and especially the colonial Christendoms (of Latin America, part of Africa, and the Christian minorities in Asia[32]) that will have to overcome coloniality and capitalist modernity by *inverting* Christendom in order to reclaim an entirely renewed *messianic* Christianity.

.

32. Asian Christians, as a religious minority, either return to being messianic, as at the Christian origins, or fail when they try to impose Christendom, which is a culture and not a religion. Mateo Ricci sought to clearly separate the two, but he was persecuted by Rome and his project failed. However, the question must be raised again, because it is at the heart of future evangelization.

4.

Doing Contextual Theology: Feminist and Postcolonial Perspectives

KWOK PUI-LAN

Through his life and scholarship, Shoki Coe (1914–1988) made significant contributions to global theological education, the ecumenical movement, and the development of third world theologies. He coined the term "contextualizing theology" in the 1970s, when he worked with the Theological Education Fund of the World Council of Churches (WCC). His theological orientations were shaped by his personal background and political engagements. Born in Taiwan under Japanese rule, Coe lived as a second-class citizen. His classmates shouted slurs at him when he attended college in Japan. He had firsthand experiences of discrimination and acrimony under colonialism and foreign aggression. As a theological educator in Taiwan from 1949 to 1965, Coe saw rapid social changes and revolutions in Asia and elsewhere, as many countries regained political independence after colonization. When leaders of African and Asian nations met at the Bandung Conference in 1955, they organized the Non-Aligned Movement, and the term "third world" became popular. In Taiwan, Coe faced political pressure from the Nationalist authorities because of his involvement in the Self-Determination Movement. He lived virtually as an exile when he left Taiwan in 1965.[1]

Coe differentiated between indigenization and contextualization, and advocated the latter approach because of the sociopolitical changes taking place in the third world. For him, indigenization means responding to the gospel in terms of traditional culture, whereas contextualization

---

1. Ray Wheeler, "The Legacy of Shoki Coe," *International Bulletin of Missionary Research* 16, no. 2 (2002): 77–80.

goes beyond this, as it "responds to the Gospel itself as well as to the urgent issues in the historic realities, particularly those of the Third World."[2] Contextualization is a dynamic process, open to change, and is future-oriented. It is a new way of theologizing and responding to God's mission in the world, because it involves the "missiological discernment of the signs of the times, seeing where God is at work and calling us to participate in it. . . . It is the conscientization of the contexts in the particular, historical moment, assessing the peculiarity of the context in the light of the mission of the church as it is called to participate in the *Missio Dei*."[3]

To honor the life and legacy of Shoki Coe, I would like to reflect on my encounter and engagement with contextual theology. As a theological student and a junior faculty member in the 1970s, I witnessed and participated in the early conversations about contextualization in Hong Kong, and later took part in the feminist and ecumenical movements in Asia. Several years before 1997, when Hong Kong was returned by Britain to China, I became involved in the development of postcolonial biblical studies and theology. Although I never met Coe, my recollections and reflections will demonstrate the far-reaching impact of his visions of contextualization in Asia and beyond.

DISCUSSION OF CONTEXTUALIZATION IN THE 1970S

The 1960s and 1970s were periods of ferment and protest in Asia and around the world. Students and protesters in Hong Kong took to the streets to fight against corruption and to demand that the Chinese language be adopted as an official language. For even though 98 percent of the people in Hong Kong were Chinese, English was the only official language until 1971. Meanwhile, in South Korea, massive demonstrations broke out on university campuses and on the streets against the dictatorial Park Chung-hee government. Park ruled the country with an iron fist: dissolving the National Assembly, suspending the constitution, and suppressing opposition. Likewise, in the Philippines, students, workers, and protesters demonstrated against the corruption and brutality of the Marcos government, which ruled under martial law from 1972 to 1981.

It was against this backdrop of political upheavals in Asia that theologians in Hong Kong began to debate about the pros and cons of indi-

---

2. Shoki Coe, "In Search of Renewal in Theological Education," *Theological Education* 9, no. 4 (1973): 243.

3. Coe, "In Search of Renewal in Theological Education," 241.

genization and contextualization. The indigenization process in China began earlier, in the 1920s, when Chinese theologians such as Wu Leichuan and Zhao Zichen interpreted the gospel with the help of Confucian classics to show that Christianity was not inherently a foreign religion complicit with Western imperialism. They argued that imitating Jesus's personal life and following his social teachings could help the national reconstruction of China. Their critical engagement with Chinese traditional culture was a way to respond to the sociopolitical situation of their time.[4] But in the 1970s in Hong Kong, indigenization had lost much of its appeal, because Confucian classics were no longer as influential in the British colony as in China of the 1920s. Contextualization, with attention to social and political issues and third world liberation, was seen as a better response to the changing political climate. Philip Shen, a theologian in Hong Kong, wrote about the effects that rising political consciousness in Hong Kong and a shifting Chinese political climate, including the downfall of four important leaders in 1976, had on contextual theology.[5]

Two events in the 1970s served as catalysts to stimulate conversations about contextual theology in Hong Kong and in other parts of Asia. The first was the 1972 World Conference on Salvation Today, held in Bangkok and sponsored by the WCC. A significant outcome of the conference was the promotion of a holistic understanding of salvation that went beyond individual redemption to include social and structural transformation. In his opening address at the conference, M. M. Thomas from India stated that Christian mission was concerned with salvation, "not in any pietistic or individualist isolation, but related to and expressed within the material, social and cultural revolution of our time."[6] This meant that theology could not be done in the abstract but had to respond to the signs of the times and its contexts. The second event was the Lausanne Congress organized by evangelical Christians in 1974. The Lausanne Covenant, a watershed document, clarified the relationship between evangelism and social justice involvements. While the Covenant insisted that evangelism meant spreading the good news of Jesus Christ, it also insisted that Christians "should share [God's] concern for justice and reconciliation throughout human society and for the

4. Simon S. M. Kwan, "From Indigenization to Contextualization: A Change in Discourse Practice Rather Than a Shift in Paradigm," *Studies in World Christianity* 11, no. 2 (2005): 242–43.

5. Philip Shen, "Concerns with Politics and Culture in Contextual Theology: A Hong Kong Chinese Perception," *South East Asia Journal of Theology* 21, no. 2–22, no. 1 (1980–81): 97–102.

6. M. M. Thomas, "The Meaning of Salvation Today: A Personal Statement," *International Review of Mission* 62, no. 245 (1973): 162.

liberation of men and women from every kind of oppression." It went further to affirm that "evangelism and socio-political involvement are both part of our Christian duty."[7] The encouragement for Christians to be socially engaged meant that Christians needed to take their contexts seriously in carrying out God's mission.

The emphasis on contextualization propelled Asian theological educators to reflect critically on the visions and practices of theological education and ministerial formation. Coe pointed out that theological education in the third world carried too much missionary baggage and was in urgent need of renewal and innovation.[8] Many theological schools still modeled their curriculum after that of the West, with heavy emphasis on learning white, Western theologies. In Hong Kong, theological educators began to include courses on Chinese and Asian Christianity and started to introduce contextual theologies, especially liberation theology, from various contexts. Latin American liberation theology captured the attention of many students. For Gustavo Gutiérrez, theology is a critical reflection of praxis, and theology without action is dead. Gutiérrez emphasized God's preferential option for the poor, the structural dimensions of sin, and God's action in history for liberation.[9] His image of Jesus as liberator was far more relevant in this turbulent time in Asia than the Christs depicted in European theologies. Other liberation theologies, such as black theology and feminist theology, were also introduced. These critiques of racism and gender oppression in white, Western theology clearly pointed to its limitations and the danger of treating it as universal and normative.

Theological educators in Hong Kong also paid attention to the various kinds of contextual theologies emerging from Asian countries, particularly those from South Korea and Taiwan, because of geographical proximity and cultural connections. South Korean theologians developed "minjung theology" as a response to the massive protests for human rights, democratic participation, and economic justice. The word *minjung* originally comes from two Chinese characters, meaning the masses or the multitude. Korean New Testament scholar Ahn Byung Mu (1922–1996) studied the *ochlos*—the crowd who followed Jesus from place to place in Mark's Gospel. The diverse groups of Galilean *ochlos*, coming from the lower class, were the audience whom Jesus's message addressed and formed the background of his activities (Mark 2:4, 13; 3:9,

7. "The Lausanne Covenant," Lausanne Movement website, https://tinyurl.com/z8peecq.

8. Shoki Coe, "Theological Education: A Worldwide Perspective," *Theological Education* 11, no. 1 (1974): 5–12.

9. Gustavo Gutiérrez, *A Theology of Liberation: History, Politics, and Salvation*, trans. Caridad Inda and John Eagleson (London: SCM, 1973).

20, 32; 4:1; 5:21, 24, 31; 8:1; 10:1). In contrast to the ruling class from Jerusalem, the *ochlos* frequently sided with Jesus against the ruling class. Minjung theologians argued that Jesus was part of the minjung, and his teaching must be interpreted in the context of the social aspirations of the people.[10] Using the social biography of the people as a critical lens, minjung theologians began to read the Bible together with the long history of suffering of the Korean people. Theologian Kim Yong Bock criticized Western domination in theology, which assumes that the cultures of Asian people are discontinuous with the gospel and do not have any positive place in theological reflection.[11] In contrast, minjung theologians emphasized that people are subjects of history and recovered the liberating potentials of Korea's indigenous traditions, such as shamanism and the masked dance. Sebastian Kim said, "Minjung theology developed into a major contextual theology intended to address the problems of the poor and the exploited . . . [it was] against the unjust system of modern and divided Korea on the one hand, and against conservative fundamentalist theologies on the other."[12]

Theologians in Taiwan developed "homeland theology" in their fight for self-determination against the Nationalist government. Taiwan had been under Dutch and Spanish rule at various times and was ceded to Japan after the Sino-Japanese war in 1895. After the Chinese Nationalist Government evacuated to Taiwan in 1949, martial law was declared, and Chiang Kai-shek's regime denied the people freedom of speech, arrested and tortured dissidents, and suppressed political movements. Taiwan faced international isolation in the 1970s, when the People's Republic of China joined the United Nations and Taiwan was expelled from it. The 1972 visit of President Richard Nixon to China paved the way for the normalization of relations with China. The Presbyterian Church in Taiwan issued three statements at the time, declaring that the homeland was a gift from God and that the Taiwanese people had the right to determine their destiny. In response to political change, theologians Wang Xianzhi and others developed homeland theology, seeing parallels between the histories of Taiwan and Israel. The Hebrew people left the land of bondage in Egypt and crossed the Red Sea to enter the promised

10. Ahn Byung Mu, "Jesus and the Minjung in the Gospel of Mark," in *Minjung Theology: People as the Subjects of History*, ed. Kim Yong Bock (Singapore: The Commission of Theological Concerns, Christian Conference of Asia, 1981), 140–41.

11. Yong Bock Kim, "Doing Theology in Asia Today: A Korean Perspective," in *Asian Christian Theology: Emerging Themes*, ed. Douglas J. Elwood (Philadelphia: Westminster, 1980), 315–16.

12. Sebastian Kim, "Minjung Theology: Whose Voice, for Whom?" in *Asian Theology on the Way: Christianity, Culture and Context*, ed. Peniel Jesudason Rufus Rajkumar (London: SPCK, 2012), 112.

land. Trying to build a community, they insisted that the land belonged to God and not to the rulers and elites. Their prophets repeatedly condemned corruption and injustice, and exhorted them to care for the poor and the marginalized. Just as in the exodus, many Chinese people crossed the Taiwanese Strait over the centuries to escape political oppression and seek a better life. In the face of isolation and uncertainty, homeland theologians insisted that Taiwan belonged not to the rulers or political parties but to all those who lived on and loved the homeland. Taiwanese people have the right of self-determination for their future and destiny.[13]

Taiwanese theologian C. S. Song played a critical role in the development of contextual theology, particularly in his insistence on using Asian myths, stories, and legends in doing Asian theology. Similar to Coe, Song lamented that Asian theologians had depended too much on models of Western theology and had come dangerously close to "disowning [their] own cultural heritage as having no useful meaning in the design of God's salvation."[14] To remedy this trend, Song suggested a process of "transposition" to describe the theological journey from Israel to Asia. Transposition is not simply a translation into another language, style, or expression, but requires "theological discussion to shift to different subjects, to face new questions, and to discover alternative approaches."[15] Through his writings and his leadership in the Programme for Theology and Cultures in Asia, Song encouraged doing Asian contextual theology with Asia's own cultural and spiritual resources.

Korean minjung theology, Taiwanese homeland theology, and other Asian contextual theologies, such as theology of struggle in the Philippines, offered new models and resources for contextualization of theology in Hong Kong. In the early 1980s, when Britain and China began to discuss the future of Hong Kong, churches needed resources and guides to face the challenges ahead. I edited the book *1997 and Hong Kong Theology*, the first book on the subject, which discussed the history and role of Hong Kong and the identity of Hong Kong people. It also offered biblical and theological reflections and recommendations for local churches and Christian schools to prepare for the political transition.[16]

13. Wang Xianzhi, *Taiwan xiangtu shenxue lunwen ji* (Collected Essays of Taiwanese Homeland Theology), vol. 1, ed. Wang Xianzhi (Tainan: Tainan Theological Seminary, 1988).

14. C. S. Song, *The Compassionate God* (Maryknoll, NY: Orbis, 1982), 7.

15. Song, *The Compassionate God*, 9.

16. Kwok Pui-lan, ed., *1997 yu Xianggang shenxue* (1997 and Hong Kong Theology) (Hong Kong: Chung Chi College Theological Division, 1983).

EMERGENCE OF ASIAN FEMINIST THEOLOGY

Contextual theologies done by Asian male theologians have often over-looked women's concerns and their struggles for liberation. Under pressure from women, the Christian Conference of Asia set up a Women's Desk, which organized one of the first conferences devoted to Asian feminist theology, in Sukabumi, Indonesia, in 1981. Elizabeth Tapia organized the conference, and Mary John Mananzan from the Philippines, Chang Sang from South Korea, and I were among the participants.

Asian women theologians were keenly aware of the ways that social and economic changes had affected women's lives. Although industrialization had enabled an increasing number of women to work outside the home, their jobs were often insecure and their working conditions were poor. Economic takeoff of countries around the Asian Pacific Rim accorded women more educational opportunities and participation in the public and corporate sectors. However, these advances did not significantly change stereotypical gender roles, and women still had limited power in both the domestic and public spheres. The Vietnam War brought unspeakable suffering and a devastating impact to Southeast Asian countries. War, militarism, guerilla fighting, and violence affected women and children disproportionately. Prostitution around the American military bases and the development of insidious forms of sex tourism in the Philippines, Thailand, and neighboring countries exploited women's sexual labor. Mary John Mananzan has written about and condemned the sexual exploitation of women and violence against women in the third world.[17]

For Asian feminist theologians, attempts at contextualization were inadequate if they failed to take into serious consideration the intersection of patriarchy with poverty, militarism, gender violence, and political discrimination. They criticized male contextual theologians when they overlooked the androcentric elements in both the Bible and Asian cultures. I have pointed out the limitations of contextualization: "First, it takes the content of the Bible and the Gospel for granted, without seriously challenging the androcentric biases both in the biblical texts and in the core symbolism of Christianity. Secondly, it identifies with Asian culture too readily, often failing to see that many Asian traditions are overtly patriarchal."[18] Thus, Asian feminist theologians had to engage

17. Mary John Mananzan, "Sexual Exploitation of Women in Third World Setting," in *Essays on Women*, ed. Mary John Mananzan (Manila: St. Scholastica College, 1991), 104–12.
18. Kwok Pui-lan, "The Emergence of Asian Feminist Consciousness of Culture and The-

in a double critique and reconstruction. While they criticized the patriarchal teachings and practices in the Buddhist, Confucian, Shinto, and Hindu traditions, they also recovered their liberating potentials. For example, some feminist theologians have recovered feminine images and metaphors of the divine in both the Asian and biblical traditions. They pointed out that many Asian religious traditions emphasized the interplay between the feminine and the masculine, yin and yang, heaven and earth, and challenged the predominant usage of male metaphors and images in liturgy, theology, and preaching in Asian churches.

As several pioneers in Asian feminist theology were active in the Ecumenical Association of Third World Theologians (EATWOT), they adopted EATWOT's theological methodology. This methodology could be conceived as a spiral process that included the following steps: critical analyses of the social, cultural, and political contexts; questioning of biblical and theological traditions from the perspectives of the oppressed; reformulation of theological doctrines and traditions; and concrete action and social praxis to change social systems and promote justice. But Asian feminist theologians took care to adapt this methodology specifically to the Asian situation. Virginia Fabella from the Philippines surmised that Asian feminist theologians had to take into consideration both their Asianness and womanness. "By 'womanness' is not meant a mere conglomerate of biological and psychological factors but an awareness of what it means to be a woman in the Asian context today. . . . Women's experience is basic to our theology," she wrote.[19]

Since the Bible occupies a pivotal place in Asian church life, interpreting the Bible from feminist perspectives is indispensable for doing contextual theology in Asia. Asian feminist theologians criticized the androcentric heritage of the Bible, but also lifted up biblical women such as Ruth and Naomi, Hannah, Miriam, Deborah, Mary Magdalene, and Mary the mother of Jesus as role models. They have also interpreted the Bible in relation to their particular social and political situations. For example, in her interpretation of Mark's Gospel, Hisako Kinukawa of Japan emphasized Jesus's crossing of ethnic, cultural, and religious boundaries. She used Jesus's example to challenge the exclusion and discrimination of ethnic minorities and migrant workers in Japan. As Jesus defied purity and religious taboos when he healed the bleeding woman (Mark 5:25–34) and the Syrophoenician woman's daughter (Mark

ology," in We Dare to Dream: Doing Theology as Asian Women, ed. Virginia Fabella and Sun Ai Lee Park (Maryknoll, NY: Orbis, 1989), 98.

19. Virginia Fabella, "A Common Methodology for Diverse Christologies?" in With Passion and Compassion: Third World Women Doing Theology, ed. Virginia Fabella and Mercy Amba Oduyoye (Maryknoll, NY: Orbis, 1988), 115.

7:24–30), Japanese Christians should reach out to and embrace their ethnic and religious Others.[20] In India, Dalit women are thrice marginalized, and have been for centuries, because of their caste, gender, and class. Dalit women are considered "untouchables" because they are regarded as polluting and unclean. Monica Jyotsna Melanchthon has developed a biblical hermeneutic from Dalit women's perspectives. She says that this hermeneutic must recognize the multiple oppression of Dalit women and affirm and transform life in all of its wholeness. This effort must be multiscriptural, for Dalit women are oppressed by patriarchal hermeneutics of the Bible on the one hand and that of the scriptures of other faiths on the other.[21]

Asian feminist theologians have also reinterpreted Christology in response to social movements for human rights and democracy. Filipino women insisted that during the struggles against the Marcos regime and in subsequent social movements, women had contributed to the liberation project just as men had. They saw Christ as liberator and political martyr. Lydia Lascano, a Catholic sister, wrote, "the passion of Christ in the Filipino people is fashioning women disciples who would accompany the suffering Christ alive among the people."[22] In South Korea, Chung Hyun Hyung and other Korean women sought inspiration from their shamanistic tradition, because the majority of the shamans are women. They saw Jesus as a symbol of females and the oppressed because of his identification with those who suffered. Jesus could be interpreted as a shaman woman, a priest who exorcised women of *han*, a feeling of hopelessness and indignation against unjustifiable suffering.[23]

Asian feminist theologians have reclaimed Mary as a co-redeemer for human salvation and a fully liberated human being, instead of a docile, obedient, and sanctified mother. Mary is seen as someone who accepts the challenge of the Holy Spirit and has a profound historical sense of the destiny of her people. As a self-defining woman, Mary challenges the cultural norms, follows Jesus to the cross, and continues his ministry after his death. As a model of discipleship, she symbolizes a woman who yearns for liberation from oppression and nurtures the hope of new

20. Hisako Kinukawa, *Women and Jesus in Mark: A Japanese Feminist Perspective* (Maryknoll, NY: Orbis, 1994).

21. Monica Jyotsna Melanchthon, "Dalit Women and the Bible: Hermeneutical and Methodological Reflections," in *Hope Abundant: Third World and Indigenous Women's Theology*, ed. Kwok Pui-lan (Maryknoll, NY: Orbis, 2010), 103–22.

22. Lydia Lascano, "The Role of Women in the Church and Society," *In God's Image* (December 1985–February 1986): 127.

23. Chung Hyun Kyung, *Struggle to Be the Sun Again: Introducing Asian Women's Theology* (Maryknoll, NY: Orbis, 1990), 65–66. See also Chung Hyun Kyung, "'Han-pu-ri': Doing Theology from Korean Women's Perspective," *Ecumenical Review* 40, no. 1 (1988): 27–36.

humanity. The dark-skinned Madonna who has great appeal to Filipino women becomes a patron for women's resistance against colonialism and oppression.[24]

Asian feminist theologians also challenge churches to recognize women as full members of the body of Christ and equal partners in ministry. The church needs to challenge its own sexism before it can serve as a beacon of hope for society. Instead of a body-denying and other-worldly form of Christian spirituality focusing on prayer and meditation, Asian women theologians develop a life-affirming spirituality that integrates body and soul, inner and outer worlds, and contemplation and social action. This ecofeminist spirituality affirms the creative power of women, the interrelatedness of all things, and the sacredness of earth. Such spirituality will enable Asian women to struggle against the exploitation of the global economic order, sex tourism, militarism, and gender oppression.

DEVELOPMENT OF POSTCOLONIAL THEOLOGY

In the 1990s, intellectuals and theologians in Hong Kong became interested in postcolonial discourse in preparation for the return of Hong Kong to China in 1997. Even though I had begun teaching in the United States at the time, the return of Hong Kong was a milestone in my personal life and in Chinese history. "Postcolonial" is a contentious term because the colonial legacy remains strong in many countries, and neocolonialism continues to ravage the world. But "postcolonial" also signifies a fighting posture and a commitment to resistance. I have defined postcolonial imagination as "a desire, a determination, and a process of disengagement from the whole colonial syndrome, which takes many forms and guises."[25] In fact, as early as 1973, Coe used the terms "postcolonial" and "post-Christendom" to describe the period following the turbulent protests and revolutions of the 1960s.[26]

Postcolonial theory has raised our consciousness of the politics and rhetoric of empire in the Bible and theological tradition, of Eurocentrism and colonialist assumptions, of hidden and submerged voices, and of the plurality and diversity within Christian traditions. Postcolonial theory first entered theological fields through biblical studies. R. S. Sugirtharajah writes, "What postcolonial biblical studies does is to focus on the

24. Chung, *Struggle to Be the Sun Again*, 74–84.

25. Kwok Pui-lan, *Postcolonial Imagination and Feminist Theology* (Louisville: Westminster John Knox, 2005), 2–3.

26. Coe, "In Search of Renewal in Theological Education," 237.

whole issue of expansion, domination, and imperialism as central forces in defining both the biblical narratives and biblical interpretation."[27] The Hebrew people and early Christians lived under the shadows of Egyptian, Assyrian, Babylonian, Persian, Greek, and Roman empires. The Bible lends itself to postcolonial and intercultural studies because it deals with the themes of travel, space and spatial construction, movement, boundaries, borderland, border-crossing, crossroad, indigenized women and populations, ethnic formation, diasporic communities, rhizomic fragments, uprooting, dis-placing place, displacement, transplantation, international power relations, and globalization processes.[28]

Because male postcolonial critics have overlooked the gender dimension in their interpretations, I have articulated several approaches of postcolonial feminist biblical criticism. First, we can investigate the symbolization of women and the deployment of gender in the text in relation to class, modes of production, state power, and colonial domination. Second, we need to pay attention to the depiction of women in the contact zone, such as Rahab, and offer reconstructive reading as a counternarrative. Third, postcolonial feminist critics scrutinize metropolitan interpretations, including those offered by both male and feminist scholars, to see if their readings support colonizing ideology. Fourth, in order to subvert Eurocentric readings, postcolonial feminist critics, especially those from Africa, emphasize the roles and contributions of ordinary and nonacademic female readers. Finally, postcolonial feminist interpreters need to pay attention to the politics of social location of the critic and the poetics of location.[29]

The application of postcolonial theory to theology is more tenuous and difficult. After all, most of the foundational postcolonial theorists harbor negative attitudes toward religion in general and Christianity in particular. For Edward Said, it was Christian Europe that constructed an inferior and negative image of the "East" to dominate and control.[30] As a humanist and a champion of secular criticism, Said insisted that critical consciousness could only flourish and criticism could only be conducted freely without the imposition of political and religious dogmas. Postcolonial theorists influenced by Derrida, such as Gayatri Chakravorty Spivak, are allergic to anything that smacks of ontotheology.

27. R. S. Sugirtharajah, *Postcolonial Criticism and Biblical Interpretation* (Oxford: Oxford University Press, 2002), 25.
28. Fernando F. Segovia discusses these themes in the Gospel of John, see "Johannine Studies and Geopolitical: Reflections upon Absence and Irruption," in *What We Have Heard from the Beginning: The Past, Present, and Future of Johannine Studies*, ed. Tom Thatcher (Waco, TX: Baylor University Press, 2007), 281–306. These themes can also be found in other parts of the Bible.
29. Kwok, *Postcolonial Imagination*, 81–85.
30. Edward W. Said, *Orientalism* (New York: Vintage, 1979).

But if Christianity has played such an important enabling role in colonialism and empire building, the study of the postcolonial will not be complete without engaging the theological. Conversely, the theological also needs the critique and contribution of the postcolonial because the theological enterprise has been laden with imperial assumptions and motives ever since Christianity became the state religion of the Roman Empire. Postcolonial theology is not an exercise in nostalgia, of trying to recuperate a pristine Christianity that has not colluded with empire. As theologian Catherine Keller has reminded us, there is no "pre-colonial Christianity": "When [Christianity] opened its young mouth to speak, it spoke in the many tongues of empire—nations and languages colonized by Rome, and before that Greece, and before that Babylon, which had first dispersed the Jews into imperial space."[31] It is delusive to find a particular moment or an Archimedean point in the Christian tradition that is not enmeshed in the power dynamics of its time. Precisely because of the prolonged imbrication of Christianity with empire, postcolonial critique is not only necessary, but also indispensable, in the reconceptualization of the theological discipline and the articulation of an alternative politics.

Postcolonial theory is particularly relevant at a time when globalization and neoliberalism have restructured the world economy, with the emergence of the transnational capitalist class, flexible production, and the flux of capital, labor, and resources. The former binary conceptualizations of the world, such as colonizer/colonized, first world/third world, and "the West and the rest" do not seem to be adequate to describe the new global relations. Postcolonial theory emerged in the 1980s amidst the global setback of resistance movements and the retreat of the political Left. It provided the theoretical impetus to examine culture and economy in ways different from the traditional Marxist approach. With phenomenal economic development in China, India, and other countries in the Asia Pacific, Asia increasingly occupies a key geopolitical position in the global political economy. Yet Marxism and socialism have long been looked at with suspicion in Taiwan, South Korea, and other countries surrounding China. Postcolonial theory offers an alternative approach to look at the power dynamics that shape the modern world.

The postcolonial approach also addresses some of the limitations of liberation theology. An important critique of liberation theology is that it is done primarily by male theologians and is still very androcentric.

---

31. Catherine Keller, *God and Power: Counter-Apocalyptic Journeys* (Minneapolis: Fortress Press, 2005), 114.

The focus has been on the preferential option of the poor, without adequate analyses of gender and sexuality. Gustavo Gutiérrez argues that Christ has come to bring political emancipation, the liberation of human beings throughout history, the liberation from sin, and communion with God. The image of Christ as liberator dispels the myth of the gentle and meek Jesus often preached in middle-class churches. But postcolonial theory has led me to question this masculinist portrayal of the savior who intervenes in human history, without a concomitant critique of androcentrism and heterosexism embedded in such an image.

I also began to see history and politics as more than just black and white. A binary construction of oppressors and the oppressed seems outdated. In *The Colonizer and the Colonized*, Albert Memmi has already argued that colonization is not possible without the collaboration of the colonized.[32] Today in our globalized and interlocking world, it is difficult to say where empire begins and where it ends. We are all implicated in the global system in one way or another, though to different degrees. It is too optimistic to claim that Christ will bring social and political liberation into the world. What happens when the oppressed are not yet liberated? How do we live in the in-between space between now and the not yet? My questions about the major facets of liberation theology led me to delve deeper into postcolonial theology.

In *Postcolonial Imagination and Feminist Theology*, published in 2005, I used postcolonial insights to interrogate some of the categories and assumptions of (white) feminist theology: women's experience, the gender of divinity, the question of whether a male savior can save women, and the relation between women and nature.[33] While many white women insist that feminist theology begins with women's experience to contest androcentrism in traditional theology, they have often forgotten that they are not only victims of patriarchy, but also imperial subjects who benefit from colonialism and its legacy. The intersection of gender and imperialism has not been theologized, even though many white women are increasingly more conscious of their racial privilege. The attention given to inclusive language and the gender of divinity overlooks the fact that other languages may not have the same problems regarding the use of masculine pronouns for God. In Chinese, for example, there is a separate pronoun for God, different from "he" and "she." The question of whether a male savior can save women is an important one, but many cultures have both male and female saviors, and the

---

32. Albert Memmi, *The Colonizer and the Colonized*, trans. Howard Greenfeld (New York: Orion Press, 1965).

33. Kwok, *Postcolonial Imagination*.

emphasis on Jesus as male overlooks the fact that many cultures have come up with different expressions of the hybrid Christ: Christ as the Corn Mother in native American culture, Christ as the feminine Shakti in India, and the Bi/Christ in LGBTQ cultures. Many Western feminist theologians argue that women are subordinate to men just as nature is to culture. But in Asian traditions, nature is not subordinated but glorified in poetry, paintings, and other media and cultural artifacts. This means that Asian ecofeminist theology must take a different direction and learn from Asian and indigenous religious traditions and sensibilities.

The development of feminist postcolonial theology has implications for theological anthropology, interreligious dialogue, and practical theology. Postcolonial theologians understand identity as fluid and changing, because boundaries are perpetually shifting or being redefined. Racial and ethnic minorities and those who have formerly been colonial subjects often find themselves living in the in-between or Third Space, having to negotiate multiple realities all the time. Homi K. Bhabha's concept of hybridity contests purity, fixed and binary categories, and the imposition of the same.[34] Hybridity is the result of the collision and coalescence of two cultures, when one is perceived as dominating the other within a colonial context. The understanding of hybrid identity and a permeable self challenges assumptions about the human in theological anthropology. The human has been variously imagined in an androcentric way—as a transcendental ego, a sovereign subject, a person with the will to power, and someone whose anxiety over freedom leads to pride and temptation. The understanding of the hybrid self requires us to speak of personhood and sin in new ways. Chinese American gay theologian Patrick S. Cheng offers new approaches of conceptualizing sin and grace. One of his definitions suggests sin as singularity, as "failing to recognize the complex reality of multiple identities within a single person, which in turn silences the experiences of those individuals who exist at the intersections of race, gender, sexual orientation, age, and other categories."[35] He cites the example that Asian American gay men are marginalized in the white lesbian, gay, bisexual, and transgender world, while their sexual identity is erased from the straight Asian American world. Grace, then, is living in hybridity with the ability to negotiate and embrace the "in-between" spaces of two or more intersecting worlds.

A postcolonial approach to interreligious dialogue needs to pay atten-

---

34. Homi K. Bhabha, *The Location of Culture* (London: Routledge, 1994), 112–16.

35. Patrick S. Cheng, "Rethinking Sin and Grace for LGBT People Today," in *Sexuality and the Sacred: Sources for Theological Reflection*, 2nd ed., ed. Marvin M. Ellison and Kelly Brown Douglas (Louisville: Westminster John Knox, 2010), 115.

tion to the ways in which religion is defined, studied, and classified. Interreligious dialogue is often based on outdated concepts of "religion" influenced by colonialism and racism. In *Empire of Religion*, David Chidester documents how knowledge about religion in the academic study of religion was produced through the complex interplay among the imperial scholars, local colonial experts, and indigenous actors.[36] Writings on interreligious dialogue are still dominated by European assumptions about religion and focus on the work of male religious leaders and elites. In many Asian cultures, many people belong simultaneously to more than one tradition, because religious identities and boundaries are defined differently from those of the West. Asian Christian women often combine elements of their indigenous cultures with Christianity in their search for religious sustenance. Women's grassroots movements have worked across religious divides to promote interreligious dialogue and solidarity in search for justice and peace. In Taiwan, Christian women and Buddhists work together for environmental protection. In Palestine, Jewish and Muslim women stand in solidarity with one another in the Women in Black movement. The involvements of women in interreligious dialogue need to be told and studied.

For practical theologians, the concerns of postcolonial theory are not new, since many are grappling with the issues of multiculturalism, intercultural identity, and pastoral practices in an increasingly diverse and globalized world. I have argued that worship and preaching can be transformed into a subversive Third Space so that the faith community can imagine new ways of being in the world and encountering God's salvific action. I have demonstrated the ways feminist postcolonial interpretation can contribute to postcolonial preaching.[37] Boyung Lee used postcolonial theory to study Christianity and culture, and offered insights into postcolonial biblical pedagogy and religious education. Her work shows sensitivities to multicultural and feminist concerns.[38] In the field of practical theology, McGarrah Sharp brings pastoral theology, ethnography, and postcolonial studies to bear in her study of intercultural understanding in pastoral care and community building across cultural differences.[39]

36. David Chidester, *Empire of Religion: Imperialism and Comparative Religion* (Chicago: University of Chicago Press, 2014).

37. Kwok Pui-lan, "Postcolonial Preaching in Intercultural Contexts," *Homiletic* 40, no. 1 (2015): 8–21.

38. Boyung Lee, "From a Margin within a Margin: Rethinking the Dynamics of Christianity and Culture from a Post-colonial Feminist Perspective," *Journal of Theologies and Cultures in Asia* 3 (2003): 3–23; Boyung Lee, "When the Text Is a Problem: A Postcolonial Approach to Biblical Pedagogy," *Religious Education* 102, no. 1 (2007): 44–61.

39. Melinda McGarrah Sharp, *Misunderstanding Stories: Toward a Postcolonial Pastoral Theology* (Eugene, OR: Pickwick, 2013).

In her book *An Aesthetic Education in the Era of Globalization*, Gayatri Spivak invites us to consider the profoundly democratic possibilities of imagination and the critical roles that art, the humanities, and literary studies can play in cultivating a profound feeling and engendering critical thinking that go beyond the logic of capital.[40] The study of theology should broaden our religious and moral horizons, and nurture in us a habit of thought that challenges both social and religious oppressive systems. As we remember the legacy of Shoki Coe, we are motivated by his example of speaking truth to power and his insistence that theology must be contextually relevant. As a theological educator, Coe was ahead of his time in challenging the colonial legacy of theological educational models and proposing renewal and innovation for the postcolonial and post-Christendom period. Without such creative attempts and collective reimagining, Christian praxis to change the world would not have been—and will not be—possible.

40. Gayatri Chakravorty Spivak, *An Aesthetic Education in the Age of Globalization* (Cambridge, MA: Harvard University Press, 2012).

5.

Religions and Scriptures in Actual Cultural Contexts: A Reflection in Honor of Shoki Coe

J. N. K. MUGAMBI

INTRODUCTION

The focus of this paper, in appreciation of the vocation of Shoki Coe, is the interrelationship between the sacred scriptures of "scripture-based religions" and the cultural contexts within which believers practice their scriptural religiosity.[1] Missionaries of scripture-based religions across cultures (including Christianity, Islam, and Buddhism) face the risk of alienating converts from cultures other than those in which the original scriptures were written. Translation of such original scriptures into other languages, as a means to enhance cross-cultural conversion, will remain incomplete until scholars from the recipient communities translate and publish the core scriptures as sole authors.[2]

Christianity is the most widespread scripture-based religion in human history. Owing to the dominance of European "Christian" cultures for nearly two millennia, there has been a tendency to portray Christianity as a "European" religion, especially in the context of European missionary enterprises abroad. Factually, however, non-Europeans embraced Christianity long before Emperor Constantine declared it the official

---

1. Shoki Coe is appreciated as one of the most articulate proponents of contextualization in Christian missiology and pedagogy. On this point see Ray Wheeler, "The Legacy of Shoki Coe," in *International Bulletin of Missionary Research* (April 2002).

2. Such feats were accomplished with the Septuagint (132 BCE); Jerome's translation (405 CE); Luther's Bible (1534); King James Version (1611). Similar translations were done in other European languages. The most recent such accomplishment in African Christianity is the translation by Professor John S. Mbiti of the New Testament from Koine Greek into KiiKamba, published in December 2014, Nairobi: Kenya Literature Bureau.

religion of his empire under the Edict of Milan in 313 CE. It was in northern Africa that the earliest doctrinal debates were the most intense.[3] In the doctrinal debates of the early church, African theologians wielded prominence in the clarification of the essence of Christianity.[4] The impact of this early influence continues, within both the Ecumenical and the Evangelical wings of Protestantism.[5] The Orthodox expressions of Christianity are much older than Protestantism, and have maintained their doctrinal and cultural identity since the Council of Chalcedon in 451. Within Africa the Orthodox ecclesial identity includes both the Coptic and Ethiopian Orthodox churches. In Tropical Africa it was not until the sixteenth century that Christianity was introduced—as an integral part of European imperial conquests. Colonization for trade in slaves, minerals, and wood was taken for granted, with provisions for chaplains to pray for the perpetrators and the victims—in life and in death! The distinction between Christian faith and European culture was blurred. This confusion lingers on.

Coe's endeavor toward clearer conceptual clarification is important and significant worldwide, although his focus was mainly on East Asia. Within the modern ecumenical movement, Coe has been among the most influential leaders from Asia. Other voices from Asia include Choan-Sen Song (Taiwan), Kosuke Koyama (Japan), M. M. Thomas and Stanley Samartha (India), and Wesley Ariarajah, Tissa Balasuriya, and D. T. Niles (Sri Lanka). Their writings have helped in presenting and proclaiming Christianity as a multicultural faith, rather than a merely European one. Coe became widely known internationally during his term as director of the Theological Education Fund (TEF), based at Bromley, United Kingdom (1972–77). Along with other colleagues, he promoted the notion of *contextualization* in theological education.[6] A series of books were published under the sponsorship of the TEF with the aim of promoting contextualized ministerial formation.[7]

3. On this point see, for example, Thomas Oden, *How Africa Shaped the Christian Mind* (Downers Grove, IL: IVP, 2006).

4. The Roman Province of Africa (*Africa Proconsularis*), from which the Continent of Africa is named, produced leading scholars and bishops, including three popes (14th, Victor I, circa 189–98 CE; 32nd, Miltiades 311–14 CE; 49th, Gelasius I, 492–96 CE).

5. For some detailed analysis of this point see Kwame Bediako, *Theology and Identity: The Impact of Culture upon Christian Thought in the Second Century and in Modern Africa* (Oxford: OCMS-Regnum, 1992); "Understanding African Theology in the 20th Century," *Themelios* (October 1994).

6. For a summary of Shoki Coe's life see Ray Wheeler, "The Legacy of Shoki Coe," *International Bulletin of Missionary Research* (April 2002).

7. Ross Kinsler, *Diversified Theological Education: Equipping All God's People* (Pasadena, CA: William Carey International University Press, 2008).

DIVINE REVELATION AND CONTEXTUAL
HUMAN RESPONSES

Promoters of outward-bound religions with sacred scriptures—especially Christianity (the Holy Bible) and Islam (the Holy Qur'an)—have a long history of proclaiming themselves as custodians of Absolute Truth, denigrating and ruling out the validity of all others. Conversion in these "missionary" religions has mainly consisted in forcing or indoctrinating people—both potential converts and actual converts—to abandon their cultural heritage and embrace that of the missionaries. Invariably, conversions of this kind have remained superficial—a ritualistic veneer or façade hardly ever penetrating beyond appearances, vestments, decorations, uniforms, dances and songs, art, and architecture. Eventually, a generation arises that questions the validity of such imposition, resulting in schisms, rifts, and splits. Islam has at least seventy-three variations, while Christianity has at least five hundred times more than that number and increasing every year. Through such ways of behaving, missionaries have elevated their cultures to a pedestal, denigrating the peoples they target for conversion and belittling the religious and cultural heritage of their potential converts.

With very few exceptions, for two millennia the missionary legacy of Christianity has been littered with denigrations of non-Christian peoples, cultures, and histories and exaggerations of the goodness of the missionary and the badness of the potential convert. In turn, younger churches have emulated their mentors and contributed to their share of "evangelization" by denigrating those they consider worse-off in the process of making more converts for Christendom. Ironically, much of that evangelization has been in already "converted" areas by luring converts from one denomination to another. Thus the focus of missionaries from Europe and North America remains in African, Caribbean, and Pacific nations that are predominantly Christian:

> The countries receiving the most missionaries per million people are overwhelmingly in Oceania and the Caribbean and have majority Christian populations. More striking, the ten countries that received the most missionaries per million non-Christians averaged almost one for every seven. This includes Samoa, at the top of the list, received more than one missionary for every three non-Christians. None of these countries was less than 90% Christian and only three were less than 95%. Suriname, with a bare Christian majority (51%), ranked 93rd on the list, while Albania, the highest-ranked country with a true Christian minority (32%), ranked 137th out of 232 countries. In addition, Samoa received one missionary for every 2.5

non-Christians. Tonga received one missionary for every 7.4 non-Christians, and Micronesia one for every 11.1 non-Christians.[8]

The self-explanatory statistics cited above are indicative of a problem that has persisted in the modern Christian missionary enterprise, raising doubts and questions about the real motivation for missionary outreach to communities that are already Christian. Kenya is another example. According to the 2009 Kenya Population Census estimates, nearly 83 percent of Kenyans identified themselves as "Christian" (Protestant 47.7 percent; Catholic 23.4 percent; Other Christian 11.9 percent; Muslim 11.2 percent; Traditionalists 1.7 percent; Other 1.6 percent; None 2.4 percent; Unspecified 0.2 percent).

With such statistics as these above, what are foreign Christian missionaries doing in areas that are already predominantly Christian, while Christianity is statistically declining in their own countries? The increasing proliferation of Christian denominations promotes the perception that Christian mission is like a parade of options in a shopping mall, where customers are free to pick whatever seems more attractive depending on the popular perceptions created using various approaches to advertising and persuasion. The conceptual distinction between "advertising" and "mission" has become increasingly blurred, especially in contexts where business and mission are so interrelated as to appear interchangeable.[9] The denominational spectrum in Kenya is so wide as to include all categories of ecclesial polity. While "freedom of worship" is a "human right," the expressions of Christianity have such a wide range of ecclesial polity that it is difficult for both outsiders and insiders to define Christianity as one religion. Such denominational proliferation is not unique to Kenya or to Africa. It seems to have become normative globally, prompting questions about the real (rather than purported) motivations for engagement in Christian mission.[10]

8. See *Christianity Today*, July 25, 2013.
9. Dennis O. Tongoi, "Business as Mission and Mission as Business: Case Studies of financially sustainable Christian mission ventures with a focus on Anglican dioceses in East Africa," Pretoria: PhD Thesis, UNISA, 2016.
10. For the spectrum of denominational polity see J. N. K. Mugambi, "Missionary Presence in Interreligious Encounters and Relationships," in *Studies in World Christianity* 19, no. 2 (Edinburgh: Edinburgh University Press, 2013).

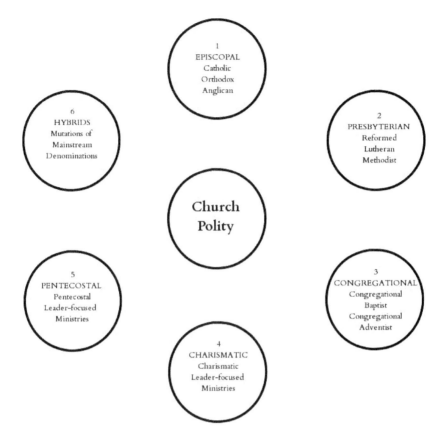

Figure 1. Culture-based forms of ecclesial polity in Christianity

At the opposite end of religious demography, some nations are depicted as nominally nonreligious. In such countries, religious identity is almost synonymous with cultural and national identity. When religious affiliations and political identities coincide, theologies and ideologies become interchangeable. This alignment is neither recent nor localized. It pervades the history of religions. In Palestine, during the first century CE the elite was identified with such alignments as Herodians, Nazarenes, Pharisees, Sadducees, Samaritans, Scribes, and Zealots. In economic terms, there were administrators, soldiers, artisans, peasants, fishermen, and traders. Jesus navigated his teaching betwixt these identities.[11] The Gospel narratives provide some clues regarding the nature of religious and ideological alignments of these groups. St. Paul, as a member of

11. On this point see, for example, John Howard Yoder, *The Politics of Jesus* (Grand Rapids: Eerdmans 1972, 1994).

the elite, could claim rights and privileges none of the disciples of Jesus enjoyed because they were members of the lower strata of society. The discourse on "contextualization" during the twentieth century is complicated by a lack of clarity regarding the relationship between religious identity and ideological alignment. At the same time, denominational identity has a tendency to be aligned with economic stratification and ideological interests. With such conceptual obscurity, discourses on contextualization are problematic.

CONTEXTUALIZATION IN THE CONTEXT OF THE REFORMATION

The fifth centenary of the dramatic publication of Martin Luther's Ninety-Five Theses against Catholic teaching was celebrated on October 31, 2017, in Germany and also in other places where Lutheranism has some influence. In protest against some papal decrees, Luther posted the list of his objections on the door of the church at Wittenberg. The event sparked a wave of protests against papal authority across Europe, in what became the Protestant Reformation. One of the symbolic events of the fifth centenary was a joint commemoration of the event by the Lutheran Church leadership and the Vatican with the launch of a commemorative publication.[12]

In 1534 the English Parliament under King Henry VIII passed the Act of Supremacy, declaring that "the bishop of Rome" (the pope) had no jurisdiction therein.[13] The Reformation was more about cultural autonomy and national sovereignty than doctrinal accuracy. The Council of Trent (1545–63) condemned any move toward national independence and at the same time launched the Counter-Reformation, culminating in the Peace of Westphalia (1648). During the sixteenth century, Christian denominational identity in Europe became one of the markers of national identity, under the maxim *cuius regio, eius religio*. Each prince reserved the right of choosing the religion of the subjects under his reign. It is this maxim that sealed the fate of Africans in Tropical Africa under imperial rule.

The First Vatican Council (1869–70) reaffirmed papal authority and upheld the condemnation of Protestantism at a time when missionary societies—both Catholic and Protestant—were already competing for

---

12. Lutheran World Federation, *From Conflict to Communion: Lutheran-Catholic Common Commemoration of the Reformation in 2017.*

13. Act of Supremacy in England, passed in 1534: https://tinyurl.com/5zwuev.

converts and assets in the colonies abroad.[14] The Berlin Conference on Colonial Questions (1884–85), convened by Bismarck of Germany, ensured that the dominant Christian denomination in each African colony would be the "national" church of the imperial power in charge. Minority denominations could send missionaries, but the power of veto was vested in the imperial power and the dominant denomination. Foreign missionary entrepreneurs function in Africa very much like investors and politicians, competing for as many "customers" as possible. Under such circumstances, contextualization was inconceivable.

One of the most eloquent African pioneer church leaders in Nigeria, Samuel Ajayi Crowther, suffered condemnation and humiliation at the hands of missionaries for insisting that the gospel must necessarily be interpreted and applied in such a way as to make sense to local believers. He was demoted from the office of bishop, sparking a rift between the missionaries and the local African leadership.[15] Such attitude and conduct of missionaries toward African clergy and laity evoked resistance that culminated in the formation of the largest number of independent churches in the entire history of Christianity in Africa, as documented by Allan Anderson, Ogbu Kalu, David B. Barrett, and other scholars.[16]

The consequence of this imperial and missionary history was a mosaic of denominational affiliations, like the spots on the skin of a giraffe, with the most conspicuous ones boldly displayed on the long neck. The cultural factor in all this is unmistakable. Denominational rivalry ended up as cultural rivalry: Lutheranism in former German colonies; Anglicanism in former British colonies; Presbyterianism in areas in former British colonies under the influence of Scottish and American missionaries; Methodism in former British colonies in areas under the influence of British and American missionaries, each group in their separate enclaves. In the meantime, thousands of African independent churches emerged, tinged with the flavor of anticolonial sentiments but distinct from militant political movements. The former emphasized the power of divine intervention, while the latter waged political and militant campaigns, evoking the wrath of imperial reprisal. One of the unexpected impacts of the two world wars during the twentieth century (1914–18 and

14. For a survey of the influence of the Catholic Church in the history of Europe see Philip Hughes, *The Church in Crisis: A History of the General Councils, 325–1870* (London: Mowbray, 1961).

15. Andrew Walls, "The Legacy of Samuel Ajayi Crowther," in *International Bulletin of Missionary Research* (January 1992).

16. Allan Anderson, *African Reformation* (Trenton, NJ: Africa World Press, 2001); Ogbu Kalu, *Christian Missions in Africa: Success, Ferment, Trauma* (Trenton, NJ: Africa World Press, 2010); David B. Barrett, *Schism and Renewal in Africa* (Oxford: Oxford University Press, 1969).

1939–45) was an unprecedented interaction of large numbers of people across cultures, both institutionalized and informal. Africans conscripted into these two wars traveled far across their colonial borders in various ranks of their respective imperial armies. Their interactions—among themselves, with their superiors, and also with the noncombatants across the frontlines—completely changed their worldview, especially in matters of spirituality and applied ethics.[17]

The modern Christian missionary enterprise introduced Christianity into Africa as a religion of peace and goodwill. In practice, however, this tenet of the gospel seemed honored more in words than in practice. As an integral part of the empire, the missionary enterprise had to comply with both imperial and colonial laws and regulations. African converts to Christianity had a tightrope to walk on—to struggle for national sovereignty without breaching their allegiance to both the Imperial Crown and their inalienable right to be free under the reign of Almighty God.[18]

The modern ecumenical movement, institutionalized in the World Council of Churches (WCC) in 1948, is a manifestation of the efforts among mainstream Protestant and Orthodox churches to collaborate on those matters and concerns they shared in common, while minimizing denominational competition and conflict in Africa, Asia, the Caribbean, and the Pacific. Fraternal relationship has been established between the WCC, the Catholic Church, and the World Evangelical Alliance. At the local level, however, division, competition, and rivalry prevail, as a legacy of the past, without any signs of abating.

THE FUTURE OF AFRICAN CHRISTIANITY IN THE CONTEXT OF GLOBALIZATION

Paradoxically, the World Missionary Conference at Edinburgh in 1910 was exuberant about the possibility of European and North American Christians evangelizing the rest of the world within their generation. Christian mission was conceptualized as a human project, with all the technology and gadgetry that the Industrial Revolution had availed itself of. The colonized peoples were taken for granted as passive recipients of the gospel packaged in Europe and North America for consumption in the rest of the world. Thus, Christianity became a commodity for export, alongside other manufactured goods, as the software of civilization and

17. See John G. Gatu, *Fan into Flame* (Nairobi: Moran, 2017).

18. On this point see, for example, Roland Oliver, *The Missionary Factor in East Africa* (London: Longman, 1950, 1970); Arnold J. Temu, *British Protestant Missions* (London: Longman, 1972).

progress. There were neither African nor Asian participants, although a few Asians were invited as observers. Not a single African was invited in any capacity. The conveners and organizers conceptualized the event as a European affair, with mission as a project of patronage and benefaction. The optimism exuded in the speeches was kindled by the scientific development that seemed irreversible.

The optimism exuded at the Edinburgh 1910 Mission Conference turned out to be short-lived. Within less than four years, the First World War erupted, causing more devastation than all previous wars combined and more deaths than in all earlier wars. The optimistic missionary plans outlined at the Edinburgh Conference had to be shelved while many Africans were conscripted as "Carrier Corps" and at similar low-level ranks. At the end of the war in 1918 the colonial demarcation of Africa had to be revised, with German colonies shared out between the victor nations, mainly Britain and France. The League of Nations was formed in 1920 and missionary partition of Africa was also revised.

Missionary-led Christianity in Africa after the world war entered a new phase, faced with the challenge of African initiatives that were critical of missionary insensitivity to African worldviews and interests. This challenge came from the colonies with substantial European presence—especially in East Africa, Central Africa, South Africa, Belgian Congo, and some countries in West Africa. Contextualization of the gospel was inconceivable under these circumstances. African leaders appealed directly to God for intervention, bypassing missionary tutelage. Even within missionary-led churches, converts appealed to the Holy Spirit instead of the resident missionary for guidance and protection.

Within two decades another war erupted, causing even more devastation than the First World War. More Africans were conscripted. Many died, but some returned home in 1945. By default, their exposure gave them courage to struggle for national self-determination. Political awareness, combined with prayer and organizational skills, facilitated the campaign for freedom. By 1963 most of the former African colonies had become sovereign nations, which launched the Organization of African Unity. At the religious level, mainstream Protestant African churches formed the All Africa Conference of Churches (AACC). Meanwhile, independent churches in Africa continued to lobby for recognition from both African governments and mainstream Protestant churches. It took another two decades for these churches to form and launch their own body, the Organization of African Instituted Churches (OAIC). Having become thus organized, they gained clout through which to lobby for recognition both religiously and politically. The OAIC is now represented in the WCC, the National Councils of Churches, and other religious forums.

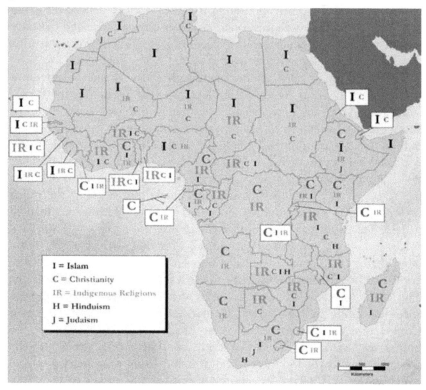

Figure 2. Complexity of African Religiosity

At the opposite end of the denominational spectrum emerged another phenomenon: Charismatic and Pentecostal churches. Among other factors, in these churches (or ministries) one saw echoes of charismatic preachers from North America, who visited various African countries during the 1960s, 1970s, and 1980s. Many young people in Tropical Africa prefer to worship in these churches rather than in the churches of mainstream denominations, both Catholic and Protestant. The first generation of this Pentecostal and Charismatic expression of Christianity is reaching middle age, with their children who are now in their teens or early adulthood. Parishes and congregations inherited from the missionary era have fewer young people attending them, and the future of these churches is difficult to predict in the long term. Young people are increasingly lured toward nonreligious lifestyles thanks to many influences and media. Globalization in Africa under these circumstances is a mixed blessing. On the one hand the utility of Information and Communication Technology (ICT) has greatly accelerated communication. On the other, influences from other cultures are destabilizing the cultural equilibrium in Tropical Africa to the extent that the younger generation is losing touch with the older.

CHRISTIAN THEOLOGIES OF CONTEXTUALIZATION AND RECONSTRUCTION

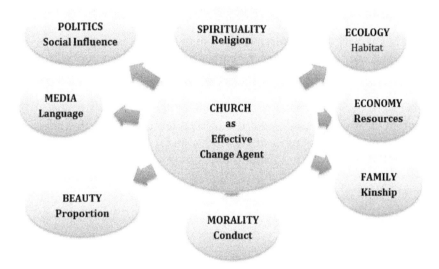

Figure 3. The future church as effective change agent.

The notions of liberation and contextualization may have had a role among the earlier generation of African Christians. Among the present generation of African youth, the greatest quest is for ways and means to utilize all the resources at their disposal, both material and nonmaterial, preparing themselves for meaningful and sustainable livelihoods in an increasingly competitive and integrated world. The mobile phone has become a pocket gadget, with activated internet access and applications to conduct various business transactions. It has become an integral part of the list of accessories, replacing a watch, camera, notebook, diary, and many other necessities that would otherwise be carried in a briefcase. If constructively utilized, these gadgets can be great assets. On the other hand, if used without proper mentoring, they can become a great liability.

Perhaps African Christianity in this third millennium can become the channel through which African youth will be able to reconstruct their social consciousness in anticipation of the future. Taking cue from St. Paul in his advice to Christians in Rome, African youth ought to avoid being conformed to the norms of the present, but instead become agents of change through the renewal of their minds. The immense volume of information beamed though the mobile phone and the internet can be an asset for a constructive future, but at the same time it can be a great liability for those who are not disciplined and are not selective in the access and utilization of ICT. There is a big gap between what ICT provides and the capacity of the church leadership to catch up with it. Perhaps the solution to this constraint is for churches to engage members who have that capacity as trainers of trainers until the whole community becomes technologically transformed.

Shoki Coe endeavored to formulate conceptual tools to help the church in Taiwan, and later in the whole world, for the effective response to the challenges of the 1970s and 1980s, both internal and external. It is our turn in this third millennium to respond to our respective contexts.

PART II

Redefining Mission and Ecumenism

6.

Implications of Shoki Coe's Thoughts on Contextualization for the Mission and Ministry of the Church

S. WESLEY ARIARAJAH

I still hold pleasant memories of the first and only personal meeting I had with Shoki Coe, on a crisp and sunny morning in August 1972 at 13 London Road, Bromley, Kent, in England. In August of the previous year, Coe, who had been an associate director of the Theological Education Fund (TEF) since 1965, was made its director. He eventually gave leadership to a fascinatingly diverse group of associate directors: Desmond Tutu from South Africa, Jim Berquist from the United States, Ivy Chou from Singapore, and Aharon Sapsezian, an Armenian Methodist from Brazil.

Speaking of the group, Desmond Tutu says,

> We were as diverse as you could ever hope to be—racially, nationally and ecumenically. Shoki was Presbyterian, Ivy Methodist, Jim Lutheran, and I was Anglican. I think Aharon was Methodist. English was the first language of only one of us, but it was the language of our organization. We were diverse in our life experiences as well. Ivy had been born on mainland China but grew up in Singapore; Jim was a US citizen who had taught in India for quite a while; Aharon came with all the memory of the Armenian genocide and the radicalness of Latin American Liberation Theology. Shoki was a refugee, an exile from his native Formosa, now Taiwan.[1]

---

1. Desmond M. Tutu, "Shoki Coe and the Theological Education Fund," in Jonah Chang, *Shoki Coe: An Ecumenical Life in Context* (Geneva: WCC, 2012), xi–xii.

Speaking of their staff meetings, Tutu says, "Our meetings were raucous and bruising in a way because each sought to carry the day and our colleagues were rigorous in their examination of each (other's) project." But the team worked well together because "Shoki was quite wonderful in his ability to remain calm and serene amidst the cacophony, and we always ended still friends despite the sharp criticism we had given and received. . . . I doubt that anyone else could have kept us as a team despite our different temperaments and interests. He believed fervently in our theological enterprise and had the skills to herd this particular collection of cats."[2]

I begin with this quote from Archbishop Desmond Tutu because it captures the impression that Coe left on me on that August morning. Calm, serene, profoundly respectful of the young man who had come to meet him, he listened with utmost interest in what I had to say. He gave the impression that his eyes were not just looking at one's face, but into one's soul. And his demeanor reflected the spiritual maturity that emanates from one who had remained faithful to God through many struggles in life. His was an inviting presence, which allowed anyone who met him to be at ease; he left a deep impression on me.

Unfortunately, by the time I joined the staff of the World Council of Churches (WCC) in 1981, the mandates of the TEF had been already brought to an end (1977), the office at Bromley had been closed, and the concern on theological education had been moved to the WCC head-quarters in Geneva under the title, Program for Theological Education (PTE). Coe, who was persuaded to continue as a consultant to the PTE, had also retired from that position in August 1979. I was pleased, how-ever, that one of the associate directors with whom I had spent just a few moments at Bromley, Aharon Sapsezian, was now one of my colleagues as the director of the PTE. During my years at the WCC, the friend-ship with Aharon was a blessing. He had the most sparkling eyes I have seen on a man, a permanent mischievous smile on the face, and bound-less enthusiasm about whatever he was called to do.

SHOKI COE AND ECUMENISM

Only after joining the staff of the WCC did I come to know more about Coe and his long and sustained ecumenical involvement at the global level, always as a true and faithful representative of the Presby-terian Church in Taiwan. His exposure to ecumenism began with his attendance at the World Youth Conference in Amsterdam as early as

2. Tutu, "Shoki Coe and the Theological Education Fund," xi–xii.

1939 and was further enhanced by his participation in the formative second World Conference of Christian Youth in Oslo (1947), which was one of the cradles from which many of the leaders of the modern ecumenical movement emerged. His ecumenical formation was further cemented by his time at the WCC Ecumenical Institute in Bossey near Geneva, Switzerland. These involvements and his deep commitment to ecumenism resulted in the invitation to join the Preparatory Committee for the second WCC Assembly in Evanston, Illinois (1954), where he began to build a network of global ecumenical friendships. These contacts resulted in the invitation to be an active participant at the meeting of the International Missionary Council (IMC) in Accra, Ghana (December 1957–January 1958), which established the TEF. He also participated in the third WCC Assembly in New Delhi (1961), which saw the integration of the IMC into the WCC as the Commission on World Mission and Evangelism.

At these major ecumenical events, he rubbed shoulders with some of the big names in global ecumenism of the time. He came to have close relationships with some of the main ecumenical thinkers and those who were directing major ecumenical programs, like Van Dusen, Stanley Smith, Philippe Maury, Robert Bilheimer (director of the WCC Division of Studies), Daisuke Kitagawa and Paul Abrecht (Department of Church and Society), Victor Hayward and D. T. Niles (Department of Missionary Studies), and many others. Despite his global ecumenical engagements, Coe deeply believed that there was only one ecumenical movement, with its local, national, and global expressions. For him, local ecumenical commitments provided the bulwark of global ecumenism. Therefore, in February 1948, at the meeting of the Ninth South Synod of the Presbyterian Church in Taiwan that met in Táu-lak, Coe strongly advocated a united church—to combine the North and South synods. And he saw it come to fruition in March 1951, when the two synods joined to form the General Assembly of the Presbyterian Church in Taiwan. This assembly, under his influence, also voted to give expression to its global ecumenical commitment by joining the World Presbyterian Alliance and the WCC.[3]

Although confessional identities could not be easily shed at that time, Coe participated in a meeting in Princeton, along with well-known theologians like John Baillie, T. F. Torrance, J. Hromadka, and Jim McCord, among others, to discuss the question: "Now the WCC has come into being and is to stay, is the Presbyterian Alliance really

3. I am indebted to Jonah Chang for the details of this information; he gives a "Chronology of the Reverend Shoki Coe" in Appendix 3 of his volume, *Shoki Coe: An Ecumenical Life in Context*, 175–80.

necessary? And, if so, what is its role? From the perspective of an ecumenical stance, what it should refrain from doing and what it should do?" After serious debate, the decision was made that the alliance would remain mainly as a fellowship of the Presbyterian churches that are too small to be part of the WCC, but that "the Alliance will refrain from activities which can be done with other communions in and through the WCC."

Coe saw denominational and confessional identities as an aberration of the church; his understanding of the church was that it is a gathered community of faith in each and all places, united by the common commitment to the message of the gospel. Coe said that the Princeton discussions on confessional families "became my guide, when I joined D. T. Niles in combating the spread of so-called 'World Confessionalism' in Asia."[4] The imported confessional identities still remain a major issue for churches in Asia. It was difficult, at that time, to take it on with the strength it required.

RETHINKING MISSION AND MINISTRY

Coe was convinced that confessionalism, isolationism from the affairs of the world, and excessive dependence on outside sources for the basic life and ministry of the churches in Asia were due to the nature of the missions that were carried out in Asia and the type of theological formation of the churches. However, like most theologians of his generation, Coe was influenced by Barthian theology, but the changing religious situation in Asia began to impact his perceptions on the meaning of evangelism in the context of religious plurality. It was at a preparatory meeting for the Evanston Assembly at the Ecumenical Institute in Bossey that Coe felt that Barth's excessive Christomonism and his sweeping view that other religions were "unbelief" was not sitting well with him. It was this meeting, he said, that "marked the beginning of my understanding of the vital importance of this thorny issue of 'dialogue with those of other faiths and ideologies' for mission in general and theological education in particular."[5]

It is of interest that it was on this occasion that Coe had the opportunity to personally meet and have a conversation with Hendrik Kraemer, who was earlier very familiar to him through his book *The Christian Message in a Non-Christian World*, written as a preparatory volume for the

4. Shoki Coe, *Recollections and Reflections* (Taiwan: The Rev. Dr. Shoki Coe Memorial Fund in New York, 1993), 208.

5. Coe, *Recollections and Reflections*, 174.

third World Missionary Conference in Tambaram (1938), near Madras, India. At Tambaram, Kraemer elaborated on Barth's contention that non-Christian religions were "part of the human rebellion against God" in order to argue for the urgency of evangelism. Coe's professor at Westminster College, Cambridge, H. H. Farmer, was one of the strong opponents of Kraemer's views at Tambaram and had discussed the issue with his students. So, Coe valued the unanticipated opportunity to meet with Kraemer.

Kraemer was at that time the director of the Ecumenical Institute and had invited Coe and a few other Asian participants for an evening conversation with him. What Coe discovered came as a surprise to him:

> Naturally our discussion that evening was mostly about dialogue with other religions, and of special interest was his position vis-à-vis that of Karl Barth. We had the strong impression that he also felt not too comfortable with Barth's outright stance. He told us that he hoped to make his "new" position clear in a forthcoming book.[6]

This experience reflects what M. M. Thomas said, that beyond Tambaram, Kraemer had himself become post-Kraemarian! However, the Barth-Kraemer theology of mission has been the primary influence in Asia and of the missionary movement that came into Asia. Unfortunately, this reality continues to this day. However, Coe found his escape from this narrow view of Christian witness, which alienated Christians from people of other religious traditions, by readily embracing the concept of *missio Dei*, the mission of God, when it was introduced at the fifth World Missionary Conference in 1952 in Willingen, Germany. He saw that this expansive and inclusive vision of mission—as something that God does to heal the world, in which we are called to participate—was very liberating. It could meaningfully include the full participation in the struggles relating to the political situation in Taiwan, the Christian witness and discipleship in the world, and a new positive relationship with peoples of other religious traditions. Thus he became highly critical of the traditional understanding of mission that made the church into an isolated community, with an understanding of its relationship to the world only in terms of evangelism and *diakonia*. For Coe, the church's involvement in the world, certainly in the historical context of Taiwan, demanded a much deeper and more authentic understanding of mission, and he found it in the concept of *missio Dei*.

Turning to the ministry, he understood the church's ministry as an extension and continuation of the ministry of Christ, to be done in the

---

6. Coe, *Recollections and Reflections*, 174–75.

spirit in which Christ performed it. For him, the ministry of the church is a "real, though imperfect, representation and continuation of Christ's ministry." And since the ministry of Jesus Christ is the "absolute standard and basis of the Church's ministry," this necessarily has service as its essential form. And it remains "open" in three ways, "to God; to the world; and to the church in the world." Coe, therefore, saw three dimensions to the ministry: God-related (liturgical), church-related (to equip the church to be the church in the world), and world-directed (toward service as the focus of mission). He further qualified this by saying that the "church-related ministry is only *existentially* for the church, since *essentially* it is for the world-directed ministry." In other words, the church's ministry is caught up in the movement of God's love for the world.[7]

To be able to achieve this, Coe believed, there needed to be a threefold formation of the church, namely, Christian formation, theological formation, and ministerial formation. And he saw the centrality of theological education to achieve these formations and for all of the other dimensions of the church: its self-understanding, its approach to its mission and ministry, to the way it expounded the scripture, did its theology, and especially to the way it understood its relationship with the world. It is no wonder that Coe was the first one to introduce the concept of "contextualization" into the TEF discussions and expounded its full implications through his ministry within the TEF.

THEOLOGICAL EDUCATION

It is of interest that in introducing the TEF team at Bromley, Tutu speaks of Shoki Coe as "a refugee, an exile from his native Formosa, now Taiwan." This was indeed the case at that time, and it summarizes eloquently how the political turmoil that engulfed Taiwan at that time—the Communist Revolution in China and the devastating political consequences it had on Taiwan, Japanese imperialism and its takeover of Taiwan, and so on—continuously affected Shoki Coe and his family, eventually resulting in their move to the United Kingdom.

Since there will be other articles in this volume on Coe's life, I will not go into details on how these events affected and shaped his life, except to note that despite the many interruptions and problems, and the number of periods in his life he had to live abroad for studies and work, Coe's heart, soul, and mind were deeply and unshakably rooted in his

7. William P. Russell, *Contextualization: Origins, Meaning and Implications* (Rome: Pontificia Università Gregoriana, 1995), 377–78.

native soil. He saw the historical vicissitudes that befell his nation, and the struggle for its independence and self-determination, as part of his own biography. All other reflections on "context" and the need to "contextualize" arose out of his determined commitment to make a faithful response to the actual social, political, and historical context of his own country and its people. It is this conviction that drove him, along with Ng Bú-tong, Lim Chong-gi, and Song Choan-seng, to initiate the internal movement of "Taiwanese for Self-Determination" on December 25, 1973, and to call for "Taiwanese Self-Determination Movements" in the US and Europe.

The discernment of the need to be responsive to the context in which one lived drove Coe to move toward contextualization of Christian theology, ecclesiology, missiology, theological education, and spirituality, and the opportunity came his way when he was invited, first to become the associate director, and later the director of the TEF.

INDIGENIZATION AND CONTEXTUALIZATION

In expounding the concept of contextualization, Coe had to first deal with the concept of "indigenization," which had been a preoccupation of some parts of the church and some of the missionaries ever since the missionary movement came into Asia. Speaking on this question, Coe says, "Throughout the three Mandates (of the TEF) there has been a continuous concern for indigenization in theological education—a term and a process which has been debated in mission circles of both older and younger churches for a long time." This, he says, "is understandable, as indigenization is a missiological necessity when the gospel moves from one cultural soil to another and has to be retranslated, reinterpreted, and expressed afresh in the new cultural soil." Why then, he asks, do we now use a new word, contextualization, in preference to indigenization?[8]

While being sympathetic to the younger churches' attempts to plant the gospel message in their own cultural soil, Coe says:

However, because of the static nature of the metaphor, indigenization tends to be used in the sense of responding to the gospel in terms of traditional culture. Therefore it is in danger of being past-oriented. Furthermore, the impression has been given that it is only applicable to Asia and Africa, for elsewhere it was felt that the danger lay in overindigenization, an uncritical accommodation such as expressed by culture faiths, the American Way of Life, etc. But the most important factor, especially since the last war, has been the new phenomenon of radical change. The new context is not that

8. Coe, *Recollections and Reflections*, 270–71.

of a static culture, but the search for the new, which at the same time has involved the culture itself.[9]

William P. Russell, in his dissertation submitted to the Faculty of Theology of the Pontificiam Universitatem S. Thomae in Urbe on *Contextualization: Origins, Meaning and Implications*, examining the use of the term within the TEF, especially between 1970 and 1972, says that Coe never described himself as a theologian, although others have referred to him in this way. "Instead, he always identified himself as a 'theological educator.'" This meant, Russell rightly claims, that "besides theology, his interest lay primarily in education and ministry."[10]

Yet, what is significant in Coe's thinking is that he did not separate theological education from ministry, ministry from mission, and mission from the life and meaning of being a church in a specific context. This wholistic understanding of "contextualization" is one of the most important contributions he made to the discussion and is valid for our discussions on mission and ministry today.

The other significant input Coe made was to make a distinction between "contextuality" and "contextualization." He remembered the warning by Jürgen Moltmann, in one of the TEF meetings, that there is a danger that academic theology may become so contextualized that it becomes fossilized theology, or that it may be caught in the opposite danger of becoming chameleon theology, changing color according to the context. This led Coe to emphasize the importance of "contextuality." For him, contextuality meant "the missiological discernment of the signs of the times, seeing where God is at work and calling us to participate in it." Thus, in his view, "contextuality is more than just taking all contexts seriously, but indiscriminately. It is the conscientization of the contexts in particular, historical moments, assessing the peculiarity of the context in the light of the mission of the church as it is called to participate in the *Missio Dei*."[11] Such conscientization, for Coe, could come only through involvement and participation in the specific context out of which critical awareness may arise.

He held that although the concepts of contextuality and contextualization should be seen as distinct, they could not be separated and should be seen as the source for doing theology in context:

> This dialectic between contextuality and contextualization indicates a new way of theologizing. It involves not only words but actions. Through this,

9. Coe, *Recollections and Reflections*, 271.
10. Russell, *Contextualization*, 362.
11. Coe, *Recollections and Reflections*, 273.

the inherent danger of a dichotomy between theory and practice, action and reflection, the classroom and the street, should be overcome. Authentic theological reflection can only take place as a *theologia in loco*, discerning the contextuality within the concrete context. But it must also be aware that such authentic theological reflection is at best, but also at most, *theologia viatorum*; and therefore contextuality must be matched by contextualization, which is an ongoing process, fitting for a pilgrim people, moving from place to place and from time to time, in awareness that there is no abiding place which is not subject also to the changes of time.[12]

According to Coe it is for this reason that the Working Policy Statement of the TEF does not speak about "contextual theology" nor "contextualized theology" but about "contextualizing" theology. Although the official documents of the TEF are the final products of group processes, William Russell, by studying Coe's writings before he became part of the TEF, shows that much of the thinking within the TEF on contextualization is drawn from Coe's own thinking. The concept itself first appears prominently during the Third Mandate of the TEF in its statement on *Ministry in Context*. The introduction to the statement says:

> The third mandate's strong emphasis on renewal and reform in theological education appears to focus upon a central concept, contextuality, the capacity to respond meaningfully to the Gospel within the framework of one's own situation. Contextualization is not simply a fad or catch-word but a theological necessity demanded by the incarnational nature of the word.[13]

The text goes on to enunciate five basic principles to expound the meaning of contextuality and contextualization:

1. It means all that is implied in the familiar term "indigenization," and still seeks to press beyond. Contextualization has to do with how we assess the peculiarity of the Third World context. Indigenization tends to be used in the sense of responding to the Gospel in terms of a traditional culture. Contextualization, while not ignoring this, takes into account the process of secularity, technology, and the struggle for human justice, which characterize the historical moment of nations in the Third World.

---

12. Coe, *Recollections and Reflections*, 273.

13. The statement on *Ministry in Context* is one of the papers in "A Consolidated TEF Policy Statement for the Implementation of the Third Mandate" (with the heading "TEF Committee, Bromley 1972," in 1972 Workbook), TEF Archives Box 29. (I owe this reference to William Russell.).

2. Yet a careful distinction must be made between authentic and false forms of contextualization. False contextualization yields to uncritical accommodation, a form of culture faith. Authentic contextualization is always prophetic, arising always out of a genuine encounter between God's word and his world, and moves towards the purpose of challenging and changing the situation through rootedness in and commitment to the historical moment.

3. It is therefore clear that contextualization is a dynamic not a static process. It recognizes the continually changing nature of every human situation and of the possibility for change, thus opening the way for the future.

4. The agenda of a Third World contextualizing theology will have priorities of its own. It may have to express its self-determination by uninhibitedly opting for a "theology of change," or by recognizing unmistakable theological significance in such issues as justice, liberation, dialogue with people of other faiths and ideologies, economic power, etc.

5. Yet contextualization does not imply the fragmented isolation of peoples and cultures. While within each diverse cultural situation people must struggle to regain their own identity and become subjects of their own history, there remains an interdependence of contexts. Contextualization thereby means that the possibilities for renewal must first of all be sensed locally and situationally, yet always within the framework of contemporary inter-dependence which binds both to the problems of the past and present and to the possibilities for the future.[14]

Undoubtedly these five principles arise from the life experiences and contexts of all the TEF staff and their consultants, but it is easy to see in each of them the imprint of Coe's reflections arising out of his own personal struggles and the challenges faced by the church back in Taiwan.

LOCAL PARTICULARITY AND CATHOLICITY

Coe was absolutely convinced about contextuality in understanding the gospel message and responding to it in context, but was, at the same time, well aware that the message of the gospel and the fellowship in

14. Cf. Russell, *Contextualization*, 34–35.

Christ cuts across all boundaries. While asking the question whether being rooted in a concrete situation presents the danger of losing the catholicity of the gospel, he raised a counterquestion, whether "there is such a theology which is not in *loco* and thus in *vacuo*?" Thus, rejecting the idea that there is some universal "utopian theology" that binds all Christians across their specific contexts, he held that the concern for the catholicity of the gospel is a legitimate one. However, his answer was that contextualization was the authentic way to that catholicity we seek.

He found this illustrated in the incarnation: "Catholicity is both a gift and a task. As a gift we must see how it was given. This was in a very concrete way, by the Word which became flesh and dwelt among us at a particular time and space. I believe, in fact, that the incarnation is the divine form of contextualization, and if this is so, the way we receive the gift is also through our following his way."[15] Expounding the concept of incarnation further, Coe has argued that true catholicity is a gift that only becomes ours as we draw our basic power from the gospel of the incarnate Word:

> True catholicity could not possibly be a colorless uniformity, but must be a rich fullness of truth and grace, which unfolds and manifests itself as we take the diversified contexts in time and space, where we are set, and respond faithfully, as the Incarnate Word did on our behalf once and for all. The true and authentic catholicity will become fully ours as we not only draw basic power from the *same gospel*, but also as we are committed wholly to *serve the same Missio Dei* in the diversified contexts.[16]

Thus, Coe did not see contextuality as something that militated against catholicity, but as something that in itself constituted the catholicity of the gospel and the church:

> In this way we can welcome with joy the emergence of black theology, and for that matter yellow theology, and the theology of liberation for the sake of the true catholicity of the gospel. There is no colorless theology. But there is all the joy of the multiplicity of colors mobilized for the beauty of the new heaven and the new earth which God has promised. Or to change the metaphor, all the sounds must be mobilized in the great symphony of the Hallelujah Chorus, to be heard not only in heaven but on earth.[17]

---

15. Coe, *Recollections and Reflections*, 274.
16. Coe, *Recollections and Reflections*, 274.
17. Coe, *Recollections and Reflections*, 275.

CONCLUSION

I am struck by the immediate relevance of what Coe has held out to the understanding of mission and ministry in Asia today, to our understanding and interpretation of the scripture, to the theological formation of the congregations, and to the Christian understanding of our relationship to the peoples of other religious traditions. Some prophetic voices are local and timebound, while others resound through the decades. If Coe's challenges were relevant when they were raised, they have become even more relevant as we look to the future of Christianity in Asia. As Jesus did, Coe could also have ended his ministry with the words, "Let those who have ears to hear, let them hear" (Mark 4:9).

It would be appropriate to conclude this reflection with the words of the current general secretary of the WCC, Rev. Dr. Olav Fykse Tveit. In his foreword to the volume *Shoki Coe: An Ecumenical Life in Context* by Jonah Chang, he says that "in many ways Shoki Coe represented the pioneering spirit of the ecumenical movement" and that "his work on the missiological concept of 'contextualization' not only extended the horizons of mission theology but opened up a new avenue for exploring the interrelatedness of the Christian message and the world in which the church is called to witness." And commenting on Coe's own life, he says: "The life and work of Shoki Coe exemplify for us what it means to be honest and faithful—to the gospel of Christ, to one's ethnic and social reality, and also to the spirit of ecumenism and its quest of mission in unity and unity in mission."[18]

I have also heard Dr. Philip Potter, a former general secretary, say that "the ecumenical movement is built on the faith and faithfulness, courage and strength and the unrelenting hope of the pioneers that have gone before us." Shoki Coe is a shining example of one of those pioneers.

18. Chang, *Shoki Coe: An Ecumenical Life in Context*, viii–ix.

7.

Contextualization, Ecumenism, and the Wider Ecumenism

EDMUND KEE-FOOK CHIA

I first came across the name Shoki Coe while researching for a paper in graduate school. It soon dawned on me that most scholars writing on the theme of contextualization employ his work as a starting point for reflection. As director of the Theological Education Fund (TEF) in 1972, Coe spelled out the essence of contextualization: "Authentic contextualization is always prophetic, arising always out of a genuine encounter between God's Word and his world, and moves toward the purpose of challenging and changing the situation through rootedness in and commitment to a given historical moment."[1] This has shaped a lot of my subsequent work, including how I think theologically on the topic of the present article.

The article will investigate the theme of ecumenism, but will do so through an Asian lens. It will first examine the reality of Christian diversity as well as the divisions that came about over the centuries of Christian history. It will then look at the events leading up to what has come to be known as the modern ecumenical movement and also the dynamics behind the belated entrance of the Roman Catholic Church into the ecumenical world. In light of these realities, the article reflects on what the quest for Christian unity entails. It takes into account the contextual issues of the native Christians' quest for nationalism and liberation in the early twentieth century as well as the phenomenon of religious pluralism

---

1. Theological Education Fund, *Ministry in Context: The Third Mandate Programme of the Theological Education Fund* (London: TEF, 1972), 20–21, cited in Simon Kwan, "A Discursive History of the Asian Theological Movement: A Critique of Its Binarism," *JTCA: The Theological Journal of Theologies and Cultures in Asia* 1 (February 2002): 104.

that came into ascendency in the late twentieth century. These reflections are attempts at contextualizing the ecumenical movement to enable it to be at once responsive to God's word as well as the challenges and situation of the given historical moment.

CHRISTIAN DIVERSITY AND DIVISION

That Christianity is divided at its core needs no further discussion. There are so many Christian denominations in the world today that the joke is even the Holy Spirit is unable to keep track of how many there are! In view of this embarrassing reality, some Christians wish for the return of Christianity to its origins when there was simply one church founded by the one Lord Jesus Christ. This is probably not going to happen and, moreover, it is a fallacy to think that Christianity was one singular and united church when it first began.

Biblical scholars such as Harold Attridge posit that "the Christian movement probably began not from a single center but from many different centers where different groups of disciples of Jesus gathered and tried to make sense of what they had experienced with him and what had happened to him at the end of his public ministry."[2] To be sure, during the New Testament era, the Christian communities were "diverse with different forms of ministries, patterns of organizations, and having a variety of articulations of faith and ways of worship which were spontaneously shaped by their different historical, cultural, and religious contexts."[3] So, diversity was the trademark of Christianity from its very beginning. That notwithstanding, the different expressions of the Christian faith did have one crucial factor that they all shared in common, that is, their faith and belief in Jesus as Lord and Savior. That Jesus Christ is the messiah who is fully human and fully divine was and continues to be the confession of all the disparate Christian communities. This central Christological proclamation became the litmus test of orthodoxy.

This original diversity, however, was compromised when Christianity was made the official religion of the Roman Empire in the fourth century. Having to now serve the political stability of the empire, uniformity was insisted upon across the board, including in beliefs, worship, and organizational structure. The ecumenical councils convoked by the

2. Harold W. Attridge, "Book of Acts Account Too Simple," in *Frontline: From Jesus to Christ, The Diversity of Early Christianity*, https://tinyurl.com/3y7jyx.

3. Kuncheria Pathil, "Theology of Ecumenism in the Asian Context: A Catholic Perspective," in *Our Pilgrimage in Hope: Proceedings of the First Three Seminars of the Asian Movement for Christian Unity* (Manila: St. Paul's, 2001), 25.

Roman emperors were meant to enforce some sort of unity in Christian beliefs. Those who did not agree or did not fit in, such as Arius or Nestorius and the Antiochian School, were expelled or separated from the mainstream.

Over the course of history numerous such divisions took place, resulting in the establishment of what the mainstream considers as a heterodox church. There was the separation of the Oriental Orthodox Communion from the dominant Eastern Church. Then there was the split between the whole Eastern Church and the entire Western Church in 1054, now better known as the Great Schism. The Protestant Reformation of the sixteenth century was another major division, this time within Western Christianity only. Since then, many more groups have splintered off to establish churches on their own. Through it all, each of the separated groups considers itself the most authentic expression of Christianity and calls itself the "one, holy, catholic, and apostolic" church.

THE QUEST FOR CHRISTIAN UNITY

Given the numerous divisions within the church of Christ over the centuries and millennia, it would be imprudent to even dream that there will one day evolve a single entity that unites all the many factions together as one church. The pluralism of the Christian tradition is something that will probably remain with us for all time. That does not mean that unity is impossible, but it might mean that unity as understood by uniformity is probably not going to happen. The one, holy, catholic, and apostolic church has to be expressed in the diversity of the many churches.

Church unity begins when each of these individual churches comes closer to Christ as the source and summit of the Christian faith. As they come closer to Christ they should also come closer with their sister churches. No one church, however, will be able to claim itself as the most accurate representation of Christ. Every single church is a pilgrim on earth, in the process of growth toward faithfulness, and can certainly learn from and with one another so as to better approximate the will of Christ. This is essentially the quest for Christian unity; it is a quest where there will be mutual support between the churches and mutual learning taking place.

This quest for Christian unity is driven primarily by two verses from the Bible, the first coming from John's Gospel where Jesus is at prayer asking the Father to ensure "that they may all be one . . . so that the world may believe that you have sent me" (John 17:22). This prayer for the disciples to be united remains relevant to contemporary disciples of

Christ. The phrase "that they may all be one" has become so popular that one often finds it as the central theme of many ecumenical gatherings.

A second verse comes from Paul's Letter to the Ephesians where he pleads with the community "to maintain the unity of the Spirit in the bond of peace" because "there is one body and one Spirit, just as you were called to the one hope of your calling, one Lord, one faith, one baptism, one God and Father of all, who is above all and through all and in all" (Eph 4:3–6). This verse affirms that Christian unity should be something that is already present in the community. It is a gift from the Lord. The contemporary Christian's task is to make visible this unity. In that way it serves as goal of the ecumenical movement. Christian unity is thus a gift as well as a goal.[4] The word "ecumenism" (Greek word *oikoumene* meaning "the inhabited world") is, therefore, used today to refer to all the activities undertaken to promote understanding and enhance relationships between different Christian denominations. Its hope is that there will come a day when we can see unity between the many different Christian communities throughout the whole wide world.

ANTECEDENTS TO THE ECUMENICAL MOVEMENT

Western historians often attribute the modern ecumenical movement to the efforts of the missionaries serving in the so-called "mission lands" in the nineteenth century. It is believed that their friendships in the missions fostered a desire for Christian unity so that they could give better witness to the native peoples. Moreover, cooperation in a variety of ministries such as Bible translations, education, and healthcare affirmed the importance of presenting a united front as one Christian community. It was this context, so the argument goes, that inspired the ecumenical movement.

Asian historians such as T. V. Philip, however, offer another perspective. They argue that ecumenism was already well and going among Asian Christians long before the missionaries thought about it. The impetus among the natives is often a reaction to how the missionaries were treating them: "It was the protest of the Indian Christians against Western denominations and missionary paternalism that led to church unity discussions in some of the missionary conferences in India."[5]

---

4. Wesley Ariarajah, "Some Basic Theological Assumptions of the Ecumenical Movement," in *Our Pilgrimage in Hope*, 38.

5. T. V. Philip, *Ecumenism in Asia* (Delhi: ISPCK, 1994), 44, as quoted in Ninan Koshy, *A History of the Ecumenical Movement in Asia*, vol. 1 (Hong Kong: World Student Christian Federation, 2004), 35–36.

Also happening in the nineteenth century was the establishment of numerous informal movements of young Christians in Europe and North America. These eventually led to the formation of both the Young Men's Christian Association (YMCA) in 1844 and the Young Women's Christian Association (YWCA) in 1855 in London. The World Student Christian Federation (WSCF), which brought together a host of autonomous national student movements, was founded in 1895 at Vadstena Castle, Sweden. The participants in these movements were not representing any churches and so interdenominational concerns never surfaced.

With the disillusionment over the European tribal wars that caused immense misery to the entire world in the First World War, the young Christian associations began to include Christian unity as one of their aims.[6] In many of these movements, key leaders such as John Mott and Nathan Soderblom emerged. They were to later become major players in international ecumenical movements. Mott, who was an American YMCA leader, served as chair to the Edinburgh Missionary Conference.

THE EDINBURGH 1910 MISSIONARY CONFERENCE

The 1910 World Missionary Conference held in Edinburgh is often regarded as the end of the missionary era and the beginning of the modern ecumenical movement. While it was pitched as an ecumenical conference, its aims were twofold: (i) to discuss ways in which missionaries could be equipped with more effective methods, and (ii) to address the problem of interdenominational competition in the mission fields. It was certainly more a missionary conference than it was ecumenical. It was apparent that Christian unity was in the service of Christian evangelism. The report of the first commission, titled "Carrying the Gospel to All the Non-Christian World," confirms the thesis that evangelism was at the foreground of Edinburgh 1910. In fact, the report begins with these words:

> It is a startling and solemnising fact that even as late as the twentieth century the Great Command of Jesus Christ to carry the Gospel to all mankind is still so largely unfulfilled. It is a ground for great hopefulness that, notwithstanding the serious situation occasioned by such neglect, the Church is confronted to-day, as in no preceding generation, with a literally worldwide opportunity to make Christ known. There may have been times when in certain non-Christian lands the missionary forces of Christianity stood face to face with as pressing opportunities as those now presented in the same

6. Koshy, *History of the Ecumenical Movement in Asia*, vol. 1, 45.

fields, but never before has there been such a conjunction of crises and of opening of doors in all parts of the world as that which characterises the present decade.[7]

Most of the other reports were also by and large oriented toward how mission can be enhanced in view of being more successful in terms of converting the natives in the mission lands to Christendom. It was only in the eighth report, titled "Co-operation and the Promotion of Unity," that the motif of ecumenism appeared.[8] Christian division was discussed not only as a liability to the missionaries witnessing in mission lands, but also as a scandal infecting the churches in Europe and North America. The Euro-Americans, therefore, looked toward unity in the missions: "The Church in western lands will reap a glorious reward from its missionary labours, if the church in the mission field points the way to a healing of its divisions and to the attainment of that unity for which our Lord prayed."[9]

While the conference's aim was specifically to better prepare missionaries for Christian mission, it also promoted better relationships between the missionaries of different denominations. Christian unity was certainly accomplished and was by no means sidelined. The desire for Christian unity was a recurring theme throughout the conference, especially during the informal sessions and also when the delegates were at prayers. "In the time of worship at the Conference, we read that in their prayers of intercession as in the debates themselves, the theme of the unity of the Church in mission continually surfaced. As one participant remarked: The ever-recurring refrain was 'that they may be one, that the world may believe.'"[10]

FORMATION OF THE WORLD COUNCIL OF CHURCHES

At the conclusion of the Edinburgh 1910 Missionary Conference, the delegates appointed a continuation committee charged with following up on the decisions of the conference and also to further the cause of uni-

---

7. W. H. T. Gairdner, *"Edinburgh 1910": An Account and Interpretation of the World Missionary Conference* (Edinburgh: Oliphant, Anderson & Ferrier, 1910), 68.

8. Edinburgh 2010, "Centenary of the 1910 World Missionary Conference," https://tinyurl.com/ybw3kfg2. The nine volumes of the 1910 conference publications are archived on this site.

9. *World Missionary Conference, 1910: Report of Commission VIII: Co-operation and the Promotion of Unity* (Edinburgh: Oliphant, Anderson & Ferrier, 1910), 131, https://tinyurl.com/y979x5zj.

10. Gideon Goosen, "The World Missionary Conference, Edinburgh 1910–2010: A Time for Reflection," *Compass* 44, no. 3 (Spring 2010): 28.

fying the many Protestant denominations. By 1921, this committee had evolved into the International Missionary Council (IMC), which had its foundation in Lake Mohonk, New York.[11] The IMC was to host major conferences in subsequent years, the principal ones being in Jerusalem (1928), Madras (1938), Whitby (1947), Willingen (1952), Ghana (1957), and New Delhi (1961).

At around the time the IMC was founded, Christians in Europe were also busy networking among themselves across denominational lines to collaborate in projects on behalf of justice and peace, which was especially relevant in the aftermath of the First World War. The former Christian youth leader Nathan Soderblom had become the Swedish Lutheran bishop by then and, together with other Christian leaders across continental Europe, hosted the Universal Christian Conference on Life and Work in 1925 in Stockholm. The Life and Work Conference became the arm of the church in Europe to address issues of international relations and social and economic life. Its starting point is that Christian social action in and for the world is very much a part of the Christian mission and plays a significant role in witnessing to the good news of Jesus Christ.

Complementing the social action dimension, the Anglican Bishop Charles Brent of the US Episcopal Church issued a call for a conference across Christian denominations to explore seriously the roots of Christian division and to facilitate theological conversations between the historically divided Protestant churches in view of restoring some semblance of unity. When it first met in Geneva in 1920, after the First World War, some eighty churches were represented. A continuation committee was appointed to plan an international conference that was held in Lausanne in 1927 where about four hundred participants representing both the Eastern Orthodox churches and a wide spectrum of Protestant churches were present. This resulted in the establishment of the Faith and Order Movement, where "faith" refers to questions of doctrine and "order" to questions of ministerial structure of the church. At the next international conference held in Edinburgh in 1937 a proposal to merge with the Life and Work Movement was adopted. This eventually led to the formation of the World Council of Churches (WCC).[12]

The WCC is a fellowship of churches along the lines of the League of Nations and was established when over one hundred church leaders voted in 1937–1938 in favor of it. The actual foundation, however, was

11. Jeffrey Gros, Eamon McManus, and Ann Riggs, *Introduction to Ecumenism* (New York: Paulist, 1998), 27.

12. "Faith and Order Movement," in *Encyclopedia of Protestantism*, https://tinyurl.com/yanarov6.

delayed by the Second World War. But when it finally became a reality and held its first assembly in 1948 in Amsterdam, 147 member churches were represented, together with the Life and Work and the Faith and Order movements. In 1961 the International Missionary Council also joined the WCC and the World Council of Christian Education did the same ten years later. Since then the ministries of the respective streams have been organized under the auspices of the WCC. It has had ten assemblies since its foundation and has 345 member churches today.

THE CATHOLIC CHURCH AND ECUMENISM

The Roman Catholic Church's ecclesiological attitude of "return" to the Catholic fold naturally meant it stayed away from both the Edinburgh 1910 event and the founding of the WCC. When Anglican Bishop Charles Brent invited Pope Benedict XV in 1919 to send Catholic participants to the Faith and Order movement, the pope declined but promised to pray that "if the congress is practicable, the participants may, by God's grace, see the light and become reunited to the visible head of the church, by whom they would be received with open arms."[13] Likewise, Vatican officials also declined when invited to participate in the first Life and Work conference.

But thinking changed with the publication of the 1949 document *Ecclesia Sancta* by the Curia's Holy Office. Ecumenism was beginning to be accepted and approval was given to Catholic experts to engage in dialogue with their fellow Christians from other denominations. The Augustinian priest George Tavard attended the Second Assembly of the WCC in 1954 and was later appointed to serve as a Catholic observer at the Faith and Order Commission conference in Montreal in 1963.[14] The Jesuit priests John Courtney Murray and Gustave Weigel were also approved to attend the Conference on Faith and Order in Oberlin, Ohio, in 1957. They were to become ecumenical giants within the Catholic Church and contributed significantly to the discourse on church unity during the Second Vatican Council and also in North America.

With the Second Vatican Council, the Catholic Church opened its doors completely to the modern ecumenical movement. Pope John XXIII established the Secretariat for Promoting Christian Unity in 1960

13. Tom F. Stransky, "Roman Catholic Church and Ecumenism," in *Dictionary of the Ecumenical Movement*, 2nd ed. (Geneva: WCC, 2002), 997.

14. The Assumptionists: US Region, North American Province, "Rev. George Tavard, A.A.," https://tinyurl.com/y6vugcoc.

(elevated to Pontifical Council status in 1988) to explore the ecumenical agenda and also to identify and invite the major Orthodox, Protestant, Anglican, and Reformed churches, and church communions to send representatives to serve as observers of the council. By the end of the council in 1965, nearly one hundred of these Christian observers who were previously known as "schismatics" and "heretics" but now called "our separated brethren" had participated in the council.

Because some of these ecumenical observers had been involved in the Faith and Order Commission, they were able to share their ideas with the Council Fathers of Vatican II. It is not difficult to notice that "Faith and Order's landmark statement on 'Scripture, Tradition and Traditions' of 1963 was contemporaneous with important developments in the way Catholics think about scripture and its relation to tradition."[15] A comparison between that Faith and Order document and *Dei verbum* will lead one "to note the dramatic convergence that emerged."[16]

Beyond texts and documents, gestures also count in assessing the Roman Catholic Church's seriousness with regard to the ecumenical agenda. One such gesture that made clear that ecumenism was advancing was presented toward the end of the council. Cardinal Franz König, archbishop of Vienna and Council Father, recounts:

> I will never forget the solemn ecumenical service in St Peter's on 7 December 1965 which marked the end of the council. I was one of a small group on the altar with Pope Paul VI. After asking the representative of the Ecumenical Patriarch of Constantinople to join him there, the Pope announced that the Papal Bull of 1054, which had declared the Great Schism between the Western and Eastern Church, was now null and void. I can still hear the thundering burst of spontaneous applause with which this announcement was greeted. For me this highlight signalled that the impulses set off by the council were already at work. The crucial process of reception, that all-important part of any church council, which can take several generations, had begun. It continues today.[17]

VATICAN II'S VISION OF ECUMENISM

The 1964 decree *Unitatis Redintegratio* (UR) was the Second Vatican Council's official statement on ecumenism. It begins by declaring that

15. William Henn, "The Achievements of Faith and Order: A Catholic Perspective," in *Celebrating a Century of Ecumenism: Exploring the Achievements of International Dialogue*, ed. John A. Radano (Geneva: World Council of Churches, 2012), 43.

16. Gros et al., *Introduction to Ecumenism*, 144.

17. Cardinal Franz König, "It Must Be the Holy Spirit," *Tablet* (December 21–28, 2002), https://tinyurl.com/y87fpwtf.

"the restoration of unity among all Christians is one of the principal concerns of the Second Vatican Council" (UR 1). It goes on to state that even as Christ founded only one single united church of God, it is unfortunate that Christians over the centuries have separated from one another: "Such division openly contradicts the will of Christ, scandalizes the world, and damages the holy cause of preaching the Gospel to every creature" (UR 1). Despite the reality of Christian division, the Second Vatican Council believes that real communion is possible among all Christians. The basis for this confidence is the one faith and baptism that all Christians share in Jesus Christ, the Lord and Savior, their commitment to the triune God, and that it is the communities of Christians and not just individual Christians who are responding to the call for the restoration of Christian unity. The Catholic Church, therefore, accepts that all those who have been properly baptized "are in communion with the Catholic Church even though this communion is imperfect" (UR 3) or exists only in different gradations among the churches. Moreover, it is also the conviction of the council that "all who have been justified by faith in Baptism are members of Christ's body, and have a right to be called Christian, and so are correctly accepted as brothers and sisters by the children of the Catholic Church" (UR 3).

The Catholic Church's acceptance of their separated brethren is premised on the principle that "some and even very many of the significant elements and endowments which together go to build up and give life to the Church itself, can exist outside the visible boundaries of the Catholic Church" (UR 3). It is the council's belief that "the Spirit of Christ has not refrained from using [the other churches] as means of salvation which derive their efficacy from the very fullness of grace and truth entrusted to the Church" (UR 3).

To that end it would be important for Catholics to "get to know the outlook of our separated brethren" (UR 9). Catholics "need to acquire a more adequate understanding of the respective doctrines of our separated brethren, their history, their spiritual and liturgical life, their religious psychology and general background" (UR 9). More important than just plain study would be the actual encounter in the flesh of Catholics with Christians of other denominations "where each can deal with the other on an equal footing. . . . From such dialogue will emerge still more clearly what the situation of the Catholic Church really is. In this way too the outlook of our separated brethren will be better understood, and our own belief more aptly explained" (UR 9). The fruits of these studies and encounters cannot be overestimated. Its benefits are not only to the Catholic, but "everyone gains a truer knowledge and more just appreciation of the teaching and religious life of both Communions" (UR 4). Dialogue implies that the Catholic also needs to share with the other what the Catholic Church teaches and how Catholics practice their faith. Ecumenical dialogues are therefore means by which Catholics can learn not only about the religious worldview of their separated brethren but can also clarify and deepen their very own Catholic worldview as well.

Besides mutual witnessing in the Catholic's encounter with other Christians, "the way is prepared for cooperation between them in the duties for the common good of humanity which are demanded by every Christian conscience" (UR 4). The impetus for reconciliation and unity between Christians is ultimately oriented toward the reconciliation and unity of the entire human race "so that the world may believe that you have sent me" (John 17:21). The church of Jesus Christ serves as light and hope for the rest of the world: "The Church, then, is God's only flock; it is like a standard lifted high for the nations to see it: for it serves all humankind through the Gospel of peace as it makes its pilgrim way in hope toward the goal of the fatherland above" (UR 2). Thus, the bishops at the Second Vatican Council "exhort all the Catholic faithful to recognize the signs of the times and to take an active and intelligent part in the work of ecumenism" (UR 4).

THE ECUMENISM OF NATIONALISM AND LIBERATION

While the agenda for interdenominational unity was being pursued by missionaries who inspired the ecumenical movement in the early twentieth century, native Christians in the mission-receiving nations were also pursuing the ecumenical agenda on their own. As mentioned briefly earlier in this article, in line with the spirit of nationalism and liberation sweeping through much of the colonial territories of the European empires, the native Christians too wanted to be freed from the control and domination of the missionaries. Like their counterparts in the civil and government services, the native Christians working under the missionaries desired more significant roles in the management and development of their own local churches. They were sick and tired of being merely servants to the missionaries who had control over what happened in the mission lands. The native Christians were asking to be respected as partners rather than treated as servants of the mission.

Some of these native Christians had in fact been holding leadership roles within their own national Christian youth movements and had had experiences that were more positive as the relationships with the missionaries in these movements were more equitable. They expected a similar relationship to be displayed in the missions and were united across churches in pursuing the same. We could call this pursuit of Christian unity the ecumenism of nationalism and liberation. Anyway, those who were present at the 1910 World Missionary Conference at Edinburgh (only seventeen out of the 1,215 delegates came from the developing world and all of them in their capacity as leaders of Christian youth movements) took advantage of the occasion to express their feelings aloud. The youth Christian leader V. S. Azariah of India had this to say when given the chance to share his experience:

> My personal observation during a period of ten years, some of which have been spent travelling in different parts of India, in mission districts worked by different Missionary societies, has revealed to me the fact that the relationship between the European missionaries and the Indian workers is far from what it ought to be, and that a certain aloofness, a lack of mutual understanding and openness, a great lack of frank intercourse and friendliness, exists throughout the country. . . . The official relationship generally prevalent at present between the missionary and the Indian worker is that between a master and servant, in fact, the word often used in South India by the low grade Indian workers in addressing missionaries is *ejaman* or master. The missionary is the paymaster, the worker his servant.[18]

On another occasion the youngest delegate at the conference, Cheng Ching-Yi, who had come from an independent, unified Chinese Christian Church and a nondenominational unity of Christians in China, pleaded with the missionaries not to impose their wishes on the native Christians but instead to view things from the perspective of the Chinese, many of whom, he said, "hope to see in the near future a united Christian church without denominational distinctions."[19] His seven-minute speech was the shortest but made one of the most significant impacts on the conference, especially in its thrust toward greater indigenization and contextualization of the churches in the missions.

Likewise, the Korean statesman T. H. Yun Chi-Ho appealed for greater participation by the native Christians in major decisions such as how and to whom money and aid should be distributed in the missions. The delegate from Japan, the Reverend President Kajinosuke Ibuka, "raised questions about the cumbersome Western creeds with their underlying complicated [Western] theologies that were being

18. "The Problem of Co-operation between Foreign and Native Workers: The Rev. V.S. Azariah," *World Missionary Conference, 1910: Report of Commission IX: The History and Records of the Conference, Together with Addresses Delivered at the Evening Meetings* (Edinburgh: Oliphant, Anderson & Ferrier, 1910), 307, 311, https://tinyurl.com/ybwrxalu.

19. Koshy, *Ecumenical Movement in Asia*, vol. 1, 54.

foisted on Japanese Christians. . . . For Japan, there had to be simpler creeds that spoke to the Japanese situation."[20] To illustrate his point he claimed that even as there was already a simple Confession of Faith for the church in Japan that had been developed in consultation with the native Christians, the missionaries were insistent that all of them had to use the doctrinal standards of Westminster. The natives, he continued, "accepted, not cordially and of choice, but simply out of deference to the judgment and wishes of the missionaries."[21]

These were just some of the interventions of the Asian delegates at the Edinburgh 1910 conference. It was clear that while interdenominational unity among the Christian churches was deemed important, unity between the Christians of mission-sending and mission-receiving countries was equally important. The Edinburgh 1910 conference was thus a truly ecumenical event in that it provided a forum to address these other dimensions of Christian unity. It also marked the arrival of the native Christians, especially those from Asia and Africa, on the world stage. As is evidenced since 1910, they have played a significant role in the development of the ecumenical movement in the last century.

THE WIDER ECUMENISM

As mentioned earlier, the Gospel verse of John 17:21 has played a central role in the ecumenical world. The part of the verse that reads "that they may all be one" focuses on the importance of Christian unity, while the part that reads "so that the world may believe" focuses on the impact of this unity on the world at large. This, according to Wesley Ariarajah, speaks to the theological conviction of the ecumenical movement "that both the church and its unity are for the purpose that God's will might be fulfilled in the world."[22] Just as the nation of Israel is the light to the nations, Christian unity serves as the sign of God's care and blessings for all the peoples in the world. That the movement toward Christian unity is called "ecumenical" (the inhabited world) means that the ultimate concern is the entire inhabited world, that is, all its people. In other words, while enhancing interdenominational relationships serves as its immediate aim, the ecumenical movement's ultimate goal is to be concerned about and address the needs and suffering of the peoples of this world, including those who are not Christian.

---

20. D. Preman Niles, "Theological and Mission Concerns in the Ecumenical Movement in Asia," in *A History of the Ecumenical Movement in Asia*, vol. 2, ed. Ninan Koshy (Hong Kong: Christian Conference of Asia, 2004), 24–25.

21. "Problem of Co-operation between Foreign and Native Workers," 296.

22. Ariarajah, "Some Basic Theological Assumptions," 41.

Wesley Ariarajah elaborates on this change of religious consciousness: "If the *oikoumene* is the whole inhabited earth, and if God is the creator of all that is and intends to bring all things to their fulfillment, it is no longer conceivable that large sections of the life of the people can be left outside the focus of the ecumenical movement."[23] The movement is fully ecumenical when it takes care of not only its *ad intra* Christian needs but also the *ad extra* problems and challenges of the world at large. The Christian community has the mission of facilitating the salvation (from the Latin word *salus*, which means "wholeness") of all its inhabitants and also the entire created world. Ironically, it is sometimes precisely the activities of service to the larger community that enables the Christians of different churches to get to know and love one another better. Where doctrinal differences between some of these churches are so severe that reconciliation is almost impossible, it is through working together in the service of the world at large that unites them as a Christian family. The oft-used slogan of "doctrine divides, but service unites" informs this optimism.

Thus the movement toward Christian unity must have at its fore the alleviation of suffering, especially of those who are poor and oppressed, and the promotion of peace, justice, and the integrity of creation. This service to the wider community is part of the Christian ecumenical movement's participation in the *missio Dei* (God's mission), which is nothing more than enabling all peoples to live life in all its fullness (John 10:10). In fulfilling the *missio Dei*, Christians realize that they are not the only ones committed to the vision for a better world and that their neighbors of other religious traditions are also very much engaged in the same mission. Besides, the problems of this world are so enormous and extensive that it would be irresponsible to think that Christians alone can resolve them on their own without the participation of peoples of other religions. As Ariarajah says, "There is an increasing recognition that the world's problems are not Christian problems requiring Christian answers, but human problems that must be addressed together by all human beings."[24] The Christian community therefore needs to be working in partnership with other religious communities if they desire to be truly ecumenical (worldwide) in scope. This is the new or wider ecumenism that they are called to: to be in dialogue with their brothers and sisters of other religions who are their partners and collaborators and not their competitors or, worse still, targets of evangelism.

23. S. Wesley Ariarajah, "The Ecumenical Impact of Inter-religious Dialogue," *The Ecumenical Review* 49, no. 2 (April 1997): 218.

24. S. Wesley Ariarajah, "Wider Ecumenism: A Threat or a Promise?" *The Ecumenical Review* 30, no. 3 (July 1998): 327.

The call for the wider ecumenism comes mainly from Christians who have been living and working in close harmony with other religious communities, especially in Asia, the cradle of all the world's religions. Ariarajah confirms this: "It is not without significance that the 'church-oriented' ecumenical movement originated in Europe and North America, while the pressure for a 'new ecumenism' comes from Asia and elsewhere."[25] He was actually echoing the sentiments of a statement of the WCC that makes explicit that "a growing number of voices from the churches, especially in Asia but also in Latin America, have spoken of the need for a 'wider ecumenism' or 'macro-ecumenism'—an understanding which would open the ecumenical movement to other religious and cultural traditions beyond the Christian community."[26] Thus the ecumenical movement, especially through the WCC, has been at the forefront in encouraging Christians to engage in dialogue with persons of other religions as part of their Christian duty and mission.

The WCC took this call to another level when, in partnership with the Pontifical Council for Interreligious Dialogue of the Catholic Church and also the World Evangelical Alliance, it issued a document titled *Christian Witness in a Multi-Religious World: Recommendations for Conduct* in 2011. This document was the fruit of a series of consultations between the three major worldwide Christian bodies over a five-year period. Under the topic of "A Basis for Christian Witness," the document posits that "Christian witness in a pluralistic world includes engaging in dialogue with people of different religions and cultures (cf. Acts 17:22–28)." The eighth principle of the document specifically spells out the nature of this engagement: "Christians are called to commit themselves to work with all people in mutual respect, promoting together justice, peace and the common good. Interreligious cooperation is an essential dimension of such commitment."

This is the new ecumenism that Christians are invited to participate in. It is how Christians witness to Christ in the increasingly multireligious world that we live in today. This is not to say that Christian ecumenism has become irrelevant. To be sure, it is still very much needed and continues to rank in importance in the mission of the church. In fact, the two forms of ecumenism are needed. The new or wider ecumenism can also give occasions to enhance the practice of Christian ecumenism. In Muslim-Christian dialogue activities, for example, the Christian participants from the different churches (perhaps one Methodist, one Lutheran,

25. Ariarajah, "Wider Ecumenism," 326.
26. "Common understanding and vision of the WCC (CUV)," *World Council of Churches* (February 14, 2006), https://tinyurl.com/ya4ze2jx.

one Baptist, one Assemblies of God, one Lakeside Church, etc.) will have to agree among themselves first on how Christianity is to be presented before they can engage with their Muslim dialogue partners. To be sure, interchurch understanding is enhanced through the process. So, the dialogue of Christians with believers of other religions can certainly serve to reinforce the dialogue between Christians of different denominations.

In conclusion, the ministry of ecumenism that leads to the wider ecumenism is integral to the mission of Christians today. Given the contextual reality of religious pluralism in today's societies, the movement toward the wider ecumenism with other religions, in line with Shoki Coe's thoughts, is a convincing sign of authentic contextualization. It becomes an especially prophetic alternative in response to situations where conflicts and tensions in the name of religious differences are allowed to fester. The invitation to the wider ecumenism arises from the genuine encounter of contemporary Christians to the word of God with the present world of many religions. It serves at once as a challenge to the complacency of Christians and the ecumenical movement and a sign that Christians are committed to changing situations that are not in keeping with God's word. Thus, when Christians reach out to their neighbors of other religions and build partnerships to address the common challenges of humanity, it shows that they take seriously the prayer of Jesus "that they may all be one. As you, Father, are in me and I am in you, may they also be in us, so that the world may believe that you have sent me" (John 17:21).

PART III

Mission and Dialogue: Universality of Contextual Theological Discourse

8.

Pope Francis as Contextual Theologian

STEPHEN BEVANS

On March 13, 2013, the Cardinals of the Roman Catholic Church stunned the world by electing Jorge Mario Bergoglio, archbishop of Buenos Aires, Argentina, to succeed Benedict XVI as pope. There were several reasons for the world to be stunned. Bergoglio was a member of the Society of Jesus, a Jesuit, and the first Jesuit ever to be elected pope. Born in Latin America, he was the first non-European to be elected pope in some 1,300 years and the first from the "New World" of the Americas.

What became even more stunning, however, was how in the first days and weeks of his pontificate Bergoglio, who took the name of Francis, differed so profoundly from his predecessor. Benedict is first and foremost a theologian, one of the great theologians of our time; Francis is much more of a pastor, having studied for but not having completed the doctorate in theology. Benedict seemed awkward and ill at ease in public; Francis quickly showed himself to be highly charismatic, clearly enjoying his contact with the people he encountered in the crowds that thronged to see him in the days and years after his election. Benedict is the quintessential European; Francis, although the son of Italian immigrants to Argentina, is Latin American to the core. Benedict seemed to love the pomp and circumstance of the papacy, preferring the liturgical style and vestments of the period after the sixteenth-century Council of Trent; Francis has shown himself a man of simplicity, preferring a simple white cassock, the weathered black shoes he had worn before his election, and the simpler vestments of Vatican II's liturgical reform. Benedict was deeply concerned with a Europe that was abandoning religious faith in the wake of postmodern relativism, and so called for greater education in the faith and orthodoxy in doctrine; Francis, although he sees the same problem, calls for the church to become more open, compassionate, tender, and merciful. To use distinctions recently proposed by philosopher and theologian Clemens Sedmak, Benedict would tend toward a "propositional" and "political" orthodoxy, while Francis would tend toward a more "existential" and "pilgrim" perspective on religious truth.[1]

Benedict and Francis differ markedly in at least one other respect, one that is relevant to this volume honoring the great Taiwanese churchman Shoki Coe. Benedict is quite wary of context, preferring a theology and church teaching rooted in the great philosophical and theological tradition of the West. In a thoughtful presentation at the University of Notre Dame's Center for Ethics and Culture several years ago, during the pontificate of Benedict XVI, historian and theologian Paul Kollman reflected on "Why Is Benedict XVI Wary of Inculturation?"[2]—"inculturation" being the preferred Roman Catholic term for what Coe called "contextualization."[3] Kollman's answer to the question is that central to the thought of Benedict is his constant insistence on not compromising the gospel message in the human appropriation of it.

Prior to becoming pope, as Cardinal Joseph Ratzinger he had opposed some of the tendencies of Latin American liberation theology and Asian religious pluralism—both contextual theologies. For several decades as well, he had voiced his misgivings about contemporary Western culture, with its tendencies to relativism and nihilism. His famous speech at the University of Regensburg in 2006 received much publicity for remarks that were interpreted by many as anti-Muslim. However, other comments he made in the same speech that were not so widely reported point to Benedict's cautious approach to inculturation or contextual theology. For him, there is a real harmony, if not identity, between Greek (or Western) thought and the Christian gospel, to such an extent that a thorough "dehellenization" of doctrine would ultimately betray it. The New Testament itself is already imbued with Hellenistic culture, to such an extent that it cannot be stripped down to a basic content that could take on the form of another culture. Hellenistic culture, therefore, has become a privileged bearer of Revelation itself, and therefore cannot be completely left behind to discover the "pure gospel."[4] If there would be any kind of inculturation or contextualization, it would be limited, it

1. See Clemens Sedmak, *A Church of the Poor: Francis and the Transformation of Orthodoxy* (Maryknoll, NY: Orbis, 2016).

2. Paul Kollman, "Why Is Benedict XVI Wary of Inculturation? Missiological Reflections," Notre Dame Center for Ethics and Culture, video presentation, https://vimeo.com/20883785.

3. See Stephen B. Bevans, *Models of Contextual Theology*, rev. and exp. ed. (Maryknoll, NY: Orbis, 2002), 26–27.

4. Benedict XVI, Speech at the University of Regensburg, Meeting with the Representatives of Science, https://tinyurl.com/ldnma24.

seems to me, to what I have called the "countercultural model" or possibly the "translation model."[5]

But while Benedict is wary of inculturation or contextual theology, Francis embraces it as the way to do theology and offer church teaching in today's world. A powerful passage in the apostolic exhortation *Evangelii Gaudium* even seems to contradict Benedict's perspective in his Regensburg speech. "We would not do justice," Francis writes, "to the logic of the incarnation if we thought of Christianity as monocultural and monotonous." He then continues:

> While it is true that some cultures have been closely associated with the preaching of the Gospel and the development of Christian thought, the revealed message is not identified with any of them; its content is transcultural. Hence in the evangelization of new cultures, or cultures which have not received the Christian message, it is not essential to impose a specific cultural form, no matter how beautiful or ancient it may be, together with the Gospel. The message that we proclaim always has a certain cultural dress, but we in the Church can sometimes fall into a needless hallowing of our own culture, and thus show more fanaticism than true evangelical zeal.[6]

What I propose to explore in this essay is how Pope Francis does indeed embrace the process of inculturation or contextualization, or, in other words, how Pope Francis is a contextual theologian. With Coe, I prefer the term "contextualization" or "contextual theology," since I fully agree with his explanation of the term as one that includes all that is understood by the term "indigeneity" (or "inculturation"), but seeks "to press beyond for a more dynamic concept which is open to change and which is also future-oriented."[7] Francis does not use the term at all, since, I have noted, the Catholic preference is for the term "inculturation." Nevertheless, his method, I hope to show, goes beyond the cultural to a more general regard for the importance of context as such, and so in this essay to honor and remember Shoki Coe, I think I am justified in calling Francis a contextual theologian.[8]

After only five years of his pontificate, Francis's teachings and writings

---

5. See Bevans, *Models of Contextual Theology*, 117–37; 37–53.

6. Pope Francis, Apostolic Exhortation *Evangelii Gaudium* (EG), https://tinyurl.com/mvreyv4, 117. From here on, all references to EG will be within parentheses in the text.

7. Shoki Coe, "Contextualizing Theology," in *Mission Trends No. 3: Third World Theologies*, ed. Gerald H. Anderson and Thomas P. Stransky (New York/Grand Rapids: Paulist/Eerdmans, 1976), 21.

8. In my own work I have suggested that "context" is made up of at least four aspects: (1) individual or social experiences; (2) a person's social location; (3) culture as the web of meanings by which a particular group of people live; and (4) social change in that culture. See Bevans, *Models of Contextual Theology*, 5–7.

are voluminous, and a study of them all would require a much larger essay than can be included in this collection. I will reflect therefore only on three of Pope Francis's major documents—*Evangelii Gaudium*, *Laudato Si'*, and *Amoris Laetitia*—and then briefly comment on his 2015 address before the United States Congress, the *Motu Proprio* "Magnum Principium," and his 2017 trip to Myanmar.

EVANGELII GAUDIUM: CONTEXTUAL THEOLOGY AND EVANGELIZATION

Francis's great statement on mission, *Evangelii Gaudium* (The Joy of the Gospel), makes a strong connection between the *need* for the church to evangelize and the *way* it should evangelize, that is, by taking the context—particularly the cultural context—seriously. After a powerful first chapter in which he calls for a "missionary transformation" of the church, Francis begins to "take up some basic questions related to the work of evangelization" by a brief sketch of "the context in which we all have to live and work" (EG 50). He does this in two major sections, the first of which focuses on the contemporary world, and the second of which focuses on the church.

In the first section, Francis calls attention to the "globalization of indifference" that a "throwaway culture" is causing (EG 53–54). He rails against the financial system that spawns the "idolatry of money" and an "inequality that causes violence" (EG 57–60). He points to the widespread indifference to religion and relativism on the one hand, and a fundamentalism and fanaticism on the other (EG 61–66). He emphasizes the growing urbanization of the world and points out its advantages and dangers (EG 71–75).

In the more church-centered second section of his analysis, while Francis acknowledges the "enormous contribution of the church to today's world" (EG 76) he names, first, a tendency of some church leaders to have a spirituality that has little or no missionary motivation (EG 78–82). He also condemns a "selfishness and spiritual sloth" in the church, as well as a "sterile pessimism" (EG 81–84). One of his strongest condemnations is the situation in the church that he calls "spiritual worldliness." He describes this as an "ostentatious preoccupation for the liturgy, for doctrine and for the Church's prestige, but without any concern that the Gospel have a real impact on God's faithful people and concrete needs of the present time" (EG 95)—in other words, a lack of regard for trying to do evangelization in context. Francis lists many other challenges, but perhaps the most serious is that of "warring among ourselves" (EG 98–101).

This is the context of the world in which the church evangelizes and the context of the church itself, but despite the many challenges, Francis insists, the church must continue preaching the gospel with its whole heart: "Evangelization is the task of the church" (EG 111). How this is done is the aim of chapter 3 of the document, titled "The Proclamation of the Gospel." It is here that Francis makes the point, I believe, that such proclamation can only be done contextually, with appreciation of culture, of people's actual situations, and people's actual struggles.

Much of this chapter talks about the sensitivity that evangelizers need to have toward culture, an emphasis which, after his analysis of the context, might be a bit surprising. One might expect a call to evangelization that is strongly countercultural in spirit. Instead, however, Francis insists that proper evangelization can only take place as (in his words) "inculturation" (EG 122), or (in Shoki Coe's) the constant doing of contextual theology that is appreciative of God's presence in culture, even when it is distorted.

"The People of God," Francis writes, "is incarnate in the peoples of the earth, each of which has its own culture" (EG 115). Cultural existence is human existence, and grace cannot exist without it: "Grace supposes culture, and God's gift becomes flesh in the culture of those who receive it" (EG 115). Culture is not only enriched by Christianity but Christianity is enriched in turn. The Holy Spirit is at work both enriching culture and, with the values of culture the Spirit offers "new aspects of revelation" and gives the church "a new face" (EG 116). Indeed, it is the Spirit who offers to the church its catholicity, the great diversity of ways of understanding the gospel. Just as the triune God is a unity that is rich in diversity, so the church exists in a unity that is grounded in God's many-faceted splendor. This is the context of the phrase quoted earlier, that "we would not do justice to the incarnation if we thought of Christianity as monocultural and monotonous" (EG 117). We cannot expect non-European peoples to imitate European Christianity of a certain age, "because the faith cannot be constricted to the limits of understanding and expression of any one culture," and no one cultural expression can completely exhaust its meaning (EG 118).

Having laid down these principles, Francis turns to acknowledging that all Christians have the duty to evangelize—they are all "missionary disciples" (see EG 24). Discipleship cannot be separated from being missionary. "We no longer say that we are 'disciples' and 'missionaries,' but rather that we are always 'missionary disciples'" (EG 120). The reason for this is deeply theological: because of baptism, Francis insists, Christians possess a deep "sense of the faith" (*sensus fidei*) that gives them a sure grasp—even if they cannot put it fully into words—of the truth of Christianity (EG 119). It is this that Christians rely on when they attempt to evangelize by taking culture and context seriously.

A principal way by which evangelization takes root in a particular people is through "popular piety," also referred to as "popular spirituality," "the people's mysticism," or a "spirituality incarnated in the culture of the lowly" (EG 122, 124). In a bold move, Francis speaks of this popular piety as a "*locus theologicus*" or "theological source," a source from which—like scripture and tradition—theology can be developed. In other words, ordinary Christian faith of ordinary people, expressed in simple but culturally meaningful forms, is a real way of doing inculturation or contextual theology. Francis insists: "Let us not stifle or presume to control this missionary power" (EG 126, 124).

The contextual way of evangelization is explained in the next section of the chapter. We are always called to evangelize, in whatever situation, but it should not be in a way that disregards particular situations or contexts. "Being a disciple means being constantly ready to bring the love of Jesus to others, and this can happen unexpectedly and in any place: on the street, in a city square, during work, on a journey" (EG 127). Evangelization, however, is "always respectful and gentle," listening to a person's hopes, concerns, and needs. When it is appropriate, a more direct approach can be taken, but even here the message is "shared humbly, as a testimony on the part of one who is always willing to learn, in the awareness that the message is so rich and so deep that it always exceeds our grasp" (EG 128).

Francis had already cautioned his readers against a kind of mechanical orthodoxy that is only about correct formulas. Earlier in the document he noted that sometimes, people can listen to "completely orthodox language," can actually misunderstand it and "take away something alien to the Gospel of Jesus Christ." We have to be careful, if we hold a formula, not to forget to "convey its substance." If we do not do that, he says, "this is the greatest danger." We need to creatively—and the implication is with some risk—find ways to renew expressions that are orthodox but have become unclear or irrelevant to ordinary people (EG 41). The need to be creative and risk-taking comes back in chapter 3, when Francis discourages the gospel message to be communicated "by fixed formulations learned by heart or by specific words which express an absolutely invariable content." We need to opt rather for inculturation or contextual theologizing, because "if we allow doubts and fears to dampen our courage, instead of being creative we will remain comfortable and make no progress whatsoever" (EG 129). To this end, Francis calls on theologians "to advance dialogue with the world of cultures and science," mindful always that the point of theology is never for itself—he calls that "desk-bound theology"—but always to promote the mission of the church (EG 133). Once again we see the strong connection between doing contextual theology and Christian mission. Neither can exist without the other.

In a second major part of this chapter 3 on the way the gospel should be proclaimed, Francis turns to the homily—that privileged form of preaching that takes place in the context of the church's liturgy.[9] "The homily is the touchstone for judging a pastor's closeness and ability to communicate to his people" (EG 135). Francis is strong in insisting that the preacher needs to be someone steeped in the word and in the Christian life, and he writes eloquently about that. He insists, however, that while a good homily comes from the contemplation of the word, it also comes from a contemplation of the people (EG 154). Quoting Paul VI's *Evangelii Nuntiandi*, Francis says that the preacher needs to link the biblical texts to the human situation, developing a "spiritual sensitivity for reading God's message in events" (EG 155).[10] And, as he says wryly, "let us also keep in mind that we should never respond to questions that nobody asks" (EG 155).

Much more could be written about Francis's appreciation of context in *Evangelii Gaudium*, but let me end this first section of our reflections by calling attention to one of the four principles that he outlines as ways to harmonize differences in both society and in the church, principles he had articulated long before he became pope.[11] The principles are: (1) Time is greater than space; (2) Unity prevails over conflict; (3) Realities are more important than ideas; and (4) The whole is greater than the part. The one that I would like to focus on, in reflecting on Francis as contextual theologian, is the third: realities are more important than ideas. What is important is that ideas serve reality, that reality is illuminated by ideas. If this way of basically contextual thinking is not operative, people are led into dead ends. The problem is that both political and religious leaders can get "stuck in the realm of pure ideas and end up reducing politics or faith to rhetoric" (EG 232) and so really betray

9. Vatican Council II, Constitution on the Liturgy, *Sacrosanctum Concilium* (SC), https://tinyurl.com/ay8y, 52.

10. See Paul VI, Apostolic Exhortation *Evangelii Nuntiandi* (EN), https://tinyurl.com/z4plkz3, 33.

11. See Austen Ivereigh, *The Great Reformer: Francis and the Making of a Radical Pope* (New York: Henry Holt, 2014), 322.

the incarnation. On the contrary, says Francis, "the principle of reality, of a word already made flesh and constantly striving to take flesh anew, is essential to evangelization" (EG 233). One of Francis's major principles, all of which he had held for quite a long time, clearly points to the importance of context in his thought.

LAUDATO SI': A CONTEXTUAL CONCERN, A CONTEXTUAL METHOD

Clear from the first days of Francis's pontificate was that one of his major concerns is the integrity of creation. In the homily at the Mass that inaugurated his papacy, given on March 19, 2013, Pope Francis spoke about St. Joseph as the "protector" of Jesus, Mary, and the church, but then he spoke about the need for all Christians—indeed all humans—to be protectors: "Protecting all creation, the beauty of the created world, as the Book of Genesis tells us and as Saint Francis of Assisi showed us. It means respecting each of God's creatures and respecting the environment in which we live. It means protecting people, showing loving concern for each and every person, especially children, the elderly, those in need, who are often the last we think about."[12] Time and again in the short homily Francis comes back to this theme of protection, especially the protection of creation. All in all he refers to the protection of creation six times, and to the respect and protection of the environment two times.

It was not long before it became known that Francis was preparing a major statement, an encyclical, on the topic of ecology. In the meantime, he referred to the ecological crisis, toward the end of *Evangelii Gaudium*, numbering the entire creation among the "weak and defenseless beings at the mercy of economic interests or indiscriminate exploitation" (EG 215). He closes this short section with the words: "Small, yet strong in the love of God, like St. Francis of Assisi, all of us, as Christians, are called to watch over and protect the fragile world in which we live, and all its peoples" (EG 216).

The highly anticipated encyclical was issued in June of 2015, to the acclaim of Catholics, many other believers, and unbelievers as well. It was titled *Laudato Si'*, words from St. Francis of Assisi's poem "Canticle of the Creatures,"[13] and was the first papal encyclical to be devoted entirely to ecology and the protection of creation. It is, to my mind, a masterpiece of contextual theology. Francis understands the destruction of our "common home" as one of the most significant crises in the world

---

12. Pope Francis, Inaugural Homily, March 19, 2013, https://tinyurl.com/pknducm.
13. See "Canticle of the Creatures," https://tinyurl.com/y87w3ey2.

today and brings the biblical and Christian tradition into dialogue with it in order to offer significant wisdom and suggestions for practice to all the peoples of the earth.[14]

The method employed by the encyclical is the contextual method of "See-Judge-Act." Chapter 1, titled "What Is Happening to Our Common Home," is a brief but well-informed overview of the causes of the ecological crisis. Francis treats the questions of pollution and climate change, of water, the loss of biodiversity, and then the results of these realities in the decline of the quality of human life, the breakdown of society, and the rise of global inequality. Francis goes on to deplore the weak responses from the world's governments, and, although he acknowledges that there are a variety of opinions about what he considers the ecological crisis, he says that the church must call for "an honest debate among experts." Nevertheless, he says, there is no doubt that the crisis is real: "We need only take a frank look at the facts to see that our common home is falling into serious disrepair" (LS 17–61; the quotes are from LS 61).

Having "seen" the facts, Francis moves into the "Judge" phase of his contextual method. In chapter 2, he offers a biblical-theological reflection on "the gospel of creation," followed by a third chapter that traces the "Human Roots of the Ecological Crisis," especially in terms of a "misguided anthropocentrism" (LS 119). As Francis explains it,

An inadequate presentation of Christian anthropology gave rise to a wrong understanding of the relationship between human beings and the world. Often, what was handed on was a Promethean vision of mastery over the world, which gave the impression that the protection of nature was something that only the faint-hearted cared about. Instead, our "dominion" over the universe should be understood more properly in the sense of responsible stewardship. (LS 116)

Chapter 4 then moves to develop a basic ecological theology, based on the Christian tradition and in critical dialogue with the mistakes that it has made. Francis's project is to articulate an "integral ecology" that attempts to balance the human concerns for a good and happy life together with the need for environmental sustainability. Key to such an integral approach is the maintenance of the "common good," one of the foundational principles of Catholic social teaching and "a central and unifying principle of social ethics" (LS 156).

The final two chapters of Laudato Si' embody the "Act" phase

14. Pope Francis, Encyclical Letter *Laudato Si'* (LS), https://tinyurl.com/o6sowft. References will be in parentheses in the text.

of Francis's contextual method. Chapter 5 lays down "Lines of Approach and Action," and chapter 6, the final chapter, outlines the elements of ecological spirituality and ways to proceed in ecological education. Francis commends and calls for a continued international dialogue on environmental issues. Here he calls for enforceable international agreements that will regulate the dumping of waste and the pollution of oceans, the development of national and local policies that protect the environment and aid the poor, dialogue and transparency in decision-making regarding ecological policies, and an honest dialogue between politics and the economy that takes into account not only profits but authentic human fulfillment. "Where profits alone count, there can be no thinking about the rhythms of nature, its phases of decay and regeneration, or the complexity of ecosystems which may be gravely upset by human intervention" (LS 190).

The basic practice of an ecological spirituality is a "new lifestyle" that lives simply, close to nature, and is generous toward others. Such spirituality will have a kind of ripple effect: "A change in lifestyle could bring healthy pressure to bear on those who wield political, economic and social power. This is what consumer movements accomplish by boycotting certain products. They prove successful in changing the way businesses operate, forcing them to consider their environmental footprint and their patterns of production" (LS 206).

In reflecting on the kind of education needed for "ecological citizenship" (LS 211), Francis writes that it cannot simply provide information. Rather, education for responsible ecological action is about cultivating the kind of virtues that will make people "able to make a selfless ecological commitment. A person who could afford to spend and consume more but regularly uses less heating and wears warmer clothes, shows the kind of conviction and attitudes which help to protect the environment" (LS 211). Practices such as using less plastic and paper, reducing waste, recycling, car-pooling or using public transportation are all practices that reflect "a generous and worthy creativity that brings the best in human beings" (LS 211).

Ultimately, education for the care of creation calls for what Pope John Paul II first called "ecological conversion."[15] Such conversion is the foundation for a rich ecological spirituality based on Eucharistic sharing and the Trinitarian life of radical interrelationship. "Everything is interconnected, and this invites us to develop a spirituality of that global solidarity which flows from the mystery of the Trinity" (LS 240).

---

15. See LS 5 for a summary of John Paul II's teaching on ecology. Francis speaks of it in LS 216–21.

AMORIS LAETITIA: A CONTEXT THAT CALLS FOR TAKING RISKS

On April 8, 2016, the Vatican released the apostolic exhortation *Amoris Laetitia* (The Joy of Love), Pope Francis's reflections after the two Synods of Bishops in 2014 and 2015 on the Family.[16] The document is a long one—256 pages of text in the official Vatican edition—and for the most part it is (at least in my opinion) although warmly written, quite unremarkable in content, except for the final chapter, chapter 8. It is in this chapter that Francis tries to find new ways to deal with the delicate issue in the Catholic Church of full sacramental participation (especially receiving the Eucharist) by women and men who are living together without being married or who have been divorced and remarried without their marriage being officially annulled. In this chapter in particular, Francis was doing contextual theology—trying to find ways of dealing compassionately with people in difficult situations that took into account their own experience on the one hand and maintaining fidelity to tradition and the gospel on the other.

Chapter 8 created a sensation. On the one hand, it appeared as a word of hope to so many women and men in the church that find themselves, often through very little fault of their own, in situations where they cannot participate fully in the church's life.[17] On the other it came under strong criticism by more conservative Catholics, including several prominent churchmen. At one point four cardinals submitted a letter that expressed their doubts as to the chapter's orthodoxy.[18] In *Evangelii Nuntiandi* Francis had recognized the need, sometimes, to take risks with traditional formulations for the proper communication of the gospel. In chapter 8 this is exactly what he did.

The theological foundation for the entire chapter is one of the major themes of Francis's papacy: God's mercy. From the first days and weeks after his election, Francis spoke over and over again of the mercy of God.[19] In 2015 he declared that the year 2016 (from December 2015 until November 2016) would be an Extraordinary Jubilee of Mercy. In the document that made the proclamation, Francis noted that "when

16. Pope Francis, Apostolic Exhortation *Amoris Laetitia* (AL), https://tinyurl.com/zlxbta4. References will be in parentheses in the text.

17. See Tom Roberts, "Reactions to '*Amoris Laetitia*'—A Leap or a Baby Step?" https://tinyurl.com/y787xlyn. See *National Catholic Reporter*'s extensive series on the document at https://tinyurl.com/y787xlyn.

18. Joshua J. McElwee, "Four Cardinals Openly Challenge Francis over '*Amoris Laetitia*,'" https://tinyurl.com/y85y3v5e.

19. See Pope Francis, *The Church of Mercy: A Vision for the Church* (Chicago: Loyola, 2014).

faced with the gravity of sin, God responds with the fullness of mercy."[20] Indeed, he writes, quoting St. Augustine, "'It is easier for God to hold back anger than mercy.' And so it is. God's anger lasts but a moment, his mercy forever."[21] In *Evangelii Gaudium* we read, as Francis refers to the frequency of his references to God's mercy: "Let me say this once more: God never tires of forgiving us; we are the ones who tire of seeking his mercy" (EG 3). It is with mercy that Francis begins chapter 8 of *Amoris Laetitia*. Quoting the final document of the 2014 Synod, he acknowledges that "the Church must accompany with attention and care the weakest of her children, who show signs of a wounded and troubled love, by restoring in them hope and confidence, like the beacon of a lighthouse in a port or a torch carried among the people to enlighten those who have lost their way or who are in the midst of a storm" (AL 291). He then refers to a favorite image of the church that he first used as pope in an interview with the Jesuit journalist Antonio Spadaro in 2013—the church as field hospital. "It is useless to ask a seriously injured person if he has high cholesterol and about the level of his blood sugars! You have to heal his wounds. Then we can talk about everything else. Heal the wounds, heal the wounds."[22]

Referring to the 2014 Synod document, Francis speaks of the need of a "pastoral dialogue" or "pastoral discernment" in order to determine how God's mercy can be understood in the context of situations of people that do not measure up to the expectations of the church in terms of their marriage (AL 293). Engaging in that dialogue or discernment, constantly referring to the documents of the 2014 and 2015 Synods, Francis recognizes that for many people the choice of a civil marriage or living together without marriage is the result not of "prejudice or resistance to a sacramental union, but by cultural or contingent situations" (AL 294). Rather than condemning these people outright, the church needs to respect them. Indeed, with such respect and no condemnation, they may often, when the time is right, seek the regularization of their union in the church.

Francis continues his pastoral dialogue and exercise of pastoral discernment when he turns to the question of divorced and remarried Catholics. Quoting a homily that he gave to new cardinals in 2015, he states that "there are two ways of thinking which recur through the Church's history: casting off and reinstating. The Church's way, from the time of the Council of Jerusalem, has always been the way of Jesus,

20. Pope Francis, *Misericordiae Vultus* (MV), https://tinyurl.com/p6y6etx, 3.
21. MV 21.
22. *A Big Heart Open to God: A Conversation with Pope Francis*, Interview by Antonio Spadaro (New York: America/HarperOne, 2013), 30.

the way of mercy and reinstatement. . . . The way of the Church is not to condemn anyone for ever; it is to pour out the balm of God's mercy on all those who ask for it with a sincere heart" (AL 296). It is important, therefore, to avoid making judgments that do not take into consideration complex situations, and "to be attentive, by necessity, to how people experience distress because of their condition" (AL 296).

Because of this, Francis says he agrees with many in the 2014 and 2015 Synods who believe that divorced and remarried people need to be "more fully integrated into Christian communities in the variety of ways possible, while avoiding any occasion of scandal" (AL 299). People in this situation should not see themselves as excommunicated but "instead as living members, able to live and grow in the Church and experience her as a mother who welcomes them always" (AL 299). Francis insists that such a perspective does not compromise the demands of the gospel because, he says, there is a strong tradition in the church of factors that mitigate personal culpability in situations often beyond people's control. Thus, "it can no longer simply be said that all those in any 'irregular' situation are living in a state of mortal sin and deprived of sanctifying grace" (AL 301).

And so, in the light of God's mercy and the often-difficult circumstances in which people find themselves, the door is open for people living together or in civil unions, and divorced and remarried Catholics, to participate more fully in the church's life. What this fuller participation consists of is not mentioned concretely, but it could mean at least being welcomed into the community with an understanding of a person's sincerity in the faith. It could mean that the person could be an active participant in parish activities like being a lector at Mass, or a volunteer in a number of parish ministries. It could also mean that the person would be able to receive communion at the Eucharist. Francis recognizes the imperfection of the situation but insists that God's love and mercy trumps a strict, legalistic approach.

Francis recognizes that there are those in the church "who prefer a more rigorous pastoral care which leaves no room for confusion." Nevertheless, he says, what he thinks is that "Jesus wants a Church attentive to the goodness which the Holy Spirit sows in the midst of human weakness, a Mother who, while clearly expressing her objective teaching 'always does what good she can, even if in the process, her shoes get soiled by the mud of the street'" (AL 308, quoting EG 45). Sometimes, Francis writes, "we find it hard to make room for God's unconditional love in our pastoral activity," and we put a lot of conditions on God's mercy. But, he exclaims, "that is the worst way of watering down the Gospel" (AL 311).

BEING SENSITIVE TO THE LOCAL CONTEXT

On September 24, 2015, Pope Francis became the first pope to address the United States Congress in Washington, DC.[23] His speech was a masterpiece in being sensitive to the local context. The first line of the speech expresses his gratitude for the invitation "to address this Joint Session of Congress in 'the land of the free and the home of the brave'"—a reference to the last lines of the national anthem of the United States. Francis then goes on to structure his speech around "the anniversaries of several great Americans," namely Abraham Lincoln, Martin Luther King, Dorothy Day, and Thomas Merton.

Referring first to Lincoln in the year of the 150th anniversary of his assassination, he quotes a line from Lincoln's famous "Gettysburg Address," remarking how he "labored tirelessly that 'this nation, under God [might] have a new birth of freedom.'" Then Francis goes on to urge the United States to work for "restoring hope, righting wrongs, maintaining commitments, and thus promoting the well-being of individuals and peoples," and to do this together with real respect for each other despite "differences . . . and convictions of conscience."

Francis then calls on Americans to work for a common good that "sacrifices particular interests in order to share, in justice and peace, its goods, its interests, its social life." Here he remembers Martin Luther King Jr. as the United States commemorates the fiftieth anniversary of the march from Selma to Montgomery, Alabama, at the height of the civil rights movement in 1965. In this context Francis reflects on the contemporary refugee crisis and the abolition of the death penalty as important issues of civil rights today. Dorothy Day is then held up as a model of social activism, justice, and concern for the poor, and her mention leads Francis to speak about the need for ecological responsibility and the importance of his encyclical *Laudato Si'*. Reflection on the tragedy of war moves Francis to mention Thomas Merton, born one hundred years ago in 1915, and also a champion of interreligious dialogue.

Francis ended his speech by saying that he had "sought to present some of the richness of your cultural heritage, of the spirit of the American people." In doing this, respecting the history and values of the United States, he also subtly but firmly called the Congress and the coun-

---

23. Pope Francis, Address to Congress, https://tinyurl.com/nafnhhw. All quotations that follow regarding Francis's speech are taken from this text.

try to work together despite differences (this was in the middle of the Obama administration, with tremendous political polarization), to work for justice for refugees, to abolish the death penalty, to work for peace. His words struck deep chords in the American people, while at the same time being profoundly prophetic.

Two years later, in September of 2017, Francis showed a sensitivity to local cultures in a decree titled "Magnum Principium," a decree that had to do with the process for approving adaptations and translations of liturgical texts in local cultures and languages.[24] The document itself is written in quite technical language and is focused on a change of wording in the Catholic Church's Code of Canon Law, numbers 838.1, .2, and .3. Its point, however, is simple and very important. Whereas the previous wording of the canons specify that the Vatican (its Congregation for Divine Worship) *approves* any adaptations and translations of the Roman Liturgy from the normative Latin text, the new wording states that it *recognizes and confirms* adaptations and translations that have been approved by local Bishops' Conferences. In other words, it is the local church in a particular context that has the basic say in terms of the particular variations in and translations of the Liturgy.

Soon after the publication of the decree, the head of the Vatican's Congregation of Divine Worship, Cardinal Robert Sarah, published an opinion that the pope had not taken away all the authority of his congregation for approval of adaptations and texts. However, in a rather unprecedented move, Francis issued a public letter to Sarah insisting that he had indeed changed some of the norms for translation and "asserted that *Magnum Principium* does in fact call for a much-reduced Vatican oversight of the translation process."[25] Francis's letter insisted on a "triple fidelity" in liturgical translations—a fidelity to the original Latin text, a fidelity to the language into which the text is being translated, and a fidelity to the comprehension of the text by the faithful in the local context.[26] Francis has clearly opted for local autonomy in decision-making, and for the importance of the local context.

A final example of Francis's commitment to contextual theologizing took place in November 2017, when Francis visited the countries of Myanmar and Bangladesh. The political situation in Myanmar was delicate. The military of the country had been involved in the systematic persecution of a Muslim minority called Rohingya, and Cardinal Charles

24. Pope Francis, *Motu Proprio* "Magnum Principium," https://tinyurl.com/yc4kmtft.

25. Richard R. Gaillardetz, "Francis's correction of Sarah shows that Vatican II is his 'sure compass," *National Catholic Reporter*, https://tinyurl.com/ycl6zjj4.

26. Elise Harris, "Pope offers clarifications on new process for liturgical translations," https://tinyurl.com/y735mga4.

Maung Bo, the archbishop of Yangon, had requested Francis not to mention that name in his public speeches in the country. It would only cause embarrassment to the government and certainly not help the influence of the church in Myanmar.[27] And so Francis did not use the term and spoke more generally about human rights and justice during his visit. Nevertheless, as soon as he landed in Bangladesh, he did use the term "Rohingya," using the striking phrase "the presence of God today is also called Rohingya."[28]

It seems to me that Francis showed a double sensitivity to local context here. Even though it most likely was difficult for him to be silent—or at least indirect—and even though he was highly criticized for it,[29] he took the advice of the person who knew the local context better than he: the Cardinal Archbishop of Yangon. But then, when he was able to, he not only used the name "Rohingya" but eloquently expressed how God was present in this terribly suffering group of human beings. The phrase about the presence of God as Rohingya was a little contextual theology in itself—one more small sign that Pope Francis is indeed a contextual theologian.

CONCLUSION

Almost fifty years ago, Shoki Coe offered to the world a new way of thinking about doing theology. This was a way that recognized that any time Christian faith seeks understanding it needs to do it by taking into account how God's presence, God's judgment, God's challenge, and even God's absence makes itself known in ordinary human experience—in human, social, historical, cultural contexts. Coe's insight was such a great one that it influenced my own conviction, as I have expressed it often, that there really *is* no such thing as theology; there is only *contextual* theology.[30]

What I have tried to show in this essay in Coe's honor and memory is that Pope Francis understands this insight profoundly. As a Latin American, he is steeped in the method of the theology of liberation. As a Catholic, he is steeped in the Catholic sacramental imagination. As a person of great humanity, he is profoundly affected by the plight of the

27. "Myanmar Cardinal urges Pope Francis to avoid the use of the term 'Rohingya,'" https://tinyurl.com/y9r7fxzn.
28. "Pope Francis: 'The presence of God today is also called Rohingya," https://tinyurl.com/y6vzw4cw.
29. See Marcello Rossi, "Rohingya challenge Pope Francis over silence in Myanmar," https://tinyurl.com/y77tvelq.
30. See for example Bevans, *Models of Contextual Theology*, 3.

world's poor, victims of a "globalization of indifference." As a deeply religious person he is overwhelmed by God's tenderness and mercy. Because of who he is, I believe, when Francis does theology—in his many speeches, in the documents he writes, in the homilies he gives, in the pastoral decisions he makes—he can only do so as a contextual theologian.

9.

Contextual Theology as Dialogue: An Asian Catholic Approach to Shoki Coe's Theological Legacy

ANH Q. TRAN, SJ

The development of Christianity in Asia after the Second World War accompanies contextual theology and the mission movement. In the wake of Vatican II (1962–1965), the appreciation for liturgy in the vernacular and for the role of the local church resulted in the inculturation model that is widely used in Roman Catholic circles. The rise of Asian theology faces the task of proclaiming the gospel as a transcultural message of salvation that is relevant not only in cultures molded by living world religions but also in countries influenced by modern civilization.

On the Protestant side, Taiwanese theologian Shoki Coe (Ng Chiong-hui/Hwang Chang-Hui, 1914–1988)[1] contributed to the development of doing theology in context. In an influential article titled "In Search of Renewal in Theological Education"[2] published in 1973,

---

1. For an account of his life, see his autobiography *Recollections and Reflections*, 2nd ed., intro. and ed. Boris Anderson (New York: Rev Dr. Shoki Coe's Memorial Fund, 1993); Jonah Chang, *Shoki Coe: An Ecumenical Life in Context* (Geneva: WCC, 2012). On his legacy see Kosuke Koyama, "Spiritual Mentors: Christ's Homelessness," *The Christian Century*, July 14–21, 1993, 702–3; Ray Wheeler, "The Legacy of Shoki Coe," *International Bulletin of Missionary Research* 26, no. 2 (April 2012): 77–80.

2. Shoki Coe, "In Search of Renewal in Theological Education," *Theological Education* 9 (Summer 1973): 233–43. This influential essay has been reprinted in part in several anthologies, notably as "Contextual Theology" in Gerald H. Anderson and Thomas F. Stransky, eds., *Third World Theologies* (New York: Paulist, 1976), 19–24; "Contextualization as the Way Toward Reform," in *Asian Christian Theology Emerging Themes*, ed. Douglas J. Elwood (Philadelphia: Westminster, 1980), 48–55. Elwood's version is more complete.

Coe and his colleagues, James Burtness and Aharon Sapsezian of the Theological Education Fund (TEF) of the World Council of Churches (WCC), introduced a new concept of doing theology. Arguably, Coe was the first Asian who advocated the use of the term "contextualization" to replace the indigenization model of theological reflection. For Coe, the term "indigenization" has the "danger of being past-oriented."[3] He saw that the theologies advanced in Latin America, Africa, and Asia up to then were no more than efforts of accommodation of the gospel message to traditional cultures. The problem, he argued, was that doing theology this way was little more than the old tree being transplanted into new soil.

The term "contextualization" was thus coined by Coe to advocate a new dynamic that is "open to change" and "future-oriented."[4] For Coe, theological reflection should begin with "missiological *discernment of the times,* seeing where God is at work and calling us to participate in it."[5] Contemporary churches in Asia vividly live in the context of now and are embedded in various cultural expressions and sociohistorical situations. Coe invited the churches in Taiwan and South East Asia to reflect on theological education and mission in their present contexts in ways that foster change and are open to the future.

This paper offers an ecumenical appraisal of Coe's approach to contextual theology. It discusses how Coe's call for contextualization has also found its parallel in Asian Catholic circles since the 1970s, namely in the Catholic bishops' efforts to renew their churches in Asia in the aftermath of Vatican II. In what follows, I will review the context and the hermeneutics that make up Asian Catholic theological thinking as it is documented in the writings of the Federation of Asian Bishops' Conference (FABC).[6] By studying their theological method, I hope to find a supplemental way to address the multicultural, multiethnic, and multireligious realities that are shaping the future of a worldwide church.

---

3. Coe, "In Search of Renewal," 240; reprint in Elwood, *Asian Christian Theology*, 51.

4. Coe, "In Search or Renewal," 241; reprint in Elwood, *Asian Christian Theology*, 52.

5. Coe, "In Search or Renewal," 241. Note that the phrase "reading the sign of the times" is also a Catholic theme propagated by the Vatican II document *Gaudium et spes* (Pastoral Constitution on the Church in the Modern World) in 1965.

6. The documents of the FABC and of its institutions and offices have been collected in a five-volume work, *For All the Peoples of Asia*, vol. 1 (1974–1991), ed. Gaudencio Rosales and C. G. Arevalo (Manila: Claretian, 1997); vol. 2 (1992–96), vol. 3 (1997–2001), and vol. 4 (2002–6) are edited by Franz-Josef Eilers and published by Claretian in 1997, 2002, and 2007 respectively; vol. 5 (2007–12) is edited by Vimal Tirimanna and published by Claretian in 2014. Since 2006, many FABC documents and papers are available online at www.fabc.org.

WESTERN THEOLOGY IN ITS CONTEXT

Traditionally, theological thinking has been the domain of Western theologians.[7] At the risk of overgeneralizing, I would characterize Western theological thinking as "academic." As *fides quaerens intellectum*, theology in the Christian West tends to favor abstractions and rational discourses, independently of context. The fact that Europe and America have been under a Christian culture for centuries certainly limits their ability to separate European culture from Christianity, as has been attested in the history of Christian mission. The effort in recent decades to contextualize theology seems to apply more to "third world theologies,"[8] whereas most theological writings coming out of Europe and North America still think of themselves as universal, and not contextual.

According to the Catholic missiologist Stephen Bevans in *Models of Contextual Theology*, all theologies are "contextual theologies."[9] Bevans argues that what makes contextual theology *contextual* is that it takes the present experience and situation of individuals and communities as the point of departure for theology (*locus theologicus*). Bevans's approach to theology echoes what Coe proposed back in the 1970s. If theology is an interpreted response of the revelatory message—in particular of the Christ event—then every generation of Christians, in different eras and locations, will express the content of faith using the language and thought pattern of their space and time. This means the honorable fifth-century Vincentian canon "at all times, everywhere, by everyone" that has been used by many to justify the universal application of the propositional truths should be under suspicion as a legitimate way to maintain doctrinal uniformity (and implicitly to maintain the status quo).

Before going into the characterization of Asian theological methodology, I find it necessary to briefly review the contexts of the development of theology in the West. This is to show that Western theology has also been a product of its own sociohistorical developments, and not as universal as people might think.[10] The fact that Christianity spread from

---

7. I use the word "Western" here in a generic sense to describe what grew out of the Latin church after the eleventh century until modern times.

8. The term "third world" reflects a Cold War mentality and is now dated. Consequently the term "third world theologies" that was popular in the 1970s and 1980s is now replaced by "world theologies," "globalizing theologies," or "theologies from the global South." See Jonathan Y. Tan and Anh Q., trans. and eds., *World Christianity: Perspectives and Insights* (Maryknoll, NY: Orbis, 2016).

9. Stephen B. Bevans, *Models of Contextual Theology* (Maryknoll, NY: Orbis, 1992, 2002), 4.

10. To give a detailed account of all the doctrinal developments in theology is beyond the scope of this paper. Many excellent histories of doctrine are available, for example, the five-volume *The Christian Tradition* by Jaroslav Pelikan (Chicago: University of Chicago Press,

Palestine to Asia Minor, and from there westward to Greece, then Rome and other parts of Europe was decisive. As soon as they moved out from a Semitic cultural milieu to the greater Greco-Roman world, Christians had to "translate" the gospel of Jesus to people who had never heard or known him, using Hellenistic expressions. With the Edict of Milan in 313 CE and the subsequent official sanction of Christianity as the state religion, Christianity took firm root in the Roman Empire. This set the stage for Augustine and other Western theologians to make their contribution to theology even though most theological debates were still carried out in the Greek language and employed Greek metaphysics.[11] An important development of the imperial era was that theological diversity was restricted in favor of doctrinal uniformity, which was seen as preserving the unity of the empire. That eventually led to the development of the Christendom of one faith, one pope, and one emperor.

During the Middle Ages, whereas the Eastern churches continued to be enriched by local languages and cultures, a Latin monoculture began to grow in the West. Isolated from the south and west by Islam and from the east by the 1054 schism, Western theologians turned inward and lost sight of their own context. Theological reflection began to take place in universities and was restricted to propositions that could be argued and refuted. Western theology reached its best in the development of scholastic theology and philosophy from the eleventh to the fourteenth century. Not all theologies were rationalistic and academic; however, mystical theology occupied a small part of Christian thinking, and it did not have a strong impact on the development of Western theology.

Beginning in the fifteenth century, Western missionaries ventured into the new world "discovered" by European explorers, carrying with them this "universal" model of culture and theology.[12] In fact, when these missionaries came into contact with other forms of Christianity in India and the Middle East, Latinization would be enforced. In the

---

1971–89). I am ignorant, however, of any standard reference in theology that links the social, historical, and cultural contexts that gave rise to theological thought or schools. In the field of history, the story of Christianity is now retold as a global movement, taking seriously the context in which the local church evolved worldwide. See Scott Sunquist and Dale Irvin, *History of the World Christian Movement: Earliest Christianity to 1453* (Maryknoll, NY: Orbis, 2001), and *History of the World Christian Movement: Modern Christianity from 1454 to 1800* (Maryknoll, NY: Orbis, 2012).

11. One should not overlook the fact that most doctrinal disputes that led to church councils from the fourth to the seventh century (the first seven Ecumenical Councils) were about Greek terminologies and concepts; Latin theology had not yet gained significance at this time.

12. One can argue that Christians, Jews, and Muslims were aware of one another's traditions, and that during the High Middle Ages there were a few philosophical and cultural exchanges. But for the most part, non-Christian traditions were judged to be inferior to Christianity and thus not worthy to be engaged seriously.

meantime, the breaking of the one Christendom in Europe during the Protestant reformations and the subsequent divisions of Protestants solidified the need for uniformity of doctrine and practice within the Roman Catholic Church. The challenges of the Enlightenment and modernism to theology from the eighteenth to the early twentieth centuries slowly resulted, though not without fierce resistance, in an awareness of the sociohistorical limitations of theological formulations.

By the middle of the twentieth century, theologians were confronted with the need to update their methodology. If the traditional method had worked out a triad of theological reflection using biblical data, denominational tradition (for Roman Catholics, the magisterium), and philosophy, Christian theologians began to consider the role of human experience as a valid theological locus. Philosophy was not the only partner (though it was still the dominant one) of theology. Other fields of humanities such as psychology, sociology, religious study, political sciences, and cultural studies began to have an impact on theological formulation.

After the Second World War, non-Western theologians began to make their voices heard. They raised the need for a contextual theology that takes seriously the social location of theological reflection. This theological insight stimulated the development of liberation theologies, feminist theologies, inculturation theologies of Africa and Asia, and theology of religions. These developments signal the end of the myth of the universally valid theologies that have come out of Western academic institutions.

The strength of traditional Western theology is its precision and clarity in the expressions of faith (a result of many centuries of theological debate) and its preservation of the Christian heritage in a logical and systematic way. The theological resources employed in Western theology (scripture, tradition, and philosophy) are useful and have made substantial contributions to the enrichment of human thought. However, Western theology is also trapped in its own parochial way. Doctrinal unity was achieved at the expense of theological pluralism. Theological agreements were not achieved by consensus, but rather by condemnation and excommunication backed up by temporal or ecclesial powers. In addition, the weight of tradition does not allow one to update the archaic theological formulas that are not culturally translatable (e.g., hypostatic union or transubstantiation). Furthermore, certain Western theological formulations, for example on the doctrine of original sin, reflect a Western bias and ignorance of Eastern Christian anthropology, and yet they claim to be universal. In short, with all the strengths and limitations of their theological methods, traditional Western theologians need to acknowledge that their theology is also contextual and should be open to other forms of interpretation.

THE CONTEXT FOR ASIAN THEOLOGY

Prior to 1500, Christian missions to Asia were sporadic and limited, but we can find pockets of its development in Syria, Mesopotamia, Persia, Armenia, and India, at least until the advancement of Islam.[13] Furthermore, what was brought to these lands is not a monolithic Christianity but rather a variety of Christianities with different languages, liturgies, spiritualities, theologies, modes of organization, and cultures. This multiplicity and variety were further increased by the varied ways in which the Christian faith was received in these countries. The expansion of Islam into West and Central Asia from the eighth to the tenth centuries isolated the small Christian communities in those areas, reducing them to an insignificant number, and arresting their theological development.

The second wave of Christian mission to the Far East coincided with the European explorers of the fifteenth century. These missionaries were Western Europeans (Portuguese, Spanish, Italian, French) who took pride in the cultural and religious superiority of Europe. With the exception of a few Jesuit efforts to study the culture and religions of the evangelized people, most Europeans were ignorant of the Asian realities, and they caused tremendous damage in the history of mission (like the Rites controversy of the eighteenth century). These isolated many Asian Christians from their fellow countrymen.

Furthermore, in the nineteenth century, most of South and South East Asia was colonized by Western powers, and Christianity grew with the aid and protection of the colonizers. During this time, foreignness is one thing that characterized the churches in Asia. Asian Christians led separate lives from the mainstream life of the people. Everything was a replica of what went on in Western Europe, from school to church, from worship to theology. While there were native leaders and clergy, all were trained in the Western theological method and were taught to distrust their cultural heritage. After the Second World War and following the independence movements of former colonies, Asian Christians slowly

13. For standard reference on early Asian Christianity, see Samuel Hugh Moffett, *A History of Christianity in Asia: Beginnings to 1500*, 2nd ed. (Maryknoll, NY: Orbis, 1998); Ian Gillman and Hans-Joachim Klimkeit, *Christians in Asia before 1500* (Ann Arbor: University of Michigan Press, 1999); John C. England, *The Hidden History of Christianity in Asia: The Churches of the East Before the Year 1500* (Hong Kong: CCA, 1998).

recovered their cultural identities. Only in the 1970s did church leaders of Asia begin to assert their independence from Western influence.

THE FORMATION OF FABC

The gathering of 180 bishops of Asia in Manila on the occasion of Pope Paul VI's visit to East and South East Asia in 1970 was a remarkable event for Asian Catholic churches. This was the first time that the bishops of Asia came together to share their experience and "to search for new ways through which [they] could be of greater and more effective service—not to [the] Catholic communities only—but also to all the people of Asia."[14] The bishops' main concern was the urgent need for the Asian church to be more truly "the church of the poor," "the church of the young," and "a church in dialogue" with all people of other religious traditions as well as with the cultural traditions of Asia. The message issued by the bishops at the end of the Manila meeting stressed the importance of cooperation with all people of goodwill in search for human development, freedom, justice, and peace, so that the church may "help bind together the new world of Asia as a true family of nations in this part of the earth, linked not only by lines of geography, but by mutual understanding and respect, by the nobler bonds of brotherhood and love."[15]

With this commitment, the twelve bishops' conferences of South and East Asia started the discussion that eventually formed the FABC as a sign and instrument of fraternal cooperation and communion.[16] From its inception in 1974 until 2016, the bishops have gathered officially in eleven plenary assemblies to address different concerns.[17] In addition, various FABC offices have organized hundreds of regional consultations,

14. Asian Bishops' Meeting (1970), art. 2, in *For All the Peoples of Asia*, vol. 1, 3–10.

15. Asian Bishops' Meeting, art. 27, in *For All the Peoples of Asia*, vol. 1, 7.

16. On the history and structure of the FABC, see Miguel Marcello Quatra, *At the Side of the Multitudes* (Manila: Claretian, 2000), 5–21, and the journalistic account of Thomas Fox in *Pentecost in Asia* (Maryknoll, NY: Orbis, 2002), 22–37. At present there are thirteen full-member bishops' conferences: Bangladesh, India, Indonesia, Japan, Korea, Laos-Cambodia, Malaysia-Singapore-Brunei, Myanmar, Pakistan, Philippines, Sri Lanka, Taiwan, and Vietnam. Those countries that do not have full episcopal conferences enjoy associate membership: Hong Kong, Macau, Mongolia, Nepal, and the Central Asian states (of former Soviet republics).

17. FABC I (Taipei, 1974): *Evangelization in Modern-Day Asia*; FABC II (Calcutta, 1978): *Life of the Church in Asia*; FABC III (Bangkok, 1982): *The Church—the Community of Faith in Asia*; FABC IV (Tokyo, 1986): *The Vocation and Mission of the Laity in the Church and in the World*; FABC V (Bandung, Indonesia, 1990): *Emerging Challenges for the Church in Asia in 1990s*; FABC VI (Manila, 1995): *Christian Discipleship in Asia Today*; FABC VII (Samphran, Thailand, 2000): *A Renewed Church in Asia*; FABC VIII (Seoul, 2004): *The Asian Family*; FABC IX (Manila, 2009): *Living the Eucharist in Asia*; FABC X (Xuan Loc, Vietnam, 2012): *Responses to the Challenges of Asia*; FABC XI (Colombo, Sri Lanka, 2016): *Catholic Family in Asia*.

workshops, seminars, and conferences on the challenges confronting
Asia and Asian churches.[18]

CONTEXT OF CONTEMPORARY ASIA

The context of the churches in Asia today shapes their theological thinking in a different way than their counterparts in the West. Postcolonial
Asia has struggled with forging its own *self-identity*. As a result, many
Asian countries have seen the rise of nationalism, which at times is exag-
gerated and manifested in anti-Western activities. Furthermore, frag-
mentation of nation-states, civil war, and political oppression have been
common occurrences in many parts of Asia in the past fifty years (e.g.,
Korean and Vietnam wars, Chinese Cultural Revolution, the killing
fields of Khmer Rouge, separatist movements in Sri Lanka, the Philippines, and Indonesia). These events made Asia anything but peaceful.

Massive poverty is a painful reality of Asia. In a continent that houses
almost two-thirds of humankind, Asia is marked with "poverty, with
undernourishment and ill health, scarred by war and suffering, troubled
and restless."[19] Many young people of Asia are vulnerable to the temptations of materialism and consumerism and easily become the prey of
ideological exploitation for they are "living under wretched conditions,
unable because of poverty to liberate themselves from the bondage of
ignorance and illiteracy, and are shackled to a life severely limited by
inadequate skills and knowledge."[20] Among the poorest are women and
children (especially girls) who suffer from discrimination and oppression of "dowry, forced marriages, wife beating and destruction of female
fetuses" because "in general, Asian society views women as inferior."[21]
While there are undeniable benefits from modernization, the coming of
globalization adds to the existing economic disparity between the rich
and the poor. The Asian bishops lamented: "It has enabled only a small
proportion of the population to improve their standards of living, leaving
many to remain in poverty. Another consequence is excessive urbanization, causing the emergence of huge conglomerations and the resultant
migration, crime, and exploitation of the weaker sections."[22]

Unlike Europe, Asia is the cradle of all major world religions, the con-

18. The plenary assembly is the highest body; all committees and offices are answerable to
it. Other important offices include the Bishops' Institute for Religious and Ecumenical Affairs
(BIRA), Social Action (BISA), Lay Apostolate (BILA), Missionary Apostolate (BIMA).

19. Asian Bishops' Meeting, art. 4, in *For All the People of Asia*, vol. 1, 4.

20. FABC IV (1986), art. 3.2.2, in *For All the Peoples of Asia*, vol. 1, 181.

21. FABC IV, art. 3.3.1, in *For All the Peoples of Asia*, vol. 1, 182–83.

22. FABC VII (2000), part II: A, in *For All the Peoples of Asia*, vol. 3, 6.

tinent of ancient and diverse cultures, religions, histories, and traditions, "a region like Joseph's coat of many colors."[23] Cultural and religious *pluralism* is a reality of Asia, and it might account for the innate toleration of syncretistic behaviors that have scandalized many monotheists. The Asian religious ethos distrusts any exclusive claim to the truth. It highlights the relational and historically embedded character of all exclusive and absolute religious claims. Indeed, this ethos challenges the very nature of Christianity itself, with its attendant notions of truth, normativity, revelation, sacred scripture, divinity, salvation, worship, dogmas, moral norms, ethical practices, cultural traditions, and so on.[24]

CONTEXT OF THE CHURCH IN ASIA

With the exception of the Philippines and East Timor, Christianity has never been a major religion anywhere in Asia.[25] It is a *minority religion* that comes with a "minority complex" that tends to adopt a defensive and ghetto mentality. Church life has little to do with the larger society but is only concerned with its internal growth and maintenance. In many areas, Christians lead a parallel life apart from the struggle of injustice of their neighbors. The Asian bishops capture this mentality well:

> But we must acknowledge too, with regret, where we have been found wanting: where we have tended to foster only narrow and "domestic" interests; where we could have shown more compassion and solicitude for the poor and have not been sufficiently vigorous in speaking out for justice and the defense of human rights; where we have not incarnated the Christian life and enfleshed the Church in ways and patterns of our respective cultures, and thus kept it alien in our lands; where we have not sought understanding of, reconciliation and collaboration with our brothers of other Christian Churches and of other faiths.[26]

The *"foreign"* factor is also a hindrance for Asian Christians. The church's historic association with colonial powers and its continued dependence on Western cultural norms, authorities, theological language, and concepts make local churches of Asia remain alien to their people's religio-

---

23. Asian Bishops' Meeting, art. 7, in *For All the Peoples of Asia*, vol. 1, 4.

24. But even Hinduism, Buddhism, and the Chinese religions, which may not make exclusive claims for themselves, are affected in diverse ways by religious pluralism insofar as whatever claims they make for themselves are shown to be historically conditioned and context-dependent.

25. While Judaism, Christianity, and Islam started out in the continent of Asia, many East and South Asians see them more as Western religions than Asian religions.

26. Asian Bishops' Meeting, art. 17, in *For All the Peoples of Asia*, vol. 1, 5.

cultural surroundings. Vatican II's mandate on inculturation has resulted in haphazard results, with strong resistance in some Christian circles. For so long, Asian Christians were taught to view their native religions as superstitions and their cultural expressions as inferior to the Christian culture of the West. The difficulty for many Christians to shake off this indoctrination results in a "superiority complex," and thwarts any effort of dialogue. If the church is believed to be the only means of salvation, then dialogue is at best a tool to wake people up from their errors, and at worse to be ignored altogether. This negative and defensive attitude is partly due to the "minority-but-superior" complex that many Christians still carry with them. The competition between missionaries for influences (e.g., Jesuits and MEPs [Missions Etrangères de Paris] in seventeenth-century Vietnam, or Catholics and Protestants in the contemporary era) reinforces the negative attitude toward dialogue. The fights and divisions among Christians have scandalized many Asians and have contributed to the hindrance of evangelization. In fact, sometimes it is easier to collaborate with non-Christians than with members of another Christian denomination. Fortunately, as Christians move into the mainstream of Asian societies, they foster an open attitude toward dialogue and collaboration.

Against these backgrounds and contexts, one can see certain repetitive themes in the FABC documents, such as the "triple dialogue," "dialogue of life," "commitment to life," "harmony," "communion of communities," and "new way of being Church," as representatives of the FABC and/or Asian theology.[27] Keep in mind that the FABC is a response of Asian bishops to the impetus of Vatican II; it takes seriously the mandate to "return to the original charism" and "reading the signs of the times" to foster a theology that can be accepted in the Asian context. By design, the FABC is an advisory body without a juridical binding authority on individual churches. Its influence on the thinking and praxis of Catholicism in Asia is due to its radical openness to a "new way of being Church," a church that is committed to becoming "a community of communities" and "a credible sign of salvation and liberation."[28] The FABC took the situation and context of the local church as the focal point for theological reflection and pastoral application.

27. In the meetings of the FABC and its offices, not only the bishops are present, but also theological experts (religious, priest, and lay). Many influential theologians of Asia such as Michael Amaladoss, Tissa Balasuriya, Jacques Dupuis, Aloysius Pieris, and Felix Wilfred have served as resource persons at these FABC assemblies and conferences. This is not to suggest that the views of these theologians are adopted uncritically by the bishops, but to point out that many FABC documents bear the theological signatures of these Asian theologians.

28. Cf. FABC VI (1995), art. 3, in *For All the Peoples of Asia*, vol. 2, 2.

FABC AND ASIAN THEOLOGICAL METHODOLOGY

Given the context of Asia, a different approach to theology must take place so that theology can be a useful tool to reflect on the conditions of Asia. Asian theology can be characterized briefly (and not exhaustively) as a theology of dialogue, a hermeneutic of religious pluralism, an inductive and pastoral response, and a regnocentric orientation.

THEOLOGY OF DIALOGUE

Regarding the theological thrust of the FABC, the Indian theologian Felix Wilfred points out:

"If we were to summarize the orientation of the FABC in one word, then it is *dialogue*. It is the focal point that the FABC's understanding of the Church and its mission revolves [around]. Dialogue frees the Church from becoming a self-centered community, and links it with the people in all areas and dimensions of their lives."[29] The churches of Asia look at its theology from a contextual perspective. At FABC I, the bishops committed to a *triple-dialogue* that characterizes their pastoral and theological orientation: a dialogue with the religions of Asia (art. 14–18), with the poor of Asia (art. 19–24), and with the cultures of Asia (art. 26, 31–32). To achieve this, the FABC has called for constructing an indigenous theology that is genuinely Asian and relevant to the multitudes of Asia (art. 33).[30]

Since the FABC places its emphasis on a contextual and pastoral approach, the theological resources are open to whatever concerns Asian peoples: their cultures, religious heritages, religious scriptures, oral traditions, popular religiosity, social movements (women's, tribal, ecological), reality of the poor, economic and political realities, and world events, in addition to the traditional Christian sources of scripture and tradition.[31] In other words, "*the totality of life is the raw material of theology*; God is redemptively present in the totality of human life" (emphasis

29. Felix Wilfred, "The FABC: Orientations, Challenges and Impact," in *For All the Peoples of Asia*, vol. 1, xxiv–xxv.

30. It was only in 1987 that an official body was set up exclusively for this purpose. It was called the Theological Advisory Commission (TAC), which was mainly a body of bishops and theologians from FABC member countries. Its task was to stimulate and facilitate theological reflections and discussions in the context of Asia. In 1997, the TAC was elevated to an office, called the Office of Theological Concerns (OTC).

31. See the descriptions of these *loci theologici* in chapter 3 of "Methodology: Asian Christian Theology" (2000), a document of the Office of Theological Concerns (OTC) in *For All the Peoples of Asia*, vol. 3, 355–64.

mine).[32] The context for Asian theologians does not only mean the background against which one does theology, but also the theological locus together with Scripture and Tradition. This means that Asian theologians are willing to use a *multidisciplinary* approach for theological reflection, going beyond the normal use of philosophy, history, and the social sciences toward other possible forms of human expressions such as arts, dance, story, folk wisdom, literature, and music.

RELIGIOUS PLURALISM AS RESOURCE FOR THEOLOGY

By religious pluralism, I do not mean a particular position of the theology of religions (such as that of John Hick, which holds that various religions are equally valid, albeit diverse, paths to the Divine or Reality). This radical view of religious pluralism does not help the cause of Christianity in Asia. The FABC's Office of Theological Concerns rejects such an approach:

> Today there are persons and groups who hold all reality to be relative. For such persons and groups, pluralism means relativism, in the sense of claiming that all points of view are equally valid. Such philosophical or theological claims are to be rejected; and in fact, all major Asian religions condemn such relativizing of reality, especially the relativizing of basic human values.[33]

While firmly rejecting any pluralistic view that naturally ends up in relativism or subjectivism, the Asian bishops see pluralism as a blessing and enrichment.[34] They embrace a view of religious diversity that shows the unity and harmony behind pluralism: "Diversity is not something to be regretted and abolished, but to be rejoiced and promoted, since it represents richness and strength. Harmony is not simply the absence of strife, described as 'live and let live.'"[35] While condemning indifferentism, they also see exclusivism as an obstacle to harmony. The root of exclusivist attitude is "the failure to view the complementarity which exists between people, cultures, faiths, ideologies, world-visions, etc. For the promotion of harmony, it is important to cultivate an all-embracing and complementary way of thinking."[36] Harmony is the central theme of many FABC meetings, notably the BIRA IV's (Bishops' Institutes for Interre-

32. *For All the Peoples of Asia*, vol. 3, 356.
33. OTC, "Methodology," in *For All the Peoples of Asia*, vol. 3, 334.
34. BIRA IV/10 (1988), art. 10, in *For All the Peoples of Asia*, vol. 1, 314.
35. BIRA IV/11 (1988), art. 15, in *For All the Peoples of Asia*, vol. 1, 321.
36. BIRA IV/11, art. 20, in *For All the Peoples of Asia*, vol. 1, 322.

ligious Affairs) second, tenth, and eleventh meetings that addressed the theology of harmony, and BIRA V's five meetings that explored the understanding of harmony in the context of interreligious dialogue.[37]

This does not mean that Asian Christians do not know of discord and division; their many wars and conflicts in recent years attest to these failures to maintain harmony. The existence of so-called religious conflicts in some parts of Asia (e.g., India, Indonesia) makes it urgent for theologians to dig into the roots of such tragic conflicts. Are there any specific reasons? Or is it only a conflict in the name of a certain religion? How can we teach and speak about God in the midst of a conflictual atmosphere? Contextual theology demands an analysis of the sociocultural, economic, religious, and political situation where the seeds of the good news are planted.

The purpose of using religious experiences of other traditions as theological locus is neither to extract some common core of religious experience that is supposed to undergird all religious traditions nor to erect on the basis of allegedly common and identical elements a universal world religion and theology. Rather, recognizing the other as "other" but not as "opposite," it is to assist Asian Christians to be in touch with their cultural heritage, to see the mutual illumination among religious traditions where differences are as important as commonalities, and to explore the ways in which studying in depth the analogies in other traditions can open up a fresh and rich understanding of their own.

The interreligious hermeneutic is evidenced in the 1997 document on the role of the Holy Spirit in Asia and the 2000 document on Asian Christian Theology, both the works of the Office of Theological Concerns. The 2000 document, in particular, spends more than half the number of pages looking at how hermeneutics is done in various Asian religions.[38] This interreligious hermeneutic has inspired comparative theology and ethics projects, not only among Asian scholars (such as Aloysius Pieris or Raimon Panikkar) but also North American scholars who research and teach Asian religions (such as Francis Clooney and James Frederick).

37. See the documents of BIRA V/1–5 (1992–96), in *For All the Peoples of Asia*, vol. 2, 143–71.

38. OTC, "Methodology: Asian Christian Theology"—chap. 4 in *For All the Peoples of Asia*, vol. 3, 365–405.

INDUCTIVE AND PASTORAL FOCUS

While giving respect to scriptures of other faiths, the FABC still places the Christian scripture as a primary source of revelation. In biblical hermeneutic, Asian theologians still affirm the primacy of the "literal sense" of scripture, that is "the meaning of a text in its original context, which is recovered through a critical, historic-literary study."[39] However, they reject the Western historical-critical method in favor of a contextual hermeneutic that is related to Asian worldviews, cultures, and sociopolitical situations. For them, the primary task of biblical interpretation is to marry biblical and Christian teaching with the concrete social situation.

Methodologically, Asian theologians achieve this by multiple approaches. In addition to the multicultural, multireligious, and the social hermeneutics (which are described in sections above), a particular attempt is to retrieve the hermeneutical tradition of the Oriental churches (especially the Syriac tradition), which emphasizes typological exegesis, accords priority to mysticism and apophaticism, and favors the use of images, symbols, paradoxes, and poetry in theological expressions. These are deemed to be in line with the Asian way of thinking, and a return to the source.[40] Another attempt is to use a "people-based" hermeneutic, which does not rely solely on the scholarly works of trained theologians, but also the shared experience of the ordinary believers themselves. This approach makes extensive use of popular myths, stories, fables, dance, and arts to interpret biblical stories, as exemplified by Asian theologians such as Kosuke Koyama and Choan-Seng Song.[41]

The main questions for Asian theologians are pastoral in nature: How can theology respond to and meet the religious needs of the people? How can theologians speak of God in popular, daily language? What kind of language(s) is to be used in doing theology? This depends much on the "audience." With and to whom are we going to speak about God? The majority of Asians are not familiar with the abstract reasoning and categories of Western philosophical tradition. The complicated lan-

---

39. OTC, "Methodology," in *For All the Peoples of Asia*, vol. 3, 366.

40. The Syriac tradition survives in South India, despite centuries of being ignored and suppressed. For a brief exposition of its hermeneutics see "Methodology"—chapter 2, in *For All the Peoples of Asia*, vol. 3, 338–46.

41. Kosuke Koyama and Choan-Seng Song advocate the use of cultural resources such as story, myths, and folk wisdom as starting points for theological reflection. Both were influenced by Shoki Coe in different ways. Koyama was Coe's student, and Song was Coe's successor at Tainan Theological Seminary.

guage used in theology makes people confused; popular everyday language needs to be used. What Asians need in their daily lives is to be conscious of the divine presence and providence. How can we show them that God exists in this world? How can we show that Jesus Christ does not only belong to Christians, but to all human beings in the world? Jesus's Asian face needs to be shown to people in Asia, that he is not a foreigner on this continent but a member of it.

A REGNOCENTRIC THEOLOGY

Evangelization and mission are major concerns for the FABC. However, its understanding of "making disciples of all nations" takes on a new meaning of "being with the people, responding to their needs, with sensitiveness to the presence of God in cultures and other religious traditions, and witnessing to the values of God's Kingdom through *presence, solidarity, sharing and word*" (emphasis mine).[42] The Asian bishops see the gospel as "leaven" for liberation and transformation of societies: "Our Asian world needs the values of Kingdom and of Christ in order to bring about the human development, justice, peace, and harmony with God, among peoples and with all creation that the peoples of Asia long for."[43]

In seeking to respond to the challenges of the Asian situations, the kingdom of God becomes a focal point. It offers the framework to understand the two major experiences of Asia: the cultural and religious plurality of its people and the prevalence of massive poverty. The FABC's understanding of the kingdom is a divine reality operating in the world: "Where God is accepted, where the Gospel value, where [hu]man is respected . . . there is the Kingdom"—a universality "far-wider than the Church's boundaries."[44] This is not rhetoric but a world-transforming force: "The Kingdom of God confronts the forces of injustice, violence, and oppression," all of which represent structures of sin, from which people need to be liberated.[45]

While insisting on the universality of the kingdom of God and its accessibility beyond the confines of the church, the Asian bishops also insist on the primacy of Christ and the gospel. From the very first assembly, they are convinced that the quests of Asians to find meaning, overcome destructive forces, shape a new society, free themselves from structural bondage, foster human dignity and freedom, and to create a

42. FABC V, art. 3.1.2, in *For All the Peoples of Asia*, vol. 1, 279.
43. FABC V, art. 3.2.5, in *For All the Peoples of Asia*, vol. 1, 281.
44. BIRA IV/2 (1985), art. 8.1, in *For All the Peoples of Asia*, vol. 1, 252.
45. BIRA IV/10, art. 8, in *For All the Peoples of Asia*, vol. 1, 314.

genuine communion among all peoples can only be realized "in and through Christ and his Gospel . . . it is in Him and in His good news that [Asian] peoples will finally find the full meaning . . . the liberation . . . the brotherhood and peace which is the desire of all."[46]

The positive affirmation of the Christian faith in Jesus as *the way the truth and the life* for the peoples of Asia is not done at the expense of other religious traditions. In fact, in the FABC plenary assemblies, one does not find any statement that compares Jesus with other religious figures or Christianity with other religions. The Asian bishops are conscious that the religions of Asia have been the source and inspiration for generations of people and have shaped the spiritual development and growth of Asia. Viewing Asian religions as "significant and positive elements in the economy of God's design of salvation,"[47] the bishops invite Christians to dialogue with them to discern how God's saving activity is in operation. In short, the FABC sees other religions as possible partners in building the kingdom of God—a bold move that takes us beyond the more theoretical questions about the uniqueness of the salvific action of Christ that dominates many conversations in the West.[48]

CONCLUDING REFLECTION

As a conclusion, I would like to quote from the FABC Office of Theological Concerns (OTC) document on Asian Christian Theology (2000) on the basic principle of the Asian theological approach:

> The Asian way of doing theology is historically rooted and concrete, a method in which we learn to face conflicts and brokenness, a method we value as one of liberative integration, interrelatedness, and wholeness, a method that emphasizes symbolic approaches and expressions, and is marked by a preference for those on the periphery and "outside the Gate" (Heb 13:3).[49]

Thanks to globalization and immigration, the West in general, and American society in particular, are becoming increasingly multicultural, multiethnic, and multireligious. As a result, being religious today means being interreligious and calls for intercultural and interreligious understanding and collaboration on both national and international levels. This need was made dramatically evident by the 9/11 event and its

46. FABC I, art. 6–7, in *For All the Peoples of Asia*, vol. 1, 13.
47. FABC I, art. 14, in *For All the Peoples of Asia*, vol. 1, 14.
48. Cf. the concern of CDF on doctrinal relativism in *Dominus Iesus*.
49. OTC, "Methodology," in *For All the Peoples of Asia*, vol. 3, 419.

aftermath. Furthermore, there has been a massive demographic shift in Christianity from the North to the South, in which almost two-thirds of its membership will reside in the so-called "Global South" or the "Majority World" (that is, Africa, Asia, and Latin America) in the next few decades.[50] This shift of the Christian population to the South, where Christians and followers of other religions rub shoulders with one another, presents Christians and others with an urgent need for dialogue.

As for theology, religious pluralism means that the shape of Christian theology will be influenced by dialogue with other religions and that the claims of Christian theology will be understood in a context in which similar claims are made by other religions. In other words, comparative theology will help to define and shape confessional theology. This will not require surrendering particular claims, but it will mean reinterpreting some of them. This should be done in a spirit of openness to the truth from whatever quarter it may emerge.

Traditional Western approach to theology is still important to clarify concepts and articulate the tenets of Christian faith, but it must be reflected on and taught critically. How far does it influence daily life? Does it help to promote dialogue? Need we find a better and a more contextual method of reflection concerning the process of theologizing? We need to be aware that all theology is contextual in its origin. The FABC theological method reminds us that perhaps it is better to start from life instead of ideas, from practice instead of theory, from a context instead of abstractions.

To be fair, Asian theology is still in its developing phase, and it is in no way trying to replace traditional Western theology as "the" theology of the future. What it highlights is a need to take contextual theology seriously, as Shoki Coe proposed more than forty years ago. Given the new reality in world Christianity, I hope to have presented some of the ways that Asians are doing theology, so that it can be helpful and enriched for the way we do theology in the worldwide church. In a world that becomes more globalized every day, mutual sharing and enrichment can benefit theologians.

---

50. The new situation of Christianity has been well documented and popularized by the work of Philip Jenkins, *The Next Christendom: The Coming Future of Global Christianity*, 3rd ed. (New York: Oxford University Press, 2011).

10.

Christian Church among Religions: Toward a Hospitable Missionary Encounter with the Other

VELI-MATTI KÄRKKÄINEN

FIRST WORDS: ECCLESIOLOGY, MISSION, AND ECUMENISM IN A NEW PLURALISTIC WORLD

Reading the latest ecclesiological investigations and reports,[1] one often wonders whether the writers and the readers live in a different world.[2] By and large, doctrines of the church—similarly to ecumenical documents—are still written as if a Christendom model were still in place, virtually making Christianity the only world religion, with established "mainline" churches as the only players on the field, and well-to-do Europeans and Americans establishing the majority of the faithful. And, of course, leaders and theologians are supposed to be mainly aging white males! Yet, how radically different is the world of the third millennium in which the global church and her mission take place. Nothing less than a radical transformation—or in the words of the Cuban-American historian-theologian Justo L. González, "macroreformation,"[3] is happen-

1. The present essay is based on and draws directly from Veli-Matti Kärkkäinen, *Hope and Community: A Constructive Christian Theology for the Pluralistic World*, vol. 5 (Grand Rapids: Eerdmans, 2015), chap. 18; the first main section also gleans from chap. 11.

2. For insightful observations about the context of ecclesiology in the current world, see Gerard Mannion and Lewis S. Mudge. "Introduction: Ecclesiology—the Nature, Story and Study of the Church," in *Routledge Companion to the Christian Church*, ed. Gerard Mannion and Lewis S. Mudge (New York: Routledge, 2012), 1–6.

3. Justo L. González, *Mañana: Christian Theology from a Hispanic Perspective* (Nashville: Abingdon, 1990), 49.

ing before our very eyes. The church of the bygone era is over and something radically new is emerging.

What I mean with this "radical transformation" is well known and well documented, so suffice it to add this brief reminder. While Christianity has grown to be the world's largest religion, with over 2.4 billion adherents, the majority of the faithful have moved from the Global North (Europe and North America) to the Global South (Africa, Asia, Latin America); by 2050, only about one-fifth of the world's Christians will be non-Hispanic whites. Rather than a wealthy Euro-American male, a "'typical' contemporary Christian . . . [is] a woman living in a village in Nigeria or in a Brazilian *favela*"[4] or a young, often poor, person anywhere in the megacities of the Global South. At the same time, the composition of the church worldwide is changing dramatically; as of now, half of all Christians are Roman Catholics, a quarter comprises Pentecostals/charismatics, and the rest are Eastern Orthodox Christians, as well as Anglicans, mainline Protestants, and members of free churches.[5] This means that Roman Catholics and Pentecostals/charismatics together constitute three-fourths of the global membership. As a result, conservative and traditional mindsets will be strengthened even when theological liberalism and pluralism reign in Western academia. The "Pentecostalization" of the Christian church in terms of Pentecostal/charismatic spirituality and worship patterns infiltrating all churches is yet another implication of the transformation.[6] Add to this the rapidly growing influence of diaspora[7] and migration,[8] and you get a picture of an unprecedented global transformation.

But there is even more to the life of the church and ecclesiological

---

4. Philip Jenkins, *The Next Christendom: The Coming of Global Christianity* (Oxford: Oxford University Press, 2001), 2. For Asia, see Peter C. Phan, ed., *Christianities in Asia*, Blackwell Guides to Global Christianity (Oxford: Wiley-Blackwell, 2011); for Africa and the Caribbean, see Bengt Sundkler and Christopher Steed, *A History of the Church in Africa* (Cambridge: Cambridge University Press, 2000); for Latin America, see Edward Cleary and Timothy J. Steigenga, eds., *Conversion of a Continent: Contemporary Religious Change in Latin America* (New Brunswick, NJ: Rutgers University Press, 2007).

5. The current statistical source is Todd M. Johnson and Brian J. Grim, *The World's Religions in Figures* (Oxford: Wiley-Blackwell, 2013).

6. For important contributions, see Neil J. Ormerod and Shane Clifton, eds., *Globalization and the Mission of the Church: Ecclesiological Investigations* (New York: T&T Clark, 2009).

7. See Stéphane Dufoix, *Diasporas* (Berkeley: University of California Press, 2008).

8. A useful reference work is Stephen Castles and Mark J. Miller, *The Age of Migration: International Population Movements in the Modern World*, 4th ed. (New York: Guilford, 2009). A standard missiological analysis is Jehu J. Hanciles, *Beyond Christendom: Globalization, African Migration, and the Transformation of the West* (Maryknoll, NY: Orbis, 2008). General migration data can be found in the continually updated database of the Pew Research Center, https://tinyurl.com/y9nyzmh9.

reflection in the beginning of the third millennium—and this is the focus of the current essay. It has to do with the massive presence and influence of religious diversity (the fact that a number of religions coexist) and religious pluralisms (ideologies, "takes" on religious coexistence). What had been expected to become a "secular" world with the progress of modernity has become even more religious. At the global level, religions are not only holding their own but are also flourishing and (in some cases) growing in numbers. Importantly, religious plurality is no longer a matter of certain locations and continents, but is now a reality over the whole globe, including the Global North.[9] This state of affairs alone should be a clarion call for Christian theology at large and ecclesiology in particular to engage seriously other religions' views, teachings, and doctrines. Because of the overwhelming continuing presence and force of religious plurality and forms of religious pluralisms, the ambitious and noble call for all Christian theologians writing on ecclesiology and laboring in mission and ecumenism would be to work toward a truly comparative doctrine of the church in an authentic dialogue with visions of community of other faith traditions.[10]

While there are certainly many "practical" reasons for the church to engage the religious other, from establishing a pedagogical contact and preparing to witness to Christ in the matrix of religious convictions to helping Christians live in a civil way with the other and so alleviating conflicts,[11] there is also a theological and ecclesiological mandate. This mandate urges Christian theology (and its integral cognates, missiology and ecumenism) to engage robustly with the religious other and religious diversity. Let us summarize this mandate under three interrelated rubrics, the last two building on and elaborating the first one:

9. Currently about a third of the world's population belongs to the Christian church (2.4 billion) and about a quarter is comprised of Muslims (1.6 billion). The 1 billion Hindus make about 15 percent, followed by Buddhists at half that number. Jews number fewer than 15 million, and over 400 million belong to various kinds of "folk religions." Only about 15 percent (1 billion) label themselves religiously unaffiliated (even though the majority of them entertain some kind of religious-type beliefs and practices). Details can be found in *The Global Religious Landscape: A Report on the Size and Distribution of the World's Major Religious Groups as of 2010* (December 2012); available at https://tinyurl.com/y8moh7yk, 9 (executive summary).

10. The first major such study is Keith Ward's *Religion and Community* (Oxford: Oxford University Press, 1999). *My Hope and Community*, Part II, introduces the visions of community and her rites, life, and "mission" among Jews, Muslims, Hindus, and Buddhists (chap. 12) and then throughout the construction of a Christian ecclesiology sympathetically and critically engages them topic by topic.

11. See Reid B. Locklin, "A More Comparative Ecclesiology? Bringing Comparative Theology to the Ecclesiological Table," in *Comparative Ecclesiology: Critical Investigations*, ed. Gerard Mannion (London: T&T Clark, 2008), 125–49. For background issues and debates concerning the rise of the ecumenical "mission as witness to people of other living faiths," see David J. Bosch, *Transforming Mission: Paradigm Shifts in Mission* (Maryknoll, NY: Orbis, 1991), 474–89.

The essential task of Christian theology—and therefore of ecclesiology as part of theology—is to pursue the question of the truth (of God) for the sake of all people; the common origin and destiny of humanity in one God; and the theology of hospitality.

THE THEOLOGICAL MANDATE OF A HOSPITABLE MISSIONARY COMMUNITY

THE PURSUIT OF TRUTH—CAN IT BE DONE IN A HOSPITABLE MANNER?

The first task, pursuing the question of the truth of God for the sake of all peoples, may strike one not only as a sort of hybrid task, but also as something easily leading to violence and oppression. How could any theologian (of any faith tradition, for that matter) claim such a task? Before dismissing the argument, let us be reminded of the obvious yet all-too-often-neglected necessary connection between monotheism—whether Islamic, Jewish, or Christian—and the assumption of the location of truth (and beauty and goodness, among other virtues) in the one and same God. The English philosopher of religion R. Trigg reminds us that "Christianity and Islam both believe that they have a universal message. If there is one God, one would expect that He would be regarded as the God of all people, and not just some." Consequently, there is an assumption of "only one world, one version of reality":

> Monotheism can have no truck with relativism, or alternative gods. Beliefs may construct gods, but those who believe in one God cannot allow for other parallel deities, even in the sense that other people have their gods while monotheists look to their one deity. Monotheism must not only imply the falsity of all other alleged gods, but, if it is true to itself, it has to proclaim it to all, loud and clear. Otherwise, by definition, it is not monotheism, or even realism.[12]

Out of this uncompromising monotheism arises not only Islam's and Christianity's missional task but also the mandate for theology to pursue God's truth. That pursuit of truth, however, does not have to be "foundationalist" in terms of expecting indubitable Cartesian certainty after modernity. Rather, our approach is postfoundationalist in which questioning and confidence mutually shape and inform each other, and the

12. Roger Trigg, *Religious Diversity: Philosophical and Political Dimensions* (Cambridge: Cambridge University Press, 2014), 115.

personal search and the communal search for truth critically cohere. Nor does this pursuit have to expect final arrival, as it were: ultimately, the search for the truth of God is eschatological and anticipatory in nature—also in keeping with the Christian communion's anticipatory nature. Nor should it be coercive or violent; rather, it should be guided by hospitality and gift giving. It is done for the sake of others and their well-being, without subsuming the other under one's own explanation. Dialogue and mutual engagement in a peaceful and honoring posture are the key.[13]

Consequently, we should seriously critique the common tendency to assume that since there are so many religions and ideologies with competing truth claims, none of them can be true and, therefore, relativism is the only way out—the view according to which "each group must live by their own truth, but there is no overarching 'truth' that all should recognize."[14] Should relativism be adopted, it would mean that religious commitments, similarly to, say, personal tastes, were taken merely as subjective choices without any role to play in the public arena.[15]

The relativist argument fails in light of the fact that "religions that only express the personal attitudes of the believer cannot claim any truth that can be rationally assessed. Faith then is merely an idiosyncrasy that some have and some do not."[16] The very fact that we continue to speak of different religions indicates that they are something bigger than just one person's—or even a group's—personal "tastes." There is a necessary intersubjective side to religion—as there is also to secularism, as far as that is thoughtfully and rationally defended. Indeed, "total subjectivism brings the threat of nihilism."[17] Common sense tells us that the content of faith matters. Just think of everyday nonreligious life: the content matters with regard to the kind of doctor or car mechanic we put our faith in.

---

13. For details, see my *Christ and Reconciliation. A Constructive Christian Theology for the Pluralistic World*, vol. 1 (Grand Rapids: Eerdmans, 2013), 1–32.

14. Trigg, *Religious Diversity*, 2.

15. Trigg, *Religious Diversity*, 15–18. A strong appeal to the subjective nature of religions is presented by the Italian philosopher Gianni Vattimo, *After Christianity*, trans. Luca D'Isanto (New York: Columbia University Press, 2002); for a critique, see Trigg, *Religious Diversity*, 26–27. For a wider critique of subjectivism, see Roger Trigg, *Religion in Public Life: Must Religion Be Privatized?* (Oxford: Oxford University Press, 2007). For a convincing defeat of relativism due to its incoherence, see Roger Trigg, *Reason and Commitment* (Cambridge: Cambridge University Press, 1973).

16. Trigg, *Religious Diversity*, 23. This has also been the persistent argument throughout Wolfhart Pannenberg's theological career; see, e.g., chap. 1 in *Systematic Theology*, vol. 1, trans. Geoffrey W. Bromiley (Grand Rapids: Eerdmans, 1991).

17. Trigg, *Religious Diversity*, 13.

I agree with R. Trigg's argument that "all faith has to be faith in something or somebody. There is no such thing as undirected faith."[18]

Nor does doubt or uncertainty, that is, the difficulty or even seeming impossibility of establishing the basis of one's beliefs, constitute relativism.[19] It just makes the pursuit of truth a lifelong, communal, and painstaking task for all. Only if one is an ontological nonrealist, that is, if one holds that all there is, is a result of human construction, could a link between doubt and relativism be made. Most of us, however, are realists (of some sort), which simply means that "reality is independent of all our knowledge and not a construction out of human knowledge." As a result, the jump from epistemology (how we know) to ontology (how things are) cannot be taken for granted.[20]

In keeping with these presuppositions, this essay builds on the conviction that in order for constructive theology to pursue the task of coherent argumentation regarding the truth of Christian doctrine, its claims must be related to not only the internal but also the external spheres. Religions certainly form an essential part of human experience and the experience of the world. In this process, the self-understanding of Christian faith may also be clarified and deepened—and if the engagement is done in an authentic and respectful way, the religious other may also benefit. A hospitable relating to the other not only makes space for a genuine presentation and identification of one's own position but also opens one for a careful listening to the testimonies and convictions of the other.[21] All faith traditions may learn from the Jewish distinction between arguing for victory and arguing for God.[22]

THE COMMON DESTINY OF ALL HUMANITY AS THE IMAGE OF GOD

The second theological reason for a robust engagement with the religious other lies in the common origin and destiny of humanity, an off-

---

18. Trigg, *Religious Diversity*, 18. See further Harold A. Netland, *Christianity and Religious Diversity: Clarifying Christian Commitments in a Globalizing Age* (Grand Rapids: Baker Academic, 2015), chap. 7.

19. For thoughtful reflections, see Netland, *Christianity and Religious Diversity*, chap. 6.

20. Trigg, *Religious Diversity*, 23–30 (27); Trigg uses the term "antirealism" for what I call here nonrealism.

21. See further V.-M. Kärkkäinen, "Dialogue, Witness, and Tolerance: The Many Faces of Interfaith Encounters," *Theology, News & Notes* 57, no. 2 (Fall 2010): 29–33. Fuller studio, https://tinyurl.com/y8yqolh2.

22. Reuven Firestone, "Argue for God's Sake—or a Jewish Argument for Argument's Sake," *Journal of Ecumenical Studies* 39, nos. 1–2 (2002): 47–57.

shoot of monotheism. This was clearly set forth in the beginning of Vatican II's statement on other religions (Nostra Aetate, #123[23]):

> One is the community of all peoples, one their origin, for God made the whole human race to live over the face of the earth. One also is their final goal, God. His providence, His manifestations of goodness, His saving design extend to all men, until that time when the elect will be united in the Holy City, the city ablaze with the glory of God, where the nations will walk in His light.

Because of this common origin and destiny, we can trust that the Holy Spirit is at work among religions in ways unknown to men and women in helping them be connected with the love of God and seek for salvation and truth.[24] As a result, all men and women "should constitute one family and treat one another in a spirit of brotherhood,"[25] including mutual love and care for one another. This reaching out and engaging in the spirit of hospitality is particularly important for the church in light of the growing interdependence of our globalizing world.[26]

THE CONDITIONS AND BENEFITS OF HOSPITALITY

Third, on the basis of these two "foundational" convictions, the mandate for hospitable relating to the other establishes itself. It seeks to cultivate inclusivism, welcoming testimonies, insights, and interpretations from different traditions and contexts, and so foster mutual dialogue as well as room for a peaceful and respectful witnessing and sharing of one's faith. A hospitable posture honors the otherness of others as human beings created by the same God and reconciled by the same Lord.

Hospitality also makes space for an honest, genuine, authentic sharing of one's convictions. In pursuing the question of truth as revealed by the triune God, the church also seeks to persuade and convince with the power of dialogical, humble, and respectful witnessing and argumentation; and this same right and privilege should be granted to other faith traditions communities if they so wish. Ultimately, this posture becomes an act of hospitality, giving and receiving gifts. This kind of hospitable dialogue is a "relationship where both parties are recognized by each

---

23. All Vatican II references are from the official Vatican website at www.vatican.va.

24. For the Catholic Church's Christocentric inclusivistic interpretation, see *Gaudium et Spes*, #22. For my proposal, see *Spirit and Salvation: A Constructive Christian Theology for the Pluralistic World*, vol. 4 (Grand Rapids: Eerdmans, 2016), chap. 5.

25. *Gaudium et Spes*, #24.

26. See further *Gaudium et Spes*, #23.

other as someone not determined by the conditions of one's own horizon, but rather as an Other, a relationship that is not part of the world
and the concrete expectations (or anticipations) of the Other. Hence, in
such a relationship one is invited into the world of the Other by means
of an open invitation."[27]

TOWARD A COMPARATIVE THEOLOGY
AND ECCLESIOLOGY

The God-centered pursuit of truth, acknowledging the deep belonging
together of all men and women, leading to hospitable dialogue and
mutual engagement, calls for and facilitates the scholarly work of comparative theology. Whereas comparative religion seeks to be "neutral"
and look "objectively" at the features of religious traditions, comparative
theology is "comparative and theological beginning to end . . . [and]
marks acts of faith seeking understanding which are rooted in a particular faith tradition but which, from that foundation, venture into learning
from one or more other faith traditions. This learning is sought for the
sake of fresh theological insights that are indebted to the newly encountered tradition/s as well as the home tradition."[28]

Comparative theological work does not brush aside or undermine
deep dynamic tension concerning religions and their claims for truth; in
the spirit of hospitality they are brought to the dialogue table. That said,
it acknowledges that "there is a tradition at the very heart of [many liv-
ing] . . . faiths which is held common. It is not that precisely the same
doctrines are believed, but that the same tendencies of thought and devo-
tion exist, and are expressed within rather diverse patterns of thought,
characteristic of the faiths in question."[29] Nor does the comparative work
reject tradition, as is typical in modernist epistemology with its alleged
"neutrality" and "objectivity."[30] Rather, remaining "tied to specific communities of faith without being trapped by these communities,"[31] the

27. Jan-Olav Henriksen, *Desire, Gift, and Recognition: Christology and Postmodern Philosophy*
(Grand Rapids: Eerdmans, 2009), 44–45.

28. Francis X. Clooney, SJ, *Comparative Theology* (Chichester, UK: Wiley-Blackwell, 2010),
10, emphasis in original; see also p. 12.

29. Keith Ward, *Images of Eternity: Concepts of God in Five Religious Traditions* (London: Dar-
ton, Longman & Todd, 1987), 1.

30. See Jens Zimmermann, *Incarnational Humanism: A Philosophy of Culture for the Church in
the World* (Downers Grove, IL: InterVarsity Press, 2012), 35–36.

31. Wentzel J. van Huyssteen, *Alone in the World? Human Uniqueness in Science and Theology*
(Grand Rapids: Eerdmans, 2006), 12.

investigation honors contextuality and the locality of human knowledge.[32]

With these theological and attitudinal assets in place, let us consider
whether a hospitable, dialogical relating to the religious other is best
done following the precepts of religious pluralisms or if there is another
way.

RELIGIOUS PLURALISMS IN A
THEOLOGICAL ASSESSMENT

THE PLURALITY OF RELIGIOUS PLURALISMS

Similarly to terms such as "modern" and "postmodern," "pluralism" is
polyvalent and subject to differing interpretations.[33] Notwithstanding
diverse meanings, there is a scholarly consensus that the roots of contemporary pluralistic theologies can be found in the philosophical-reli-
gious views of leading (post-)Enlightenment thinkers from Hume, Kant,
and Hegel to his famed pupil D. F. Strauss and others.[34] Building on
his teacher's idiosyncratic philosophical idealism with "incarnation" as
a formative idea,[35] Strauss's massive two-volume Life of Jesus Critically
Examined widened the manifestation of the divine to encompass in some
way the whole of the human race.[36] In twentieth-century pluralistic
interpretations,[37] this program of nonexclusive Christianity was taken
to its logical end with alleged openness to embrace the religious other
without any demanding Christian identity.

In order to differentiate and analyze forms of pluralism, I have come
to speak of two kinds of families of pluralisms,[38] the first of which is

32. See van Huyssteen, *Alone in the World?*, 36.

33. See G. Larson, "Contra Pluralism," *Soundings: An Interdisciplinary Journal* 73, no. 2/3
(1990): 303–26.

34. For a highly useful recent account, see Netland, *Christianity and Religious Diversity*,
47–54.

35. For an important investigation, see Peter Hodgson, "Hegel's Christology: Shifting
Nuances in the Berlin Lectures," *Journal of the American Academy of Religion* 53, no. 1 (1985):
23–40.

36. David F. Strauss, *The Life of Jesus Critically Examined*, trans. from the 4th German edition
by George Eliot. 2nd ed. in 1 vol. (London: Schwann Sonnenschein; New York: Macmillan,
1892), 779–81; this par. (151) comes under a telling heading, "The Last Dilemma."

37. A leading contemporary example is John Hick, *The Metaphor of God Incarnate: Christology
in a Pluralistic Age* (London: SCM, 1993).

38. For details, see my *Christ and Reconciliation*, chap. 9, and my *Trinity and Revelation: A
Constructive Christian Theology for the Pluralistic World*, vol. 2 (Grand Rapids: Eerdmans, 2014),
chap. 14, respectively.

"first-generation pluralism." It refers to the pluralistic Christian theologies of religions that arose in the second half of the last century, building on the modernist epistemology and ethos, as briefly noted above. These emerged both in the Global North (by the Protestant John Hick and the Roman Catholic Paul F. Knitter, among others)[39] and in Asia (by the Protestants Stanley Samartha and M. M. Thomas, as well as the Roman Catholic Aloysius Pieris, among others).[40] Even those coming from Asian soil, while shaped by the multireligious context of that continent, draw their main inspiration from the European Enlightenment and its subsequent developments, including classical liberalism. They represent by and large the replacement of Christocentrism with theocentrism.

Although what I call "second-generation pluralists" share a common vision with their predecessors, namely, negotiating the interfaith impasse of exclusivism, their approach differs significantly in that they do not make the rejection of a particularly religious identity the primary goal, nor do they intentionally try to subsume the religious other under their own explanation but rather make every effort to honor both identities. The late Hindu-Christian Catholic Raimon Panikkar, half Indian, half Spanish, and the American Baptist S. Mark Heim represent those orientations in their own distinctive ways. The key asset in these second-generation pluralisms is not only a tolerance toward diversity but even its enthusiastic embrace. Indeed, they argue that religions may be so fundamentally different that for a pluralism to be really *pluralism*, differences should not be denied nor seen as an obstacle. In Heim's case, it even leads to an affirmation of diverse religious ends to adherents of different religions.[41] Ultimately, however, against their best intentions, I fear even the second-generation pluralists end up compromising Christian identity in a way that is beneficial neither to the Christian church nor to the religious other.

So, what are the liabilities and problems of pluralistic ideologies when relating to the religious other? Why do they eventually lead to an impasse and fail to deliver lofty promises?

---

39. In *Christ and Reconciliation*, chap. 9, I have engaged the American Roman Catholic Knitter's eco-liberationist pluralism particularly from the perspective of Christology.

40. In *Christ and Reconciliation*, chap. 9, I have engaged the Sri Lankan Roman Catholic Pieris's liberationist pluralism particularly from the perspective of Christology.

41. Mark S. Heim, *The Depth of the Riches: A Trinitarian Theology of Religious Ends* (Grand Rapids: Eerdmans, 2000); for a critical engagement, see my *Trinity and Religious Pluralism: The Doctrine of the Trinity in Christian Theology of Religions* (Aldershot, UK: Ashgate, 2004), chap. 9 (see also chap. 8 on Panikkar).

HEALING THE BROKEN PROMISES OF PLURALISM(S)

The leading Roman Catholic comparative theologian of England, Gavin D'Costa, has offered a sharp criticism of pluralisms, particularly of what I call the first-generation type; this essay endorses his critique. D'Costa considers pluralisms at their core to be representations of modernity's "hidden gods." Ultimately, these pluralisms fail to deliver the promises of the Enlightenment: "Despite their intentions to encourage openness, tolerance, and equality they fail to attain these goals (on their own definition) because of the tradition-specific nature of their positions." Why so? Because, "in granting a type of equality to all religions, [the Enlightenment] ended up denying public truth to any and all of them."[42] Not for nothing, D'Costa laments the fact that even though pluralists present themselves as honest "brokers to disputing parties," they in fact conceal the fact "that they represent yet another party which invites the disputants to leave their parties and join the pluralist one, namely, liberal modernity." In the true sense of the word, this represents a concealed form of exclusivism and even "liberal intolerance."[43]

With D'Costa, I contend that the remedy to pluralisms is not exclusivism but rather an attitude that takes delight in the potential of an encounter with the other without denying either party's distinctive features. "The other is always interesting in their difference and may be the possible face of God, or the face of violence, greed, and death. Furthermore, the other may teach Christians to know and worship their own trinitarian God more truthfully and richly."[44] The aim is to make room for a "critical, reverent, and open engagement with otherness, without any predictable outcome."[45] That kind of engagement does not water down real differences, as happens when modernity's epistemology is followed. Too easily, pluralisms tend to deny the self-definitions of particular religions and to do so from a distance.[46]

In contrast to these flattening tendencies of pluralisms, I recommend an approach aiming at openness that becomes "taking history seriously." Differences are honored rather than dismissed or suspended. Tolerance,

42. Gavin D'Costa, *The Meeting of Religions and the Trinity* (Maryknoll, NY: Orbis, 2000), 1–2.

43. D'Costa, *Meeting of Religions*, 20, 22, 24 (24). See also my "The Future of Pluralisms—and Why They Likely Will Fail," in *Christianity and Religious Plurality: Historical and Global Perspectives*, ed. Wilbert R. Shenk and Richard J. Plantinga (Eugene, OR: Cascade, 2016), 284–309.

44. D'Costa, *Meeting of Religions*, 9.

45. D'Costa, *Meeting of Religions*, 9.

46. See further D'Costa, "Christian Theology and Other Religions: An Evaluation of John Hick and Paul Knitter," *Studia Missionalia* 42 (1993): 161–78, and Hick's response, "Possibility of Religious Pluralism," in *Studia Missionalia* 42 (1993): 161–66.

rather than denying tradition-specific claims for truth—which in itself, ironically, is one more truth claim among others—becomes the "qualified establishment of civic religious freedom for all on the basis of Christian revelation and natural law." Equality becomes the "equal and inviolable dignity of all persons," which naturally leads to taking the other seriously, dialoguing with the other with willingness to learn from the other and teach the other.[47]

Plurality and diversity of religions itself is not the problem. On the contrary, ultimately it is the case that "for a religious person, to accept disagreement is to see it as within the providence of God"—even disagreement due to diversity of religious beliefs and convictions. Religions are not here without God's permission and allowance. The continuing challenge, particularly for the staunch monotheist, is how to reconcile the existence of one's own deeply felt (God-given?) beliefs with different, often opposite, kinds of convictions.[48] This calls for careful reflection on interfaith hospitality that also allows convictions and identities.

A TRINITARIAN THEOLOGY OF INTERFAITH HOSPITALITY OF WITNESS AND DIALOGUE

THE TRINITARIAN SHAPE OF INTERFAITH ENGAGEMENT

In keeping with the vision of a truly Trinitarian ecclesiology (attempted in my *Hope and Community*, Part II)—following the Trinitarian unfolding of Christian theology at-large—Trinity is a proper framework for interfaith dialogue and hospitality.[49] In the triune God there is both unity and plurality, communion and diversity. The Trinity as communion allows room for both genuine diversity (otherwise we could not talk about the Trinity) and unity (otherwise we could not talk about one God). The Trinity "unites transcendence and immanence, creation and redemption," thus facilitating true dialogue.[50]

Many problems in theologies of religions derive from a less-

47. For a brief statement, see D'Costa, *Meeting of Religions*, 13.

48. Ward, *Religion and Community*, 25, emphasis in original.

49. This section borrows directly from my two earlier essays, "Theologies of Religions," in *Witnessing to Christ in a Pluralistic World: Christian Mission among Other Faiths*, ed. Lalsangkima Pachuau and Knud Jørgensen, Edinburgh 2010 Studies (London: Regnum, 2011), 110–18, and "Theologies of Religions," *Evangelical Interfaith Dialogue* 1, no. 2 (Fall 2011): 3–7, available at https://tinyurl.com/yd7zzrqm.

50. Risto Jukko, *Trinitarian Theology in Christian-Muslim Encounters: Theological Foundations of the Work of the French Roman Catholic Church's Secretariat for Relations with Islam* (Helsinki: Luther-Agricola-Society, 2001), 221.

than-satisfactory conception of the Trinity, including the typical plural-istic pitfalls of turning to "theocentrism" in an effort to replace Jesus as the Way, or turning to the "Spirit" in order to get around the central-ity of Jesus and the Father, as if the Spirit's ministry were independent from the other Trinitarian members. Similarly failing are approaches to other religions and mission that have a tendency to minimize the church and only speak of the kingdom of God and the building of the kingdom as the only goal.[51] That constitutes a failure to recognize the fact that the kingdom, the rule of God, is in itself a Trinitarian process: the Son comes in the power of the Spirit to usher in the Father's righteous rule, graciously allowing the church, the body of Christ, to participate in its coming. Of course, the kingdom is far wider than the church; but the church serves as a sign, anticipation, and tool of the coming rule of God.

Borrowing from the biblical scholar Walter Brueggemann, I make the term "other" a verb to remind us of the importance of seeing the reli-gious other not as a counterobject but rather as a partner in "othering," which is "the risky, demanding, dynamic process of relating to one that is not us."[52] What matters is the capacity to listen to the distinctive testi-mony of the other, to patiently wait upon the other, and to make a safe space for him or her. Similarly, that kind of encounter gives the Christ-ian an opportunity to share the distinctive testimony of the love of God. An important aspect of the process of "othering" is to resist the tendency, so prevalent in secular societies of the Global North and in the various forms of religious pluralisms, to draw the other under one's own world explanation and thus deny the existence and possibility of genuine dif-ferences among religions. It is an act of insult rather than a sign of tol-erance to tell the believer of another faith that—contrary to his or her own self-understanding—no real differences exist in beliefs, doctrines, and ultimate ends.

RELATIONAL ENGAGEMENT

In a profound reflection titled "The Holy Spirit's Invitation to Relational Engagement,"[53] D'Costa speaks of the Spirit's call to "relational engage-ment." Other religions are important for the Christian church in that they help the church penetrate more deeply into the divine mystery and so also enrich their own spirituality and insight. While testifying to the

---

51. See my *Christ and Reconciliation*, 231–35.
52. Walter Brueggemann, *The Covenanted Self: Explorations in Law and Covenant* (Minneapo-lis: Augsburg Fortress, 1999), 1.
53. Section title in D'Costa, *Meeting of Religions*, 109.

salvation in Christ, the Trinitarian openness toward other religions fosters the acknowledgment of the gifts of God in other religions by virtue of the presence of the Spirit—as well as the critical discernment of these gifts by the power of the same Spirit. "If the Spirit is at work in the religions, then the gifts of the Spirit need to be discovered, fostered, and received into the church. If the church fails to be receptive, it may be unwittingly practicing cultural and religious idolatry."[54] This kind of mutual engagement holds great promise. In the words of the postcolonial feminist Mayra Rivera, there is the "possibility of transformation . . . in the encounter with the transcendence in the flesh of the Other."[55] Similarly, another postcolonial feminist, Luce Irigaray, speaks of "touching which respects the other."[56]

What might more specifically be some "practical" implications of this theological framework for the church's mission and existence in a pluralistic and secular world of the third millennium? Although they are too often juxtaposed with each other, there is ecumenical consensus that mission and dialogue, proclamation and interfaith engagement belong together and are not alternatives: "In mission there is place both for the proclamation of the good news of Jesus Christ and for dialogue with people of other faiths,"[57] including common service, healing, and reconciliation,[58] in keeping with the multilayered ministry of the missional communion.[59]

In accord with this ecumenical consensus, the recent Catholic interreligious document "Dialogue and Proclamation" encapsulates in a few pregnant sentences a holistic understanding of interfaith engagement by listing the principal elements of mission in terms of Christian "presence and witness; commitment to social development and human liberation; liturgical life, prayer and contemplation; interreligious dialogue;

---

54. D'Costa, *Meeting of Religions*, 115.

55. Mayra Rivera, *The Touch of Transcendence: A Postcolonial Theology of God* (Louisville: Westminster John Knox, 2007), 118.

56. Luce Irigaray, *I Love to You: Sketch of a Possible Felicity in History*, trans. Alison Martin (New York: Routledge, 1996), 124.

57. "Mission and Evangelism in Unity Today," #61 in *"You Are the Light of the World" (Matthew 5:14): Statements on Mission by the World Council of Churches, 1980–2005*, ed. Jacques Matthey (Geneva: WCC, 2005), 59–89; so also *Christian Witness in a Multi-Religious World: Recommendations for Conduct*, World Council of Churches, Pontifical Council for Interreligious Dialogue, World Evangelical Alliance, 2011.

58. Ulrich Duchrow and Franz J. Hinkelammert, *Transcending Greedy Money: Interreligious Solidarity for Just Relations* (New York: Palgrave Macmillan, 2012).

59. Consult also Veli-Matti Kärkkäinen and Michael Karim, "Community and Witness in Transition: Newbigin's Missional Ecclesiology between Modernity and Postmodernity," in *The Gospel and Pluralism Today: Reassessing Lesslie Newbigin in the 21st Century*, ed. Scott W. Sunquist and Amos Yong (Downers Grove, IL: InterVarsity, 2015), 71–100.

and finally, proclamation and catechesis." The document stresses that "proclamation and dialogue are thus both viewed, each in its own place, as component elements and authentic forms of the one evangelizing mission of the Church. They are both oriented towards the communication of salvific truth."[60] In other words, interfaith dialogue includes and makes space for both proclamation, with a view to persuasion by the power of truth and love, and dialogue, with a view to facilitating mutual understanding, reconciliation, and harmony.

LAST WORDS: WITNESS, DIALOGUE, AND TOLERANCE AS THE WAY FORWARD

As mentioned, religious plurality in itself is not the problem for the church. On the contrary, as the British comparative theologian Keith Ward brilliantly puts it, ultimately it is the case that "for a religious person, to *accept* disagreement is to see it as within the providence of God—even disagreement due to diversity of religious beliefs and convictions. Religions and secularism are not here without God's permission and allowance. The continuing challenge, particularly for the staunch monotheist, has to do with how to reconcile the existence of one's own deeply felt (God-given?) beliefs with different, often opposite, kinds of convictions."[61] In this respect I find useful and fully affirm the veteran American evangelical philosopher and missiologist H. Netland's wise principles for how to do witnessing in our kind of world:

1. Bearing witness to the gospel of Jesus Christ among religious others is not optional but is rather obligatory for the Christian church.

2. Christians are to bear witness to the gospel in accordance with God's love.

3. Christian witness must be respectful of others and be conducted with humility and moral integrity.

4. Christian witness should include appropriate forms of interreligious dialogue.

5. Christians are to reject violence and the abuse of power in witness.[62]

60. Pontifical Council for Inter-Religious Dialogue, "Dialogue and Proclamation" (May 19, 1991); available at https://tinyurl.com/435qjs.
61. Ward, *Religion and Community*, 25.

A true dialogue does not mean giving up one's truth claims but rather entails patient and painstaking investigation of real differences and similarities. The purpose of the dialogue is not necessarily to soften the differences among religions but rather to clarify similarities and differences as well as issues of potential convergence and of impasse. A successful and fruitful dialogue often ends up in mutual affirmation of differences, divergent viewpoints, and varying interpretations.

The contemporary secular mindset often mistakenly confuses tolerance with lack of commitment to any belief or opinion. That is to misunderstand the meaning of the term "tolerance." Derived from the Latin term meaning "to bear a burden," tolerance is needed when real differences are allowed. Tolerance means patient and painstaking sharing, listening, and comparing notes—as well as the willingness to respectfully and lovingly make space for continuing differences.[63] To foster tolerance and heal conflicts between religions, in collaboration with representatives of other faiths of goodwill, Christians should do their best to help governments and other authorities to secure a safe, noncoercive place for adherents of religions to present their testimonies without fear.

The late missionary bishop Lesslie Newbigin reminds us that while for Christians the gospel is a "public truth," it has nothing to do with a desire to return to the Christendom model in which the state seeks to enforce beliefs.[64] That should be unacceptable to all religions. In a truly pluralist society, decision for beliefs can never be a matter of power-based enforcement. When Christians, Muslims, Hindus, Buddhists, Sikhs, Confucians, and followers of other faiths can without fear and threat meet each other in a free "marketplace" of beliefs and ideologies, genuine missionary encounters are also possible.[65] Importantly, the famed American Catholic Hindu-expert and comparative theologian Francis Clooney reminds us that engaging not only the diversity within the globalizing Christian church but also the religious diversity is a huge challenge. It takes us often to the edge not only of our intellectual capacities but also of our emotional comfort zones. Clooney puts it well:

62. Netland, *Christianity and Religious Diversity*, 234–42.

63. A highly useful discussion is Netland, *Encountering Religious Pluralism*, chap. 4.

64. For details, see my "The Church in the Post-Christian Society between Modernity and Late Modernity: L. Newbigin's Post-Critical Missional Ecclesiology," in *Theology in Missionary Perspective: Lesslie Newbigin's Legacy*, ed. Mark T. B. Laing and Paul Weston (Eugene, OR: Pickwick, 2013), 125–54.

65. See the WCC document "Religious Plurality and Christian Self-Understanding," #27 (February 14, 2006); available at https://tinyurl.com/ydawrcmf.

If we are attentive to the diversity around us, near us, we must deny ourselves the easy confidences that keep the other at a distance. But, as believers, we must also be able to defend the relevance of the faith of our community, deepening our commitments even alongside other faiths that are flourishing nearby. We need to learn from other religious possibilities, without slipping into relativist generalizations. The tension between open-mindedness and faith, diversity and traditional commitment, is a defining feature of our era, and neither secular society nor religious authorities can make simple choices before us.[66]

66. Clooney, *Comparative Theology*, 7.

PART IV

Text and Context

11.

Engaging the Context of the Tower of Babel and Listening to the Voices in the Text

ARCHIE LEE

TEXT, CONTEXT, AND CON/TEXTUAL INTERPRETATION

The word pair "text and context" has been around and extensively adopted in articulating the rationality and legitimacy of doing theology in regional and local settings around the world, and it is especially the case in Asian theological construction since the 1960s. Theological imagination in modern days could hardly become possible, and therefore meaningfully relevant, without the notion of "text" and the awareness of "context," as well as the genuine engagement of the two. In this volume dedicated to an outstanding Asian theologian, Shoki Coe, there is no way not to recognize the pioneering role he played in impacting the religious thinking and theological methodology in Asia, which are, in one way or the other, the effect and result of his call for the renewal of Christian formation and theological education in terms of "contextuality and contextualization."[1] Coe raised the important idea of "text and context" in the inaugural address of the Northeast Asia Association of Theological Schools in 1966 and he further explained the perception of the notion of a "double wrestle" that involves "textual cum contextual criticism" in "wrestling with the Text from which all texts are derived and to which they point, in order to be faithful to it in context; and wrestling

---

1. Shoki Coe, "Contextualization as the Way Toward Reform," *Recollections and Reflections*, intro. and ed. Boris Anderson (New York: The Rev. Dr. Shoki Coe's Memorial Fund, 1993, 2nd ed.), 267–75. The article is an extract of Part II and III of Coe's paper in *Theological Education* (Summer 1963), the Association of Theological Schools in the United States and Canada, 237–43.

with the context in which the reality of the Text is at work, in order to be relevant to it."[2]

This article intends to apply the dynamics of text and context to biblical studies and to demonstrate the fruitful engagement of the "double wrestling" in the rereading of the story of tower of Babel in Genesis 11. It is now well recognized by scholars that the biblical text must not only be interpreted contextually in its literary and historical context, readers must also be invited to listen to the plurality of voices in the text. There are also other texts co-opted by the present passage under study. These "texts" are adopted, subverted, and transformed in a rewritten form to constitute the text as we have it in the tower of Babel story.

Scholars have long noted the difficulties of the conventional reading of the story of the tower of Babel in Genesis 11 as mainly an account of the diversity of language and human dispersion in the world. Such a reading undermines the richness of the multiplicity of languages and the challenge of the plurality of cultures, perceiving these social realities as divine punishment for human hubris. The biblical God is strangely, and perhaps very unfortunately, portrayed as a timid and easily scared deity whose heavenly abode does not stand any human act of constructing a structure on earth with "its head high in heaven" (11:4).

This overall view of the "confusion of tongues" and "dispersion" of the human race[3] as an explanation for the origin of languages and diversities of human communities, which are interpreted as "a divine judgment on the presumptuous impiety,"[4] has been persistently upheld in general, even among critical, textual critics. However, this reading is in contradiction with the previous chapter of Genesis 10 in which diversity of human races, languages, communities, and division into tribes and social groups on the face of the earth are explicitly stated (10:5, 20, 31). Genesis 10 understands racial, cultural, and linguistic diversities as a matter of natural fact in the so-called "Table of Nations" in the postdiluvian expansion and multiplication of the descendants of Noah's three sons, Shem, Ham, and Japheth after they left the Ark.

The majority of interpreters reading Genesis 10–11 in the literary sequence did not fail to see the introduction and presentation of the con-

2. Coe, "Contextualization as the Way Toward Reform," 268. He points out that the term "double wrestle" was the theme of the Consultation on Theological Education held in Indonesia a year or two before then.

3. Hermann Gunkel separates the passage into two distinct legends, one on the name Babel (city recension) and the other on a certain memory of some ruined tower (tower recension), *Genesis, Translated & Interpreted*, trans. Mark E. Biddle (Macon, GA: Mercer University Press, 1997), 94–99.

4. See John Skinner, *Critical and Exegetical Commentary on Genesis* (Edinburgh: T&T Clark, 1930), 223.

temporary empires as perceived by the biblical author(s)/redactor(s) at the time of writing or redacting. The narrator of the tower of Babel specifically mentions in the beginning the locality of "Shinar" where the story takes place. The name is first listed as a place ruled by the first hunter and empire-builder named Nimrod. Ancient readers, such as Josephus, have already pointed out the identification of Nimrod among the descendants of Ham with the kingdom of the Babylonians and the Assyrians whose major cities, Babel, Erech, Accad, and Calneh are in the land of Shinar.

> And Cush begot Nimrod; he began to be a mighty one in the earth.
>
> He was a mighty hunter before the Lord; wherefore it is said: 'Like Nimrod a mighty hunter before the Lord.'
>
> And the beginning of his kingdom was Babel, and Erech, and Accad, and Calneh, in the land of Shinar. (Gen 10:6–10)

In *Antiquities of the Jews*, Josephus proposes that it was Nimrod who led the people astray against God and became an oppressive power by turning his government into one of tyrannical rule. It was also understood that he led the people astray from God and had in mind the building of a high tower.

> Now it was Nimrod who excited them to such an affront and contempt of God. He was the grandson of Ham, the son of Noah, a bold man, and of great strength of hand. He persuaded them not to ascribe it to God, as if it was through his means they were happy, but to believe that it was their own courage which procured that happiness. He also gradually changed the government into tyranny, seeing no other way of turning men from the fear of God, but to bring them into a constant dependence on his power. He also said he would be revenged on God, if he should have a mind to drown the world again; for that he would build a tower too high for the waters to be able to reach! and that he would avenge himself on God for destroying their forefathers![5]

This interpretation of Josephus has been noted by scholars interested in the theme of the Bible and the "empires," especially those in the field of postcolonial studies who have drawn our attention to the oppressive tower builder and the imposition of one-language policy in the Babel

5. Flavius Josephus, *The Genuine Works of Flavius Josephus: Containing Five Books of the Antiquities of the Jews* (New York: Duyckinck, 1810), book I, chap. 4. See a recent discussion on Josephus's discourses of Jewish history, Gottfried Mader, *Josephus and the Politics of Historiography: Apologetic and Impression Management in the Bellum Judaicum* (Leiden: Brill, 2000).

story.[6] But there has not been any reading in identifying who the speakers and the builders are and their relationship. The story begins with narrating a migrating community: "And it came to pass, as they journeyed east, that they found a plain in the land of Shinar; and they dwelt there" (Gen 11:2). This group of people then is concerned with settling down and building houses: "Come, let us make bricks . . ." Would this group of new migrants be interested first and foremost in building a tower with its top in heaven while they had to adapt to the new building material of clay in the new environment? In order to settle down in the new place, they had to learn the new technology of building houses with bricks and slime and to adjust to the different ways of living in a brick culture ("And they had brick for stone, and slime had they for mortar," Gen 11:3). In what ways were these new settlers identified with the construction of the city and the tower of Babel, especially in respect to the interpretation of Josephus and most contemporary scholars in linking up the city with the great Babylon and its impressive and gigantic structure of the ziggurat? Why was the human proposal a project God must take the action of descending to earth to reject and stop completely? This paper will address these questions by rereading the text with a special attentive ear to the three speeches of "let us . . ." (. . .נ הָבָה, Havah n . . .). I will start with the contextual issue of how the colonial and triumphal reading of the tower of Babel story was interpreted by the Protestant missionaries who went to China and how they rendered the Chinese culture they encountered into a rebellious and idolatrous other. They demonized the Chinese and their language in terms of the negative traditional understanding of the tower of Babel. The Chinese were present at Babel and punished by God with the dispersion and confusion of tongues. Being expelled from Babel, they finally ended up in China, carrying with them the idols and the sin of an attitude of pride from Babel. Chinese scholars would be shocked by the missionaries' understanding of non-Christian cultures being evil and rebellious to God and that they bear the burden of being punished by God to disperse from West Asia to the East. The very fact that these people speak many languages alien to the missionaries was taken as an indication of God's punishment of sin at Babel. This paper is therefore a genuine quest for an alternative reading of the context and listening to the voices in the text in Genesis 11:1–9 in order to better understand the text in context and to counteract the colonial interpretation represented by some missionaries to China.

---

6. *Philip Chia*, "On Naming the Subject: Postcolonial Reading of *Daniel* 1," *The Postcolonial Biblical Reader*, ed. Rasiah S. Sugirtharajah (Oxford: Blackwell, 2006), 171–84.

THE TOWER OF BABEL IN CHINA AS INTERPRETED
BY MISSIONARIES

Some Christian missionaries of the colonial era in Asia used to characterize and even demonize the so-called "pagan culture" and its "strange religious practices" by applying their preconceived negative aspects of the church's interpretation of the Bible to religio-cultural matters in the mission field. Those who came to China are examples of how some missionaries superimposed their interpretation onto the culture of China, which was often seen as embodying abomination and idolatry. Colonial discourse constructs forms of racial/cultural/historical otherness in terms of differences, foreignness, and impurity. Some of the missionaries described the people in the mission field in binary terms of "us-and-them"[7] as we will see in the following paragraphs. The Chinese were often perceived as the opposite of the Christian West and were therefore dealt with as the cultural and religious "other." They represented transgression and corruption and were urgently in need of conversion to the Christian gospel, which provides the only salvation brought from the Christian West. A few Western missionaries redefined and hence also exercised their manipulation of the Chinese culture and its people as a homogeneous entity consisting of a sinful and backward people left from Babel. Such colonial mindset has the tendency of perceiving the story of the tower of Babel as a powerful image to highlight the irreconcilable cultural and linguistic differences between the Christian West and the gentile East.

A couple of examples will bring out the colonial, imperialistic reading of the Bible in the Chinese context. The first is taken from the writing of Andrew Patton Happer (1818–1894), the founder of the Canton Christian College in 1886 and a missionary educator to Guangzhou. During his visit to Beijing (Peking), he was amazed to find points of similarities and contrasts between the imperial worship at the Altars of Heaven, Earth, Sun, Moon, and the Gods of the Grain and the Land.[8] He further tried to make sense of his observation of the alien other by rereading, in the Chinese context, the canonical biblical text, which to him had great authority and explanatory power. "The most natural surmise to account for these striking resemblances of the forms of worship, in countries so remotely separated, is this: that the forms of worship were carried by

---

7. Edward Said, *Orientalism* (New York: Vintage, 1978), 299, 335.
8. A. P. Happer, "A Visit to Peking," *Chinese Recorder* 10 (1879): 23–47.

the ancestors of the several people at their dispersion from the Tower of Babel, as they came down to them from their common ancestor Noah."[9]

Andrew Happer was one of the earliest missionaries sent to China by the American Presbyterian Mission, North (AP) in Philadelphia. He arrived in Macau on October 22, 1844 to begin his work in establishing a boarding school for boys in 1845. Three years later he moved with another missionary named John Booth French to Guangzhou and opened a few churches in the city from 1860 to 1890. Since Happer was trained as a medical doctor at the University of Pennsylvania (M.D., 1844) in addition to his theological education at the Western Theological Seminary, he involved himself in building churches, hospitals, medical schools, and nursing schools in Guangzhou and nearby regions. He also contributed a lot to the field of education by establishing a university and two secondary schools, one for boys (Pui Ying School) and another for girls (True Light Girls School) and the Canton Christian College (renamed Lingnan College in 1907), all of which are still in operation in Hong Kong. His publications include *Questions and Answers in Astronomy*, the first Chinese book on astronomy, *The Religion of China* (1881), *Influence of the College in the Civilization of the World* (1895), and *A Visit to Peking* (1889); in addition, he was the editor of *Chinese Recorder* in 1880–84.[10]

Learning of the intellectual and educational background of Happer, one can be sure that his position to reckon Chinese ancestors as unrepentant descendants from the tower of Babel was not one of ignorance, but a deliberate imposition showing, in Edward Said's terminology, both forms of orientalism: the latent and the manifested.[11] As a missionary, his aim was to convert the Chinese and to turn them from an inferior, rebellious, and idolatrous disposition. He applied the traditional negative interpretation of the Babel story to the Chinese and saw them as a sinful residue from Babel. From the colonizer's point of view, the way of salvation for the Chinese was to overcome and conquer their sinful culture by eliminating the evil element inherited and passed on from ancient times to the present day.

The second example is furnished by Thomas Booth McClatchie

9. Happer, "A Visit to Peking," 43.
10. Loren W. Crabtree, "Andrew P. Happer and Presbyterian Missions in China, 1844–1891," *Journal of Presbyterian History* 62 (1984): 19–34. See also R. G. Tiedemann, "Happer, Andrew Patton, 1818–1894," *Ricci Roundtable: Biographies*, https://tinyurl.com/ybnz587r.
11. Said makes a distinction between two forms of orientalism: the latent and the manifest. The former refers to the unconscious certainty of what the Orient really is while the latter points to orientalism being spoken and acted upon. See his book *Orientalism*, chap. 3, esp. p. 206. For further discussion of the two terms see Karl-Heinz Mayer, *Latent and Manifest Orientalism as Seen by Edward Said and His Critics* (Munich: Grin, 2014).

(1814–1885), the founder of the Church Missionary Society in China. He went further than Happer in his interpretation of the Babel story and its relevant application to the Chinese. He sought to find an explanation for the unusually strange and peculiarly queer language that the Chinese speak. Obviously, Chinese is a very difficult language to learn for Western missionaries, though a lot of them have mastered the language quite well. McClatchie was of the opinion that the Chinese were heavily punished at Babel, and with the curse of the confusion of language they were dispersed to China. They had some memories of what happened at Babel and had the same attitude of arrogance and ambition. He further took the Temple of Heaven at Beijing as "the local transcript of the tower of Babel."[12] The Chinese are blamed for reproducing pagan worship of Babel in Beijing, though there is no mention of idols or idolatry in Genesis 11 in its telling of the tower of Babel story. From the textual studies of the chapter, any notion of the sin of the people at Babel as being idolatry must be challenged.

As a matter of fact, McClatchie was well versed in the Chinese language. He went to Shanghai in 1844 as one of the founders of the Church Missionary Society work in China and later became the Canon of St. John's Cathedral in Hong Kong and then Shanghai. He was the first to translate the *Book of Changes* into English in 1876[13] and was convinced that the first two hexagrams referred to phallic worship of the yin and yang in China, which had aroused some scorn and objections. Among those who dismissed McClatchie's work was James Legge, one of the greatest missionary sinologists, who published his own translation six years later. McClatchie also published his book on Confucian Cosmology in 1874.[14]

Homi Bhabha in his "The Other Question" formulates the important feature of colonial discourse in the construction of the other by the concept of "fixity." He characterizes "fixity" as "a paradoxical mode of representation" that "connotes rigidity and an unchanging order as well as disorder, degeneracy and daemonic repetition."[15] Colonial discourse uses stereotype as its major discursive strategy to assert "an ambivalent mode of knowledge" of the object—"that otherness which is at once an object of desire and derision, an articulation of difference contained within the

---

12. Thomas McClatchie, "Paganism, v," *Chinese Recorder* 8, 56.

13. Thomas McClatchie, *A Translation of the Confucian Yik King or the Classic of Change* (Shanghai and London).

14. Thomas McClatchie, *A Translation of Section Forty-Nine of the Complete Works of Philosopher Choo-Foo-Tze.*

15. Homi Bhabha, "The Other Question," in *Contemporary Postcolonial Theory: A Reader*, ed. Padmini Mongia (London: Arnold, 1996), 37.

fantasy of origin and identity."[16] R. S. Sugirtharajah, a Sri Lankan scholar who worked at Birmingham on postcolonial criticism and the Bible, uses "the collusion between colonialism and exegesis"[17] to characterize the Eurocentric construction of Christian origins. How often it is for biblical interpretation to collaborate with a colonialist perspective to foster a negative view of the cultures of the colonized other and to promote the monistic attitude of Western expansionist Christians! These two examples of missionary interpretation of Chinese culture from the traditional doctrinal perspective of the tower of Babel well illustrate the colonial superimposition of Western superiority and imperial attitude. The other is always looked upon as inferior and backward. There is a need to read the biblical text from the other side and the underside, paying attention to the voices of the weak and oppressed in the text. Texts are historically and culturally conditioned and their complexities should always alert us readers to exercise our hermeneutics of suspicion to expose hegemonic discourses, and to take a critical view of the colonial subjugation of the native by powerful empires.

AN INTERPRETATION OF THE TOWER OF BABEL
AS POLYPHONIC TEXT

There have been quite a lot of studies on the tower of Babel story in Genesis. Major critical issues range from whether the text in Genesis 11:1–9 is to be seen as a unity or a combination of literary sources[18] to that of whether the nature of the sin of the people be regarded as pride or read as the deliberate refusal to disperse to fill the earth as commended by God.[19] Scholars have also noted the issue of the West Asian (Ancient Near Eastern) background of the tower as referring to the Babylonian ziggurat. In this case, the whole narrative has, therefore, been understood as embodying a satire and mocking perspective targeted at the Babylonian pride of the city's temple having its top in heaven. Reference is often

16. Bhabha, "The Other Question," 38.
17. R. S. Sugirtharajah, *Postcolonial Reconfigurations: An Alternative Way of Reading the Bible and Doing Theology* (St. Louis: Chalice, 2003), 13.
18. H. Gunkel, *Genesis Die Urgeschichte und die Patriarchen (Das erste Buch Moses)* (Göttingen: 1911), 95–98. Based on the doublets of building a city and a tower; God coming down twice (11:5 and 11:7); and the two accounts of confusing of language and scattering of the people, H. Gunkel concludes that there are two layers: city recension (11:1, 3a, 4[part], 5, 6a, 7, 8b, 9a) and tower recension (11:2, 3b, 4[part], 5, 6b, 8a, 9b). See also Claus Westermann, *Genesis 1–11, A Commentary*, trans. John J. Scullion, SJ (Minneapolis: Augsburg, 1974), 536–40.
19. P. J. Harland, "Vertical or Horizontal: The Sin of Babel," *Vetus Testamentum* 48 (1998): 515–33.

made to *Enuma Elish* for its temple and tower building project in line
55–64.[20] The Babylonian connection is taken as confirmed by Gordon
Wenham, who points to the brickmaking technique in contrast to the
use of stone for construction by the Canaanites.[21]

There are quite a few scholars who are not satisfied with the traditional
approach and the doctrinal conclusion and seek to come to the text from
a liberation perspective.[22] But there has not been anyone, as far as one
can tell, who ventures to make a distinction between the two "Let us
. . ." in Genesis 11:3–4. Scholars take the two lines as from the same
speaker and representing the same community. My experience of the
discussions on the return of Hong Kong's sovereignty to China and the
subsequent debates on political reforms on the future of Hong Kong has
taught me the hard reality of conflicts and the difference in power relationship within the same community.[23] The literary expression and linguistic features of the text of Genesis 11:1–9 also support the reading of
a possible differentiation of the speaking subjects in the narrative.

There are three short speeches that begin with "Come, let us . . ." (הָבָה
נ, Havah n . . .) (vv. 3, 4, 7). The first one comes from the "they" in
verse 2, who "found a plain in the land Shinar, and they dwelt there."
They are the new settlers who "journeyed east" and arrived at Shinar.
The story does not tell us who they are and where they come from. Shinar is the only geographical reference. It may be productive if we go
to some intertextual passages to see how Shinar is being perceived and
remembered by the authors of biblical writings. In the Abraham story
there is a description of the battles between the four kings and the five
kings; one of them is the king of Shinar (Gen 14:9). John Sasson is of
the opinion that it is a general name referring to Sumer and Akkad.[24]
But this geographical term may embody more than the physical plain in
Mesopotamia. It may remind the first listener of the story of some experiences of bitterness and griefs as to the people of Israel who experienced
the exile. Shinar is not only in a foreign land, but also a name of shame
and pain as it brings about memories of the exilic suffering in the hands

20. James Pritchard, ed., *Ancient Near Eastern Texts Relating to the Old Testament* (Princeton: Princeton University Press, 1969), 68–69.

21. Gordon J. Wenham, *Genesis 1–15* (Waco, TX: Word, 1987), 237.

22. Severino Croatto, "A Reading of Story of the Tower of Babel from the Perspective of Non-Identity," *Teaching of the Bible: The Discourse and Politics of Biblical Pedagogy*, ed. Fernando Segovia and Mary Ann Tolbert (Maryknoll, NY: Orbis, 1998), 203–23.

23. Archie C. C. Lee, "Biblical Interpretation of the Return in the Postcolonial Hong Kong," *Biblical Interpretation* (Leiden: Brill, 1999): 164–73. (Collected in *Voices from the Margin, Interpreting the Bible in the Third World*, ed. R. S. Sugirtharajah [Maryknoll, NY: Orbis, 2006], 281–96).

24. John Sasson, *From Sumer to Jerusalem: The Forbidden Hypothesis* (Oxford: Intellect Books, 1993), 90–91.

of the empire and it is a constant reminder of the destruction of the temple with its treasure and vessels taken to Shinar:[25]

> In the third year of the reign of King Jehoiakim of Judah, King Nebuchadnezzar of Babylon came to Jerusalem and besieged it. The Lord let King Jehoiakim of Judah fall into his power, as well as some of the vessels of the house of God. These he brought to the land of Shinar, and placed the vessels in the treasury of his gods. (Dan 1:1–2 NRSV)

At the time of the exile there were Israelites who were captured and sent to Shinar. In Isaiah's prophecy there is an assurance of God's gathering of the remnant of Israel from foreign lands, including those in Shinar:

> On that day the Lord will extend his hand yet a second time to recover the remnant that is left of his people, from Assyria, from Egypt, from Pathros, from Ethiopia, from Elam, from Shinar, from Hamath, and from the coastland of the sea. (Isa 11:11 NRSV)

Therefore, the mention of Shinar and the settling there may not bring about a pleasant mood. On the contrary, the accounts may convey the memory of the plight of a people on a journey (בְּנָסְעָם) eastward, encountering a different cultural environment in Shinar. "Come, let us make brick . . ." (11:2) may very likely be an attempt and effort to start a new page of life again in a foreign land.

The third quotation, "let us go down and mix" (11:7), is clearly from God who descended to put a stop to the building project of a city and a tower with its head that reaches heaven. God went down to see the building project and resolved to end the human proposal of city and tower building.

> And the Lord came down to see the city and the tower, which the children of men built.

> And the Lord said: Behold, they are one people, and they have all one language; and this is what they begin to do; and now nothing will be withheld from them, which they purpose to do. (11:5–6)

The speaker of the first speech refers to the people who took a journey and finally arrived at Shinar: "And as they migrated from the east, they came upon the plain in the land of Shinar and settled there" (11:2). They are a people in migration. The word "east" (מִקֶּדֶם), which is used

25. There are scholars who think Shinar is a place of pagan idolatry. See André LaCocque, "Whatever Happened in the Valley of Shinar? A Response to Theodore Hiebert," *JBL* 128 (2009): 32.

twenty-three times in the Hebrew Bible, including five times in the
first thirteen chapters of Genesis (2:8; 3:24; 11:2; 12:8 [×2]; 13:11), is of
much significance, but its presence in the text is often neglected. Scholars have been interested with the text to be rather read as in the Hebrew
Masoretic tradition "from the east" or as in the Greek "to the east." Taking either "from the east" or "to the east," the word "east" resonates with
other appearances of the word in passages that come before and after the
tower of Babel story. The first appearance of מִקֶּדֶם in the Bible is in
the passage on the Garden of Eden: "And the Lord God planted a garden eastward in Eden" (2:8). This is closely linked with the following
chapter where the word is used again in relation to the garden and with
regard to the fate of the human being in the garden: "So God drove out
the human being; and God placed Cherubim at the east of the Garden
of Eden" (3:24). After the third appearance in 11:2 we encounter a double usage of the word in 12:8, a verse that connects with the tower of
Babel story in several ways: "And he (Abram) moved from there (מִשָּׁם)
to a mountain in the east (מִקֶּדֶם) of Beth-El and pitched his tent, having
Beth-El on the west, and Hai on the east (מִקֶּדֶם); and there (שָׁם) he built
(וַיִּבֶן) an altar to the Lord, and called upon the name (בְּשֵׁם) of the Lord"
(12:8). It is interesting that the builders in Babel wish to make a name
for themselves (שֵׁם-לָנוּוְנַעֲשֶׂה) and in Genesis 12 God said to Abraham:
"I will make your name (שְׁמֶךָ) great" (Gen 12:3). It all happens "there"
(שָׁם) in the "East" (מִקֶּדֶם). The last appearance of מִקֶּדֶם in Genesis is
also instructive: "Then Lot chose for himself the valley of Jordan; and
Lot journeyed (וַיִּסַּע) east (מִקֶּדֶם), and they separated (וַיִּפָּרְדוּ) themselves, one from the other" (Gen 13:11). The words "to the east" will
well remind the reader of the reality of being expelled from Eden, and
like Abraham and Lot who are still on the journey and seeking to settle
down. They say to each other: "Come let us make bricks" (11:3). Abraham will not expect to make a name for himself and the nation, but he is
promised to have his name made great by God.

The speakers of the second speech of "Come, let us build for ourselves
a city and a tower . . ." cannot be easily identified by the readers of the
story as being the same as that of the first speech. Before we address the
text and the context of the speech momentarily, let us look at the usage
of "Come, let us . . ." in the Bible besides the three appearances in Genesis 11. It is interesting that the phrase is found only once outside the
tower of Babel story in the Pentateuch, and it is in the Exodus narrative.
It refers to the nameless Pharaoh who says to his people: "Come, let us
deal shrewdly with them . . ." (1:10). He implements his evil scheme of
enslavement of the Israelites. The parallels between the Exodus narrative

and the Babel story are not limited to the literary form of the speech. The specific reference to the hard service in "mortar and brick" in Exodus echoes the story of the tower of Babel. The description of the affliction of the people of Israel in Egypt is similarly framed by the Egyptian oppressor's speech (Come, let us . . . [הָבָה נ], Exod 1:10). It is also in the Exodus story that we hear of God's decision to descend to intervene (I have come down to save [לְהַצִּילוֹ וָאֵרֵד], Exod 3:8). Furthermore, the building project of the Egyptians is also characterized as hard labor (קָשָׁה בַּעֲבֹדָה) in mortar (בְּחֹמֶר) and in brick (בִלְבֵנִים) (Exod 1:14), and both words are used in Genesis 11. Another linguistic resonance is the fear expressed by the Egyptians of the people of Israel—"lest they multiply" (יִרְבֶּה-פֶּן) (Exod 1:10). This echoes a parallel fear of the empire-builder in Genesis 11—"lest we be scattered . . ." (נָפוּץ-פֶּן) (Gen 11:4). These two threats cause real concerns for empires: either we be scattered or the enemies multiply.

The new settlers in the story intend to adapt themselves to the new cultural environment of using bricks for building. The sentence "they had brick for stone and bitumen for mortar" (Gen 11:3) represents the writer's description of the people's former environment of a stone culture and the new context of brick culture. It is also indicative of their memory of exploitation under the Pharaoh's oppressive building project ("made their lives bitter with hard service in mortar and brick and in every kind of field labor," Exod 1:14) and may very well connect the building event in Exodus with that in the Babel story. The people are in forced labor in the empire's building project.

What is therefore proposed is that the second "Come, let us . . ." (Havah n . . .) comes from the empire-builders who force the new settlers into hard labor for empire-building projects and enforce the empire's one-language policy. The story begins with the entire land (not necessarily the whole world as we know it today) having one language (שָׂפָה אֶחָת) and one single project (אֲחָדִים דְּבָרִים). The conventional translations of the two phrases are to take them as referring to the linguistic aspect (NIV: "one language and a common speech"). But the second phrase can well be "the same words," "the same things," "the same events," "the same set of commandments" (Exod 20:1, etc.). These two phrases are used to pinpoint the twofold project of the empire-builder. Eleazar S. Fernandez is right to take "one language" as the "univocal linguistic code of the Babylonian Empire, a code of centralized power and control."[26] He further comments that the empire's building pro-

---

26. Eleazar S. Fernandez, "From Babel to Pentecost: Finding a Home in the Belly of the Empire," *Semeia* 9 (2002): 33.

jects inevitably involve an element of exploitation as gigantic structures are, more often than not, "erected on the back of others, especially the marginalized" and new settlers are "conscripted for the construction of Babylonian projects."[27] The concluding remark of the tower of Babel story ("Therefore it was called Babel, because there the Lord confused the language of the land," v. 9), which resonates with the beginning, is a reorientation, a postcolonial perspective that denounces totalitarianism, absolutism, essentialism, and imperialism. Turning the name Babel (בָּבֶל), the "the Gate of God" (Akkadian bab-ilu) into "balel" (בָּלַל, confusion) is "a surprise to the people of Babylon."[28] The building of the Babylonian tower-temple (ziggurat) is being mocked and it becomes a satire in the eyes of the narrator of the tower of Babel. John Skinner comments that the Babylonian temple tower represents "a meritorious approach to the gods" and it "appealed to the imagination of the nomads as a god-defying work."[29] Skinner further says:

> It is evident that ideas of this order did not emanate from the official religion of Babylonia. They originated rather in the unsophisticated reasoning of nomadic Semites who had penetrated into the country, and formed their own notions about the wonders they beheld there.[30]

The discussion above on the three speeches shows that it is not the innocent nomads penetrating into Shinar in Babylonia who just formed an unsophisticated notion of the tower. The story is told from the perspective of the new settlers who anticipated being liberated from the oppressive power of Babel (Babylon) in its single-language policy and empire-building ambition. While they said to one another, "Come, let us make brick" (v. 3), they were reminded of the oppressive voice of the empire-builders' "come, let us build a tower and a city" (v. 4). What God did was an act of termination of the empire's ambition to establish its power (name) and its building project that exploited the settlers. Since the tower symbolizes, in Fernandez's words, "imperial praxis" that seeks to achieve "perpetuation of the imperial name," God's interference can be taken as a counterproject to "deconstruct the dominant metanarrative."[31]

27. Fernandez, "From Babel to Pentecost," 31.
28. Richard Elliott Friedman, *Commentary on the Torah* (San Francisco: HarperSanFrancisco, 2001), 46.
29. Skinner, *Critical and Exegetical Commentary on Genesis*, 226.
30. Skinner, *Critical and Exegetical Commentary on Genesis*, 228.
31. Fernandez, "From Babel to Pentecost," 32.

CONCLUSION

This article has revisited the three repetitions of "Come, let us . . ." (3, 4, 7) and suggested that they represent three groups of speakers: the migrating community, the oppressing empire-builder, and the divine adjudicator who decides to intervene in the human world. Babel is the contesting site between the enslaving empire, the new settlers, and divine intervention. The sin of the empire is one of totalizing power and monolithic imposition. It is the voice of the weak migrating community in the speech of "Come, let us make bricks" that is immediately overshadowed by the voice of the powerful order of "Come, let us build a tower and a city." Through a postcolonial reading on the text and context of Genesis 11:1–9, this paper recovers the lost voice of the oppressed immigrants in facing the power of the empire-builder. As Sugirtharajah points out, in a postcolonial perspective, it is the first time "the colonized other was placed at the center of academic discourse"[32] in postcolonial studies. Tensions and ambiguities exist among the unidentified "they" who were on a journey to the east and intended to adopt the local building culture of using the local building material for their houses ("Come, let us make . . .), but their life's aspiration was turned into an ambitious voice of the empire (Come, let us build . . .). What God did was a speech-act ("Come, let us go down . . .") of counterproject against the twofold project of the empire-builder as it is introduced in the first verse: "one language" and a "totalizing project." Thus, we are invited to engage with the context of the tower of Babel, listen to the different voices in the text, and make distinction between them as they are being spoken in our daily life today.

---

32. Sugirtharajah, *Postcolonial Reconfigurations*, 13.

12.

Contextual Rereading of the Bible to Construct Hope in a World of Oppression and Marginalization

DHYANCHAND CARR

According to Ray Wheeler,[1] Shoki Coe was one who roiled the pond of missiological thinking in a fast-changing world and came out with brilliant insights on contextualization of the Christian gospel.

When indigenization had become the accepted norm for doing theology in Asia among those who were trying to get out of the Western moorings of theology, Coe saw the trend as not altogether a healthy one. This was because some of their eager attempts to be relevant to the local community resulted in falsely construed theological ideas being assimilated into the gospel. A lively debate began on the extent of syncretism permissible. Another reason why indigenization was inadequate was that theology was not always truly indigenous, as it was sometimes imposed from outside or it was unmindful of the cultural dominations that had religious sanctions in the local contexts. Therefore, even when it came from within there was little willingness to challenge the existing endorsements in hierarchically ordered cultures. Disparities that had cultural sanctions were left untouched and only the indigenization of philosophical and art forms, for example in liturgical music, was attempted. In a place like Tamil Nadu in India, even classical music maintained a Brahmanical exclusivity and snobbishness. Folk music and its instrument, the drum, were anathema to classical music. Some caste converts to Christianity retained their caste names, showing that they would want

1. Ray Wheeler, "The Legacy of Shoki Coe," *International Bulletin of Missionary Research* 26, no. 2 (2002): 77–80.

to maintain their assigned higher status over the majority Dalit Christians.[2]

What comes to my mind, although not specifically mentioned by Coe, is the life of Robert de Nobili, an Italian Jesuit missionary to India who adopted the Brahmanical lifestyle, ostracized himself from local Christian priests of deemed lower-caste origin, and tried to win Brahmin converts. He declared that for one to become a Christian one need not give up his/her caste identity. Such a stance is near blasphemy, as those committed to Dalit theological persuasion would argue. According to conscientized Dalit Christians, the primary purpose of the gospel is to challenge all forms of supremacist consciousness of those who claim to hail from upper-caste backgrounds. Salvation implies humanization by which we hope that a new humanity devoid of the walls of separation would emerge by the grace and power of God's inclusive love that engulfs all human lives. The most important challenge of the gospel as far as the Indian context is concerned, therefore, is to annihilate caste.

Quite a few early missionaries, however, refused to challenge the supremacist caste consciousness among its converts from the caste background and seriously compromised the gospel. Until such time that Christians from the Dalit background had a voice in the church, two separate cups for communion, one for caste Christians and another for Dalit Christians, were used in many places. Therefore Coe was right in saying that all contexts were not in accordance with God's will and that contextualization should include within its ambit the sociocultural and political issues of a place. This is not to say that Coe was opposed to indigenization, but he insisted that we were to live in the present as if we were already living in the hoped-for future. The hoped-for future, of course, is the New Humanity devoid of barriers and social inequalities. So he coined the term "contextualization" and suggested that the work of contextualization was best done by the local community, which was very much part of the context and was well aware of its merits and demerits in the light of the gospel. Therefore contextualization has to be incarnational. Therefore, the local community that is conscious of mission should wrestle with the scripture to discern its meaning and bring the challenge of the gospel call to repent in the full awareness that God is already present in the context. Such a mindset will not make us withdraw

2. Who are the Dalits? The root word "dal" means crushed/trampled upon in Hebrew and Sanskrit. So "Dalit" is a self-designation accepted by the conscientized people whose tasks were deemed polluting and made to live on the outskirts of villages; they were untouchables and were made to walk without slippers and live with many other indignities. Nearly 25 percent of the Indian population belong to this category. An awakening among them was created chiefly by Dr. B. R. Ambedkar, the Chairperson of the Constituent Assembly, who declared that Dalits are not Hindus.

from the world but, on the contrary, impel us to delve into the context and be incarnate in the context in order that the gospel challenge to participate with repentance in the making of the not-yet-of-God's-future becomes a reality. The task is not just theological; it has to impact the sociopolitical realities of the context as well.

True to the perception of contextualization that he advocated, Coe himself was very much involved in the self-determination struggle to make Taiwan, his motherland, an independent nation-state. He suffered humiliation at the hands of his Japanese schoolmates who called him a Taiwanese slave because Taiwan was under Japanese occupation. Coe started working for the independence of Taiwan vigorously. However, he advocated only nonviolent struggle as befitting Christian involvement. There were other personal and family crises he suffered, which in fact equipped him, as it were, to delve fully into the movement for the independence of Taiwan. This experience led him to develop the theological concept of contextualization, which mandated that all traditions—theological, cultural, and political—needed to be brought under the challenge of the gospel call to repent.

For an anarchist like me, this is grist to the mill. Having been involved from time to time in the struggles of local Dalit communities for dignity and freedom, I have come to the conclusion that the widely internalized God image across religious borders needs to be questioned. God is understood as the Almighty Sovereign Lord. Therefore all things, including differences in social status, different hierarchies, disparities in wealth distribution, are understood as ordered by God. More significantly, the Christian view of a retributive and arbitrary God who predestinates and elects some people for salvation and who has deemed it fit to save the elect for eternal salvation by imputing the legitimate punishment of death due to them upon Jesus needs to be questioned boldly. As long as such views prevail, it is not possible to argue with logical consistency for a God of inclusive love who has planned to renew the whole of humankind and to redeem and restore all creation. What follows, therefore, is a bold questioning of the prevalent popular as well as the philosophical/theological understanding of God that is a hindrance to articulating any theology of liberation.

It is not as if there had not been attempts to articulate different liberation theologies earlier. But the problem all have faced is that the same God is claimed to be on the side of the oppressor as well as on the side of the oppressed. Phrases such as "God's preferential option for the poor" cut no ice as long as God is spoken of as God of the metaphoric descendants of Cain and also of victims like Abel and Hagar. For, the Almighty and all-knowing God of systematic theology as well as of popular religion and even a large part of the Bible seems to be on the side of the race/caste supremacists, of the male gender's privileges and dominance over women, and God forever is understood as one who keeps showering his bounty on capitalist entrepreneurs.

For those involved in Dalit struggles the question arises: "Does this God, the God of the metaphoric descendants of Cain, exist?" If he does exist, of what use could such a god be to the vast majority of the poor and the oppressed of the world and of the local context? Or, better still, is it proper to use the name God for such a monarchical and arbitrary power? In fact, would it not be proper to give another name for the imperial power of evil that rules the world? This imperial power is confused with the merciful and just God and, of course, seems to be welcomed by the metaphoric descendants of Cain who are in fact the visible agents of the invisible prince of the power of the air, as Paul would name it.

To be able to see a vision of God as one whose love is inclusive and whose justice is perfect and who has purposed to create a new humanity of peace, equality, and justice and who is always with the victims of the world, we need, as Jesus said, a pure heart. This purity of heart consists in the preparedness of those who say "yes" to God's agenda without any reservation for bringing about a new humanity and a renewed earth. By a pure heart, Jesus implied all those who were wholeheartedly committed to be part of the kingdom that belonged to the poor in spirit. They would put themselves out to bring solace to the war-ravaged, the landless, and all those who suffer denial of justice. (See further below the expanded list of the partners of God as found in the Beatitudes of the Sermon on the Mount.)

Oftentimes the imperialist and arbitrary god of the metaphoric descendants of Cain is confused with God as a result of the human tendency to make God serve their ends rather than live to serve God. Therefore the nonretributive God whose love is inclusive and whose concern is focused on those who are denied justice is not recognized as such.

Because of this confusion it is not going to be an easy task to differentiate the true God from the false claimant. In traditional ways of understanding God, God is seen as one who rewards piety and punishes the impious and the wicked. God promises protection and well-being to those whom God chooses to be favorably disposed toward. The god of domination and tyrannical political powers is often confused with the true God of love and compassion for all. At many points the two images are interwoven. One seems to act concurrently with the other. This is because in the minds of quite a few of the biblical authors and also of the philosophically inclined there cannot be two power centers. So it is believed that good and evil come from the only God. Evil is seen as synonymous with divine punishment. However, biblical voices are not unanimous in endorsing this confusion. In the First Testament, the Book of Job stands out in challenging such a view and, of course, Jesus clearly saw the power of evil as a strongman and as the ruler of the world. But Jesus's insistence that God is nonretributive is not given full weight as Jesus himself seems to speak of some people who would not in the end be saved. But that needs to be understood as self-exclusion—people themselves preferring not to be part of the company of those within the purview of God's inclusive love and choose to be in the darkness of hatred and spite (Matt 8:11–13). People who willfully refuse to recognize that God is with the victims of arrogance and wickedness here on earth will inevitably find it hard to live in the company of people like Lazarus who enjoy special privileges and compensatory comfort in the divine presence. To bring it down to earth, people who are opposed to egalitarian ways of life, preferring higher privileges, will certainly not fit into the new humanity of God.

The true God, however, is most determinedly nonretributive and so the word "punishment" does not find a place in his vocabulary. Such a claim goes against not a few texts but against the whole gamut of scripture.

The most difficult to reinterpret is the understanding that God's wrath demands a just punishment of eternal death for all humans, for all have sinned and fallen short of the image of God in which they are created. Therefore God, who is also being merciful, chose to impute that punishment to Jesus and grant salvation to those who accept this in faith. We shall see later that this way of understanding can be reinterpreted without doing damage to God's love made known in Jesus. It is the Son of Man who offers forgiveness on behalf of all the victims of human history inasmuch as he shared their fate of indignity, deprivation, and excruciating suffering.

If Luther could declare that the letter of James should be removed from the canon, we can also challenge texts that speak of God being involved in the handing out of any punishment. The idea that Jesus bore our punishment is abhorrent.

For example, the god of the metaphoric descendants of Cain being the more well-known one as if he were God Almighty who ordered all things, there is little wonder that many believe in a deterministic life. If it does not seem to fit with the God of grace, so be it; it is due to the inscrutable will of God. Thus the true God of grace and inclusive love, who respects human freedom and chooses to be nonintrusive, is pushed to the background. This is because we only hear the laments of the persecuted and the oppressed and rarely see the God of compassion being able to effect any spectacular deliverance. God is always with the oppressed, providing companionship in suffering and enabling them to find their own solutions, as God was with Hagar, for example. But it is necessary to identify painstakingly the different images made to blend together by the clever lies of the power of evil to which even devout people, believers in Yahweh of the burning bush, easily fall prey (John 8:37–56). Therefore we need to learn to separate one from the other.

Let us take the story of Cain and Abel and also of Hagar and Sarah. I shall do a slightly different narrative in keeping with the understanding of God's nature as revealed by Jesus.

God first rejects the offertory brought by Cain. Although God warned him that his offering was rejected because he had allowed sin to crouch at his door, we are not told what kind of sin it is. It is clear, however, that Cain knew it but was unrepentant. Out of jealousy, he then murders Abel. God, though angry with him at first, does not punish him in keeping with God's nonretributive nature and also perhaps because he heard the cry of Abel as not pleading for vengeance but for clemency. See Hebrews 12:24, where the writer compares the plea of the blood of Abel with the blood of Christ as a matter of degree (better) and not of contrast. That is, whereas Abel's blood cried for vengeance, Christ's blood pleaded for mercy.

The unrepentant Cain who escaped punishment spins a story that not only did God not punish him but also promised lifelong protection! Cain seems to have attributed his escape to a clever ploy of manipulating God and conveys the idea that whatever he does God will be there to prosper and protect him, a calculated abuse of the nonretributive nature of God. What really happens is that the god of this world, the power center of evil, becomes the god of all the metaphoric descendants of Cain from that point on. This can be discerned from the way Lamech, the fifth-generation descendant of Cain, tells his wives that although he murdered a young man for some challenge (in all probability the victim was someone like Abel, and Lamech's story that he injured him was something he made up as an excuse for his unprovoked atrocity) he would be protected seventy times seven (Gen 4:3–16; 19–25). This is a paradigmatic myth to show how all the metaphoric descendants of Cain manage to show that God is on their side.

Cain prospered as a city-builder and became the father of many kinds of founders of different trades and skills. With this increasing prosperity, his descendants also grew in arrogant confidence that whatever atrocity they resorted to against the poor and the vulnerable, their god would protect them. So there is a gradual merger of the God of love and the god of this world. To read the story slightly differently from what is narrated in Genesis 4 needs a conviction that God is nonretributive. God's forgiveness was on behalf of the victim Abel. This story is by no means unique. It is a typical paradigm of the present-day world of the exploiter/oppressor/imperial colonizers/caste and race supremacists who boast that God goes with them wherever they go and endorses whatever they do. Not only do the metaphoric descendants of Cain exploit and oppress, but they also plunder the earth and contribute to desertification and climate change.

God leaves the responsibility of restraining evil to humankind, whom God has endowed with freedom and wisdom to know right and wrong. Humankind created in the image of God is entrusted with the responsibility of the care of creation, is given the wisdom to make laws and the power to implement justice in society. God's compassion should be seen, however, as being channeled via and on behalf of the victim. This is perceived by the author of the Letter to the Hebrews.

We now turn to the story of God and God's partners—the marginalized and oppressed of humanity. We take Abel and Hagar as paradigmatic of this story of salvation which in our understanding is humanization.

At first God seemed not to approve of Hagar seeking liberation from her jealous and cruel mistress Sarah. The Bible indicts Sarah only for her disbelief that she would bear a son in her old age. It does not say a word of reprimand about her reprehensible treatment of Hagar. Being a foreign slave, Hagar was expendable as far as Abraham and Sarah were concerned. It is even said that it was God (the god of Cain, perhaps) who asked Abraham to listen to his cruel wife and send Hagar and her young son Ishmael away. That was surely to whitewash Abraham's unacceptable behavior. For even the narrator must have been embarrassed to tell this story. So he was ready to throw the blame on God. But the whitewash is too thin. Abraham sends his wife Hagar away with just a loaf of bread and a flask of water into the wilderness. Soon the flask runs out of water and Hagar is desperate and is resigned to the fact that her son is going to die of thirst. But God saves them both not by any miracle but by enabling Hagar to discover a source of water. We do not hear anything more about Hagar. Ishmael grew up. The biased biblical narrator paints him as one who grew up like a wild ass. This is belied in the narrative itself. In Genesis 25:8 and 9 we are told that Ishmael, together with

Isaac, gave a decent burial to their father Abraham. So Ishmael seems to have been brought up by Hagar as a good human being without resentment against Abraham. Though her son, the firstborn of Abraham, was disinherited and abandoned to die of hunger and thirst by his father, she nurtured in him no resentment against his father or his estrangement.

Just as the Jewish people claim Abraham as their forefather via Isaac, the Arab Muslim community claims Abraham (Ibrahim) as their forefather via Ishmael. They hold Hagar in high regard. There seems to be a different memory line that attributes Abraham's attempt to sacrifice his son, Ishmael, and Hagar knew it but rebutted Satan who tried to drive a wedge between the devoted wife and her erratic husband. This act of Hagar chasing Satan away is sacramentally enacted in the Haj pilgrimage. In spite of all the ill-treatment she suffered, Hagar retained her faith in God and brought up Ishmael as a good human being. Forgiveness seems to come more easily to those who suffer than to those who inflict pain, and so they are the real channels of God's love. This is very true of the Dalit community in India. Their docility is not because they have internalized the myth of karma and fate that makes them untouchables and unworthy of human relationship with those who think they are of upper-caste origin. Just as Hagar remained faithful to her husband and brought up Ishmael as a decent young man after having suffered humiliation as a foreign slave and was taken for granted to become a surrogate mother to a child of the master and then suffered ill-treatment at the hands of her jealous and cruel mistress and finally was thrown out by the very same patriarch who had abused her, so too many Dalits of India and many Africans who were made slaves have become forgiving people by the grace of God.

John Newton, the slave trader-turned-Christian priest who inspired Lord Shaftesbury and William Wilberforce, two young parliamentarians, to initiate the movement to abolish the slave trade, speaks of an experience of being surrounded one day by the spirits of the slaves he had captured and sold to American plantations and also had killed when they tried to free themselves as they were being taken in a ship.

He was frightened to the core of his being. But he came to know they had not surrounded him to seek vengeance but to offer forgiveness and friendship. He felt "amazing grace" overwhelming him. He then wrote the famous song "Amazing Grace." Some biographers, however, try to give a different context to the composing of the song. But it is a fact that he repented of his sinful life as a slave trader and left it and became a priest and songwriter. Why should people who once endorsed the slave trade find it difficult to admit that he experienced forgiveness from those whom he had hurt most? Racial pride, like caste pride, does not die easily. The supremacists are ready to push uncomfortable histories and biographies under the carpet rather than repent and become real human beings created in God's image. Christ as the Son of Man forgives on behalf of the hurt victims of humanity, even the not-so-easily-detected crooked ways of the perpetrators.

THE STORY OF THE TRUE GOD

If God is nonretributive and if God does not interfere in human freedom so that human history is man-made, without God having a share in it, what does God do? How does God keep working together with all God's partners toward the goal of the new human community of peace with justice? In order to find an answer, we need first of all to identify all God's partners.

The Beatitudes of the Sermon on the Mount provide a clear list. God's election of the true descendants of Abraham form another part of the partners of God and, finally, the role of the Son of Man complements and completes God's plan. When we refer to Jesus's saying that only those with a pure heart can see God, we understand it as the ability to recognize and identify the partners of God as listed in the Beatitudes of the Sermon on the Mount.

GOD'S PARTNERS AS LISTED IN THE SERMON
ON THE MOUNT

The Sermon on the Mount is not a new code of ethics. It is the mission mandate and lists God's partners.

The poor in spirit of Matthew 5:3 and those who suffer for the sake of justice (v. 10) are both involved in the "already functioning" kingdom, as the saying "Theirs Is God's Kingdom" is used in the present tense in both cases.

The poor in spirit are all those whose God-endowed spirit of human dignity and worth has been drained away from them. One such group is mentioned in Isaiah 61:3. It refers to those grieving over their war-ravaged country and in whose hearts lurk the nagging question, "How could God have allowed this to happen?" In Matthew's Gospel they are the Galilean refugees in Syria who had fled the Roman tyranny after the failure of the Zealots to oust Roman rule. In today's world, they include the people of Wanni in the north of Sri Lanka who supported the militant struggle for a free Tamil land and were devastated by the Sri Lankan forces who were supported secretly by neighboring states. Today their population is reduced to a third of their original number, leaving behind a large number of widows. The lands they cultivated have been taken away. The ratio of men to women is one to six. Yet these devastated people have not given up. They struggle to survive in very hard circumstances and also keep alive the hope that one day their dream will come true. They do not hate the Sinhalese people, as they know well that the real reasons for the devastation lay elsewhere. The world of humanitarian concern is gradually waking up to express solidarity with them.

All the Dalit people of India (nearly 25 percent of the Indian population) who are treated like scum, whose women are treated like Hagar by caste Hindus, also belong to those robbed of their spirit. They go about sustaining life through various jobs assigned to them. A majority of them are daily wage-earning agricultural laborers. They have a sense of vocation. They do their job for low wages and tell themselves that they are those who feed the world. Then there are trafficked women who are sexually exploited. One of them in a radio conversation once said it was because of their services that many other vulnerable women escape from being raped.

God is concerned that all those who lose their land like the Palestinian people, the Kashmiri people, should get their land back. They are meek in that they are unable to do anything to keep what is theirs as their own.

The above are only a few examples of the poor in spirit. There are those who hunger and thirst for restoration of justice: just wages, equal opportunities in a world of unfair competition and corrupt bureaucracy, and fair treatment in gender-based denials. The promise is that their hunger and thirst will be satisfied. How? Through the commitment of the pure in heart and their associates. It is pertinent to mention that there are humanistic atheists, though Hindu by origin, who fight against the Hindu fundamentalist raj. There are advocates for a caste-free society who accept Dr. B. R. Ambedkar's revolutionary principles for caste annihilation. God is present with the oppressed and empowers them to survive without losing hope and faith. God is also with all those who struggle and suffer for justice. This is how God's kingdom (reign) functions. For, the word *reign* should not be associated with any power display. Service, participation in struggle and suffering as a consequence yet persisting in faith, desisting from violence but always forgiving—these are the ways God's kingdom functions with the partners of God.

In the recent past a few whistleblowers were murdered. Even judges

known to be fair minded in sensitive cases involving political heavy-
weights have been killed; journalists exposing corruption and violence
too are not safe in the country. But God's kingdom is continuing to
function through these replicas of the cross of Christ.

It should be noticed that Jesus uses the third person plural while referring to the above-mentioned partners of God. They are not mentioned
as having any religious convictions. Purity of heart is all that matters.
Therefore all who are wholeheartedly committed to justice even if they
are atheists should be counted as God's partners. Their atheism should be
seen as questioning the god of the metaphoric descendants of Cain.

GOD'S ELECTION OF ABRAHAM AND
HIS TRUE DESCENDANTS

Abraham was important for Jesus as also for Matthew, Luke, John, and
Paul. It was through the Jewish people that the hope for the Messiah was
sustained for well over eight centuries. This hope got refined gradually
from a nationalist hope to a universalist hope (Isa 11:1–9).

We need to be careful therefore not to suggest that the Jews, the people who have physically descended from Abraham, have been disinherited and their place given to those who accept Jesus as the Messiah. Paul
made this mistake in his letter to the Galatians, but by the grace of God
retracted it when he wrote Romans. The early church made this mistake, and the hate campaign unleashed against the Jews continued for
centuries until the Holocaust. It is difficult to erase this memory. But
the question, "Who are included among the metaphoric descendants of
Abraham?" is still important for understanding God's election and the
covenant God made with Abraham in an inclusive way. For it extends
to believers in Jesus and becomes universally applicable to all those who
are denied participation in community, all those who are subject to the
harassment of the powers of evil and in general victimized by the agents
of the god of the descendants of Cain.

God's love is inclusive. Paradoxically, God intended this truth to be
perceived by the people of Israel—that their election was in fact for God's
purpose of blessing all nations through Abraham. The early church had
to learn the hard lesson of crossing the Jew-gentile barrier. Therefore,
God commanded those who returned from slavery in Egypt to remember that they should treat aliens as fellow citizens and their slaves with
kindness and give them Sabbath rest. When that did not happen because
of the incorrigible exclusivist attitude of the people of God, they got
reduced to a remnant of their own making.

Then God hoped that the Christian church grafted into the remnant of the Jewish people would rise to God's expectations. The intended wave, from the particular to the universal, did not happen easily because of human intransigence. Through a wrong interpretation of the meaning of the suffering of the Son of Man as a vicarious punishment, individualism, heavenward orientation, and snobbish exclusivist understanding crept into the gospel. But God has not given up.

That the cross of Christ was in fact an expression of God's solidarity with all the victims of the descendants of Cain is beginning to dawn on those who have woken up to a real understanding of the nature of God and God's purpose. Jesus expressed this solidarity with the suffering people by echoing the cry of the psalmist in Psalm 22. It is not often noticed that all psalms of lament in the Book of Psalms as well as those of prophets Jeremiah and Habakkuk are in fact affirmations of faith of the Son of Man community, that is, the Abel-Hagar group. As the cross of Christ is a "through time event," this community is expanding. It is through them that the real children of Abraham will be identified. In other words, the true descendants of Abraham are all those who would be part of the new humanity of peace and justice.

This is how we should understand how God is involved in the history of human renewal through particularistic but nonexclusive election and covenant and also through the partners of the oppressed and those in solidarity with them. Christ the Son of Man provides the integration of all the different strands already outlined in the discussion above.

CONCLUSION: THE HOW OF CONTEXTUALIZATION

To be involved in our society we need to know the how of contextualization. We also need to know the kind of misinterpretations of the humanizing universal gospel that is being individualized and made to lend itself to an exclusivist understanding. We do not need to work for conversion to become Christians like this. What is needed is a Christianizing/humanizing of the world. So let us briefly describe our own situation first:

THE CONTEXT OF INDIAN (HINDU) RELIGION
AND SOCIETY

The religion of the majority people of India is Hinduism. The philosophical part of it is very small. At a popular level there is the worship of Siva and Vishnu, and also many female deities such as Durga and Kali. Hinduism itself evolved through assimilative syncretism. Many local deities were taken in and given particular status in accordance with the caste to which it was the favorite deity. Local priests were replaced by Brahmin priests and different myths were created. For example, Mariamman (goddess of rain; Mari means rain and Amman means goddess) was turned into a fierce deity. Then she was given the status of a concubine of Siva because her original worshipers were from the lower caste.

The Laws of Manu is a secondary scripture that gives validity to the caste system through the theory of births and rebirths; according to it, Dalit people (deemed impure and untouchable) were born of the dust from the feet of the God-man from whom all other castes emanated. Rebirth depends on how each one conducts one's life on earth. If Dalits remain faithful to their dharma, that is, do all the menial jobs assigned to them, they could be reborn at a higher level. Gandhi, the so-called Mahatma (saint), also upheld this theory. He said untouchability should be removed, but caste duties had to be fulfilled. He thought the whole fabric of Hinduism would collapse if Manu Smriti were annulled.

Thus, assimilative syncretism, popular piety, and Manu Smriti endorse the caste hierarchy, and Dalits who comprise nearly 25 percent of the population are ostracized from society and all the hard and dirty work is assigned to them.

The church comprises different caste groups and a vast majority of them are from the Dalit background. It has already been mentioned that the people who consider themselves to have upper-caste lineage adamantly keep their caste loyalties.

Because Christian faith is understood in terms of individual salvation from death and damnation, individualism rules the hearts and minds of the caste Christians. Christian leadership has done little to challenge this. The emphasis on indigenization has only helped consolidate this tendency.

Therefore contextualization would first and foremost mean relearning of the gospel to mean humanization by breaking down all barriers. This will be a hard task. Only then the church will become fit to incarnate itself into the Hindu society. Dr. Ambedkar had already initiated a movement to annihilate caste. Dalit liberation consciousness is catch-

ing on among Dalit Christians. All those committed to Dalit liberation should join hands to participate in the struggle for Dalit liberation
at the national level. Dalit Christians should also challenge their fellow
believers. The most difficult would be to restate the gospel in terms of
humanization and interpret the cross of Christ as an expression of God's
solidarity with those who keep praying psalms of lament. The idea that
Christ bore God's punishment should be deleted with determination, as
it is blasphemy against the nonretributive God.

PART V

Theology out of Context: Contextual Theologies of the Marginalized

13.

Startling Paths in Latin American Theologies

DIEGO IRARRÁZAVAL

INTRODUCTION

When theological concerns about humanity and creation take into account historical wounds and multidimensional demands for life, they may be responding to the good news. If that does not happen, language becomes irrelevant and shows a lack of awareness of the Spirit. When theological activity deals with itself and its sacred institutions, it digs its own grave. What is at stake is faithfulness to the Spirit of Jesus.

Latin American endeavors are assessed in several ways. In this essay, allow me to examine only methodological issues (the "how"). In general terms, there is a shift from deductive reasoning to historical hermeneutics. In recent decades, several paths have unfolded, and there have been methodological achievements, difficulties, flaws, and challenges. When our tasks are more critical and constructive, more practical and symbolic, our understandings of faith touch the depth of human existence. It is like a window into the heart of God. It implies prayerful and thoughtful communities, which carry out responsibilities that deal with local and global contexts and are courageous in their epistemological journeys.

Throughout our continent, theological paths, fostered by common people's wisdom of faith, have their strengths and limitations. On the one side, they have a shared thrust (often called liberation) and also have particularities, plenty of fellowship, and mutual challenges. On the other side, there are frequent tensions with "owners of the truth" and with monocultural thinkers. I offer you methodological issues that may prompt readers toward further research and dialogue. A thorough study requires more debate in each theological dimension, and a lengthy bib-liographical analysis.

Within and outside of this continent, so-called progressive theologians are often seen as focused on ethical contemporary agendas. But the com-mon denominator is to train persons (among the elites) focusing on scripture and church teachings. Several paths and paradigms (seen as "marginal") have been developed at the grassroots, in churches, in acad-emia, and for secular struggles for justice and peace. This happens, not in the mainstream, but rather among communities that chart their own course, listen to the Spirit present in the universe, and embrace God's revelation.

Procedures and goals require careful assessment. These pages outline key steps in biblical work, in systematic reading of the signs of our times, and development of feminist, indigenous, Afro-American, and ecotheo-ologies. In each of these endeavors, there is dialogue with sciences, and in some cases there is also interaction with people's experience and rit-uals. Methodological outlines are not only theological. We have eyes of faith, but these go hand in hand with scientific discourses and with peo-ple's capacity to survive and be happy.

The downtrodden seek and find life. I like to use the metaphor "star-tling paths" because theology, by its style of thinking, is full of surprise and historical contemplation. As persons and as networks, we experience a kind of pilgrimage to the depth of existence. We move together with others, have insights, uncertainties, failures, new beginnings, and viable dreams. We become aware of unexpected gifts and enjoy God's grace. In other words, many of us are on a theological pilgrimage in Latin America; it is not narrowly academic, nor is it church-centered. Rather, it is becoming aware of "startling paths," of rediscovering the gospel in solidarity with the downtrodden and in justice and peace strategies. Sojourners are on an unending pursuit. Insights into a loving mystery do not have a "stop" sign; nor are they one's intellectual property or a merely ecclesiastical enterprise.

May I again underline choices and shortcomings? Challenging choices are relevant among members of the people of God (and not within mainstream institutions). They are startling because they examine suf-fering and take the road of compassion, of struggles for life, of critical and constructive thinking, of genuine empowerment due to relational experiences. These are acknowledged as signals of the Spirit. My essay examines insightful methods and shortcomings in Latin American the-ologies. A gamut of achievements (and also obstacles and lack of vision) are spelled out. Hopefully, it will encourage more interaction between Asia and America.

BACKGROUND: EMPOWERMENT IN THE MIDST OF SUFFERING

Over the past fifty years, unceasing activities and networks have reshaped ways of doing theology in Latin America. Such transformation may be socially explained in terms of critical modern rationality, of abandoning Eurocentric patterns, of contemporary decolonization, of interaction with grassroots wisdom and faith. In methodological terms, there have been major factors: the biblical movement and its impact in academic circles, church renewal in Catholic and Evangelical institutions, acknowledgment of *loci theologici* and of new paradigms. The latter deserves to be underlined here (since we are dealing here with Latin American languages of faith).

MEANINGS OF CONTEXT AND OF METHOD

What comes to the forefront are not only "contexts" but all that is implied by the relevant understanding of our Christian tradition. In Latin America, when we speak of methodological characteristics, several dimensions are considered: communities with their specific understandings of faith; subjectivity, which goes together with truthful statements, history, and praxis; modern communication that is critical of metaphysical arguments; narrative theology; and a holistic and interdisciplinary discourse.[1] So, huge question marks may be placed over the meaning of context and of method. What do they mean in terms of procedures? They need assessment.

Key concerns have been emerging throughout the world and in our regions: intercultural and interreligious frameworks, hermeneutical approaches that replace monocultural concepts, categories due to feminism and gender that touch all theological work, ecological demands, ethical views that confront globalism with its exclusions, utopias, symbolic forms of theology, mystical factors in liberation.[2] These concerns and types of thinking have their foundations. They are due to faithfulness to signs of God's presence in our world. Moreover, some caution

1. João Batista Libanio, "Diferentes paradigmas na historia da teologia," in Marcio Fabri Dos Anjos, org., *Teologia e novos paradigmas* (São Paulo: Loyola, 1996), 35–48.
2. Juan Jose Tamayo-Acosta, *Nuevo paradigma teológico* (Madrid: Trotta, 2003).

seems necessary. In epistemological terms, Latin American works may not be narrowed down to "schools" (contextuality, reform, liberation, inculturation) that are not complementary. There is no uniformity or incompatibility in terms of our methodologies.

In other words, there is a plurality of paths, some (although not enough) interaction among them, and a dispute with uniformity. Latin American paths are not better than others and are not the only ones that respond to the needs of liberation. But they do show forth creativity and are becoming meaningful in several parts of the world. In a global/local world, there is a need for shared intellectual and practical inquiries into truth, and a need for alternative theologies (so understood when compared with hegemonic patterns in academia and in the churches). It so happens not only because of individual talents, but mainly because thought grows within limit-situations, where common people cry for a decent life and they become empowered and rethink their faith. Such experiences are sustained by grassroots spirituality, by dialogue with secular paths of faith, by connections to sacred energies, by critical and constructive examination of God-language.

For example, for many centuries people of the Maya civilization have been led by empowering spirits; Juana Vásquez praises the "*maya* way of thinking in which persons and other beings of mother nature have *nahuales* or spiritual protectors that become present in several forms."[3] These *nahuales* are spiritual energies with earthly and cosmic dimensions. They are seen unjustly (by foreigners and by some locals) as mere animism.

In general terms, liminal understandings of God's presence imply historical compassion with suffering individuals and peoples. Mercy leads to well-being. In a global world besieged by idols, the gifts of love among humans and all beings are due to divine sources of life. Theological methodologies are nurtured by people's empowerment in the midst of structural violence. When people enjoy peace, theologies may respond adequately.

There is a rainbow of interpretations about what is being done and how it is done (and each of them has its arguments): theology lived from the underside of history, ethical understanding of communion with God and neighbor, evangelical option for the poor and the excluded and their wisdom, care for the earth that is our home, feminism and other challenging languages, and epistemologies of the South.

---

3. Juana Vásquez, "Producción desde la Espiritualidad," in Juan y Otros Tiney, *Tierra y espiritualidad maya* (Guatemala: Ak'Kutan, 2000), 120.

Any creative thinking has controversial dimensions. In our region, many have a radical critique of hegemonic patterns (not only in the West, since they are incorporated throughout the world) and are seeking and finding paradigms. A deductive methodology is slowly becoming irrelevant, and uncharted theological agendas have gradually emerged. Status quo rationality has collapsed. Forms of fundamentalism cause confusion.

In the midst of debates, ways of understanding and practicing the faith are changing courageously. During several centuries the predominant procedure was to explain principles and norms, fashioned by North Atlantic piety and reasoning. Since the 1950s, astonishing steps have been taking place. Such steps are due to biblical and pastoral renewal, systematic work with inductive methodologies, spiritual empowerment, humble learning from people's experience of faith, and interfaith and intercultural dimensions.

HISTORICAL SUFFERING NOURISHES THOUGHTS

In the midst of colonialism and forms of violence and structural suffering, there has been significant countercultural and evangelical witness.[4] Bartolomé de las Casas and others among autochthonous people saw Christ being oppressed in their mistreatment by the colonizers; this has been highlighted by Gustavo Gutiérrez and José Oscar Beozzo in their scholarly works. Manifestations of Mary on the side of the so-called animistic populations have been examined by Maria del Pilar Silveira, and devotions to Guadalupe have been appreciated by Jeanette Rodriguez, Virgilio Elizondo, Clodomiro Siller, and Leonardo Boff. Slavery and struggles for dignity in Brazil have been underlined by Antonio da Silva, Eduardo Hoornaert, and Silvia Regina da Silva, who follow in the footsteps of James Cone and Dwight Hopkins with their systematic and challenging Afro-American perspectives in the United States.

Therefore, historical wounds and healing are assessed at the heart of theology (and are no longer an appendix). That requires courageous interdisciplinary work that is not co-opted by neutrality. Some colleagues emphasize contextuality, economy, and culture. Some of us in the Americas and in Asia underline new paradigms, such as thinking

---

4. Gustavo Gutiérrez, *Las Casas: In Search of the Poor of Jesus Christ* (Maryknoll, NY: Orbis, 1995); Jeanette Rodriguez, *Our Lady of Guadalupe* (Austin: University of Texas Press, 2005); Antonio A. Da Silva and Sonia Q. Dos Santos, *Teologia Afroamericana II* (São Paulo: Atabaque, 2004).

from the margins and contributing to liberation.[5] It may be said that at the heart of each of these endeavors there are responses to historical injustice and pain and that they foster epistemologies of freedom. Since in God's plan we are saved together with others, shared empowerment means that suffering is healed due to reciprocity. Day-to-day miracles of resilience take place. Moreover, there are unceasing signs (often marginal signals) of unconditional forgiveness, reconstruction of harmony, and joyful celebrations that confront violence.

When rooted in such experiences, intellectual work does not shrink into ahistorical concepts, but rather it flourishes with understandings that confront cruel pain and that include plans of liberation. Therefore it appreciates merciful behavior among wounded people, who, in explicit or implicit ways, become sacraments of a kenotic and risen Lord. In other words, daily resilience and struggle make it possible to be closer to a crucified and risen Christ. Millions and millions of Latin American people are not only victims, but they also have strategies for survival, are able to organize, and celebrate each step toward authentic life. Thus in spite of oppression, postponed people of the earth who have greater compassion and courage (with its symbolic forms) offer signals of transformation in today's world. They are also acknowledged as signals of divine light in the midst of darkness.

Thinking is thus built due to what happens in each context. In the midst of structural violence, communities throughout the continent stand up when there are economic-political-military dictatorships and cry "nunca más" (never again; no more institutional violence). Women and men harassed by patriarchy have been using banners saying "ni una menos" (not one more woman killed); since 2015 public protest has been taking place in about eighty cities of Argentina and spreading into other regions.

In Spanish, it is said that salvation comes from the poor (*la salvación viene de los pobres*).[6] It is remarkable how God's saving power is acknowledged as coming from below. Because of what has been happening, theologies are not neutral and are significantly nourished by ordinary people's structural hardships and their small and at times public movements toward justice. In other words, postponed peoples of the earth, as they empower themselves, easily associate with a poor and risen Christ. Although mainstream religion often misunderstands marginal commu-

5. Felix Wilfred, *Margins: Site of Asian Theologies* (Delhi: ISPCK, 2008); Marcio Fabri Dos Anjos, *Teologia e novos paradigmas* (São Paulo: Loyola, 1996); Juan Jose Tamayo-Acosta, *Nuevo paradigma teológico* (Madrid: Trotta, 2003).
6. Jon Sobrino, *Fuera de los pobres no hay salvación* (Madrid: Trotta, 2007), 77.

nities, they continue to witness to the faith and intuitively produce prophetic theology.

Being positive does not mean being naïve. Unfortunately, people's wisdom and prophetic talents are not welcomed in mainstream discourse. The latter uses secluded concepts and belongs to spaces of power that have religious elements. This undermines teaching and training of leaders and the clergy in our continent. For example, programs that speak of quality education give priority to elites who are set apart from the poor. Moreover, leadership programs underline issues about secularization, although our contexts overflow with spirituality and all kinds of religious paraphernalia. Overspecialized academic programs and research seldom engage with common people's faith journeys, church renewal, or ethical questions about idols of today. These are major problems. Fortunately, people go ahead with their own agendas of faith.

In inhuman situations, people find deeper experiences of God. The common ground (in South, Central, and North America) is resilience, resistance to evil, journeys of freedom. These theological paths are in the hands of people who cry for dignity and who are empowered by a living Spirit. There is hopeful wisdom, particularly among those uninvited who end up being the first to enjoy the banquet of a merciful God.

INTUITIVE AND COMPREHENSIVE ROADS

Ways of thinking the faith have methodological procedures that may be seen as what they really are: mediations. These exist in limited and provisional forms. Unfortunately, thinking often becomes a function of elite power structures. Theological discourse that is not rooted in the faith experience of communities and lacks a critical assessment of modern patterns (such as techno-scientific pragmatism with some spiritual support) may be functional to the sacred structures of the elites. However, when inquiries have adequate mediations, then two dynamics may take place. On the one hand, specific human languages humbly take into account other meanings of life, are open to revelation, and are enlightened by the Spirit. On the other hand, challenging spiritual experiences contribute to life-giving liberation among humans that is in harmony with the environment.

A combination of intuitions and rationalities seem to be characteristic of epistemologies of the South. It is said that it is a heart-filled understanding (*sabiduría cordial*, in Spanish). The acknowledgment of *gnosis* and *agape* has been underlined by Aloysius Pieris of Sri Lanka. Felix Wilfred in Chennai, India, dwells on rediscovering the meaning of harmony in the context of contradictions. To see theology as *intellectus amoris* has been proposed by Jon Sobrino in Central America. These attitudes are meaningful in specific contexts and also universally, since they reflect human journeys of faith. They arise not because of scholarly fantasy, but rather—as Bingemer points out—they respond to God's mystery present in the world.[7]

As has often been said, in the Americas there is no uniform procedure. Rather, people honestly unfold intuitions and systematic thinking according to contexts and points of view. We enjoy traveling by different roads toward a common goal, toward an understanding of love throughout history and a contemplation of truth that makes all free.

LATIN AMERICAN CREATIVITY

Taking into account that Latin America is a wide and changing spectrum of situations, it has a gamut of intellectual and social resources. Moreover, debates arise continually about methods and goals. Are there, in terms of methodology, major trends and achievements? Understanding love within and beyond history has been and continues to be a common vision. Jon Sobrino's formula, *intellectus amoris*, may be seen as a summary of our many paths and common vision.

Moreover, a classical standpoint is due to Gustavo Gutiérrez: "Each Christian community does groundwork . . . (and) theology is a critical reflection on historical actions under the light of the Word."[8] Therefore, inductive methods belong to people's traditions, to the understanding of loving relationships, of actions on behalf of justice and peace, of being faithful to the word that confronts and enlightens everyone.

In other words, priority is given to the comprehension of faith within history (instead of emphasis on doctrinal statements). The former has mediations, such as *Sophia*-insights, systematic examination of signs of the times, analogical and mystagogic paths. In concrete terms and in each context the key questions are about signals of human and divine love. It seems it is so when thoughts are shown a passion for life and are not framed by colonial standards, when critical discourse leads to dignity and peace and when there are genuine efforts to hear the word and be faithful to its demands.

7. Maria Clara Bingemer, *O Mistério e o Mundo. Paixão por Deus em Tempos de Descrença* (Rio de Janeiro: Rocco, 2013), 298.

8. Gustavo Gutiérrez, *Teologia de la Liberacion, Perspectivas* (Lima: CEP, 1984), 15, 32.

Another major characteristic is to acknowledge how common people receive gifts of God's love and faithfully respond to such gifts. This has an impact on inquiries of faith and experiences of grace. Spiritual gifts do not lead to individual haughtiness, nor are theological methods self-centered. Rather a double task takes place: a response to the otherness of God who has the first and last word, and at the same time a response to the otherness of the downtrodden in this world. With human sensibilities, each community—with its limitations—becomes open to the Spirit when it listens to the cry of the poor and of the earth. It gives thanks for life in the midst of difficult human situations, and it grows in solidarity with people whom God loves.

Within these circumstances, different resources are useful and complementary. Some of them are due to Western thinking, and most of them are relatively seeking non-Western paths toward truth. Also, all scientific questions and interpretations may be part of human dialogues seeking truth. In this sense, genuine thinking has no sacred human owners. Rather God's revelation and ethical demands are meant for universal well-being. They have an unconditional and universal status. These may not be claimed by Christians alone. Since many of our Latin American situations are defined as being Christian, it is most important to be non-sectarian and to respect other human experiences.

Another obstacle is that Latin American elites naïvely assume Western deductive patterns. So, it is difficult to shift toward intuitive wisdom and rigorous contextual inquiries. Here we are prompted by what is done in different regions. For example, the Togan theologian Mikaele 'O Paunga honestly asked: When one's faith is contextualized, does one remain Christian and Catholic, and what is required so that theology is relevant to Pacific contexts?[9] Moved by Asian prudence, as shown by F. Wilfred and D. Pilario, a foundational theological training asks and seeks relevant answers to contemporary understandings of the faith.[10] In Taiwan, and in his leadership within the World Council of Churches (WCC), Shoki Coe (1914–1988) spearheaded contextual theology throughout the world. As he explained: in faithful responses see "the sign of the divine contextualization unfolding for the liberation and salvation of mankind."[11] These and other guidelines lead Latin American people to learn from their Asian colleagues.

9. Mikaele 'O Paunga, *The Oceania Bishops* (Suva: Bluebird Printery, 2006).

10. Felix Wilfred and Daniel Pilario, *Evaluation of Selected Theological Institutions in the Philippines* (Manila, 2011).

11. Shoki Coe, "In Search of Renewal in Theological Education," *Theological Education* 9, no. 4 (1973): 243.

Grassroots intuitions are fertile grounds for comprehensive work that has its methodologies. Hopefully, each theological activity is expected to dialogue with common people's wisdom and with scientific resources. With eyes of faith, political, economic, and cultural situations are examined so as to see signs of God. In a global and constantly changing world, concerns born out of faith interact with human efforts to be more human and more respectful of the environment.

This implies a critical study of religious consumption, of ego-centered spiritual recipes, of sacralized postmodernity. Any theology that wishes to be relevant, and not naïve, engages in debates about market control over religions, and engages in discourses of transcendence that go beyond forms of idolatry. Moreover, a reflexive community confronts any monocultural or any monoreligious way of action. This is demanded from our plural and always relevant Christian heritage. The world is pluralistic and evolving toward good and toward evil. We coexist among different—and ambivalent—journeys of faith.

PATHS WITH PARADIGMATIC THRUST

Not only is there a shift from deductive methods to more inductive reading of the signs of the times and understandings of a vital Christian tradition, but such changes also include efforts to dialogue with human sciences and with the wisdom of common people and to reconstruct theological models. So, we may now consider several paths, in the manner of paradigmatic thrusts, that are being carried out throughout our continent.

This has been happening (since the second half of the twentieth century) because both inside and outside of academia and of church programs, associations and persons have drawn their own agendas. In Latin America, major breakthroughs have been taking place when reflexive communities (fed by biblical scholarship) embrace the gospel and its personal and historical demands. This has been fertile ground for systematic work (done by theologians often called "liberationists" and by different kinds of thinking).

Toward the end of the twentieth century and particularly during the first decades of the twenty-first, feminist thinking, so-called indigenous or autochthonous understandings of faith, Afro-American perspectives, and a gamut of ecotheologies built their own methodologies and contents. Creativity has been due to many persons, networks, institutions, and in several nations and regions of the Americas, and not only due to a few individual publications. Paradigmatic thrusts do happen when many people participate in creative developments. (Being part of several of those developments, I can vouch for that.) The following paragraphs briefly note down the methodological dimensions.

Latin American theological renewal has mainly grown out of contact with a life-giving word. Carlos Mesters explains five pillars:[12] The Spirit is acknowledged in the universe; God walks with us throughout history; grace grows in the tree of human life; the word is our framework and also our journey; due to its eyes of faith, the church grows with the word. These may be called pillars (as done by Mesters) or principles developed by grassroots communities and their biblical assistants. Interpretations of God's presence are outstanding in quality and quantity. Both in broad exegetical work and, in particular, women's community leadership, these talents are admired by all. For example, since the 1970s, Elsa Tamez of Costa Rica (and other scholars) have examined human, and specifically marginal people's, liberation struggles. Also thanks to readings of the word, epistemological and sociopolitical challenges have been unfolded by Carmiña Navia in Colombian urban realities, Ana Maria Tepedino in Brazil, and Margot Bremer among *guaraní* communities in Paraguay. Anyone can see and admire how narrative and symbolic methods and day-to-day justice and peace engagements by women are nourishing theological areas (in spite of androcentric prejudices). It did not happen in the past.

No label (not even that of feminism) explains their creativity in most theological disciplines. In a few decades, women doing theology have moved beyond predominant rationalism, clerical obstacles, censorship in academia and in local churches. Some writings are better known and translated into languages other than Spanish and Portuguese. In the forefront are those like Ivone Gebara, Mercedes Lopez, and Maria Clara Bingemer in Brazil; Consuelo Velez, Carmiña Navia, and Maria Vivas in Colombia; Virginia Azcuy and Maria Jose Caram in Argentina; Sandra Robles and Judith Ress in Chile; and Elsa Tamez and Regina da Silva in Central America. A few publications are in the field of philosophy, others are mostly biblical, others fully systematic. Yet others are historical narratives, and some others are artistic productions. Their inputs may not be summarized only in terms of gender. Women are joining all theological endeavors and also prompting themselves and us men to confront androcentric patterns.

Moreover, even if there are only a few intercontinental productions, they are very significant. For example is Virginia Fabella's interpretation of collective and personal steps happening all over the world and in

---

12. Carlos Mesters, *La persona de Jesucristo* (Estella, Spain: Verbo Divino, 2004).

a special way her fellowship among "emancipating Asian women—whether they are Christian or not—who dig into the roots of patriarchy on the continent and at the same time uncover the liberating aspects in their cultural and religious heritage."[13] A pan-Asian EAT-WOT (Ecumenical Association of Third World Theologians) Congress held in India concludes that "women are aware that the world has resources to satisfy everyone's need but not few people's greed. . . . Women's resistance is growing to all that is anti-life, as they become pioneers in the quest for new forms of harmonious living."[14] Postcolonialism, interfaith, and daily harmony are key Asian concerns.

With regard to ecotheologies, some of them deal with specific environmental issues and use interdisciplinary methods; other reflections include doctrinal aspects and ecotheological systems. In our continent, for more than two decades, Leonardo Boff and others in Brazil have done outstanding research and public witness about the modern crisis. They include cosmology, physical and quantic sciences, the global and urgent ecological crisis, spirituality of Gaia, virtues, sinfulness, ethics, new understandings of God, of Christ and the Spirit. What is at stake is "feeling, loving, thinking as Earth (and acknowledging) the category of Kingdom in God's project over all of creation."[15] All of this is both theoretical and practical.

Ecofeminists throughout the world are also developing a realistic and mystical enlightenment. "Our theological, ethical, spiritual center is the body . . . humanity, internal and external cosmic dimensions, our being part of 15 billion years of cosmogenesis."[16] Within Catholic communities, Pope Francis's holistic epistemology in his 2015 encyclical, *Laudato Si: On Care for Our Common Home*, has become part of an ecotheological movement and also motivated peoples of other faith traditions, and scientists and politicians all over the world.

During the long history of Christian thinking, there has been a wide gamut of theological "schools," "epistemological horizons," written productions, and mystagogic experiences. João Batista Libanio examines traditional methods (sacred science, scholasticism, doctrinal dualism of true and false), modern existential and subjective paradigms, narrative,

---

13. Virginia Fabella. *Beyond Bonding: A Third World Woman's Theological Journey* (Manila: Institute of Women's Studies, 1993), 96.

14. Marlene Perera and Stella Baltazar, *Towards a New Dawn: Asian Women's Theology and Spirituality* (Chennai: EATWOT, 1999), 113.

15. Leonardo Boff, *Ecología, grito de la tierra, grito de los pobres* (Madrid: Trotta, 1996), 235, 249.

16. Mary Judith Ress, *Reflections on Latin American Ecofeminist Theology.* (Santiago: Conspirando, 2012), 210.

hermeneutics, historical and practical theology.[17] Antonio Almeida fears that churches only see issues of today and ecclesiastical problems and lack the "ability to deal with a humanly dignified and sustainable future."[18] We are also challenged while confronting an epochal change, a shift of civilizations. Carlos Palacio in Brazil has warned of the total crisis of modern rational Western civilization, where even theology of liberation has been at home. Part of such a crisis is that transcendence is seen in non-ontological categories, and Christian faith is comprehended beyond Western absolutes.

IDENTITIES AND EPISTEMOLOGIES

The Americas not only have systematic reconstructions, radical biblical work, ecotheologies, and feminist epistemologies, but our regions also treasure indigenous, mestizo, Afro-American, and Asian American voices and epistemologies. They belong to sociocultural and spiritual realities, where wounds and healing give birth to thinking. They promote intellectually and spiritually amazing new constructions. Drinking from their own spiritualities and symbolic understanding, indigenous, African Americans, Asian Americans, and the gamut of "mestizo" identities, migrant peoples (through qualified representatives) unfold their ways of doing theology.

Such constructions normally have local and region-specific dynamics. Since they are sustained by intercultural dynamics, they often have many syncretic elements. Christian communication is thus qualitatively narrative and symbolic. Many inquiries include art and drama, joyful celebrations, memory of martyrdom, organizations and actions toward more justice and peace. (Nevertheless, almost nothing is translated so as to be published in other languages, so it is unknown in other parts of the world.)

Autochthonous understandings of faith are well summarized and examined by the Mexican Eleazar Lopez, who has leadership among indigenous groups of the continent. On the basis of Central American realities, Lopez explains a "God who speaks, and a speaking of God, praises community singing, rituals and myths that are danced, prayer in all circumstances, rituals so as to understand future events and social conflict, other persons as models and guides, fruitful counseling, spiritual

17. João Batista Libanio, "Diferentes paradigmas na historia da teologia," in Marcio Fabri Dos Anjos, org., *Teologia e novos paradigmas* (São Paulo: Loyola, 1996), 35–48.

18. Antonio Jose de Almeida, "Os desafios dos novos paradigmas para a prática teológica," in SOTER, *Teologia aberta ao Futuro* (São Paulo: Loyola, 1997), 136.

language through nature, interpretation of dreams, historical narratives."[19] In regions of the Americas, representatives of First Nations have been nurturing their own wisdoms and theologies.

Why are they described as wisdoms? Unfortunately, scientific endeavors are mostly rational and elitist. Common people—and intellectuals in their midst—are rooted in the earth and in everyday historical events. That is why wisdoms are described using metaphors. In general terms, Latin American thinking and also these autochthonous wisdoms are ways of producing *intellectus amoris* (Jon Sobrino). They are ways of being in the world and among spirits. It is the mystery of sharing well-being, even though most suffer injustice. In spite of inequality in terms of resources and being victims of social discrimination, being alive is a transcendental gift.

Other regions use different metaphors. A fascinating and undefinable experience in China is described as a road: *Tao*. Buddhist populations all over Asia seek and find enlightenment. Traditions in India enjoy harmony and love: *bhakti marga*. Such realities are a wonderful polymorphic journey into the heart of existence. Recently, in areas of Latin America, groups and institutions have developed a strategy of "full life," *Sumaq Kawsay* (in indigenous *quechua* language). Thus, in different ways throughout the universe, persons and communities are becoming listeners of ancient and contemporary wisdom. Such kinds of knowledge are local, but they have no boundaries.

Concerning Afro-American thinking, carried out in the Caribbean, North America, Brazil, and areas of the Pacific coast, its background against slavery and its struggles for dignity have shaped their understanding (and critique) of Christianity. In a long essay that draws on family, church, and theological experience, Catherine Chalá (of Ecuador) shows how black people's history of suffering and exploitation, loss of identity, resistance, and trust in the God of life became *loci theologici*.[20] She also gives witness to how theology is produced by black communities, by some churches in dialogue with Afro-American religious traditions in the Americas, in the midst of daily social struggles, and encounters with God and sacred beings. (I was one of the many who praised her inputs in a gathering in Brazil.)

---

19. Eleazar Lopez, *Teología india. Antología* (Cochabamba, Bolivia: Verbo Divino, 2000), 99–103.

20. Catherine Chala, "Elementos indispensables para uma teologia afroamericana," in *Teología Afroamericana II* (São Paulo: Atabaque, 2004), 124–33.

Sadly, there are yet only a few signs of Asian American theological intuitions and systematic work, with the exception of communities in the Caribbean, the Pacific coast, and areas of Brazil, where migrants from Asia have strong roots and cultural manifestations. Moreover, in North America, Asian theologians have their own thinking and symbols of wholeness and enlightenment. Outstanding work has been done by Peter Phan (*Christianity with an Asian Face*), by the Koreans Chung Hyun Kyung, Sang Hyun Lee (*From a Liminal Place: An Asian American theology*), by the Taiwanese theologians C. S. Song and Shoki Coe, by Rita Nakashima Brock (*Journeys by Heart*). In the Caribbean and Brazil, Christians with an Asian background (for example, theologian Jung Mo Sung of São Paulo) are opening new roads.

Individuals and associations within the people of God have charted their own epistemologies. Each one has its particular knowledge of gospel values, intimacy with God, and patterns of understanding solidarity. All this thinking is externally defined as contextual, indigenous, sociocultural, and geographical. These labels have certain shortcomings, since they easily lead to caricatures.

What is really happening is the unfolding of several contemporary paradigmatic changes in our experiences of the Ultimate. On the one hand, there is a consistent and interdisciplinary critique of unilateral Western rationalism. In positive terms, what has been developing are several kinds of understandings of the signs of the times, reconstructing meanings of the Christian heritage, dealing with unpredictable future events, and interacting with symbolic, mythical, ritual, ethical languages present in the Americas.

These developments may be called a paradigmatic change and have new and open agendas. In slightly more than half a century (since the 1960s) in the Americas there have been intuitive and heart-filled inquiries into truth. They are provisional and limited (like any intellectual journey), but they are also comprehensive and systematic. It is not only a matter of a few voices, nor a matter of underdeveloped thinking (when compared with North Atlantic achievements). Rather, with limited resources and in the midst of cultural inequalities toward "ignorant multitudes," communities of faith are empowered by the Spirit of God and have resilience and wisdom so as to deal with theological questions and themes.

ACHIEVEMENTS AND OBSTACLES

Since humanity and also nature are demanding compassion and justice, theological methods (in the Americas, in Asia, and elsewhere) may not remain neutral or detached from historical change. Each Christian community has to respond to the signs of the times. There are signals of evil, corruption, destruction of nature, patriarchy, and so on. On the other hand, we rejoice with signs of mercy, of resistance, of tireless efforts to be more human, of taking care of the pressing needs of others, of more openness to God's love.

In these circumstances we have experiences of grace and intimacy with God and the neighbor. At times we undergo frustration, make mistakes, face obstacles, and become aware of sinful complicity with evil.

Since we are in the final part of this essay, allow me to underline fertile possibilities and also to recall inadequate methodologies. What is also most important is that interaction take place between Asian wisdoms (and forms of dealing with social evils, and responses to plural paths of faith) and us in the Americas (where hopefully there may be less arrogance and more dedication to rebuilding paradigms). Dialogue without impositions requires humility. Better connections take place "from below," and have integral and holistic goals. With these concerns we move forward to the final section.

STORIES WITH UNEXPECTED TRUTHS

Prophetic responses and literary reconstruction of God's words have become a common ground for work done in Asia, America, and elsewhere. Such creative work is carried out in places and by persons who are on the underside of history. As has been already pointed out, grassroots biblical work is the foundation of Latin American theologies. Such work is developed within all kinds of communities where women have strong leadership and where daily experiences and stories allow us to rediscover the gospel.

What has been happening in Asia is different and it is also foundational. It happens when ancient texts and new rituals become part of interfaith ways of being Christian. On the one hand, jewels of ancient traditions and of contemporary visions are placed together, and on the other, a Judeo-Christian understanding of life becomes relevant through everyday events. This implies a methodological model: narrative biblical activity is meaningful for "ordinary" situations in marginal regions.

For example, there is the work done in the Philippines by Nina Tomen and Bishop Ambo David. A layperson and a church leader are theologizing through stories of men, women, and children in their contexts. Their concrete human journeys are acknowledged as "signs of the times." They allow all to see divine miracles through historical mercy and justice. Faith is nurtured through tenderness and solidarity that change local situations. So people go beyond oppression and, above all, they enjoy life.

As Ambo David says: "Stories help . . . to express for ourselves as Filipinos what mercy is about, and how it reveals for us the face of God in the person of Jesus Christ, whose image and likeness we are called to be."[21] Instead of speculative language, we have stories like the case of a garbage collector Totoy and his Christmas wish, or the experience of social worker Joel who becomes a biblical expert, or Junjun's "garden of love." These and other windows into the heart of revelation mean that faith-understanding begins with everyday concerns. It is a matter of divine signs among the poor of the world.

Other startling reconstructions of truth happen when communities reformulate their symbols of faith and when celebrations strengthen sociocultural intimacy with God. Some years ago, I enjoyed a reconstruction of the Creed by the indigenous communities of South America (where I was doing my research and ministry); later I was part of an inculturated Catholic liturgy in an institute in Bangalore, and also joined persons of many faiths in a Christian ashram with its silence before God. Throughout Asia, Oceania, the Caribbean, Africa, and the Americas we share small and fascinating efforts to leave aside colonial patterns of thinking and praying and to courageously reinterpret our Christian heritage. This implies discovering anew interreligious and intercultural mediations that are crucial today. (This is often misunderstood by religious leaders who prefer fewer challenges and more uniformity.)

As far as Latin American theologies are concerned, their plurality and creativity do not mean that they are sacred and beyond critique. Each practical and theoretical effort is limited and provisional and needs growth and debate. Our paths require intellectual humility, particularly by whoever belongs to the elite who walk among marginal people. Our main challenge comes from salvation history, where the last ones are the first in terms of knowing and loving God.

21. Pablo David and Nina Tomen, *The Gospel of Mercy according to Juan/a* (Makati City, Philippines: St. Paul's, 2016), xii.

So intuitions and thoughts do not arise out of discussions among experts, nor do they when doctrinal patterns are reproduced naïvely. Rather, what is priority is any program established through dialogue with the people of God. In other words, communities rooted in the gospel are able to do constructive and critical readings of the "signs of the times." Theological activities become relevant when they are faithful to the Spirit and thus offer concrete service in the local and universal church.

This needs to be underlined, since there are misunderstandings about the experience of faithful truth. Contextual methodologies are due to human journeys shared by the people of God. They are not merely written productions by lonely experts, or by well-subsidized international and regional events, or by so-called "academic excellence." Although each of these is meaningful in its own realm, long-lasting achievements belong to reflexive communities among the people of God. They understand and witness to God's unconditional mercy and justice. They echo what the Gospels say of the last ones being intelligent, as in Luke 9:48 and 10:21 and in Matthew 11:25–27. Since truth comes from below, theology grows in such fertile common ground.

FRUITFUL INTERACTION BEYOND BARRIERS

In different parts of our planet we are linked by material desires, by financial, technological, and spiritual networks. Different routes allow communities to listen to God's revelation, which benefits all humanity and all creation. When so many centuries of Asian journeys of faith are compared with what is done in the Americas during just a few centuries, so much has to be learned from them. This means not only being aware of contents and contexts of their classical heritages. It also means appreciating their interfaith and justice perspectives.

In regions of the Global South, scholars are continually examining changing circumstances, debating how a rational and violent modernity shifts toward self-centered security, postmodern hedonism, and forms of idolatry. Some also predict global breakthroughs due to epistemologies of the South. An outstanding contribution is done by Boaventura de Sousa Santos and others at the University of Coimbra[22] who see the world with the hearts and minds of the Global South. In each region, human beings are objects of internal and external colonialism, but we are also able to share compassion and thoughtfully build roads of justice and harmony.

---

22. Boaventura de Sousa Santos, *Epistemologies of the South* (New York: Routledge, 2016).

Interaction is needed and desired within and between regions that often have only fragmentary knowledge of what is different and what is there in common. In our situations (speaking from a South American experience) we lack permanent links among emergent (and also traditional) ways of thinking, and links with other regions of the world.

Therefore, a priority is to listen to wise and prophetic voices, in our contexts and elsewhere, and to move ahead. Why? It is not a strategy to be up to date or merely be "world citizens." What is at stake is being radically human and faithful in the midst of global changes. One is called to listen and be silent. On that basis, organizations are established and discussions take place, and each one is able to engage in small and meaningful actions. Moreover, there may be consensus on alternatives, since in the midst of global and local mutations, there are inescapable responsibilities.

It may be said that consciously or unconsciously everyone flows in the rivers of paradigmatic shifts. What do we do with past achievements? What was planned, prayed, dreamed through local initiatives, regional and global actions by the WCC, by renewal movements in our Catholic community, and so on, may not be secluded in the past; nor may they be merely praised and reproduced like photocopies. Nor is it wise to join any spectacular event. Often there is nostalgia for sacred patterns, for identity and indigenous languages, for postcolonial labels.

Rather, courageous and viable landmarks open to the future must be welcomed. For example, it is significant—according to Shoki Coe's proposals—to leave behind what is not relevant or urgent. In Taiwan and other parts of the world, scholars remember how Coe promoted prophetic proposals and actions. Persons may do theology in such a way that new spiritual-cultural and sociopolitical factors are seriously taken into account. On that basis, churches may focus better on their own contributions to human transformation. Such a process has been described in several forms; being faithful to the gospel demands in each place and time, or in terms of contextualization, reforming church principles so that they are not self-centered but rather are evangelical ways of responding to the birth pangs in the universe.

Intercultural and interfaith thinking is slowly becoming an adequate methodology for some (and seen as a scandal by others). In the past decades (and in some places up till now) such perspectives were only *ad experimentum*, they were not part of theological studies and not allowed in official ceremonies. Concerning these problems, it is most important to be once again rooted in Jesus and in Paul's evangelization.

As is well known, the prophetic ministry of our Lord took place in a so-called pagan Palestinian and gentile land where Israelites struggled for their place. Instead of being a one-sided follower of rabbinical norms and doctrines, Jesus of Nazareth did not reject the Samaritans or the gentile population. He did enjoy fellowship with persons labeled as sinners (so labeled by rigorists in Jesus's context). Moreover, the Son of Man was scorned (according to John 7:52) because "no prophet comes" from an unknown town (like Nazareth), nor from areas influenced by gentile cultures and religions. In the case of Paul, his mission and friendship with gentiles implied unmerciful persecution and discrimination. However, evangelization went forward in unexpected ways and beyond barriers.

In contemporary situations, something similar happens to the genuine followers of Jesus and to those who have Paul as a model in terms of ministry and social interaction with other faiths and cultures. Hopefully this may become common practice so that Christianity is again rooted in Jesus and Paul and be globally relevant today. (In some contributions to dialogue with Asian theologies I have also underlined being followers of a Galilean Jesus who is Palestinian and Semitic. In this sense he may be considered an Asian prophet and healer, who is certainly meaningful today for all peoples.)

Another major concern is methodological faithfulness to the living God, which implies being not church centered or being subdued by socioeconomic standards. Ecclesiastical attitudes and material absolutes contaminate languages of faith. These are moreover influenced by paradigms of worldly success, and they often foster dependency on intellectual elites. These obstacles are subtly present in much of our theological discourse (even though Christian sources are not in favor of such mistakes). So, it is urgent to have thoughtful interaction among people that encounter similar challenges and calls for conversion.

Going beyond barriers is more than an emotional and social enterprise. In today's world, people (and theology) have decided to cross borders and have pluri-dimensional interactions. There are intellectual, political, cultural, and economic dimensions. This obviously changes daily responsibilities. As we teach and work with other people, we use only Western rationalistic paradigms and leave aside our own. There are influences of a market hegemony and of ego-transcendence. These and other dimensions place barriers in communities of faith and also harm theologies.

Nevertheless, peoples in Asia (and elsewhere) have their own resources, develop methods of research, and walk wisely toward a full humanity and environmental harmony. It is surprising how, in the midst of violence and destitution, people in the Global South give witness of joyful freedom and truth. These ancient and also contemporary values imply alternatives to neocolonial theological dependency.

Taking care of human relationships, of all living beings, and of the environment, may be acknowledged as journeys within the mystery of life. What is done in Asia and in the Americas, and all over the South, with their peculiar epistemologies, may be enlightened by inexhaustible sources. According to our tradition, humanity walks with the spirit of Jesus when there are daily forms of solidarity and prophetic forms of wisdom.

14.

Black Liberation Theology USA and Global Cross-Cultural Leadership

DWIGHT HOPKINS

In his pioneering book *Black Religion and the Imagination of Matter in the Atlantic World*,[1] James A. Noel makes a strategic theoretical intervention in the study of black religion. He writes the following:

> I have tried to situate black religion within a broader geo-temporal framework than America and place it within the Atlantic World—a world comprised of Europe, the Caribbean, South America, and North America. . . . [This broader framework] is not merely a matter of moving a particular subject of knowledge from one compartment to another. It entails redefining the subject of knowledge in relationship to other phenomena that appear in making such a move. We do not know what anything is until we view it in relationship with other materialities that account for its appearance.[2]

Noel argues that all investigations into African American religion fall short unless these examinations link intentionally the United States' domestic situation with what he calls the black Atlantic world, meaning the historical bonding of African peoples circumscribed by the Atlantic Ocean from Europe, Africa, the Caribbean, South America, and the United States of America. Noel's astute conceptualization brings added clarity on two levels at this juncture at the beginning of the twenty-first century.

First, his sharp thought is a clarion call, a crucial reminder, to reconnect black religious studies in the US to Africa. Specifically, from 1619 to 1990, enslaved Africans and blacks post-slavery have always and actively

1. New York: Palgrave Macmillan, 2009.
2. Noel, *Black Religion and the Imagination of Matter*, 197 and 199.

tied their domestic North American affairs with international affairs in Africa.[3] From August 1619, when the first group of seventeen men and three African women were brought by force to Jamestown, Virginia, until Nelson Mandela was released from prison in February 1990, black Americans have continuously linked themselves to Africa. But since Mandela's freedom, there has been an almost twenty-year break in relations. Noel challenges us to bridge that post-1990 gap and make a vital contact with Africa again.

On a second level—here we speak more about a broader significance—Noel's insights push us to reconceptualize black theology to take on the global reconfigurations and opportunities brought about by the rapidly shrinking world of fast-paced global international contacts.

Restating the two claims of Noel, we conclude the following. In the specificity of the genealogy of black theology, we need to reweave complex ties with Africa. This claim is based on tradition. And in the generality of the larger worldwide intertwining of technologies and economics, we need a new type of black theological leader for the twenty-first century. This claim is based on today's international challenges.

Elsewhere, I have already written on the black theology and Africa connection, thereby responding to Noel's argument to rebind black Americans to Africa.[4]

Hence, this paper explores Noel's second directional implica-

3. The Spanish brought the first group of enslaved Africans to St. Augustine, Florida (in the so-called New World), in 1565. They were Spanish-speaking Roman Catholics. See Cyprian P. Davis, *The History of Black Catholics in the United States* (New York: Crossroad, 1995). However, the first English-speaking settlement of enslaved Africans was at Jamestown, Virginia, a British Colony in August 1619. See Dwight N. Hopkins, *Down, Up, and Over: Slave Religion and Black Theology* (Minneapolis: Fortress Press, 1999) and Gayraud S. Wilmore, *Black Religion and Black Radicalism* (Maryknoll, NY: Orbis, 1998). This 1565 Florida settlement of Africans is an important correction to the historical misconception that August 1619 marks the first arrival of enslaved Africans in western European colonies in the "so-called New World." Also what is at stake in this dating is the importance of recovering the pioneering role of enslaved and black American Roman Catholic theologians in their impact on black religion and black theology until now. Furthermore, one must avoid black Protestants assuming an exclusive false narrative about their Christian heritage, which, in fact, is a late starter in North American colonies. Yes, August 1619 was a Protestant landing that became the first permanent North American settlement of enslaved African peoples in the thirteen colonies, but not the first arrival in what would become North America. St. Augustine was the northern territory of Spain's Caribbean empire. Jamestown was the foundation of the origin of the thirteen British colonies.

On April 9, 1865, or June 2, 1865, (depending on the historian) the Civil War (to abolish the enslavement of Africans and black Americans) in the United States ended, thus one speaks of post-slavery in the United States after this date. On April 12, 1861, eleven southern states seceded from the United States of America to form their own Confederate States of America, an independent nation separate from the northern United States of America. From this perspective, it was not a civil war but a War Between the States—an armed struggle between the Union government (of the north) and the Confederate government (of the south).

4. Dwight N. Hopkins, *Black Theology USA and South Africa: Politics, Culture, and Liberation*

tion—what is the relationship between black liberation theology and the worldwide phenomenon of close local and global interconnectivity?[5] There exist varied approaches to this relationship. For instance, one might argue that black liberation theology needs to boycott globalization in the sense of living as if it is absent from reality, thus abhorring any participation in globalization. Another might suggest that black theology remain on the periphery and, from an oppositional position below, wage a major fight against the hegemonic, anti-people essence of globalization. A third position might claim that black theology must recalibrate its perspective and seek to join the unfolding narrative of the dominant globalization by leading inside of globalization at its highest offices of power. And finally, people might bury and burrow themselves into local community organizing and individual church development with no attention to global dynamics.

In this essay, I assert none of the above. Rather I think that today's black liberation theology must craft a new type of global cross-cultural leadership because of the worldwide interconnectivity between the local and the international. This is what I take Noel to mean when he writes: "[This broader framework] is not merely a matter of moving a particular subject of knowledge from one compartment to another. It entails redefining the subject of knowledge in relationship to other phenomena that appear in making such a move." In other words, black theology has to redefine the nature of its ministry in relationship to global phenomena that appear in front of us now.

Here is my thesis. Black liberation theology has to include practical ministry along with its prophetic and priestly ministries. Prophetic ministry demands a counterattack on unjust structures. Priestly ministry requires those trained in healing. But practical ministry looks at the local and international connections and works on enhancing a leadership that will construct a new society through governing wealth and people. Restated, practical ministry responds to the following opportunity. *As global cross-cultural leaders, how do working-class and poor families govern wealth (i.e., earth, air, and water), people (i.e., through policies for*

(Eugene, OR: Wipf & Stock, 2005; originally published by Orbis Books in Maryknoll, NY, 1989).

5. See my "The Religion of Globalization," in *Religions/Globalizations: Theories and Cases*, ed. Dwight N. Hopkins et al. (Durham, NC: Duke University Press, 2001). In that essay, I take a definite position that globalization is a form of religious worldview and practice. Also, that essay presents different definitions and expressions of globalization. In this current essay, I simply posit "globalization" as an objective phenomenon confronting the contemporary period, perhaps commencing with the reintegration of the world after the Second World War and definitely shifting into hyper-gear with the invention of the internet and the 1991 breakup of the Union of Soviet Socialist Republics.

healthy families), and technology (i.e., the latest means of communication) in the twenty-first century?

Here are my presuppositions. We keep the prophetic dimension of speaking truth to bad structures of power and we keep the priestly aspect of healing the emotional and physical hurts caused by unjust structures of power. Yet, at the same time, at the start of the twenty-first century, we need to focus more on practical ministry, which for me means nurturing a new type of global cross-cultural leadership to govern resources.[6]

And here is the implication. If we do not expand our ministries to international possibilities, black liberation theology will fall behind the opportunities that global cross-cultural relationships can offer young people in poor and working-class communities. We will become trapped in a vicious cycle of mostly reacting to bad systems and not using the majority of our energy thinking about how to link practically to the new global situation so that poor and working-class black families have access to and enjoy all of God's creation. That means working with those living in the urban and rural areas throughout the US to own their own businesses and create their own jobs. From its inception, black theology rightly claimed service to the black poor and working class and, indeed, all oppressed families and communities. This is the epitome of liberation.[7] But unfortunately and by design, rather than enjoying access to earth, air, and water (the essentials for having a full life promised by God to all human beings), working people are riding an acute wave downward statistically and materially.

Therefore, as a reorientation forward, this presentation engages the relation between black liberation theology and global cross-cultural

6. I am aware of the pioneering work on how black pastoral theology has evolved. For example, Edward P. Wimberly, *Relational Refugees: Alienation and Reincorporation in African American Churches and Communities* (Nashville: Abingdon, 2000); Archie Smith Jr., *The Relational Self: Ethics & Therapy from a Black Church Perspective* (Nashville: Abingdon, 1982); James H. Harris, *Pastoral Theology: A Black-Church Perspective* (Minneapolis: Fortress Press, 1991); Homer U. Ashby Jr., *Our Home Is over Jordan: A Black Pastoral Theology* (St. Louis: Chalice, 2003); Lee H. Butler Jr., *A Loving Home: Caring for African American Marriage and Families* (Cleveland: Pilgrim, 2000); Emmanuel Y. Lartey, *Pastoral Theology in an Intercultural World* (Cleveland: Pilgrim, 2006); Anthony G. Reddie, *SCM Core Text in Black Theology* (London: SCM, 2012); and Dale P. Andrews and Robert London Smith Jr., eds., *Black Practical Theology* (Waco, TX: Baylor University Press, 2015). I expand these notions toward constructing new institutions and new human beings who are in control of their communities and themselves. Thus I accent healthy communities and healthy individuals in communities. I also see how all ministries intertwine. For example, Howard Thurman's *Jesus and the Disinherited* (Boston: Beacon, 1996) combines priestly and prophetic ministries.

7. See James H. Cone, *A Black Theology of Liberation*, fortieth anniversary (Maryknoll, NY: Orbis, 1990) and his *God of the Oppressed*, new rev. ed. (Maryknoll, NY: Orbis, 1997). Also review J. Deotis Roberts, *Liberation and Reconciliation: A Black Theology*, 2nd ed. (Philadelphia: Westminster, 2005).

leadership. The discussion unfolds around two parts. The first analysis explores what type of leadership the founding generation of black liberation theology developed. And what the social conditions were that impacted the leadership of this first generation.[8] The second part of our discussion, in a similar fashion, correlates twenty-first-century conditions and how these changing contexts demand broadening the type of leadership needed for black liberation theology today.

To sum up, the first generation of black liberation theology was forced to wage a culture of protest; resultantly the black theology activities of the founding generation emerged as a leadership of prophetic necessity. In contrast, the beginning of the twenty-first-century daily worldwide interconnectivity requires expanding black liberation theology activities into global cross-cultural leadership. The 1960s society and theology had to marshal a Herculean amount of energy to deconstruct rigid exclusive political and economic structures in society and rigid theological and religious systems in higher education. Now, while maintaining the prophetic and priestly ministries, we must expand to a practical leadership with global perspective: one that governs the material necessities of life (i.e., owning earth, air, and water) and one that governs the political policies (i.e., managing institutions) impacting working-class and poor families. Before expounding on these needs for today, we first explore the conditions and contexts of black theology's first generation.

FIRST GENERATION BLACK LIBERATION THEOLOGY

The 1950s efforts by Negro Americans to exercise their constitutional rights as US citizens and the 1960s call for black power to share in the material benefits of America drove black pastors in 1966 to create contemporary black liberation theology. On the side of the civil rights movement, numerous factors spurred the iconic Montgomery bus boycott of 1955, which was headed by Rev. Dr. Martin Luther King Jr. For example, we discover at least these two background contexts: the open-

---

8. See Gayraud S. Wilmore and James H. Cone, eds., *Black Theology: A Documentary History, 1966–1979* (Maryknoll, NY: Orbis, 1979); Gayraud S. Wilmore, *Black Religion and Black Radicalism: An Interpretation of the Religious History of African Americans* (Maryknoll, NY: Orbis, 1998); James H. Cone, *For My People: Black Theology and the Black Church* (Maryknoll, NY: Orbis, 1984); J. Deotis Roberts, *A Black Political Theology* (Philadelphia: Westminster, 1974); J. Deotis Roberts, *The Seasons of Life: By Grace and Gratitude. A Memoir* (Largo, MD: Charp Communications, 2007); and Diana L. Hayes, *And Still We Rise: An Introduction to Black Liberation Theology* (Mahwah, NJ: Paulist, 1996); Dwight N. Hopkins, *Black Theology: Essays on Global Perspectives* (Eugene, OR: Cascade, 2017); and Dwight N. Hopkins, *Black Theology: Essays on Gender Perspectives* (Eugene, OR: Cascade, 2017).

casket funeral of the deformed body of Emmett Till, and the international experience gained by Negro GIs who had served abroad in the Second World War and the Korean War.

Emmett Till was a fourteen-year-Negro boy from the South Side of Chicago sent to spend the summer with his uncle in Money, Mississippi. Following a dare of his local Mississippi cousins, Till went into a grocery store and, upon leaving, said "Bye baby" to the white female cashier, who happened to be the wife of the owner. Till was kidnapped at gunpoint by the husband and his brother. On August 28, 1955, they beat Till's body so terribly that his uncle could only identify the little boy by a ring on his finger. Till's mother insisted that his Chicago funeral have an open casket. *Jet* magazine carried that grotesque picture of the disfigured dead Till to almost every black home in America. Such a brutal outrage helped spur Negro impatience with the legal system of white power.[9]

In a similar fashion, Negro soldiers returning from military tours of duty abroad injected invigorating energy into Negroes' expectations.[10] To travel the world, interact with others as normal people in foreign lands, to don the uniform of one's country and, in certain instances, wield weapons of war in defense of one's nation, catalyzed a large segment of Negro GIs to return to the US and forbid any persons or situations from blocking them in the execution of their civil rights and their God-given rights as human beings. Consequently, when Rosa Parks,[11] a Christian, began the civil rights movement in Montgomery, Alabama on December 1, 1955 (a little over three months after the Emmett Till lynching), not only was the local Montgomery Negro population ready. Indeed, nationwide Negro communities had already been primed by the over-the-top sadistic Emmett Till murder and the enthusiastic determination of many Negro GIs returning home.

Eleven years later in 1966, the youth and student wing of the civil rights struggle combined various intuitions and thus crafted the black

9. Mamie Till-Mobley and Christopher Benson, *Death of Innocence: The Story of the Hate Crime That Changed America* (New York: One World Ballantine, 2003); and Devery S. Anderson and Julian Bond, *Emmett Till: The Murder That Shocked the World and Propelled the Civil Rights Movement* (Jackson: University Press of Mississippi, 2015).

10. Maria Hahn and Martin Klimke, *A Breath of Freedom: The Civil Rights Struggle, African American GIs, and Germany* (New York: Palgrave Macmillan, 2010), and Kimberley L. Phillips-Boehm, *War! What Is It Good For? Black Freedom Struggles and the US Military from World War II to Iraq* (Chapel Hill: University of North Carolina Press, 2012).

11. See Rosa Parks, *Rosa Parks: My Story* (London: Puffin, 1999); Douglas Brinkley, *Rosa Parks: A Life* (London: Penguin, 2005); and Jeanne Theoharis, *The Rebellious Life of Mrs. Rosa Parks* (Boston: Beacon, 2014).

power movement.[12] Their commonsense wisdom wondered why they had to allow their physical bodies to be damaged and killed by legal and illegal structures of white power in order to practice their constitutional rights. They felt duped by what they called white liberals on the federal level promising citizenship and the American dream but instead allowing the number of Negro bodies and the wounded to pile up at the hands of legal white policemen and illegal white paramilitary groups. In contrast, the youth and student wing of the civil rights movement sensed potential allies in the national liberation movements occurring in Africa, Asia, and South America. Thus the 1950s and 1960s served as a watershed whirlwind in the ongoing American experiment to realize democracy for all its citizens.

For the black pastors who initiated black liberation theology in 1966 (the same year as black power), God offered a kairos opening in the second half of the twentieth century—a divine window of grace and opportunity. And so they felt called to respond as the extension of biblical prophets from Jeremiah and Amos in the Old Testament to the historical Jesus of the New Testament. These pastors crafted a black liberation theology of prophetic ministry, speaking truth to structures of asymmetrical American power, and they participated in priestly ministry, healing the wounds of many African Americans across the country. In this regard, we can frame the founding generation of black liberation theology as one of prophetic and priestly leadership.

TWENTY-FIRST-CENTURY GLOBAL
CROSS-CULTURAL LEADERSHIP

Now we argue for expanding prophetic and priestly ministries to include twenty-first-century global cross-cultural leadership, which means developing ways of governing resources, institutions, and people's daily lives. The key is ownership of and access to wealth; that is, earth, air, and water. How can a global cross-cultural leadership of wealth accumulation and policy administration assist the black working class and the poor in inner cities to own their own businesses, generate jobs, and manage where they live? How do we expand the prophetic and priestly to practical ministries?

Such a leadership development of linking inner cities with the worldwide situation has direct impact on how people see themselves as proactive agents in their neighborhoods and internationally. And it directly

12. Stokely Carmichael, *Ready for Revolution: The Life and Struggles of Stokely Carmichael (Kwame Toure)* (New York: Scribner, 2005).

impacts tithes and offering for black churches, the shrinking of gang activities, the reduction of illegal industries, how police see black bodies, the presence and guidance of black fathers in the home, and the tax base required to improve streets, sidewalks, alleys, and bridges in the so-called American ghettoes.

Specifically, it includes preparing teenagers and young adults to govern locally and globally or else we stunt the future leadership of black America as well as of the US and the world. It entails preparing our children and our young people for governing material, human, and institutional resources in an intercultural earth neighborhood. It consists of equipping our youth to lead the fourth industrial revolution.[13] These dynamics of nurture will enable our young people to accumulate capital and manage communities for social responsibility to help themselves. Together with priestly and prophetic ministry, they can then better wield constructive and positive power in the US.

Clearly, with manufacturing jobs abandoning inner cities, our youth require training and retraining in Information and Communications Technologies, finance, service industries, and new manufacturing, all of which are now globally intertwined. Are we even aware of virtual reality, augmented reality, smart homes, robotics, 3D printing, and the internet of things? How does global finance operate in inner cities? What is the future of manufacturing and how do inner cities fit within such strategic plans? Where are the ecological sustainability industries? How does technology help to integrate all the systems required to make cities livable? What potentialities present themselves for black urban America and Africa to conduct educational exchanges and trade deals? And where is Jesus in all of this? To relish and respond to these emerging theological challenges today, black liberation theology now pivots to practical ministry, reconnecting the local with the international to govern earth, air, water, and people.

Several reasons justify why black liberation theology today requires intimate involvement in global cross-cultural leadership as a form of practical ministry in the twenty-first century.

First, black theology, since its founding, had already integrated its constructive theological statements with what it called the third world.

13. Klaus Schwab, *The Fourth Industrial Revolution* (Geneva: World Economic Forum, 2016); Foreign Affairs, *The Fourth Industrial Revolution: A Davos Reader* (www.foreignaffairs.com: Foreign Affairs, 2016). The fourth industrial revolution entails how technology becomes embedded in our society and our bodies. It is a digital revolution merging biological, physical, and digital realities into one. It is the fastest technological processing ever, one encompassing all of human reality and all human and natural systems. However, we do realize that the fourth revolution applies to the US and the developed nations. Some countries do not even have electricity yet. But this paper is about the US.

From its start, the first generation of black theologians eagerly sought out the All Africa Conference of Churches and held joint meetings on the African continent.[14] Then James H. Cone immersed black liberation theology USA in the yearly activities of the Ecumenical Association of Third World Theologians (EATWOT), the only worldwide organization comprised of all first-generation liberation theologians from Africa, Asia, the Caribbean, the Pacific Islands, and South America (i.e., the third world).[15] Simultaneously, black liberation theology USA and black liberation theology South Africa conducted bilateral meetings and conferences.[16] One of the important glues holding these pioneering gatherings together was their essential deconstructive and prophetic ministry. Hence, we today pursue the global as one expression and continuation of the long tradition of black theology, though expanding that conversation into a different direction.

Second, Jesus addresses ownership of wealth, governing people and resources, and technology enabling freedom. Specifically, when we view Luke 4:1–13, Jesus undergoes three forms of temptation. And in my theological imagination, I interpret them in the following way. He refuses the first temptation to turn stone into bread, which can signify wealth because it necessitates earth, air, and water to produce bread. He refuses the second temptation to rule over all the kingdoms of the world, which can signify policy management of resources and people. And he refuses the third temptation to fly into the air and rely on the techniques of the angels to aid him. On the surface one could claim that Jesus avoided and denied wealth, rulership, and technology for freedom. But actually he refuses these opportunities not because they exist as bad things in and of themselves. Rather, Jesus refuses to accept these offers because they provide gifts for *his own* individual, personal benefit, and because the giver embodies concentrated negative energy or extreme individualistic spirit.

Indeed, the evidence for this interpretation surfaces in Luke 4:16–20 where Jesus announces the only reason why he came to earth; that is to say, to liberate the poor and the oppressed. To proclaim good news to the poor entails the promise of a new life on earth and beyond. To proclaim freedom for the prisoner means providing the needed material necessities so that poor and working-class people will not go back to

14. National Committee of Black Churchmen, "A Message to the Churches from Oakland, California," in *Black Theology: A Documentary History, 1966–1979*, ed. Gayraud S. Wilmore and James H. Cone (Maryknoll, NY: Orbis, 1979), 103–7.

15. James H. Cone, *My Soul Looks Back* (Maryknoll, NY: Orbis, 1986). J. Deotis Roberts, *Black Theology in Dialogue* (Philadelphia: Westminster, 1987).

16. Simon Maimela and Dwight N. Hopkins, eds., *We Are One Voice: Essays on Black Theology in South Africa and the USA* (Johannesburg: Skotaville Press, 1989).

jail. Recovery of sight for the blind connotes both spiritual and physical sight to remove oneself from unjust structures. To set the oppressed free denotes the abolition of that which causes unfreedom. Jesus came to earth for this one purpose. To fulfill his vocation, Jesus also will work with people to enjoy an abundant life for themselves and their families. This Christian story remains a major contribution to the world's religions, spiritualities, and self-cultivation practices. The poor, the prisoner, the blind, and the oppressed can have ultimate hope in life.

Therefore, elements within this Luke 4:16 proclamation narrative of liberating working-class, poor, and oppressed families include facilitating their ownership of and access to wealth (i.e., earth, air, and water), governance of the resources and people where they live, and ownership of the technology essential for functioning in a globally connected, twenty-four-hour-cycle world. Returning to Luke 4:1–13, we see that the problem is that the three temptations were not offered to communities of working-class, poor, and oppressed families. And thus Jesus refused any temptations geared to his individual self and personal aggrandizement. Remember in Matthew 25 in the sheep and goat commandments, he clarifies how our relation to him hinges on how we deal with the least in our societies, not on his glorified status in and of itself.

Moreover, Jesus says no to the three temptations because the one making the offer exemplifies a concentrated power of internal negative energy or spirit.

Third, in addition to the tradition (of black liberation theology) and the Bible (Luke 4:1–13) motivating my suggestion that black theology be involved in global cross-cultural leadership, commonsense logic also points in this direction. For instance, one of the beautiful contributions Christianity makes to the international family of religions, spiritualities, and self-cultivation practices is faith in Immanuel (which translates into God's spirit with us in Jesus; Matt 1:23, NIV). Immanuel means, regardless of the heights and depths of our living, Jesus (God's spiritual revelation on earth) is with us through it all. Some world religions add the dimensions of reincarnation or the presence of the ancestors. But Christianity gives us a God ever present, everywhere. Thus rituals of Christianity do not exist in and of themselves, separated from the needs of global cultures and societies.

Instead, Jesus reveals himself like a permanent and reliable mountain in local and international circumstances, in our immediate neighborhoods, in our houses and apartments, and with our global neighbors brought close to us through technology and economics. Christianity deals with all of human beings' cultural necessities around the world.

There is no separate reality where Immanuel is absent. There is no separate space where Jesus does not live. Immanuel is not a tribal, provincial, and national religion, but a world religion insofar as it aids global neighbors to embrace their own particular cultures while affirming the best in other nations' cultures. Because Immanuel lacks a ceiling or walls of containment, we too must follow that path wherever it takes us globally.

Finally, experience warrants black liberation theology's crafting of a practical ministry defined by global cross-cultural leadership. For example, I initiated and managed a fourteen-country network called the International Association of Black Religions and Spiritualities.[17] The network consisted of Hawaii, Fiji, Australia, Japan, India, South Africa, Botswana, Zimbabwe, Ghana, Cuba, Jamaica, Brazil, England, and the US. The programmatic thrust focused on exchanging youth and students from different countries around the world. It became clear that the future leadership of the fourteen countries resided in those young people eager to envision their own global cross-cultural leadership. Indeed, where such a yearning, creativity, and practical implementation took place, one discovered pockets of energy, innovation, and local-global connections.

As I traveled globally, visiting and living in the fourteen countries and several other nations outside of the network, I experienced a comparative lesson in intercultural and cross-cultural hope for planet Earth. Despite the particularities of various cultures, all peoples wanted the same thing: stable families, education and a future for their children, productive jobs, access to technology, healthy local communities, sustainable ecologies, and world friendship, safety, and peace. What impeded successful productive international relations was low cultural intelligence about other countries' cultural presuppositions. To be harmonious neighbors on planet Earth entailed, at the minimum, learning about cultures of other nations.

At this point, let us recapitulate our line of thought. So far our conversation has followed James A. Noel's call to redefine "the subject of knowledge in relationship to other phenomena that appear in making such a move." Along that way, we noticed the factors undergirding the 1960s black liberation theology's stress on prophetic and priestly ministries. We then turned to a spectrum of opportunities calling black liberation theology to practical ministry; that is, twenty-first-century global cross-cultural leadership. Prophetic ministry demands a counterattack

17. See Dwight N. Hopkins, *Black Theology: Essays on Global Perspectives* (Eugene, OR: Cascade, 2017), especially chapter 11, "The International Association of Black Religions and Spiritualities"; and Dwight N. Hopkins and Marjorie Lewis, eds., *Another World Is Possible: Spiritualities and Religions of Global Darker Peoples* (London: Equinox, 2009).

on unjust structures. Priestly ministry requires those trained in healing. But practical ministry looks at the local and international connections and works on enhancing a leadership that will construct a new society through governing wealth and people. Having made the case for new leadership, how do we implement this vocation of linking the local with the global? What do we need to carry out the Luke story about Jesus spreading bread, rulership, and technological freedom to the least in our inner cities and rural areas while stretching forth their hands beyond their borders? In which direction does black liberation theology have to expand its work with black working-class and poor families and neighborhoods?

BUILDING GLOBAL CROSS-CULTURAL LEADERSHIP

As an incentive for discovering an answer, we circle back to Noel's book *Black Religion and the Imagination of Matter in the Atlantic World* where he writes the following:

> Atlanticization of the world through slavery, [and] colonialism made the world "global" for the first time in history. This meant that increasingly everything that occurred anywhere in the world had the entire world as its context. Consequently, we can view things happening in different parts of the world as being interrelated not due to simply linear causality but to the influence of the broader global context of those [events'] occurrence.[18]

I would parallel Noel's theoretical framework of the Atlanticization of the world beginning in 1492 with today's globalization of the world during the last quarter of the twentieth century. Atlanticization made the Western world global for the first time. However, now the ability of digital technology to compress time and space has enabled everyone in the global community to potentially experience events and people in real time. Everyone in the world with the appropriate technology can see any event in the world simultaneously. Likewise, digital technology of WeChat and Skype can put into immediate conversation together, live and in color, a person in Chicago, Dalian, Kauai, Accra, Bangalore, London, Rio, Havana, and Dubai in an ongoing video conference call.

More particular for our purposes, we want to underscore Noel's claim when he writes "that increasingly everything that occurred anywhere in the world had the entire world as its context. Consequently, we can view things happening in different parts of the world as being interrelated not

18. Hopkins, *Black Theology*, 187.

due to simply linear causality but to the influence of the broader global context of those [events'] occurrence." This analysis brings vital insight to the imperative for black liberation theology to implement a global cross-cultural leadership. Particularly, we aid black poor and working-class families to bridge their local contexts with international dynamics. Restated, we prepare our youth and young adults for their possible local-global cross-cultural leadership. The spirit of the times is one of interconnecting planet Earth. Indeed, systems are already interconnected now. Many churches (obviously in the advanced economies, but also increasingly in large churches in the developing world) broadcast live services to world audiences. And even US inner-city youth have cell phones, which can become smartphones wired into international knowledge.

For me this ongoing dynamic of aiding working-class and poor families is profoundly a theological one. Specifically learning from the 1960s black theology's first-generation question of "where was Jesus in the civil rights and black consciousness movements?" we too can pose a similar query for today: Where is Jesus in the immediate, split-second international interconnectivity? If Jesus already precedes us from the perspective of his world leadership, then we are called to follow him on his path. Therefore, for the reminder of our conversation, we wish to consider three ways of moving black liberation theology as it serves working-class and poor people along this journey.

In a word, how do we forge ourselves and those at the bottom of society into networks enabling us to consciously extend our hands across the oceans to build healthy communities and healthy individuals in communities? In fact, the ultimate goal of bridging cultures from the experiences of the bottom of societies is a new reality "on earth as it is in heaven" (Matt 6:10, NIV). For me, this entails helping the bottom of society govern wealth (i.e., earth, air, and water) and people and harmonizing the sacred breath internal to their bodies in such a way that their breathing is in line with the energy of nature.

And the first step for black liberation theology to consider on the path to global cross-cultural leadership is to assist working-class and poor families to focus on *knowing oneself*. Scientific research on worldwide leadership assists us here in unpacking the importance of knowing oneself. There are decades of accumulated practical experiences, published books and articles, and curricula and classes taught on the vocation and art of global cross-cultural leadership as intentional and meticulous appreciation of self-understanding.

Specifically, we draw lessons from Bill George, known for his research and writing on leadership of national and international organizations. Bill George describes five dimensions of authentic leadership for knowing oneself: (1) understanding our purpose; (2) practicing solid values; (3) leading with our heart; (4) establishing long-term relationships; and (5) having personal self-discipline.

We understand our (1) purpose by becoming more intentional about the passion driving what we do. How many of us take time to think about the passions we had growing up and the passions we hunger for today? As a theologian, I see one's vocation emerging out of the connection between passion and purpose. God has called us for a purpose and God gives us the passion to witness to that purpose.

Purpose, clarified by passion, is followed by being true to our (2) values, the second aspect of knowing oneself. Under pressure, what values do we practice in the crucible of adversities or temptations? When I use my values to make a decision, would I be comfortable if these values and this decision appeared on the front page of my local newspaper? As a theologian, I translate this to mean, what Christian non-negotiables are my anchors in times of storms?

Next after values, we encounter leading with our (3) hearts, which includes expressing compassion for others. One of the clearest criteria in the Jesus story is the unleashing of the human capacity to have empathy for someone who has fallen on emotional and material hard times.[19] Compassion consists of both praying for the spiritual well-being of each person and assisting the person with material resources so he or she can control his or her own material well-being.[20] Compassion also emphasizes each of us having compassion for our own selves, especially when we have made mistakes or done wrong. In fact, a key to success is going through and learning from many failures. Thus self-compassion is to recognize that we are still children of God and to maintain hope of eventually achieving our goals. We extend our hearts to ourselves for faith affirmation in our sacred creation and in the lessons of leadership development.[21] That is to say, after the deep darkness of the many midnight

19. In John 8:1–11, even though the law called for stoning a woman who had committed adultery, Jesus refused. He had compassion for her and set her free from the established religious leaders.

20. Note in Mark 6:34 where Jesus feeds five thousand people because he has compassion for them.

21. I think the second of the two great commandments is mainly about developing a healthy individual self (in order to love the neighbor). An individual who has unbalanced spirit inside the body is not in a healthy condition to love the neighbor. ("Love the Lord your God with all your heart and with all your soul and with all your mind and with all your strength. The second is this: 'Love your neighbor as yourself.' There is no commandment greater than these" [Matt 12:30–31 NIV].)

hours of our efforts, joy and success will eventually come in the morning.

The fourth aspect of knowing the self resides in an orientation of nurturing (4) long-term friendships. Leaders are people who share their stories and remain open to hear the stories of our local and global neighbors. This dynamic enables the process of building long-term friendships instead of using people for short-term gain. Long-term friendships suggest that we see people as human beings first; we actually look at the many neighbors across the earth as bearing the *imago Dei* (i.e., the image of God) underneath their disparate political, ideological, cultural, and economic outer garments, so to speak. And fifth and finally, all authentic leaders for the twenty-first century should practice (5) self-discipline. Bill George writes the following:

> To be authentic, leaders must behave with consistency and self-discipline, not letting stress get in the way of their judgment. They must learn to handle any kind of pressure and stay cool and calm. Handling unexpected challenges requires being in peak condition. Like a professional athlete, they need consistent habits to keep their minds sharp and their bodies in shape.[22]

22. Bill George, *Authentic Leadership: Rediscovering the Secrets to Creating Lasting Value* (San Francisco: Jossey-Bass, 2003), 41. Also review p. 18 and all of chapter 2, "The Transformation of Leaders." Bill George elaborates on this point of knowing yourself in his next book, *True North: Discover Your Authentic Leadership* (San Francisco: Jossey-Bass, 2007) especially in chapter 4, "Knowing Your Authentic Self." Here he expounds on how framing our life stories will reveal to us our passions, which as mentioned earlier, brings our purpose to the surface. He has an apt saying: the framing of our life stories is not mainly retelling the facts; rather, it is how we want to look back to discover the passions and moments we felt alive throughout our lives.
   With his take on global leadership studies, Warren Bennis presents guiding vision, passion, integrity, trust, curiosity, and daring. The first four probably seem commonsense wisdom. Hence I underscore the notions of curiosity and daring. Black liberation theology in twenty-first-century global cross-cultural leadership needs to reconnect to these two ingredients, which manifested more clearly with its 1966 origins. One might call Warren Bennis the father of leadership development. Review his *On Becoming a Leader: The Leadership Classic*, revised and updated (Philadelphia: Basic Books, 2009), 33–35.
   If Bennis is the father, then Peter F. Drucker holds the genealogical title of grandfather of global organizational, wealth, and people governing/management leadership. In one of his many classic texts, *The Effective Executive: The Definitive Guide to Getting the Right Things Done* (New York: Harper Business, 2006), xi, he presents the following attributes of an effective leader: "They asked, 'What needs to be done?'; They asked, 'What is right for the enterprise?'; They developed action plans.; They took responsibility for decisions.; They took responsibility for communicating.; They were focused on opportunities rather than problems.; They ran productive meetings.; They thought and said 'we' rather than 'I.'"
   A fourth generation of global leadership development research includes, but is not exhausted by, David Cottrell, *Monday Morning Leadership: 8 Mentoring Sessions You Can't Afford to Miss* (Dallas: CornerStone Leadership Institute, 2009); his *The Magic Question: A Simple Question Every Leader Dreams of Answering* (New York: McGraw-Hill, 2013); C. Otto Scharmer, *Theory U: Leading from the Future as It Emerges* (Oakland, CA: Berrett-Koehler, 2009); and Otto

Self-discipline includes exercise, sleeping, and eating healthily; and, George strongly emphasizes the importance of daily meditation and a deep faith in God. For black liberation theology, this stands as the plumb line for knowing oneself.

After knowing oneself, the second major category for implementing global cross-cultural leadership of poor and working people is *knowing the culture of one's own home country*. Cross-cultural leadership tells each person to bring his or her knowledge, appreciation, and love of one's home culture to the global conversation and exchange of ideas. For example, when we talk about knowing the culture of the United States of America, two of the many subcultures constituting the US are the western European heritage and the black American contribution. We could make a strong argument that the *best* of the western European values in US culture are compassion (from ancient Israel), individual rights (from ancient Greece), representative government (from ancient Rome), and hope (from the origin of the Jesus story in Christianity). (I am not naïve enough to forget when a spirituality of wickedness has influenced the USA.) Similarly, the black American tradition offers four cultural values: nature with the Conjurer figure; reversal with the Trickster protagonist; ambiguity with the Outlaw character; and liberation for the poor with the Christian representatives. Knowing one's own culture basically answers the question: What foundational values make your country unique in the world?[23] Since black liberation theology comprises two cultural traditions—African and American—it needs to embrace a profound self-understanding of its western American and African American dimensions to fully be self-confident as it builds friendships with other cultures around the world.

The third and final major category for implementing global cross-cultural leadership of those at society's bottom is *knowing the culture of at least one foreign country*. The scholarly research on facilitating global cross-cultural interconnectivity assists us here. The purpose of this literature is to teach us how to develop leadership for approaching other global cultures. What general framework do we use to identify the unique cultures of diverse nations? Within this discourse, Andy Molinsky presents the worldview and practice of what he calls "global dexterity." He writes:

Global Dexterity is about learning to adapt your behavior across cul-

Scharmer and Katrin Kaufer, *Leading from the Emerging Future: From Ego-System to Eco-System Economies* (Oakland, CA: Berrett-Koehler, 2013).

23. See my chapter "A Black American Christian Theological Anthropology: Black, United States, and China," in my *Black Theology: Essays on Global Perspectives* (Eugene, OR: Cascade, 2017).

tures—no matter what culture you come from, what culture you are going to, or the situation you find yourself in . . . so that you are effective and appropriate in that setting without feeling that you are losing yourself in the process . . . adapting behavior across cultures.[24]

His adapting behavior model teaches us how to read and practice cultural codes in a new country or new cultural situation. Molinsky claims that all countries and all groups of people have a six-dimensional framework that constitutes global dexterity. These six dimensions define how members of that country or culture operate. They are: "Directness: How straightforwardly am I expected to communicate in this situation? Enthusiasm: How much positive emotion and energy am I expected to show to others in this situation? Formality: How much deference and respect am I expected to demonstrate in this situation? Assertiveness: How strongly am I expected to express my voice in this situation? Self-promotion: How positively am I expected to speak about my skills and accomplishments in this situation? [And] personal disclosure: How much can I reveal about myself in this situation?"[25]

Regarding knowing other cultures, some scholars introduce the notion of living into what they describe as CQ, or cultural intelligence. For Christopher Earley and Soon Ang, CQ entails three aspects: cognitive, motivational, and behavioral skills.[26] The cognitive includes knowledge of self, social environments, and information handling. The motivational underscores one's internal drive toward and curiosity about diverse cultures. And behavioral means having the skills to put into practice our knowledge and desire.

Similarly, David Livermore describes drive, knowledge, strategy, and action as the four elements of CQ required for global cross-cultural interconnectivity. His nuance is to foreground CQ drive before knowledge; thus, we have to have interest, confidence, and drive to adapt cross-culturally. And before we can get to action, we need a clear strategy.[27]

In addition, in her text, *The Culture Map*, Erin Meyer offers us another paradigm comprised of how diverse cultures communicate, evaluate, persuade, lead, decide, trust, disagree, and schedule time.[28] And finally,

24. *Global Dexterity: How to Adapt Your Behavior across Cultures without Losing Yourself in the Process* (Boston: Harvard Business Review Press, 2013), ix.

25. *Global Dexterity*, 14.

26. P. Christopher Earley and Soon Ang, *Cultural Intelligence: Individual Interactions Across Cultures* (Stanford, CA: Stanford Business Books, 2003), 9, 12, 59, 68–86.

27. David Livermore, *Leading with Cultural Intelligence: The Real Secret to Success*, 2nd ed. (New York: American Management Association, 2015), ix–x, 4–5, 27–30, 38.

28. Erin Meyer, *The Culture Map: Breaking Through the Invisible Boundaries of Global Business* (New York: Public Affairs, 2014), 16.

coauthors Trompenaars and Hampden-Turner draw on their empirical and theoretical studies of global cross-cultural work from the last twenty-five years, a period in which they conducted 1,500 cross-cultural training programs in over twenty-five countries. They shrink their conclusions down to the following observations about the basic characteristics that all cultures embody: All countries are concerned about relationships with people, attitudes toward time, and attitudes with regard to the environment. Thus, all cultures revolve around these three plumb lines.[29]

Our point here is simply to exhibit the rich and diverse literature on the subject of building global cross-leadership through knowledge of oneself, knowledge of one's own home country, and knowledge of at least one foreign culture.

CONCLUSION

Let us conclude our discussion. We have used a method of correlation for two claims. First, what conditions in the 1960s gave rise to black liberation theology's leadership? That context resulted in prophetic and priestly ministries. Second, what contemporary factors challenge black liberation theology's ministry? Circumstances today require us to maintain the priestly and prophetic while *we now expand practical ministry into a global cross-cultural leadership of working-class and poor families who govern wealth (i.e., earth, air, and water), people (i.e., through policies), and technology (i.e., the latest means of communication) in the twenty-first century.* We drew on the Christian tradition of black theology, the biblical stories of Jesus, commonsense logic, and a social analysis of the present moment to reach this conclusion. If black liberation theology still adheres to Jesus's liberation anchored in the poor and oppressed throughout the world, then global cross-cultural leadership has to link the local urban and rural areas of black poor and working-class people with the

29. Fons Trompenaars and Charles Hampden-Turner, *Riding the Waves of Culture: Understanding Diversity in Global Business*, 3rd ed. (New York: McGraw-Hill, 2012), 10–13. Other works include Edgar H. Schein, *Organizational Culture and Leadership*, 4th ed. (San Francisco: Jossey-Bass, 2010); Edgar H. Schein, *The Corporate Culture Survival Guide*, new rev. ed. (San Francisco: Jossey-Bass, 2009); Geert Hofstede, Gert Jan Hofstede, and Michael Minkov, *Culture and Organizations: Intercultural Cooperation and Its Importance for Survival* (New York: McGraw-Hill, 2010); Dean Allen Foster, *Negotiating Across Borders: How to Negotiate Business Successfully Anywhere in the World* (New York: McGraw-Hill, 1992); Jeanne M. Brett, *Negotiating Globally: How to Negotiate Deals, Resolve Disputes, and Make Decisions Across Cultural Boundaries*, 3rd ed. (San Francisco: Jossey-Bass, 2014); Aimin Yan and Yadong Luo, *International Joint Ventures: Theory and Practice* (Armonk, NY: M. E. Sharpe, 2001); and Kate Berardo and Darla K. Deardorff, eds., *Building Cultural Competence: Innovative Activities and Models* (Sterling, VA: Stylus, 2012).

rapid interconnectivity of the world. We then concluded our conversation with theoretical and practical models from leadership development
and twenty-first-century intercultural research.

In James A. Noel's language, we are pushing to redefine "the subject
of knowledge in relationship to other phenomena that appear in making
such a move." Therefore, we redefine the subject of black liberation theology to expand into a practical ministry because the phenomena of the
twenty-first century appear in making such a move. From a healthy
materiality in which poor and working-class families have agency, we
can imagine their new form of leadership; one defining a practice of
ministry where they govern their own wealth, people, and technology in
their own communities and even the world. However, that move necessitates working with them to link their local eyes to the international
horizons in global cross-cultural leadership. As Immanuel—a global spirit
of liberation—Jesus is already ahead of us in developing new communities and new individuals. Why? Because the Christian story recounts
Jesus's resurrected spirit already traveling the pathways of the world and
bringing comfort and hope that another material world is possible for the
majority lacking wealth. Thus, the role of theology is to consciously link
the vision, values, and passion of the human condition with the future
insights and joyful possibilities offered by Jesus to all of humankind now.

As a final example, let me share some of my own work in this area
where working-class and poor black men daily confront the world in
their local neighborhoods. Since 1998, I have been part of a men's
ministry on the South Side of Chicago. From this experience, we discover that young teenage boys and young adult men are already caught
up in the relation between the local and the global. Increasing black
male unemployment is directly connected to manufacturing jobs going
abroad. In a similar fashion, one could make a strong case that the drugs
and illegal guns flooding the South Side have international ties. Moreover, brothers and sisters who are immigrants from other countries own
quite a number of small shops in this inner-city area. Even the building of jails and maintenance of prisons are linked to private companies
operating on a world scale. Disproportionately, black and brown teenage
boys and young men occupy this profitable incarceration business.

Furthermore, in sports, many of these inner-city males follow their
favorite American football and basketball teams that are more and more
playing exhibition games in Europe. Relatedly, they watch particular
black athletes in the Olympics all over the world. Concerning the cost of
goods on which these black males spend their money, pricing is linked
to international factors such as Brexit, the dynamics in China and India,

the bankruptcy of Greece, the underdevelopment of Africa, and other processes. And these teenagers and young men are already plugged into or have the potential to get involved in the global. Specifically, although many might not have computers at home, many have cell phones that can be converted into smartphones, thus allowing them to have instantaneous connections to each of the 194 nations in the world. Part of lifting their eyes from the local to the global and back again consists of exposing them to other possibilities beyond their current space and time and, simultaneously, helping them to gain wealth and jobs in order to stabilize their lives.

The emergence of new contemporary factors (distinct from the 1960s black liberation theology) has direct implications for communities of faith and other forms of religious and nonreligious leadership in African American communities. For instance, a prophetic church ministry encourages the working class and the poor to speak truth to unjust structures so that the powerful will eventually leave their wayward path and come back to a path of sharing God's creation with all people. A priestly church ministry enables them to appreciate the harmony and balance of life energy inside of each breath internal to their bodies so that as unjust structures become more democratized, they can move into leadership positions based on the harmony and balance of their breathing inside of their bodies. With prophetic ministry changing external structures and priestly ministry changing the calmness of their spirit inside their bodies, practical church ministry means working with these teenagers and young adults to govern wealth, people, and technology for a healthy society and healthy individuals in society in their local communities. Yet the novelty of today's interconnectivity requires a theological vision and implementation linking the local with the new global.

In a word, black liberation theology works with the church and other religious and nonreligious organizations to remain on the path of the Jesus story of the Bible and the journey of liberation and practice of freedom for poor and working-class people locally and throughout the world. Forging global cross-cultural leadership thus presents an exciting challenge for new life for those whom Jesus called the least in society.

15.

Shoki Coe and Contextualization in African Christian Theology

AUGUSTINE CHINGWALA MUSOPOLE

> Contextualization as Coe envisioned it was a way of making missiological sense of the incarnation, the ultimate (and divine) form of contextualization: God came to humanity in the form of a human for the sake of humanity.
> —Matthew Paul Buccheri

INTRODUCTION

I never met Shoki Coe, but having worked in Taiwan and taught at Tainan Theological College and Seminary, where he was the first Taiwanese principal, I have come to know about him and to love him. His theology has impacted tremendously my own theology as an African. Coe's name is synonymous with theological contextualization. When Coe propounded his concept, it was an idea whose time had come in the midst of changing political situations, especially in Africa and Asia. It was like a bombshell to which many people reacted positively or negatively. He was an Asian speaking on the global stage, addressing the powerful and dominant players, especially as far as theology and missiology were concerned. Just as the idea of dialogue as a missionary method was popular within liberal circles, the idea of contextualization caught the attention of the evangelical family where it was debated vigorously. The idea of contextualization was a critique of both missionary enterprises and Western theological hegemony, and it provided a much-needed corrective to the discourse.

There is much in common to the Taiwanese and African contexts. As people who have been colonized and oppressed on the one hand

and then denied their own identity on the other, context becomes very important in the self-definition and self-understanding of our doing of theology. I am grateful for the opportunity to share in this celebration of an illustrious life in the theological field both locally and globally. This presentation is a panoramic view of contextualization within African Christianity.

GOD ACTS CONTEXTUALLY

God is a contextual God who delights in variety. God's revelation is equally contextual but done to reach all of humanity since God loves the whole world and is also the judge of the same. The saying "Think global, act local" acts as a clue to the covenant relationship with Israel and finds its culmination in the incarnation. Abraham was told in his calling that "all the people of the earth will be blessed through you."[1] God's vision was for the entire *oikoumene*. God reminded the descendants of Abraham through the prophet Isaiah that they had been appointed to be a light even for the gentiles, a mission that they had forgotten.[2] Jesus confirmed this mission as his own mission, which he came to fulfill, as testified to in the Gospels of Matthew and Luke.[3]

Therefore, Coe's discovery of contextualization was not limited to the Taiwanese context or the Asian context but was for the whole world. It was a challenge to the Western theological hegemony that was philosophically and theologically hedged in by the universality of Christian dogma as formulated by the West in a one-size-fits-all approach; it was the same in theological formulation. The incarnation as pointed out is a model par excellence of divine contextualization. When Coe was announcing his new missionary paradigm, the African theological scene was dealing with issues similar to those he was concerned with. In 1958, at the All Africa Church Conference in Ibadan, Nigeria, African theologians wrestled with issues of revelation and African beliefs. Ever since, they have been in search of a theological methodology that is contextual. They have talked of indigenization, Africanization, black liberation theology, inculturation, theology of transformation, women theologies, and Umunthu (Ubuntu) theology. Let us briefly look at each one of these and some of the leading proponents. When Coe started talking of contextualization, he never realized that he was opening the theological floodgates in Africa too. The stopper had been removed from the dog-

1. Genesis 12:3.
2. Isaiah 42:6–7.
3. Matthew 5:17; Luke 4:18–19.

matic theology of the West and the theological air could not be put back in the bottle, thus prompting new attempts at theologizing in African Christianity.

THEOLOGICAL CONTEXTUALIZATION IN AFRICA

In 1957 Ghana gained independence from Britain as colonialism started to unravel and by 1994, most of the countries north of the Zambezi River had gained their independence. Missionaries turned over their mission work to local leadership, and this set them on the path to redefining themselves theologically, thus giving birth to African theology. Countries south of the Zambezi River continued to exist under white rule and racial discrimination. Mozambique was under the Portuguese; Zimbabwe had declared independence from Britain but was still under white rule; Namibia was under white-ruled South Africa as a mandate colony since the end of the First World War. South Africa was the bastion of white rule with its discriminatory policy of apartheid. The result was that two theological trends developed in Africa. The independent north pursued what came to be known as African Christian theology and focused on the relevance of the gospel to African cultures, spirituality, and philosophy. Those still under colonialism developed an African Christian theology of liberation that came to be known as black theology of liberation.

PIONEERS IN AFRICAN THEOLOGY

African culture was vilified by most of the missionaries and European explorers: Africa was the Dark Continent, its people were dark in appearance, were ignorant and benighted, and pagan through and through. It was the stone that the builders rejected that now became the chosen one for this new generation of theologians. These theologians engaged themselves in an exercise to retrieve traditions of wisdom that have sustained African communities from time immemorial. The missionaries had left a Christianity with its Western theological perspective, which proved inadequate for African Christians. Therefore, they sought to contextualize theological understanding, a task that is continuing to this day.

African Christian theology developed in stages. Initially it was called indigenous theology and its leading proponents were, among the Protestants, Prof. Emmanuel Bolaji Idowu of Ibadan University in Nigeria, J. B. Danquah of Ghana and Harry Sawyerr teaching at Fourah

Bay College in Sierra Leone, and Kwesi Dickson of Ghana. Among the Roman Catholics there were John Mary Waliggo and Charles Nyamiti. Their methodology was one of matching Western theological and dogmatic thoughts with African thought forms. For instance, the doctrine of the communion of saints was related to the concept of ancestors in African religion and culture. John Mbiti of Kenya sought to identify divine attributes within African cultures in his book *Concepts of God in Africa*. These theologians were accused by Okot p'Bitek, an anthropologist from Uganda, of clothing African deities in Greek attire. In other words, they did not go far enough in their indigenization program. For these theologians the racial question was not an issue since their countries had been decolonized.

John Mbiti, who belonged to the indigenous school, provided a bridge to move on to an African theology with emphasis on culture and religious philosophy. Roman Catholic theologians picked up this orientation in order to develop what has come to be called inculturation tinged with liberation elements. The leading proponents of this are Vincent Mulago; Jean-Marc Ela and Engelbert Mveng, both of Cameroon; Bénézet Bujo and Bishop Tharcisse Tshibangu of the Democratic Republic of Congo; Fabien Eboussi Boulaga, Charles Nyamiti, and Laurenti Magesa, to mention a few.

BLACK LIBERATION THEOLOGY IN SOUTH AFRICA

For theologians in the south of the Zambezi River, however, colonialism was still an issue. It was compounded by racism, the worst of which was the apartheid system in South Africa and Namibia. What was needed for them was the adoption of the black theology of liberation as expounded in the United States by leading lights such as James Cone and Albert Cleage, among many others. Therefore, young South African black theologians took up the task of theologizing within the context of racism and apartheid. Among them were Allan Boesak, Itumeleng Mosala, Simon Maimela, Bishop Manas Buthelezi, Augustine Shutte, and Archbishop Desmond Tutu. When South Africa got its independence in 1994, black theology of liberation fizzled out as the majority of its proponents were sucked into the new administration. In its place emerged Ubuntu theology and philosophy when Rev. Dr. Gideon Khabela, himself supervised by Prof. James Cone, organized a conference on Ubuntu just before the Federal Theological Seminary of Southern Africa closed its doors.

CIRCLE OF CONCERNED AFRICAN WOMEN THEOLOGIANS

Women theologians, however, have reacted critically to the inculturation efforts in doing theology. Given the dominant patriarchal cultures of Africa, women have found themselves to be victims of oppression in a variety of ways. While they work the most, they never enjoy the full benefits of their work. Therefore, the Circle of Concerned African Women Theologians, which was started by Prof. Mercy Amba Oduyoye of Ghana, has championed women's liberation in both African cultures and Christianity. African women theologians have proved very productive in terms of theological work, with special emphasis on HIV/ AIDS, the scourge of Africa. They have also highlighted issues relating to domestic violence and the plight of the girl child owing to patriarchal cultural hegemony. Biblical studies have played an important part within the Circle and the contextual challenges related to hermeneutics. Even as they have critiqued African cultures for their patriarchal hegemony, they have also found within African cultures empowering and liberating motifs, and traditions of wisdom to warrant their usability in theology.

THEOLOGY OF RECONSTRUCTION

There have been differing approaches and motifs to this task of contextualization. After indigenization, inculturation, and liberation, some theologians have found these approaches inadequate for the challenges that Africa is facing today, for instance, neocolonialism, poverty, diseases, underdevelopment, globalization, free-market economics, and global cultural hegemony. The Exodus motif was not sufficient to inspire African Christianity to be involved in the current challenges. To this end, Prof. Jesse Mugambi of Nairobi University in Kenya has proposed a theology of transformation based on the words of Nehemiah:

> You see the trouble we are in. Jerusalem lies in ruins, and its gates have been burnt with fire. Come, let us rebuild the wall of Jerusalem, and we will no longer be in disgrace.[4]

Along with Charles Villa-Vicencio, Jesse Mugambi felt strongly that the motif of Exodus and liberation had become irrelevant at a time when all of Africa had been liberated politically. What was now required was the rebuilding of Africa from the ruins of colonialism. Jesse Mugambi also

4. Nehemiah 2:17.

felt that the motif of culture retrieval and inculturation were anachronistic in view of the modernization of Africa. Therefore, the most appropriate theological motif was one of building or reconstruction. The reconstruction theological motif is meant to address many challenges that Africa and the African church are facing, namely, poverty, disease, globalization, and underdevelopment. This did not mean that inculturation was not important, but that it was one of the most important factors within the new and modern context.

UMUNTHU OR UBUNTU THEOLOGY

The newest methodology to emerge on the continent, especially in the southern part, is that of Ubuntu or Umunthu theology. It is based on anthropology or humanness as seen in the face of Christ as the incarnate one who preferred to call himself the Son of Man. Much ink has been spilled over the Christological task of explaining this title. Some see its roots in the Hebrew scriptures where they find the expression in the book of Daniel. In its application to Ezekiel as a title, it points to his humanity. However, Jesus tended to insist on it for himself as a characteristic of his being. There are several such words that speak of the characteristic of a person and not to be understood biologically as one born of a father and mother. The term *boanerges* was applied to John and James on account of their fiery anger. The name Barnabas meant "son of encouragement," and when we meet a person of that name, we see nothing but one given to encouraging another, for instance, Mark and Paul. Therefore, Son of Man means someone with a characteristic of authentic humanness, which the Gospel of John describes. It was related to his incarnation that he is described as the Word that became human and dwelt with humanity. He was a uniquely divine glorious sight that was full of grace and truth. In other words, Jesus manifested authentic human character.[5] Therefore, Ubuntu or Umunthu theology takes its cue from this as a theology informed by humanness as seen in the face of Christ. It has nothing to do with a fallen sinful humanity which he came to restore, but the revelation of a new humanity. It has to do with human transformation that conforms to the image of Christ. In this manner, it goes beyond a theology of transformation that is a mere intellectual paradigm; Ubuntu or Umunthu theology starts from human transformation as both a spiritual, historical, and existential reality. This is what St. Paul meant when he stated,

5. John 1:14.

So from now on we regard no one from a worldly point of view. Though we once regarded Christ in this way, we do so no longer. Therefore, if anyone is in Christ, he is a new creation; the old has gone, the new has come! All this is from God who reconciled us to himself through Christ and gave us the ministry of reconciliation: that God was reconciling the world to himself through Christ, not counting men's sins against them.[6]

Without this profound existential transformation, any other form of transformation is only skin-deep, external, material, and without the blessings meant for humanity from the beginning of creation. This theology sees both creation and salvation as having to do with humanization as seen in the face of Christ. It is more than salvation of the soul, that Greek relic which has distorted the gospel for a couple of millennia. Humanity was created and redeemed for glory.

AFRICAN EVANGELICAL THEOLOGY

Another theological typology that has been playing itself out on the African continent is what is called African evangelical theology vis-a-vis African ecumenical theology, which has tended to associate itself with the work of the World Council of Churches (WCC). It presumes that the ecumenicals consider themselves liberal theologically while the evangelicals are conservative. It is not easy to disentangle the two since African Christianity is missionary in origin, and all missionaries were from conservative Christianity in the West. For all practical purposes, African Christianity is the most conservative and those who are associated with the WCC are also actually conservative ecumenical evangelicals. Just as global evangelicals have been affected by the contextualization movement, African evangelicals also have been challenged to engage in the debate. However, within evangelical circles in relation to contextualization, we encounter three groups.

The first group rejects contextualization completely and for this group it is tantamount to syncretism. The leading proponent of this attitude was the late Byang Kato, the then general secretary of the Association of Evangelicals of Africa and Madagascar (AEAM), but now simply known as the Association of Evangelicals of Africa (AEA). In his book *Theological Pitfalls in Africa*, Byang Kato accused pioneering African theologians of being purveyors of liberal theological ideas based on African culture. He rejected African culture as a source of theology but insisted on what he termed biblical theology and Christianity. He was joined here by

6. 2 Corinthians 5:16–19.

many leaders of the various charismatic and Pentecostal ministries, most of whom were university professors. Evangelicals acknowledge the context as important, but only for the dangers it poses for what is understood as pure gospel leading to the salvation of souls.

The second group has cautiously engaged with contextualization and leading this group is Tokunboh Adeyemo, who succeeded Byang Kato as AEA's general secretary. In his book *Salvation in African Tradition*, he is more sympathetic with the idea of contextualization. While taking the context seriously, evangelicals tend not to affirm African religious heritage as important but view it as a danger and warn about syncretism. Other notable evangelical theologians in this group are Tite Tienou and Yusuf Turaki. This is also the case with Kwame Bediako, who has welcomed the idea of contextualization as demonstrated in his book *Christianity in Africa: The Renewal of a Non-Western Religion*, in which he seeks to understand the meaning of the gospel within an African cultural ethos. Another scholar is Lamin Sanneh, who has championed the idea of the gospel as translation. Jesse Mugambi is another scholar who has taken contextualization seriously in his theology of reconstruction. Therefore, the debate among evangelicals is on the role the African worldview should have in the proclamation of the gospel and the doing of theology. However, the paradox is that more often than not, the liberalism of today paves the way for the conservatism of tomorrow.

THE IMPORTANCE OF CONTEXTUALIZING

The methodological approaches discussed above are some of the contextual ones that have emerged partly as a reaction to those methods that we have inherited from our various church traditions, which continue to inform the theological discourses in our churches. Such theologies were constructed on the assumption that theology was universal, the one-size-fits-all approach. Now we know that that is not the case. Theology is local and is such that it contributes to a global theology. As a consequence, there have emerged new attempts at theologizing informed by socioeconomic, political, and religio-cultural contexts, especially in Asia and Africa. The contexts that have given rise to these theologies are marked by a colonial past, poverty, economic exploitation, political domination, oppression by the powerful, cultures of patriarchy, past genocides, racial discrimination, spiritual possession, oppression, disempowerment, gender discrimination, caste, classism, sexism, and many other negative characteristics. Such contexts require their own theological methodologies and not theologies tainted by the Atlantic slave trade, colonial domination and exploitation, or tolerance for patriarchal hegemony.

Shoki Coe saw the task of contextualization as the reconceptualization of the Christian faith in the light of the living context of Asia. Po Ho Huang states,

> The idea of contextualization was proposed by Shoki Coe, a Taiwanese theologian who was then working as director for the Theological Education Fund (TEF). . . . Shoki Coe contended that contemporary contextualities must be taken into account for theological education. While aware of the changing nature of contexts, he said that contextualization must be followed by de-contextualization and re-contextualization. Therefore, he suggested, the concept of this theological terminology must be changed to contextualizing.[7]

Po Ho Huang mentions two problems related to contextualizing, namely, (1) the separation of text and context, and (2) the relation of the gospel to culture. What is of methodological importance is the affirmation of culture as a theological source and the use of cultural learning methodologies for use in theology. This is a new challenge to African and Asian contexts. As M. P. Joseph observes, "Unfortunately, the Asian church and its theology lack a thought form that corresponds to the precolonial traditions and realities. It has been conditioned by a Christendom model transplanted by missionaries."[8]

In *No Longer a Stranger*, Po Ho Huang identifies four points that distinguish contextual theologies from Western theological approaches.

- Theologies should not start from conceptual hypotheses, but from experience. By treating God as a concept, Western theologies turned the covenant God, the I am who I am, into a philosophical concept to be defined by humanity. This is not the God of the Bible, the Father of our Lord Jesus Christ who is related too through love.

- Theology should not develop from above but from below. This makes the incarnation very critical in the doing of theology. Jesus was made incarnate to reveal God.

- Theology is not the "holdings" of theologians, but of people. In Jesus, God became Immanuel, that is, God with us, and whose dwelling will be with humanity in the end.

7. Po Ho Huang, *From Galilee to Tainan*, ATESEA Occasional Papers, no. 15, p. 76, 2005.

8. M. P. Joseph, "Introduction," in Po Ho Huang, *From Galilee to Tainan*, ATESEA Occasional Papers, no. 15, p. 7, 2005.

- Theology is in the service of the "oppressed," and not of the oppressor.[9] The Gospel of Luke speaks of Jesus identifying himself with the prophetic word of Isaiah when he declared at Nazareth: "The Spirit of the Lord is on me, because he has anointed me to preach good news to the poor . . ." He then finished by saying, "Today, this Scripture is fulfilled in your hearing."[10]

Furthermore, Professor Deotis Roberts, a leading theologian of the black theology of liberation in the United States, has suggested the following methodological principles for the creation of contextual theologies:

- Theology is to be interdisciplinary by taking the social and natural sciences more seriously. Applied to Africa, it means that the African worldview has to form the prolegomena to the teaching of theology since no meaningful contextualization can take place without a thorough knowledge of this context.

- Theology has to be ecumenical. Theologians cannot continue to confine themselves to narrow denominational views. God is greater than any one denomination since God has loved the world and gifted it with Jesus Christ. God's love is all-embracing.

- Theology has to embrace the whole world and thus there is the need for interreligious engagement and the need to develop a theology that is informed by various cultural, religious, and philosophical streams of meaning of life and understanding. After all, it is God's intention to unite all things in Jesus Christ, things in heaven and earth. Suppose Jesus had been made incarnate among the Masai of East Africa, how would his gospel be communicated to the rest of humanity? It would still be the gospel of love, the universal language for all human activities and relationships.

- Biblical interpretation is critical if the Bible is to have a formative role in theology. Prooftexting and literal or allegorical interpretations are not enough and are not the best hermeneutical methods. It has to be the Jesus way of understanding the scriptures that he came to fulfill.

9. Po Ho Huang, *No Longer a Stranger* (Tiruvalla, India: CSS Books, 2007), 53.
10. Luke 4:18, 21.

- The historical perspective is to be maintained and not be sacrificed to symbolic interpretations. There is often too much spiritualization of the scriptures as distinct from sound theology. Furthermore, spirit and matter do not have to be separated, and so too spirituality and sexuality. They are two sides of the same coin and define each other.

- Theology is to be rooted in the life and worship of the church, that is, the believing community. It needs to be concerned about its mission and ministry. It has to be both priestly and prophetic. This worship is done on behalf of the whole creation. Humanity gives voice to creation just as humanity is the face of creation, as M. M. Thomas declared, "salvation is humanization."

- Theology should be political and nonpartisan. Theology should be sensitive to injustices and violations of human rights. This should lead to humanization beyond the Christian fellowship and the covenant of faith.

- Theological reflection in context should seek to be holistic, thus establishing a relationship between the sacred and the secular, body and soul, rationality and feelings, practice and wisdom.

- Theology must be particular but not provincial—contextual orientation combined with a universal vision. Theology has to be about the humanization of all humanity.

- Theology needs to be passionate without being irrational, that is, having intellectual integrity and religious fervor as guided by love and wisdom.

TASKS FOR CONTEXTUAL THEOLOGICAL METHODOLOGIES

There is a need to identify the tasks required for the performance of contextual theologies; this is about contextual theological methods. The implications of the bombshell that Shoki Coe dropped are far-reaching and continue to reverberate globally as new young theologians continue to wrestle with the issues that he raised. Coe unleashed a creativity and richness unseen before. It was theologically revolutionary just as the

Reformation was. It ushered in a theological divergence, but that challenges us also to struggle for unity in diversity through love. Contextualization was an idea whose time had come when Coe declared it, and to God be the glory.

16.

Beyond Context: An Intercultural Perspective from the UK

MICHAEL JAGESSAR

I drank from the calabash of my ancestors.
To free the memories shackled in the mind.
—Martin Carter, in *University of Hunger* (2006)

FRAMING THE CONVERSATION

This essay is a contribution to a volume focusing on the legacy and contributions of the late Rev. Dr. Shoki Coe.[1] As I am asked to write from the context of the United Kingdom and specifically the United Reformed Church, I will focus on Coe's idea of "contextual theology" as a point of critical conversation on the current challenges and opportunities for mission and ministry before the United Reformed Church, as it renegotiates its intercultural life together on a changing and diverse landscape.

I come to this essay, like Coe, as a traveler to the shores of England. I am not native to the UK. Hence, my take on Coe's relevance will be influenced by own experience and contextual realities. It is impossible to jump over one's own shadow. I am not Jamaican, but I am from the Caribbean. I am not Brazilian though I am also South American. I am not British or European, but I pay UK, Dutch, and French taxes. I look

---

1. My two main sources of engagement with the life and work of Shoki Coe will be *Recollections and Reflections* (1993) and *Shoki Coe: An Ecumenical Life in Context* (2012). The former is an edited version of some of the writings/manuscripts of Shoki Coe, who, for various reasons—contextual realities always on the forefront of his engagement with doing theology—was unable to write the volume himself. The latter is written by one of his former students.

Indian but I am not a Hindu or Muslim, though my parents and siblings are, and my outlook is shaped and blessed by these influences. I am a complex diasporic Caribbean traveler who understands his frail attempts to walk the way of God in Christ—a vocation of dislocation, of moving out of zones of comfort, of multiple belonging, and delighting in the "positive vibrations" of displacement for the sake of the gospel.

As both an insider and outsider to the United Reformed Church, I will explore Coe's agency to context and its relation to text and its implications for our strapline of "multicultural church, intercultural habit." What can the United Reformed Church learn from Coe as we re-vision discipleship for today and try to live out our intercultural vocation? What questions will an intercultural optic have for Coe's contextual insights with its own limitations? In so doing, we need to be mindful that Coe's "contribution to the universal church was much more than simply presenting a 'term' for defining what must be done for Christianity to be relevant to the world in which it was called to bear witness." As Olav Fykse Tveit notes, Coe "presented the church with both a conceptual and procedural tool for formulating a method of authentic witness that held in creative tension the scriptures (text) and the dynamic changes in the society (context) in which it was read, interpreted and applied."[2]

LOCATING SHOKI COE—AN INTERCULTURAL HERITAGE

But first, some locating of Shoki Coe for this essay, while not reciting what is already known about Coe's biographical life.[3] I wish to underscore that Coe embodied an intercultural dialogue that influenced him, though he may not have reflected on and given this much thought. This fact influenced his approach to the church, ministry, theology, and life in the public square. There is the small but critical matter of his name—a reflection of his life under empire and of belonging and multiple identities.[4] Then there is the fact of exile and dislocation because of occupation, war, marriage to a foreigner, and his role on the global ecumenical

2. Desmond Tutu, "Foreword," in Jonah Chang, *Shoki Coe: An Ecumenical Life in Context* (Geneva: WCC, 2012), viii.

3. See Jonah Chang, *Shoki Coe: An Ecumenical Life in Context* (Geneva: WCC, 2012); and Shoki Coe, *Recollections and Reflections*, 2nd ed. (Taiwan: Taiwan Church News, 1991).

4. "Over his lifetime Shoki Coe had four different ways to officially pronounce and spell his name. In his Taiwanese tongue, his name was Ng Chiong-hui, although among church people, friends, schoolmates, or his students, he was known as Ng Bok-su (Pastor Ng). During the Japanese occupation of Taiwan, in schools or on official occasions, the same name was pronounced Shoki Ko. During the rule of Chiang Kai-sek, in which the official language was Mandarin Chinese, his name was officially changed to Chang-hui Hwang (commonly called C. H. Hwang) to comply with the new pronunciation. In 1965, when he left Tainan Theological

frontline. His mixed and multiple and cultural/religious heritages are significant. The fact that half of his life was spent outside Taiwan is also significant. Of those, he spent many years in England for studies (and with the outbreak of the Second World War could not return home), and working with the Theological Education Fund (TEF) of the World Council of Churches (WCC) based in Bromley. In Seaford (Sussex) where he retired with his spouse, Winifred, Coe served as an elder in the local United Reformed Church.[5]

One can reasonably contend that Coe's wrestling with identity became quite prominent in the UK context in a situation of war and occupation (Japan), his marriage to a white British woman, and his own discomfort with a sense of exile and displacement in a "foreign place." We should not underestimate the "cost" of being married to a white British person at that time. It would not have been an easy undertaking for either party, given that miscegenation in British society was frowned upon, with churches even teaching against it. Though Coe has not written extensively about this, there are instances when he noted the challenges of racial and cultural prejudice.[6] It is not our intention to dismiss the generosity and hospitality that the Presbyterian Church (later the United Reformed Church) showed to Coe. For instance, the Presbytery of South London granted Coe the status of Candidate for Ministry, declaring him to be fully qualified to be ordained should he receive a call. No such call materialized and one may ask why, especially as it is the case today that many minority ethnic colleagues still find it a challenge to receive a call in the United Reformed Church. The church, though, did find other ways to support Coe's work in England.

UNDRESSING CONTEXTUAL, CONTEXTUALIZATION, AND CONTEXTUAL THEOLOGY

Contextual theology and contextualization have become phrases associated with the developing world, though context is about everywhere. It is about all "worlds" though the dominant ones tend to operate as if only theirs matter. I agree with the view that the term "contextualization" was born in the early 1970s within the framework of the TEF.[7]

College and took up residence in England and subsequently was naturalized as a British citizen, he used Shoki Coe as his legal name" (Chang, *Shoki Coe: An Ecumenical Life in Context* 16).

5. Chang, *Shoki Coe: An Ecumenical Life in Context*, 140.

6. Chang, *Shoki Coe: An Ecumenical Life in Context*, 71.

7. Theological Education Fund, "Ministry in Context: The Third Mandate Programme of the Theological Education Fund" (1970–77), Bromley T.E.F. Fund, October 1972.

The initial thrust was a plea for self-determination and self-reliance. But more than that, it represented a conceptual hermeneutical and experiential disruption, even a discontinuity with the inherited ecclesial and theological traditions, as each in one's own context grappled with the meaning and relevance of the gospel in one's own environment. And collectively, contextual theologies are diverse, "encompassing cultural theology, ecological theology, feminist theology, liberation theology, narrative theology."[8] In an effort to give it biblical content, Coe located contextual and contextuality as "wrestling with God's word in such a way that the power of the incarnation" is seen as "the divine form of contextualization" offering the church motivation to contextualize.[9] Coe saw contextualization as an open and "painful process of decontextualization, for the sake of recontextualization."[10]

While Coe highlighted the dynamic nature of the process and method (between text and context), what is involved in the process is more than eating roti/rice cakes and drinking rice wine at Holy Communion or even deploying contextual idioms in theological discourse. At the heart of the process and method is "reconceptualising the basic tenets of the Christian faith in the light of Asian realities."[11] This led Choan-Seng Song[12] to underscore the need to locate text within context and to be mindful of contextualizing a text in another context. To this end, he invested much of his time and energy in helping the church in the Asian context to seriously consider doing theology with its own cultural resources. Song was also critical of Coe's dependence on theologians such as Karl Barth and urged the Presbyterian Church in Taiwan to search for new theological horizons that would generate theological discourses belonging to the Taiwanese. In a way, he was pushing Coe's thinking on contextualization as incarnation beyond good intentions and inherited theological limitations. I wonder how much of Coe's "contexting" gave agency to the indigenous realities of Taiwan.

8. John S. Pobee, "Contextual Theology," in *Dictionary of the Ecumenical Movement*, 2nd edition, ed. Nicholas Lossky, Jose Miguez Bonino, John Pobee, Tom F. Stansky, Geoffrey Wainwright, and Pauline Webb (Geneva: WCC, 2002).

9. Shoki Coe, "Theological Education—a Worldwide Perspective," *Theological Education* 11, no. 1 (Autumn 1974): 5–12.

10. Shoki Coe, "In Search of Renewal in Theological Education" in *Theological Education* 9, no. 4 (Summer 1973): 233–43.

11. R. S. Sugirtharajah, *Frontiers in Asian Christian Theology* (Maryknoll, NY: Orbis, 1994).

12. Choan-Seng Song books include: *Third-Eye Theology: Theology in Formation in Asian Settings* (Maryknoll, NY: Orbis, 1979); *Theology from the Womb of Asia* (Maryknoll, NY: Orbis, 1986); *Jesus, the Crucified People* (New York: Crossroad, 1990); *Jesus and the Reign of God* (Maryknoll, NY: Orbis, 1993).

MULTI-CONTEXTS—CATCHING A GLIMPSE
OF THE DIVINE

What can the pioneering spirit of Coe connecting the Christian message and the world in which it is called to witness offer to the multicultural landscape of the United Reformed Church and the UK? We all live in multi*cultural* worlds. I understand cultural/culture as all that constitutes our way of life: meaning that it is more than ethnicity, skin pigmentation, geographical location, language, and so on. Cultures wrap us in their tantalizing embrace—yet porous and leaking into each other, while we humans argue for purity and authenticity. It is complex, layered, dynamic, and impure. As cultural beings we are part of a daily perichoretic[13] remixing dance. In spite of theological/religious and ecclesial efforts at making a case for "pure" and "purity" and trying to remain true to an "imagined authenticity," all of life, creation, and cultures suggest "adulteration" as part and parcel of human existence. We are interrelated and interdependent—whether by choice, historical events of domination, interventions by dominant power groups, forced displacements, or by the relationships we find ourselves in. Ecclesial and religious traditions are yet to find a theology to touch and embrace people with multiple religious identities and experiences—travelers, not cemented long-term boarders.[14] As far as I can tell, Coe did not reflect on such, and the contextuality espoused was more about contexts in general terms rather than the intradiversity within a particular context.

One of the weaknesses of multiculturalism is the idea of culture proscribed into authentic zones with pure histories that need to be awarded grudging dignity by policies of diversity, as the benevolent multiculturalists treat the concept of culture as a homogeneous and ahistorical thing that can be appreciated, but that remains far outside the enclosed ambit of one's own cultural box. Multiculturalism with a distance forgets our hybrid history and the long waves of linkage that tie people together in ways we tend to forget. It is a denial of the porosity and the over-

---

13. *Perichoresis* is a Greek term used to describe the triune relationship between each person of the Godhead. It can be defined as co-indwelling, co-inhering, and mutual interrelating—which allows the distinctiveness of each to thrive while underscoring that each shares in (or is integral to) the life of the other. An image often used to express this idea is that of a "community of being," in which each person, while maintaining one's distinctive identity, belongs to the other and shares the identity of the others (and vice versa). In trying to find words to describe the Trinity, theologians of the early church described *perichoresis* as the dance of love. The relationships between the three Persons of the Trinity—"dynamic, interactive, loving, serving"—form the model for our human dance steps.

14. Cf. Donna E. Schaper, *Raising Interfaith Children: Spiritual Orphans or Spiritual Heirs?* (New York: Crossroad, 1999).

lapping that happens. But this is not only a problem with benevolent multiculturalists: it is also the case with those of us who locate ourselves as "minorities." Most pundits would agree that totalizing tendencies (or penchant for homogeneity) are among the curses of empire and imperialism we desperately need to exorcise!

We are all adulterated, however much we strive to position our God-talk as pure or culture-bound. The theological term we employ is incarnation. The reality, however, is that when the good news of God in Christ reaches a cultural context—it is never value free: it comes wrapped up in a cultural garb. Perhaps what takes place is not inculturation but an *encounter* of cultures! The inculturation bit lends itself to leaving uninterrogated the linking of "civilized and purity" with notions of whiteness and normativity.[15] Contexts are often more complex than our God-talk may care to admit, which raises questions around authenticity. Emmanuel Lartey, for instance, observes that though his context is Ghanaian, his "own reality has been shaped and influenced by multiple cultures and traditions" to the extent that his "own reality is itself pluriform." In other words, his "own people are a whole bunch—and diverse to the core."[16] Thus Lartey approaches pastoral theology interculturally, that is, by "respecting context, expecting difference of perspective and allowing many, including conflicting voices to be heard."[17] The critical question is "how are persons of different ethnicities, cultures, genders, faiths and socio-economic circumstances to live together reasonably on one earth, the resources of which are not unlimited, in the light of historic relations of dominance and subjugation?"[18] Lartey sees the need to move from a multicultural to an intercultural vision of our life together—journeying from a static description of our diverse life together to a more dynamic recognition of interaction, mutual influence, and interconnectedness.

Coe and others have rightly contended that our God-talk is influenced by our location and experience. However, no one theological perspective can embrace the complexity, the intradiversity and dynamic

15. See also Anthony Reddie, "Black Problematics in Imperial and Contemporary British Christianity," in *Churches, Blackness, and Contested Multiculturalism: Europe, Africa and North America*, ed. R. Drew Smith, William Ackah, and Anthony Reddie (New York: Palgrave Macmillan, 2014), 13.

16. Emmanuel Lartey, *Pastoral Theology in an Intercultural World* (Peterborough, UK: Epworth, 2006), 10; see also *Postcolonizing God: New Perspectives on Pastoral and Practical Theology* (London: SCM, 2013).

17. Lartey, *Pastoral Theology in an Intercultural World*, 11.

18. Lartey, *Pastoral Theology in an Intercultural World*, 128.

nature of contexts.[19] In my view, God-talk, which gives much agency to context and particularity, needs to critically reflect on how faithful it is to complexities and intradiversity, vis-à-vis the experiences of all black peoples. The danger for all contextual/liberative theologians is to unconsciously operate with homogenizing and static tendencies about particular experiences and contexts. Bias/prejudice is not only a habit of dominant white groups! So, while we (black and Asian theologians) argue for cultural agency before the "dominant" audience and in the company of our own punters, we can also become astute agents for the "leveling" of our intracultural dynamics, ignoring our own cultural biases, the undeconstructed inherited traditions that we have internalized and continue to perpetuate.[20] Reddie refers to aspects of this by naming it as "religio-cultural-theological-dissonance"![21]

If any liberative form of God-talk is about embodying change and transformation, intercultural conversations, with necessary caveats, are a necessary undertaking. What will an intercultural vocation in contextual liberating God-talk look like? Mindful of my own complicity, the limits of understandings, and the unlevel "playing field," how do I participate in shaping a moral imagination that will open expansive intercultural possibilities?

At the heart of an intercultural method or habit is the need to work together to enhance each other's well-being, and thus encouraging transformation through internal and mutual critique of our motives. The habit can be compared to the biblical imagery of salt losing its form/ being to flavor a dish—while at the same time maintaining its distinctive taste to be of use for the common meal. The point here is that if we simply maintain individual and solitary forms we fall into our own enclave and exist within a minority and identity politics. At the same time if we lose our identities without keeping what is distinctive we become merely assimilated into the dominant culture.

RISKING ALL FOR FULLNESS OF LIFE: SPACES FOR AN INTERCULTURAL VOCATION

An intercultural habit has always been at the heart of my theological journey, even though I have only been able to name the habit when

19. This point is also made by others in different contexts. See Jione Havea and Clive Peterson, *Out of Place: Doing Theology on the Cross-cultural Brink* (London: Equinox, 2010), 3.

20. Randall C. Bailey, "The Danger of Ignoring One's Own Cultural Bias in Interpreting the Text," in *The Postcolonial Bible*, ed. Sugirtharajah (Sheffield: Sheffield Academic Press, 1998), 80 [66–90].

21. Reddie, "Black Problematics," 19.

doing my research on Wilson Harris, Caribbean/British writer (1987), and Philip Potter (1990), ecumenist and theologian. While the former speaks of limbonality and cross-cultural imagination, the latter is the first theologian to articulate the dialogue of cultures on the ecumenical landscape. Both contend that to avoid the danger of reading reality in one rigid way (often resulting in polarizing positions), we need to perceive our cultural practices, in critical conversation, through the eyes of "the other" and different perspectives. For Potter, intercultural engagement reveals "the many-sided grace and wisdom" of God in Christ which fills us with God's fullness, in spite of all the ambiguities that we embody. In the richness and diversity within the body of Christ there is potential for "richness and diversity in the fullness of life."[22] The mutual sharing of riches, of gifts, of *charismata*, of the whole of life is an ongoing process that demands critical, honest, and open conversations around difficult questions, understandings, and misunderstandings, as well as the virtues of understanding and sympathy, humility, and readiness to listen and learn. Only then can change and transformation happen.

Moving from academia to greater participation in the life of my adopted ecclesial tradition (the United Reformed Church), with specific responsibility for racial justice and multicultural ministry, I quickly realized that if there is going to be any constructive movement in engendering spaces, opportunities, and actions that will bring about change and transformation, there is an urgent need to move beyond discourses about a multicultural, inclusive church, and diversity that have been guilty of over-racializing/gendering/minoritizing human relations in unhelpful ways. While space(s) to affirm diversity and minority groups are very critical and important, there is evidence to suggest that we have also placed too much emphasis on separate rather than common needs/vision, which in practice have/has contributed to the further marginalization of minorities. Power and its dynamics remain in place. Empire remains undefeated as we play the game by its rules! And in the process what remains largely uninterrogated are the privileges and power base of the dominant group and their positions.

By and large, I have found my church open and welcoming. That my ecclesial tradition elected me (a visible minority) as a moderator of its General Assembly, however, is not necessarily indicative that more space was and is being created or is renegotiated around the table to include

---

22. Philip Potter, "Confessing Christ in Different Cultures," *Report of a Colloquium*, ed. John Mbiti (Geneva: WCC, 1977), 35. See also Michael Jagessar, *Full Life for All: The Work and Theology of Philip A. Potter* (The Netherlands: Boekencentrum, 1997); Michael Jagessar, Andrea Frochteling, et al., *At Home with God and in the World: A Philip Potter Reader* (Geneva: WCC, 2013).

the difference and culturally shaped giftings I bring. To be accepted and to be listened to, I have to largely fit into a white-male-extrovert-heterosexual-able-bodied framework. The habit of everyone around the table being *mutually inconvenienced* for the sake of a fullness economy of the host (God in Christ) and in the specific context of finding a new identity is proving to be far too uncomfortable and demanding. Many liberal-thinking white colleagues in my tradition thrive on the sort of minority politics that will "give" or "allow" minorities space to operate within the tradition while gatekeeping their powerbase and privileges. And, my evangelical white colleagues' mantra on the other hand will be "we are one in Christ" while denying the multiplicity within the oneness—effectively unable to recognize the difference I embody. Both camps push minorities into unhelpful dualistic/totalizing habits. I find, however, liberalism the more elusive and dangerous while affirming cultures, nationalities, and religions. It pretends to be "neutral" and unbiased when in fact it "promotes a particular agenda and a particular conception of the good" and who fits into that framework.[23] Diversity is affirmed, but for the minority members this will often mean the surrendering of their collective identity for full rights as individual members/citizens.[24] And we need to be honest: when we do not all have the same understanding and criteria of what it means to include, becoming communities where all are included will continue to be a challenging journey in need of constant renegotiating.

It has become clearer to me that the issue is not about one of belonging: it is about how, given the reality of our diversity, we are able to renegotiate belonging together—to adjust to the fact of belonging for all in the light of the "fullness of life" project of Jesus. Implicit here is a call for an intercultural move. An intercultural habit reminds me of a verse of Psalm 31: "You have set my feet in a spacious place" (Lord). We struggle, however, to make use of this spaciousness, the opportunities it provides for the perichoretic dance—to keep turning, moving, finding new direction. Instead, we have become stuck or glued to particular spots. The adventure of an intercultural habit is a call to get unstuck—moving backward, forward, outside, and "limbo-ing" to a third space or in-between spaces simultaneously in our border-crossing and transgressing journeys, unable to return to the same place. Like a dancer, we savor moments of transition; like a musician we strive to discern and handle

23. Mark Griffin and Theron Walker, *Living on the Borders: What the Church Can Learn from Ethnic Immigrant Cultures* (Grand Rapids: Brazos, 2004), 10.

24. David Biale, Michael Galchinsky, and Susannah Heschel, eds., *Insider/Outsider: American Jews and Multiculturalism* (Berkeley: University of California Press, 1998), 18–19, as quoted by Griffin and Walker (2004).

pauses between the notes as we experience the Divine in unlikely spaces and moments. This requires an awareness of diversity and positionality (especially in relation to power and privileges) in order to engender the creation of critically informed spaces for encountering and deepening relations toward respect and mutual regard. The vision/commitment is for transformation of our ecclesial life into spaces where new paradigms of mutuality, decolonization, polycentric power and cultures, and openness to God's possibilities are practiced. What an intercultural habit does is to initiate a shift toward critical and constructive conversations on multiculturalism and contexts "that [facilitate] the possibility of negotiating values, practices, and even identities in order to live a more sustainable shared life."[25]

Perhaps, we ought to see God's offer of "fullness of life" and talk about the kingdom of God as pointing to spaces where the Christian community can bring imagination and memory—in a constant ebb and flow—to open up alternatives to the world's kingdoms—a common counterculture story of salvation, redemption, and liberation.[26] In enabling spaces for intercultural engagement geared toward more inclusive communities our hearts, like seas, are restless until they rest in God!

"BORN PEOPLE, WE STRUGGLE TO BE HUMANS"

What, then, would an intercultural habit mean for our contextual God-talk? I am envisioning this as a third-space along postcolonial lines and the suggestion of the intercultural habit as a perichoretic dance or the creating of perichoretic spaces.[27] To be clear, an intercultural habit is not about ignoring the realities of racism and all related forms of marginalization that are real in our society. Mindful of the complexity of oppressed/oppressor (or empire relationships) it is quite a challenge for those who have been and are on the margins to share the same space around a table with those of the dominant and powerful group and vice versa. And while it may not easily feel like a safe place, what is intended is a commitment to working together across all forms of injustices to enable transformation—ushering in a different reality, a life-affirming

---

25. José R. Irizarry, "Toward an Intercultural Approach to Theological Education for Ministry," in *Shaping Beloved Community*, ed. David V. Esterline and Ogbu U. Kalu (Louisville: Westminster John Knox, 2006), 30 [28–42].

26. Cf. Irizarry, "Toward an Intercultural Approach to Theological Education for Ministry," 38.

27. See Sarah Travis, *Decolonizing Preaching: The Pulpit as Postcolonial Space* (Eugene, OR: Cascade, 2014), 126–43, for a more recent exploration of perichoretic spaces in the context of preaching.

one.[28] By virtue of the fact of our belonging to the one body of Christ we need to rediscover our mutual dependency made possible by God's incarnating (con-text-ing) of perichoretic love in Christ and so making space for others to enter our lives as we enter theirs. We are all in need here. Making an intercultural habit incarnate will mean taking cognizance of the different ways power is deployed—always asking whose interests are being represented, the values being promoted by the engagement and who are the beneficiaries.

An intercultural habit will expose the underpinnings of power that must be recognized, disclosed, analyzed, and redeployed—as our belonging is renegotiated in the context of our diversity. The transformative vision of becoming intercultural renders all of us ethnic/cultural—and it is especially an eye-opener for those who are open to learning how being "white," "male," (whatever the pigmentation and gender) and "straight" functions with all its privileges. At the same time, no one group can be guaranteed that it will not be inconvenienced and called to move out of its comfort zones: all groups will strive to transcend their narrow ways of thinking and living. Here, movement, space, and displacement are important. As Melinda McGarrah, writing in a different context, puts it, "a model of good enough intercultural relationality adopts an in-process provisional understanding that recognizes the web of tensions in which we live."[29]

A moral imagination is vital for becoming intercultural. Imagination evokes a "passion for the possible" (that dissents from static) arrangements. It encourages desire. Imagination refers to the power to sort, to shape, and to integrate disparate elements of varied social worlds using images, symbols, stories, theories, and rituals. To imagine is to make constellations of things that matter, which prod, comfort, surprise, shock, and give meaning. In particular, I am interested in moral imagination as a resource for churches' integrity to express their intercultural vocation in public. The moral imagination of becoming intercultural seeks to move *beyond* dialogue and inclusion to justice in the making. Inclusion can be problematic if the assumption is that one individual or group is in a position to decide whether to "include" or "exclude." It is an invitation to practice "cultural transgression," a habit of disobedience characterized by a "critical attitude and moral disposition to denounce and challenge oppressive cultural practices and patterns in one's own culture in order

28. Maria Pilar Aquino and Maria Jose Rosado-Nunes, eds., *Feminist Intercultural Theology: Latina Explorations for a Just World* (Maryknoll, NY: Orbis, 2007), xxvi.

29. Melinda A. McGarrah Sharp, *Misunderstanding Stories: Toward a Postcolonial Pastoral Theology* (Eugene, OR: Pickwick, 2013), 175.

to change it."[30] In this regard, what is important is a habit that nurtures solidarity across marginalized groups, including the marginalized within minority groups. Systemic transformation will not happen unless we counter any proclivity toward a hierarchy of oppression within the body of Christ and beyond.

An intercultural habit is about "inhabiting the borderlands,"[31] that is, spaces where we can break out of ghettoized and restrictive cultures/contexts and "risk engagement with the culture at large." This will necessitate a habit of unlearning or a "de-colonizing of the mind"—our internalizing of the economy of the oppressor or empire to deny even our own a space around Christ's table. As God-talk is always about learning tentatively, and given that what I am proposing here is a conversational habit, there will be much to learn and relearn. Whatever our cultural and theological perspectives, here is an invitation to expand our hearts and our minds, and a challenge for us to move beyond our comfort zones, to dare to embody and experience transformation. I have learned that the nature of the critical engagement means that we must become more introspective about our theological views. An intercultural habit forces us to question our motivations, hence more self-interrogation and self-reflection must happen. This is particularly crucial as we continue to inhabit spaces within powerful structures and systems.

"FREEING MEMORIES SHACKLED IN THE MIND"—UNENDING NOTES

All God-talk is contextual and is like a jigsaw puzzle: we are unable to understand and articulate our views and perspectives without understanding and having a picture of how the pieces function on their own, but more importantly compose a picture together. If we are ever going to learn anything we will have to learn it together and from people who are different from us. The reality is that the present and the future (as has been the past, though played down) is *mestizo*, that is, one of multiple belongings.[32] This means that we inhabit spaces where identities are fluid and must perpetually be renegotiated. This applies to all of us and

---

30. Luis R. Rivera-Rodriguez, "Resources for Intercultural Transformation of Theological Education from the Latino/a Margins," in *Shaping Beloved Community*, ed. Esterline and Kalu, 66.

31. Griffin and Walker, *Living on the Borders*, 139.

32. Virgilio P. Elizondo, *The Future Is Mestizo: Life Where Cultures Meet*, rev. ed. (Boulder: University of Colorado Press, 2000).

it means that God-talk that is reflexive and liberative must necessarily be intercultural. Justo González writes:

> There is indeed a Christian community that is held together by bonds of a common faith. But within that community we each bring our own history and perspective to bear on the message of the gospel, hoping to help the entire community to discover dimensions that have gone unseen and expecting to be corrected when necessary.[33]

And, if transformation is to happen we need a larger picture than our own context. Such a habit is dangerous and subversive—all will have to be converted, to be mutually inconvenienced—each called to journey beyond their perspective (context). For we are all in need! All liberative and contextual God-talk ought to desire and model openness to a multiplicity of voices and their polyphonic cultural intonations toward that end concert that incarnates (in word and actions) a harmony, whose music will move us to a level that transcends debilitating polarizations that kill the human spirit.

---

33. Justo L. González, *Mañana: Christian Theology from a Hispanic Perspective*, foreword by Virgilio P. Elizondo (Nashville: Abingdon, 1990), 22.

17.

Asian Contextual Theology: Location and Methodology—An Indigenous Perspective

WATI LONGCHAR

The development of liberation theologies in the two-thirds world is part of a larger movement for liberation and determination of selfhood. Though contextualization of theology has been the way of doing theology throughout the history of Christian thought, recent liberation theologies in the two-thirds world, such as Dalit theology, minjung theology, theology of struggle, and feminist theology, differ significantly in their methodology, approach, focus, and content from dominant theological paradigms. Despite the primary focus and goal of these theologies being liberation, their approaches to liberation are different. For example, feminist/womanist theology reflects the struggle of women in the context of their experience of oppression and marginalization in male-dominated structures, and a major focus is on women's liberation. Black theology reflects "black experience" and the struggle of black people. Minjung theology is the product of the struggle of the Korean people against the dictatorial regime in the 1970s. Dalit theology's focus is to dismantle the oppressive caste structure and liberate Dalits from caste discrimination. Indigenous theology,[1] born out of various forms of injustice and oppression in different stages of history, gives a distinct theological methodology and perspective. This paper attempts to highlight indigenous people theology.

All contextual theologies in Asia are larger movements of the liberation struggle of the oppressed. Many people think that liberation theology was academically reduced to a piece of history after the fall of the

---

1. Also known as theology of aborigines, tribal theology, and so on. It is identified differently in different contexts.

Berlin Wall at the end of the 1980s. Liberation theology still has great relevance. One-sided extractive development processes and globalization serve as new systems of oppression. Economic and political poverty have continued under democratic capitalism. This brings new challenges in doing theology. We need to address new questions like how contextual theologies can make a difference in the context of continuing marginalization. How do contextual theologies unravel the complex nexus of globalization, climate justice, and survival of marginalized communities? How do contextual theologies relocate in the context of the margins? This essay attempts to highlight those issues dealing with the context of indigenous people.

MARGINS—LOCATION OF CONTEXTUAL THEOLOGY

Liberation theology is determined by the location of those living under oppressive structures. It speaks of a hermeneutic of circle because it comes back to the location again and again to break new ground. In today's context, where do we have to relocate liberation theology? Revisiting the location time and again is imperative to safeguard theology from being elitist. To clarify the location of contextual theology in modern times, let me start with the parable[2] of the rich man and Lazarus as recorded in the Gospel of Luke.

> There was a rich man who was dressed in purple and fine linen and who feasted sumptuously every day. At his gate lay a poor man named Lazarus, covered with sores, who longed to satisfy his hunger with what fell from the rich man's table; even the dogs would come and lick his sores. (Luke 16:19–21 RSV)

This parable tells us about two persons: the rich man and Lazarus. In whose context do we locate our theology? How do we discern what it means by doing contextual theology in these two contrasting contexts? What does it mean in the context of the systemic denial of justice to the poor and marginalized?

THE RICH MAN

Notice how the rich man was dressed "in purple and fine linen" (v. 19a), every day, not just for special occasions. It is very striking that the rich

---

2. Some ancient commentators are of the opinion that this parable is a "real" story because of the fact that personal names appear in it.

man is identified with the clothes he wore—purple and fine linen attire. He is not identified with his name but with his wealth. Sea purple was a precious and rare dye that was scarcely used even by princes and nobles of high position. In the Bible, purple and fine linen are mentioned in a few places (Rev 18:12; Prov 18:12; Ezek 27:7). This most luxurious fabric was associated with royalty or quasi-royal dignity. This signifies the extreme wealth of the rich man in the parable.

Notice how the rich man ate. Since he had everything at his disposal, it is said he "feasted sumptuously every day" (v. 19 b). Notice the reference to "every day." The diet of ordinary people was simple and at times the poor passed the day without even a proper meal. For the rich man, a banquet was a daily occurrence. The parable says that he feasted lavishly, not just on special occasions. Feasting on special occasions seems reasonable, but every day? Thus, with all the accompaniments of grandeur, this nameless mighty and rich person lived. We can imagine that his halls were filled with noble guests in rich attire and his antechambers with servants. Everything that could make life splendid and joyous was in profusion.

His wealth was certainly acquired at the expense of the poor as a result of the oppressive system of his time. The system was such that wealthy patrons lent money to poor clients at usurious interest rates. When the clients failed to pay their loan, their land was confiscated. A rich man like this one would have accumulated massive wealth due to this unjust system.

Notice how he lived. The rich man lived in a "house" with a "gate," not a door. Some New Testament scholars say that the gate suggests that he lived in a large ornamental mansion. Here Jesus is alluding to some of the most powerful families of the times, who were both rich and corrupt. What does a gate symbolize in today's society?

Is there any person without a name? We even name our pets, flowers, fruits, plants, animals, mountains, and more. Not to name someone is an insult to them, especially to a rich person or someone in high position.[3] Having no name means that the person is a nobody, worthless, and identity-less. But Jesus does not take account of a person's wealth. Is Jesus's action not radical?

---

3. For further detail of the interpretation in the context of indigenous people refer to Wati Longchar, *Returning to Mother Earth: Theology, Christian Witness and Theological Education—An Indigenous Perspective*, Study Series no. 4 (Kolkata: Sceptre, 2014), 24–55.

POOR LAZARUS

Where did Lazarus live? At the gate of the rich man. "And at his gate lay a poor man named Lazarus" (v. 20a). To live at somebody's gate waiting for the leftover food or burnt bread is terrible and painful. It is indeed a humiliating condition. He was waiting with the dogs.

In the past, people baked bread on a fire and it is said that nobles and high priests would not eat burnt bread. Eating such a portion was characterized as a sign of impurity. This implies that the rich man is pure and holy, while Lazarus is impure, unholy, and untouchable, and faced a societal stigma.

"Covered with sores, who longed to satisfy his hunger with what fell from the rich man's table" (v. 20b and v. 21a)—Lazarus was not only hungry and thirsty but was covered with sores, carrying a loathsome disease (perhaps leprosy). He was not only untouchable but was also extremely sick. He was a sign of impurity, pain, and suffering. He was indeed a disabled person.

Apparently, he could not get around to moving by himself because of hunger and illness; he was as good as dead. Since he was an untouchable person, Lazarus would not have had any relatives, friends, or helpers. He was left alone, except for the dogs who kept him company. Some commentators say that the dogs were wild, homeless stray dogs scavenging the streets. The Bible says that things associated with dogs were unclean. This is another sign of the poor man's outcast condition (see Exod 23:31; 1 Kgs 21:19, 24; Ps 21:16; Matt 15:26–27; Mark 7:27–28). The story also suggests that Lazarus was defenseless in that he could not even ward off the dogs. The dogs licked the pus that oozed from the afflicted man's sores and ulcers. Hungry, sick, and with dogs licking his sores, he was in a pathetic condition. Lazarus's presence also threatened to pollute others.

Was Lazarus a sinner? According to some, yes, he was a sinner and cursed by God. In Jesus's time, a beggar would have been regarded as a sinner, and poverty, or indeed incurable disease, was often spoken of as punishment from God. People were encouraged not to touch or associate with such people. Lazarus was seen as a person cursed by God.

But what happened? Jesus called him by his name! The Greek name *Lazarus* is derived from two Hebrew words, *Eli-ezer*, meaning "God helps/God helped." Calling someone by his name is to recognize the person's identity and rights. With a name, a person becomes somebody. Jesus addressed him by his name. Lazarus was no longer a nobody, but somebody with rights, dignity, and worth.

The distinctiveness of contextual theology is its location—the margins;

it is not a mere option, but it is imperative. People who are unable to participate in their political, religious, and economic systems due to the imposition of unjust ideologies, cultural practices, and economic, social, and political structures that hinder their experience of abundant life are the site of God's revelation. Much like in the time of Jesus, in today's world a few rich people at the center control and manipulate wealth, finances, public discourse, and decision-making processes, denying life to a large segment of people. Today, where people like Lazarus live, the margins, are the site of doing theology; the site of God's revelation—in Felix Wilfred's words, "the space of God's visitation."[4] To quote:

> The agenda from the periphery is the agenda of God. The real future of humanity comes from here and not from the decisions and deliberations of the centres that dominate the world. This is so because they constantly challenge the established order for its ways of exclusion and strive towards a world of inclusion and justice. In this way they are part of the agenda of God for the future of humanity. It is from the site of God's visitation—the margins—that a new world, a new Asia will take shape. This is our hope.[5]

The moment contextual theologies detach from the location of the margins they lose their relevance. Liberation theologians speak of a hermeneutic of circle because it comes back to the location time and again to break new ground. Revisiting the location time and again is imperative to safeguard theology from being elitist.

MARGINALIZED PEOPLE IN TODAY'S WORLD

In the contemporary world, we often hear and read about farmers' suicides just because they are unable to repay their loans. Or about parents forcing or selling their girl children for commercial sex work for survival. There have been newspaper reports about a mother killing her child by throwing it from a balcony or throwing the child in a pond or river, unable to face the uncertainty of their future. Such tragic deaths have become everyday affairs in Asia today. On the contrary, we hear of rich people vying with one another for the construction of sky-high buildings with facilities such as an Olympic-size swimming pool, gym, spa, recreational center, and helipads. The disparity between the rich and the poor today reminds us of the time of the prophet Amos and Jesus. Today's situation is no different from that mentioned in the parable of the rich man and Lazarus.

4. Felix Wilfred, *Margins: Site of Asian Theologies* (New Delhi: ISPCK, 2008), xix.
5. Wilfred, *Margins*, xviii.

The global market economy operates in such a way that the poor are pushed into abject poverty. While some rich people have accumulated so much wealth that they do not know how and where to invest their wealth, poor people are dying of hunger on the streets. The economic situation today is such that the ten richest Asians get about $5,000 in a few seconds or minutes, while millions of people do not earn even a dollar a day. Asia has 40 percent of its population living in abject poverty and who cannot afford to have a square meal a day. Their livelihoods threatened, thousands of farmers take their own lives. Lack of clean drinking water leads to 5 to 10 million deaths in third world countries. So whose context is crucial in doing theology?

An indigenous activist narrates his experience of modern development activities as follows:

> Many unfortunate tribes have already taken farewell from the world. Civilization has squeezed them out of this world. The rest are facing a serious threat of extinction or a life of slavery. Our big brothers want us to be their coolies; when we refused, they plan to finish us. Ruthless exploitation, deprivation from human rights, alienation from land, suppression of our ethnic identity and derogation of our culture and traditions has been almost paralyzing us.[6]

It reflects the experience of struggle, pain, and uncertainty brought about by modern development activities. The poor are not only politically and economically powerless, extractive industries are threatening their very survival. With the slogan "minority should sacrifice for the sake of majority," indigenous people are forced to sacrifice land and water. The dominant extractive growth model has become a threat to the life of indigenous people, their identity, and spirituality. Unmindful extraction of natural resources of all kinds—of minerals, natural gas, petroleum, timber, and hydropower, among others,

- threatens the waters that are sacred to tribal/indigenous people and signify life for all human beings and all of creation;
- removes tribal/indigenous people from their traditional lands and threatens the food web that we and all creation depend upon;

---

6. R. J. Kr. Kootoom, "Tribal Voice Is Your Voice," *Tribal Voice of the Persecuted Tribals* 1 (15): 1.

- leads to what is akin to genocidal murders, where tribal/indigenous peoples, vulnerable peoples, and the poor are displaced, poisoned, and killed so that multinational economic systems can reap benefits for the sake of a few.

Further, the consumeristic culture objectifies indigenous people's culture, bodies, and spirituality. For example, with booming commercial tourism, indigenous women are seen as mere objects of sexual pleasure, making them "sex objects," with scant respect for their personality or dignity. Many indigenous women are forced into the flesh trade, the environment is reduced to a mere spectacle, beaches are seen only in terms of sunbathing, and cultural practices are reduced to performances. Exploitation and violation of human rights are rampant and beyond measure. Indigenous people's customs, rituals, sacred shrines, places of worship, sacred music, ceremonial dress, traditions, and handiwork are commercialized. Sacred music and dances of indigenous people are seen as mere cabaret acts for enjoyment.

The Pre-Assembly gathering of Indigenous Peoples at the World Council of Churches (WCC) in Busan (November 27–29, 2013) issued a statement highlighting their context thus:

> Besides spiritual and theological colonialization, Indigenous People continue to experience various forms of oppression, exploitation, marginalization and suffering of a vast number of peoples and nations. The ancestral lands and sacred forest, grounds of Indigenous People are being commercialized, desecrated and abused through unmindful extractive developmental activities. Many Indigenous communities have been displaced, dispossessed, uprooted, evicted and even annihilated in genocidal scale. Indigenous People's cultures, practices, customary laws have been abused, misused and misrepresented and commercialized without respect. Today Indigenous People constitute the poorest section of the society. Many of them are poor, landless, homeless and hungry. Those Indigenous Peoples who organized themselves to resist for their right and justice are being killed, harassed and persecuted. God of life, leading us to justice and peace will have little relevance without addressing the ongoing and historical oppression of Indigenous People, and mobilizing solidarity among Indigenous Peoples to collectively resist against unjust systems, forces and institutions. Affirmation of God of life, justice and peace involves reclaiming of our identities, wisdoms, language, re-possession of our lands and sacred grounds.

This statement highlights the context of indigenous people in today's world. All indigenous people have stories of intense conflict with the forces of so-called development, especially in mining and other extractive industries. Today's context challenges us to relocate theology among the people who are forcefully pushed to the margins. It is here among the voiceless, people who are deliberately muscled out, that the incarnation of God takes place to give life and hope. The birth of Jesus in the manger is a sign of the embodiment of God in the margins. It is a sign of God's intervention to transform them from nobodies to somebodies. He has journeyed with them in creating and rebuilding their identities. The Bible testifies that the concerns of people on the periphery are the agenda of God. The real future of humanity has come and will come from the people in the margins but not from the decisions of the center that dominate the world. This is so because they constantly challenge the established order for its way of exclusion and strive toward a world of inclusion and justice. Therefore, it is in this context—the margins—that liberation theology needs to take shape in today's context.

> The deliberate option of Jesus to speak for Lazarus tells us that our churches and the ecumenical movement must be located in the context of people in the margins. Our theological reflection will miss the core focus of its vision if we miss this location. There cannot be authentic theology if we fail to locate it in Lazarus's context.

Lazarus, who was in a miserable, inhuman condition, knew what it was to be thirsty, hungry, in pain, and be begging in front of someone's gate without dignity. Therefore, indigenous people, Dalits, persons with disabilities, and other marginalized groups have the epistemological privilege of knowing what affirms life and denies it; what helps communities and what hurts them; what contributes to their well-being and what circumvents it. From the margins, they bring firsthand knowledge of the suffering that accompanies exclusionary practices and they unmask the forces that work against God's will in the world.[7] Through their lives and struggles for life, they hold forth what God wants in the world while also bringing a reservoir of hope, resistance, and perseverance that is needed to remain faithful to the promised reign of God.[8]

THE GOD OF THE MARGINS

The God of the Bible is someone who journeys to and with the margins. The Bible testifies that the Divine participates in history to defend those who are victims of power. James Cone writes:

7. A draft WCC document on "Mission from the Margins," a process initiated by Just and Inclusive Community, October 2012, p. 1.
8. "Mission from the Margins," 1.

Yahweh is known and worshipped as the One who brought Israel out of Egypt, and who raised Jesus from the dead. God is the political God, the Protector of the poor and the Establisher of the right for those who are oppressed. To know God is to experience the acts of God in the concrete affairs and relationships of people, liberating the weak and the helpless from pain and humiliation. For theologians to speak of this God, they too must become interested in politics and economics, recognizing that there is no truth about Yahweh unless it is the truth of freedom as that event is revealed in the oppressed people's struggle for justice in this world.[9]

God is the God of the poor, and God revealed Godself as liberator who stands against the manipulators of justice. The central question of Western theological inquiry is to counter the challenges posed by secularism and therefore it is a wrestling with the problem of how to prove the existence of God rationally. Influenced by the patriarchal culture, the God-world-human relationship is perceived hierarchically and dualistically. Instead of perceiving God as liberator, God is perceived as an incomprehensible being, omnipotent, omniscient, or omnipresent. God is projected as a pure transcendental and spiritual being. The world is created out of matter; it is considered sinful and destined to destruction. Therefore, it is taught that the Holy God does not come into contact with the sinful material world but is separated from it. Within this framework, we uphold patriarchal, success-, beauty-, and perfect-oriented images of God, such as Ruler, Lord, King, Almighty, Father, Master, and Warrior. These are all military and success-oriented images of God. This theological construct holds no value for the poor and the marginalized, and in a pluralistic context. M. P. Joseph argues that today "these false gods come with fashionable names such as economic growth, prosperity and development. The function of the false Gods is to legitimize various systems of oppression including patriarchy, class domination, race discrimination and ecclesiastical hierarchies."[10] These images have made Christianity a religion of, and for, the rulers, the elites, and the upper class. Any theology that measures life in terms of blessings, money, perfection, and success can be called prosperity theology. This is not the teaching of the Bible, but the domestication of God. It is equal to the worship of Mammon.

The Bible affirms that God became flesh, became Immanuel. Jesus is the incarnation of God and gave his life for downtrodden people. He touched, cared, loved, and worked for the liberation of people in the

---

9. James H. Cone, *Black Theology of Liberation* (Maryknoll, NY: Orbis, 1970), 57.

10. M. P. Joseph, "Foreword," in *Doing Contextual Theologies in Asia: Essays in Honour of Huang Po Ho*, ed. Wati Longchar, PTCA Series No. 8 (Kolkata: Sceptre, 2014), xi.

margins who were excluded, discriminated against, and stigmatized in society. Any language about God that fails to answer the cry of marginalized people, such as persons with disability, wounded women, indigenous people, minjung, Dalits, and people living with HIV, or for total freedom and right to fullness of life is not holistic. God-talk should be free from the institutionalized-patriarchal-hierarchical-dualistic views of life; instead it should be a living reality for people. We need a new theological paradigm in which God is perceived as a fellow sufferer, companion, and great comforter, a divine power that is not dominating or controlling. Rather than a dialectical power in weakness, this is a liberating and transforming power that is effective in compassionate love, care, and service.[11] This nature and power of God is effectively revealed in the life and ministry of Jesus Christ.

CONTEXTUAL THEOLOGY:
A METHODOLOGICAL CONSIDERATION

The continuing marginalization of indigenous people around the world calls for contextual theology to address wider issues of injustice. Like other contextual theologies, indigenous people's theology is born out of the experiences of various forms of injustice and exploitation in the context of their assertion of rights and identity. They attempt to express Christian faith in the sociocultural, religious, traditional, and liturgical thought patterns, drawing resources from their experience and earth-centered spirituality. They articulate the issue of ethnic, cultural, and political identities based on the subjectivity of people, their land, and sacred power.

The voices of marginalized people today show the interrelationship between social and ecological justice. It is clear that a crucial element missing in liberation theologies today is the spiritual connection with the mystery of the earth's family. Unless we rediscover the spiritual connection of people with the earth's family, it is not possible to talk about liberation and a community where all people are treated justly. It is like attempting to liberate oneself after killing one's mother. That means from the indigenous people's perspective, an authentic liberation theology is possible only in relation to the protection of land. Indigenous people affirm progress, development, and liberation as important components of human life, but without neglecting their spiritual connection with the earth's family. One of the major roots of crisis in the world

11. K. C. Abraham, *Liberative Solidarity: Contemporary Perspectives on Mission* (Tiruvalla, India: Christava Sahitya Samithi, 1996), 172.

today is the negligence of the spiritual connection with space/earth/creation for human liberation.

Though indigenous theology is part of a larger liberation theology, methodologically speaking, the point of departure of indigenous theology from other liberation theologies is that indigenous theology seeks liberation from the perspective of "space." In our search for liberation, the issue of space is central and crucial. As we have affirmed earlier, a peculiar character of the indigenous worldview is that culture, religion, spirituality, and even the Supreme Being cannot be conceived without "creation/land" or "space." Humans always understand themselves as "an integral part of creation/land and not apart from it." Therefore, in the indigenous worldview, the issue of "space" is not merely a justice issue to be set alongside others. But it is the foundational theology of self-understanding out of which liberation, justice, and then peace will flow naturally and necessarily.[12] That means poverty, oppression, ethnic conflict, and identity issues cannot be understood without relating to the integrity of creation/land. Justice to creation/land is the key to liberation and human dignity and fullness of life. That is why harmony with the "land" is the starting point of indigenous people's theology and their search for liberation.

Creation is the first act of God's revelation. God cannot be perceived without water, wind, trees, vegetation, sky, light, darkness, animals, human creatures. In this first act of revelation, God revealed himself/herself as *co-creator* with earth. The most striking aspect in this first act of God's revelation is "God is actively present in creation." The presence of God makes this earth sacred. That is why God entered into a covenant relationship with all creatures. There are many stories, myths, parables, and even fairy tales of how the Sacred Power and land sustain life together. This means "the whole earth is full of God's glory" (Isa 6:1–3). People always conceive of God-world as very much attached to them in their everyday life. To perceive God detached from creation/earth or as a mere transcendental being who controls life from above is not biblical faith. We believe in God because God as the creator is present and continues to work with land, river, and sea in order to give life and hope. This affirmation is the foundation of life. The major problem in theology is the faith articulation of human history without mother earth's family.

12. For this insight, I owe deep gratitude to Prof. George Tinker's articles (1981, 1994). See George Tinker, "American Indians and the Art of the Land," *Voices from the Third World* 14, no. 2 (December 1981): 22–38; George Tinker, "Spirituality and Native American Personhood: Sovereignty and Solidarity," in *Spirituality of the Third World*, ed. K. C. Abraham and Barnedatte Mbuy (Maryknoll, NY: Orbis, 1994), 125–36.

The first act of liberation is justice to creation itself. "When we do justice to the land, then love, nurture, care, acceptance, and peace flow naturally and necessarily."[13] When there is justice in the land, the fields, and forests and every living thing will dance and sing for joy (Ps 96:11–12). Thus an awareness of being one with the whole creation is the spiritual foundation of indigenous people.[14] Jürgen Moltmann also argues that an authentic liberation can be experienced only when we take into consideration the following levels: (a) struggles for economic justice against the exploitation of humans, (b) struggles for human dignity and human rights against political oppression of humans, (c) struggles for peace with nature against the industrial destruction of the environment, and (d) struggles for hope against apathy in asserting the significance of the whole in personal life.[15] Throughout their histories, indigenous people have affirmed this interrelationship of poverty, political oppression, economic exploitation, and justice with land. In different forums, indigenous people have made it clear that the question of identity, hunger, diseases, illiteracy, culture, and religion are inseparably related to space, and the survival of indigenous people is an integral part of total cosmic justice.

Therefore, from indigenous people's perspective, one cannot do authentic liberation theology without relating to the issue of "space." A theology that addresses humanity alone and emphasizes soul-winning but leaves the rest of the cosmos unaddressed is an incomplete theology. Theology becomes impotent when it addresses only humanity. There is no theological and biblical justification to reducing theology to a mere liberative or transformative activity of humanity. Therefore, the challenge before us is to commit ourselves to struggle for the transformation of the poor, the weak, and disfigured humanity and to curtail the overexploitation of nature. Without restoring justice to space, the indigenous and oppressed communities will not be able to attain liberation and fullness of life in Christ.

The core of human suffering is inseparably connected with the violation of space: Our selfishness, greed, and exploitative attitude toward our mother earth bring poverty, oppression, ethnic conflict, and many other forms of injustice. The moment we cut ourselves off from a reverential relationship with land, we are uprooted from the world of mystery and we live a life of indecency. Never-ending exploitation of earth's limited resources results in a few affluent individuals causing the majority of the poor to live in misery and hunger. This disparity makes peo-

---

13. Tinker, "Spirituality and Native American Personhood," 127–28.
14. Tinker, "Spirituality and Native American Personhood," 127–28.
15. Jürgen Moltmann, *The Future of Creation* (London: SCM, 1979), 110–12.

ple turn against one another; everyone becomes a threat to the other's peaceful existence. This happens state-wise, nationally, and locally. Suspicion, doubt, and selfishness take precedence over trust, love, care, and acceptance. Our rootlessness makes life lose meaning and purpose.[16]

We need to reexamine our orientation toward the mystery of nature. With the advancements in science, people believe that there is nothing amazing about the cosmos. The physical world is viewed merely as a sum total of many material components and energies. Humans can understand, predict, and control everything. We are separated from, and are master of, the earth. Nature is something "out there," apart from us and also apart from God. This wrong notion justifies manipulation and domination of land and its resources. Without any religious restraint, land and its resources are exploited and abused, denying the rights of everyone. Today land and natural resources that have sustained life for centuries are forcibly taken away in the name of development without providing proper alternatives. Indigenous people have not only lost their soil-centered culture but have been reduced to bonded laborers on their own land.

And finally, we lack a proper orientation toward God, who is the source and the sovereign Lord of all creation. Instead of affirming the divine presence in the universe, human beings consider themselves as lord and master of all. Every person wants to control and manipulate land and its resources, threatening the rhythm of the universe. "Therefore, the land mourns and all who dwell in it languish and also beasts of the field and the birds of the air and even the fish of the sea are taken away" (Hos 4:3). When there is an attempt by the servant to take over the place of the master at home, it provokes other servants who are also struggling for lordship, and the home becomes a battlefield. No one is at peace. Therefore, for indigenous people, doing justice to land is the foundation of life. When we do justice to God's world, people will find a healthier life.

16. P. P. Kochappilly, *Celebrative Ethics: Ecological Issues in the Light of the Syro-Malabar Qur-bana* (Bangalore: Dharmaram, 1999), 29–40.

PART VI

Contextualizing
Theological Education

18.

Toward the Renewal of Theological Education and Church Ministry: A Reflection on Shoki Coe's Views on Theological Education

CHEN NAN-JOU

INTRODUCTION

The book *Communicating for a Change*, written by Andy Stanley and Lane Jones on preaching, was translated into Mandarin Chinese in 2010. The Chinese title of this book literally means *Untaught Preaching Secrets in the Seminary*.[1] Although the original English subtitle of this book is *Seven Keys to Irresistible Communication*, it has nothing to do with related courses in a theological seminary, nor does the preface written by Andy Stanley mention anything about theological training in a seminary. Why then was the Chinese edition so titled? Is it a kind of sales strategy? Did the translator or the Chinese Christian publisher think that this completely different title would attract readers who are familiar with the Chinese language? Why would this new title be attractive to ministers using Chinese? Do the translator, the publisher, or even ministers who use Chinese in their ministry consciously or unconsciously think that theological seminaries have to teach everything? Or do most Christian ministers using the Chinese language take it for granted that theological seminaries should teach all things that they need in the church ministry? What does theological training mean to translators, publish-

---

1. Andy Stanley and Lane Jones, *Communicating for a Change: Seven Keys to Irresistible Communication* (Colorado Springs, CO: Random House, 2006). The traditional Chinese edition was published by CCLM, Taipei, Taiwan in 2010. The translators are Hsiao Sian-Yi and Wang Nai-Chun.

ers, and ministers? It is sad that such statements as "theology is useless" or "I have never learned this from the seminary" prevail among church ministers today in Taiwan. The churches in Taiwan are also churches familiar with the Chinese language. How do ministers in Taiwan understand theological education and church ministry? What sort of theological education do they expect to receive?

This article attempts to construct a renewal of theological education and church ministry through a reflection on Shoki Coe's views on theological education and church ministry, mainly from two of his articles: "Theology and Church: Editorial"[2] and "A Rethinking of Theological Training for the Ministry in the Younger Churches Today."[3]

THEOLOGY AND CHURCH

Shoki Coe, also known as Ng Chiong-Hui or Chang-Huei Hwang, principal of the Tainan Theological College and Seminary (TTCS) of the Presbyterian Church in Taiwan (PCT) from 1948 to 1965, was also the first Taiwanese principal of the TTCS. On the occasion of the eightieth anniversary of the TTCS, he discussed issues relating to the necessity of theology and the relationship between theological training and the ministry of the church. In an editorial of the journal *Theology and Church*, Coe said that theological study was a kind of adventure.[4] To buttress his arguments, he posed several questions: "'Is it worthy to do this adventure?' This is also a legitimate question to ask, for theological study, in fact, creates disputes, even divisions! 'Do we really need theological study?' 'Does the Church need theology?'"

He further asked, "'Does the Church need a theological seminary?' . . . The journal *Theology and Church* is to serve and to contribute to these discussions and reflections."[5] It is obvious that the mission of *Theology and Church*, from its inception, as its title suggests, has been to explore the relationship between theology and the church. Coe pointed out that "the question 'Does the Church need theology?' is already a theological argument. And 'The Church does not need theology' is also a theological conclusion, and theological understanding, including a false 'Ecclesiology,' and a false 'Christology.' If our understanding of Christology

2. Ng Chiong Hui, "Sîn-hȧk kap Kàu-hōe: Hoat-khan sû" (Shoki Coe, "Theology and Church: Editorial," *Theology and Church* 1 [March 1957]). Shoki Coe's article was written in Romanized Taiwanese. The English translation is done by the author of this article.

3. C. H. Hwang (Shoki Coe), "A Rethinking of Theological Training for the Ministry in the Younger Churches Today," *South East Asia Journal of Theology* 4, no. 2 (July 1962): 7–34.

4. Coe, "Theology and Church: Editorial," 1.

5. Coe, "Theology and Church: Editorial," 3–4.

is false, our understanding of God will be false, and so is of Human being, for the central issue of the Christian faith is the question raised by Christ to his disciples on the way to the villages of Caesarea Philippi, 'But who do you say that I am?'"[6] For Coe, expressions like "theology does not help the Church" is already a kind of theological understanding, a false theological understanding indeed. Coe said that when Jesus's disciples gave various answers to the question "who Jesus is," Jesus did not mention anything about his church. Only when Peter responded with "You are the Messiah. The Son of the living God," did Jesus mention the church.[7] Coe said, "In this response, Simon became Peter, Simon became Rock, on which the Lord Jesus will build his Church."[8] Coe stated that Peter's response was, in our language, a confession. "Where there is no confession, there is no Church."[9] In fact, we may also say that Peter's confession is based on his theological understanding. Confession is an act of faith, and a theological statement derived from reflection on faith.

After clarifying the relationship between confession and the church, Coe started to explain what theology is. He said, "A confessional church has inevitably to humble itself and ask, 'Is my confession right? Is my confession in accordance with God's will? Or is it only my bias?' Theology is derived from this sort of self-evaluation of the Church."[10] It can be noted that Coe did not think that theology is only a kind of knowledge, but a sort of reflection on faith, a reflection made by the church in her life. Then, Coe went on to say that "the necessity of self-reflection for the church will be more obvious when we associate it to the mission of the Church."[11] This again showed us that for Coe, theology is a reflection on faith, and it is eventually relevant to the mission of the church. He himself illustrated this relationship. He said that the confession of the church included making confession to others, namely, to witness, to show people that Jesus is Christ, the Son of the living God, and to proclaim the gospel, making people know that "for God so loved the world that he gave his only Son, so that everyone who believes in him may not perish but may have eternal life."[12]

It seems to me that Coe tried to illustrate the relationship between theology and the church through the mission of the Christian church. The most basic task of the church is to proclaim the word of God. Coe said that a humble church that revered God would be aware that

6. Coe, "Theology and Church: Editorial," 4.
7. Coe, "Theology and Church: Editorial," 4.
8. Coe, "Theology and Church: Editorial," 4.
9. Coe, "Theology and Church: Editorial," 5.
10. Coe, "Theology and Church: Editorial," 5–6.
11. Coe, "Theology and Church: Editorial," 6.
12. Coe, "Theology and Church: Editorial," 6.

she faced a crisis in proclaiming the word of God. How can people of unclean lips who live among a people of unclean lips proclaim the word of God? How can human beings use their languages to proclaim the word of God? In the process of proclamation, the discontinuity between the word of God and the words of human beings should be marked by continuity. If there is no continuity, there is no proclamation of God's word.[13] Coe stated,

> The persons proclaiming the Word of God have this expectation in their mind; however, they should not, and dare not take it as a self-evident event, thinking that human beings have the possibility to proclaim the Word of God. For he or she has to realize that he or she is standing under a kind of judgment when he or she is proclaiming. "The treasure" he or she is going to proclaim is from heavenly God, and the tool of proclaiming is only an earthly "clay jar." [That] proclamation can be done is a miracle, . . . and because it is a miracle, the Christian churches are standing under the grace of the Lord. Churches should not over-estimate their accomplishment for they are under the inseparable grace of the Lord and the judgment of the Lord.[14]

Theology originates from this situation that churches face the grace and judgment of the Lord at the same time. Coe made the following explanation: "In her humbleness, the church develops her theology to demonstrate that her first and the most important task is to be responsible to her Lord, and standing before the judgment and grace of the Lord. All of these can be true because 'the Word became flesh and lived among us.'"[15] Coe borrowed Karl Barth's viewpoint and said that when the church proclaimed courageously, she had to ask herself at the same time: Is the language of proclamation based on her Lord Jesus Christ? Is her proclamation in accordance with the gospel of Jesus Christ? Does her proclamation lead people to come to Jesus Christ?[16] He quoted Barth and said,

> When a church makes self-reflection and self-evaluation, it is the church's theological effort. Therefore, theology makes sense in claiming the theology of the church only when it takes place inside the church, and for the church. Theology stands behind the proclamation of the church sometimes, walks side by side with the proclamation of the church sometimes, and stands in front of the church to lead the proclamation sometimes. Whatever position the church takes, theology cannot be separated from the church, and the church should not forget her double crises and give up her effort in

13. Coe, "Theology and Church: Editorial," 6–7.
14. Coe, "Theology and Church: Editorial," 7.
15. Coe, "Theology and Church: Editorial," 8.
16. Coe, "Theology and Church: Editorial," 8.

theological study. The meaning of "and" in *Theology and Church* is based on this understanding.[17]

At the end of the editorial, Coe emphasized that both theological study and church ministry have to always remember the word "and" in *Theology and Church*. Both theology and the church are under the judgment of the Lord and the grace of the Lord. Both theology and the church have to humble themselves to proclaim the word of God and to do theology courageously.[18] He stated that "theology cannot save the church, but it is helpful in keeping the church conscious that real salvation is the judgment and the grace of the Lord."[19]

It is quite clear from what Coe said in the editorial of *Theology and Church* that for himself and his colleagues in the TTCS, theological study, theological research, and theological learning are never useless for the church. Theological education and the church are closely related. The church exists and comes out from the confession of faith, and theology is the basic element of the existence of the church. For the church, theology is necessary and helpful. Those who say that theology is useless are people who fail in theological reflection, and are thus ignorant and faulty by speaking an immodest theological viewpoint. This sort of theology is completely useless.

THEOLOGICAL EDUCATION AND CHURCH MINISTRY

On other occasions, Coe went further to explore the relationship between theological education and church ministry. He presented a paper titled "A Rethinking of Theological Training for the Ministry in the Younger Churches Today" in a consultation of the principals of theological colleges and seminaries in the Southeast Asia region, held by the Association of Theological Education in South East Asia, in November 1961. The same paper was delivered on the occasion of the meeting of the Theological Education Fund (TEF) of the World Council of Churches (WCC) in 1962.[20] That Coe gave the same contents on two different occasions to different people showed that he was confident about the theological argument he presented. This paper revealed three

---

17. Coe, "Theology and Church: Editorial," 8.
18. Coe, "Theology and Church: Editorial," 8–9.
19. Coe, "Theology and Church: Editorial," 9.
20. The article "A Rethinking of Theological Training for the Ministry in the Younger Churches Today" was translated into Chinese and printed in *Theology and Church* 3, no. 2 (May 1963) and nos. 3 & 4 (February 1964).

themes, namely, the younger churches, church ministry, and theological training or theological education.

By "younger churches," Coe referred to the churches in Asia and Africa, which are historically younger compared with the churches in the West, namely, the churches in America, Britain, and continental Europe. It also referred to the churches situated in a postcolonial era in Asia and Africa in comparison to the churches of a post-Christian era in the West. Coe took the term "younger churches" to demonstrate that the situation and mission contexts in Southeast Asia were very different from those in the Western churches, which had long histories and old traditions. And he raised a question that he thought was an uncomfortable one but nevertheless had to be faced with seriousness: Regarding theological education and church ministry, is it suitable for theological seminaries and churches in Southeast Asia "to uncritically repeat and imitate the particular pattern which we happened to inherit" from the West?[21] Quoting Richard Niebuhr, Coe said, "We tend to repeat customary actions unaware that when we do today what we did yesterday we actually do something different, since in the interval both we and our environment have changed; unaware also that we now do without conscious definition of purpose and method what was done yesterday with specific ends in view and by relatively precise means. Education in general and not least ecclesiastical education is subject to this constant process of deterioration and hence in need of periodic self-examination."[22]

Coe argued that "behind every pattern of theological education lies an implicit image of the ministry."[23] If a theological seminary wants to evaluate its theological education, it must evaluate the understanding of the church about the nature and significance of the church ministry, namely the essential questions such as "What is the church?" "What is the ministry?" and "What is the relationship between them and this dynamic, revolutionary world of ours?"[24] Coe said that "only inasmuch as we face these basic questions courageously and squarely shall we be liberated from mere repetition and imitation in our theological education and move forward creatively for the training of the ministry."[25]

For Coe, "The ministry must first and foremost be understood Christologically as the ministry of Christ. . . . The ministry of Christ is theo-

21. Coe, "A Rethinking of Theological Training for the Ministry," 8.

22. Coe, "A Rethinking of Theological Training for the Ministry," 8. Quoted from H. Richard Niebuhr, *The Purpose of the Church and Its Ministry* (New York: Harper & Bros, 1956), viii.

23. Coe, "A Rethinking of Theological Training for the Ministry," 9.

24. Coe, "A Rethinking of Theological Training for the Ministry," 9–10.

25. Coe, "A Rethinking of Theological Training for the Ministry," 10.

logically expressed as the ministry of the Triune God-of-the-Father, in the Son, and through the Holy Spirit in and for the world."[26] He argued, "So far as our ministry is concerned, the Church is first the receiver and only then the bearer; first the object and then the subject of the ministry of Christ. As the Revealer, Bearer, and the Fulfiller of the Divine Ministry, the ministry of Jesus Christ is the absolute standard and basis of the Church's ministry."[27] Then, what is the uniqueness or characteristic of Christ's ministry? Coe thought that it "can be expressed in the servant image of the New Testament." And it is "another decisive factor for the re-thinking of the Church and its Ministry."[28] Coe illustrated his argument through our Lord's servant image in Mark 10:45, Luke 22:27, and John 13:1. He said, in our Lord's servant image, "His ministry has a threefold direction—to God, His Father; to the 'many,' for whom He gave His life as ransom; and to His disciples who were in the World."[29] He went on to explain that "Thy will, not mine, be done" was Christ's life prayer unto death. This is Christ's "God-directed" ministry. And Christ's whole ministry was also directed to the many for whom he came and gave his life. This is Christ's "world-directed" ministry. Christ called out from the world a few to be with him, and he directed his ministry wholly to them, as though they were his entire concern. This is Christ's ministry to his disciples.[30] Coe made this conclusion, "In His capacity as *the diakonon*, Christ carried out His three-fold ministry—to God, to the many (the world), and to the few (the New Israel—the Church); and so perfect was His servitude that He who served unto death became once for all the Lord of the ministry—the Servant Lord."[31]

Coe then came to talk about the church. He said, "As the community of the firstfruits, the Church must carry out its entrusted ministry in the form laid down by the Servant Lord. As His servant people, the ministry of the Church is also open in three directions—to God, to the world, and to the Church in the world."[32] The relationships of this threefold ministry, according to Coe, are God-directed or God-centered.[33] And because the world is the one to which God gave His Son and for which Christ died, a truly God-directed ministry becomes truly world-directed.[34] And the church-directed ministry is only existentially for the

26. Coe, "A Rethinking of Theological Training for the Ministry," 10.
27. Coe, "A Rethinking of Theological Training for the Ministry," 10.
28. Coe, "A Rethinking of Theological Training for the Ministry," 10.
29. Coe, "A Rethinking of Theological Training for the Ministry," 10–11.
30. Coe, "A Rethinking of Theological Training for the Ministry," 11.
31. Coe, "A Rethinking of Theological Training for the Ministry," 11.
32. Coe, "A Rethinking of Theological Training for the Ministry," 12.
33. Coe, "A Rethinking of Theological Training for the Ministry," 13.
34. Coe, "A Rethinking of Theological Training for the Ministry," 13.

302   TOWARD THE RENEWAL OF THEOLOGICAL EDUCATION

church, since essentially it is a world-directed ministry.[35] Therefore, we may have a clear conclusion that for Coe, the ministry of the church has a threefold direction, namely, to God, to the world, and to the church in the world. However, these three directions are closely related. The ministry to God and to the church is inevitably a ministry to the world.

How did Coe understand theological education and its practice in Asia and Africa? Quoting a report by the United Presbyterian Church in the United States of America, Coe said: "Appropriate theological education is the education of the whole church for its mission in the world. . . . The base of this theological education of the whole church is naturally the local congregation as it is nourished through worship and preaching, teaching and pastoral care, and as it becomes a true community of shared responsibility in which the members are strengthened for their life and witness in the world."[36] He further said, "Theological education is a necessary discipline and function of the Church in view of and for the sake of its entrusted ministry in and for the world. It is equipping God's people (church-directed) for work in His service (world-directed), to the building up the body of Christ (church-directed)."[37] It is obvious that for Coe, theological education and church ministry are inseparable. Furthermore, the purpose of theological education is not only to train ministers, not to mention a few distinguished theologians, but also "to equip the saints for the work of ministry, for building up the body of Christ." For Coe, theological education is education for all members of the church.

If all members of the church are entrusted to do the ministry of Christ and theological education is for all members of the church, why do we need theological education for a "set-apart" ministry?[38] This is a question we have to ask ourselves seriously with regard to the theological understanding of the Reformation, that is, the doctrine of the priesthood of all believers. Coe argued that "there is a set-apart ministry regarded as essential in the New Testament, and yet there is no fixed pattern, rather it is kept open and flexible; and we must ask why."[39] Therefore, Coe stressed that "on the one hand, the set-apart ministry is essential to the special charismata within the charismatic body—and so there is a givenness determined from above; while on the other hand, this ministry must

35. Coe, "A Rethinking of Theological Training for the Ministry," 14.
36. Coe, "A Rethinking of Theological Training for the Ministry," 14. Quoted from *An Advisory Study* (New York: Commission on Ecumenical Mission and Relations, the United Presbyterian Church in the United States of America, 1961), 42.
37. Coe, "A Rethinking of Theological Training for the Ministry," 15.
38. Coe, "A Rethinking of Theological Training for the Ministry," 15.
39. Coe, "A Rethinking of Theological Training for the Ministry," 17.

face the existential reality of the needs either within the Church or in the world—and so there is a changeableness determined from below."[40] He elaborated this argument further and said that each of the three-fold ministries, namely the God-directed, the world-directed, and the church-directed ministry, was in a living and organic relationship to the other two.[41] Coe reminded us that "this threefold ministry in the hands of the church-in-the-world is constantly exposed to the temptation of becoming 'lopsided' in any one of three ways—either in the direction of 'liturgical' mysticism (God-directed), or of 'priestly' ecclesiasticism (Church-directed), or else of 'social' activism (world-directed)."[42] He then concluded that "the set-apart ministry is representative, functional, and relative to the total ministry of the whole church as the intention is to the dimension, so its boundary must be flexible and open to the various charismata given from above and to the various needs within the church and the world from below."[43] However, Coe criticized the prevailing theological education in some churches that concentrated on a small group for the set-apart ministry without first paying serious attention to theological education at the local congregational level.[44] He stated: "I believe, . . . the ministry into which all members of the charismatic body are called to participate, and for which each member is given a special gift for the common good, and the set-apart ministry into which some are called to intentionalize this and some are called to intentionalize that . . . [may be] understood in the light of the one essen-tial ministry of Jesus Christ which fulfilled once for all the ministry of the Triune God in and for the world."[45] It is clear that for Coe, theological education is an essential part of Christian education. Theological educa-tion is not only for training ministers for the church or for cultivating a few distinguished scholars in theology, but also for all the Christians in the pews. All Christian education of the church should be theological, and it should be for members of the congregation. Theological educa-tion and church ministry are inseparable.

It must be noted that Coe argued that theological education should take history seriously, for it takes place concretely in a historical setting.[46] He urged the younger churches in the postcolonial world in Asia and Africa to be aware that their theological educations were going to take place in their particular situations in which their churches were

40. Coe, "A Rethinking of Theological Training for the Ministry," 17.
41. Coe, "A Rethinking of Theological Training for the Ministry," 17.
42. Coe, "A Rethinking of Theological Training for the Ministry," 17.
43. Coe, "A Rethinking of Theological Training for the Ministry," 18.
44. Coe, "A Rethinking of Theological Training for the Ministry," 18.
45. Coe, "A Rethinking of Theological Training for the Ministry," 19.
46. Coe, "A Rethinking of Theological Training for the Ministry," 19.

located. And he considered this issue from two realities that the younger churches face today: pressures from within churches on theological education—the problem of imported patterns; and the pressures of the world on theological education.[47]

(a) Coe illustrated four aspects of the pressures of imported patterns of theological education. The first one is that the pattern imported by missions is "church-directed," and the need of theological training for the younger church is "world-directed."[48] The imported pattern assumed that everyone was Christian, and this led theological education to being "church-directed," or "pastoral-oriented." However, the younger churches are located in a non-Christian society. The theological training of the younger churches has to find a new pattern appropriate for a "world-directed" church. It must be reoriented so as to build churches to become a missionary community.[49]

Second, the imported pattern of ministry is denominational, and the need of the younger churches is for an ecumenical encounter in theological education.[50] Denominational-oriented theological education presents a dividing feature that contradicts the teaching of our Lord that his disciples should be one so that the world may know and believe. Coe argued that "theological educational institutions today must become the place of a real ecumenical encounter for the churches. They must be constantly in search of a pattern which will make the ecumenical encounter possible and creative, and in so doing they must also serve the churches in their search for the new pattern of life appropriate for the missionary community in and for the world of nations."[51]

Third, the imported pattern of ministry is "mono-tary," and the need of the younger churches for theological education is for varieties of ministries.[52] Coe argued that varieties of ministries were urgent concerns for the missionary community in strengthening the voices of equal participation of gender and in dealing with the dynamic situation of social revolution.[53]

Fourth, the imported pattern of ministry is "paid" professional ministry, and the need of the younger churches for theological education is for "open ministries."[54] Coe argued that "the pattern of the 'paid' ministry is impoverishing the life and mission of the younger churches in

---

47. Coe, "A Rethinking of Theological Training for the Ministry," 20–33.
48. Coe, "A Rethinking of Theological Training for the Ministry," 20.
49. Coe, "A Rethinking of Theological Training for the Ministry," 21.
50. Coe, "A Rethinking of Theological Training for the Ministry," 21.
51. Coe, "A Rethinking of Theological Training for the Ministry," 21–22.
52. Coe, "A Rethinking of Theological Training for the Ministry," 22.
53. Coe, "A Rethinking of Theological Training for the Ministry," 23–25.
54. Coe, "A Rethinking of Theological Training for the Ministry," 25.

more than one way. . . . We are driven to seek an open pattern of the ministry, so that it can be free to respond responsibly and creatively."[55]

(b) Coe illustrated three aspects of the pressures of the world on theological education, that is, the pressures from the existential situation of the world. The first one is the pressure from the area of education. Coe argued that there was a need for open dialogue in theological education.[56] He stated that "theological education is a dialogue, horizontally between teachers and students and vertically between teachers and students together and this mysterious One, who, though unseen, is yet heard. As they take part in this dialogue, the Bible becomes alive for them, for it becomes for them a dialogue between the Lord and His people in which they are called to participate."[57] He emphasized that the field of open dialogue should include the content and organization of the curriculum, determining the methods of teaching and deciding the proper combination of theory and practice in theological education.[58]

The second pressure is the one from the renaissance of culture and non-Christian religions, and Coe argued that "theological training for ministry, to be a real open dialogue, must take place concretely and faithfully in this setting of religious and cultural revival."[59] According to him, only the church takes indigenous cultures and religions seriously, and we may go toward the right way to indigenization.[60]

The third is the pressure from rapid social change, and Coe argued that theological education had to take place in the midst of this existential and exacting context.[61] He said: "I am convinced that this encounter and response between church and society is going to be the test case as to whether the younger churches are really going to be missionary communities of the firstfruits for the New Creation or irrelevant ghettos whose lone hope is directed to an 'other world,' which has nothing to do with the here and now."[62] Coe pointed out that the younger churches in general had problems such as an irrelevant theological outlook, ignorant of the real world, and did not know how to face secular religions, extreme nationalism, or to deal with a society that had suddenly become dynamic.[63]

At the end of this article, Coe stated that "we must (as we have empha-

55. Coe, "A Rethinking of Theological Training for the Ministry," 25.
56. Coe, "A Rethinking of Theological Training for the Ministry," 26.
57. Coe, "A Rethinking of Theological Training for the Ministry," 27.
58. Coe, "A Rethinking of Theological Training for the Ministry," 28.
59. Coe, "A Rethinking of Theological Training for the Ministry," 28.
60. Coe, "A Rethinking of Theological Training for the Ministry," 28–30.
61. Coe, "A Rethinking of Theological Training for the Ministry," 31.
62. Coe, "A Rethinking of Theological Training for the Ministry," 31.
63. Coe, "A Rethinking of Theological Training for the Ministry," 32–33.

sized again and again) re-think our church-directed congregational life and its pattern of ministry from the point of view of a world-directed one. Theological education for the ministry must take this redirection seriously."[64] He went on to say that "I believe that only in this way can theological training for the ministry become both true to Biblical insights and relevant to rapid social change. For only in this way will the ministry become open again—open to God, and so to the World, and so to the church, and back again in dynamic and organic interpenetration and interaction. When it is open, it will become mobile and flexible, instead of being institutionalized into rigidity."[65] Coe concluded his article with these words, "The task for Christians today is not just to 'attend a church' conceived in a four-walled building, but to 'be the church in and for the world,' in the power of Christ to exercise that ministry with which His whole body is now entrusted till He comes in glory. The Churches must search in all earnestness for a pattern of congregational life, which is appropriate to this entrusted ministry; and an open pattern of the set-apart ministry which is free to serve and lead in total ministry of His Church."[66]

Having quoted much from Coe's discourse on theological education, we may, therefore, reasonably conclude that, for him theological education is based on the ministry of Christ and is for the ministry of the church. Theological education has to be aware of the situation where the church is located. Younger churches in Taiwan or in other places in Asia and Africa should not import the theologies of the West or imitate ministries that are derived from Western churches uncritically. Younger churches have to do their theology and develop their theological education in their own contexts, especially without failing to pay attention to traditional cultures, people's religions, and social change.

These were not only Coe's theological arguments but were also his ways of doing theology and administering the TTCS. Under Coe's leadership, the TTCS became a center for research and extension during the "Double Church Movement" (PKU) of the Presbyterian Church in Taiwan. It was a time of rapid social change in Taiwan, and the church had launched enthusiastically into the evangelical movement. Coe demonstrated the close connection between theological education and church ministry when the TTCS was under his administration. Later, he recalled, "During the ten years of the [PKU] Movement, many meetings were held in the college in connection with it—study sessions, planning sessions, committee meetings and so on—some at the request of

64. Coe, "A Rethinking of Theological Training for the Ministry," 33.
65. Coe, "A Rethinking of Theological Training for the Ministry," 33.
66. Coe, "A Rethinking of Theological Training for the Ministry," 34.

a particular presbytery, some under the auspices of Synod or, later, of the General Assembly. The college became a center for study, not just for future ministers, but for all ministers and for lay men and women. They were all concerned in evangelism, not just as a theory or in a general way, but with a specific focus—the work of PKU."[67] In his *Recollections and Reflections*, Coe said,

> The PKU movement developed during a period of history in Taiwan when new and unexpected problems sprang up year by year. Yet now, looking back . . . , I see it as a most exciting period in my life as a theological educator—and, I believe, in the life of the college as a whole. In many ways it was a most constructive period. All those study sessions, planning groups and committees stimulated us to dream of and plan for the development of the college as a theological centre, a "brains trust," a workshop, a laboratory for our church, enabling her to become not just a growing minority, but a creative minority in every walk of life in Taiwan.[68]

CONTEXTUALIZING THEOLOGY

Thereafter, Coe became the director of the Theological Education Fund (TEF) of the World Council of Churches (WCC). In the TEF Policy Statement, "A Working Policy for the Implementation of the Third Mandate of the Theological Education Fund," he and his colleagues argued that theological education had to do contextualization, contextualization in mission, church structures, theology, and education.[69] Later, Coe himself illustrated his argument on "indigenization" and "contextualization" and said that "indigenization is a missiological necessity when the Gospel moves from one cultural soil to another and has to be retranslated, reinterpreted, and expressed afresh in the new cultural soil. Why, then, do we now use a new word, contextualization, in preference to indigenization? Indigenous, indigeneity, and indigenization all derive from a nature metaphor, that is, of the soil, or taking root in the soil. It is only right that the younger churches, in search of their own identity, should take seriously their own cultural milieu. However, because of the static nature of the [soil] metaphor, indigenization tends to be used in the sense of responding to the Gospel in terms of traditional cultures. Therefore, it is in danger of being past-oriented. . . . [I]t was felt

67. Shoki Coe, *Recollections and Reflections*, 2nd ed. (New York: Formosan Christians for Self-Determination, 1993), 193.

68. Coe, *Recollections and Reflections*, 195.

69. TEF staff, eds., *Ministry in Context: The Third Mandate Programme of the Theological Education Fund (1970–77)* (London: Theological Education Fund, 1972), 11–33.

that the danger lay in over-indigenization, an uncritical accommodation such as expressed by the cultural faiths."[70] Coe stated: "So in using the word 'contextualization,' we try to convey all that is implied in the familiar term 'indigenization,' yet seek to press beyond for a more dynamic concept which is open to change and which is also future-oriented."[71] He went on to explore the very core of this new theological approach: "Authentic theological reflection can only take place as the *theologia in loco*, discerning the contextuality within the concrete context. But it must also be aware that such authentic theological reflection is at best, but also at most, *theologia viatorum*; and therefore contextuality must be matched by the contextualization which is an ongoing process, fitting for pilgrim people, moving from place to place and from time to time, in awareness that there is no abiding place which is not subject also to the changes of time. Thus, the TEF does not speak about 'contextual theology' nor 'contextualized theology' but about contextualizing theology."[72] He said, "I believe, in fact, that the incarnation is the divine form of contextualization."[73] However, Coe stated, "Authentic contextualization must be open constantly to the painful process of de-contextualization, for the sake of re-contextualization."[74]

On the basis of the discourses mentioned above, we may say that Coe argued for a dynamic approach in doing theology. He stressed the living context in which the church is doing theology. There is no static context, and the church has to reflect on its faith constantly in doing theology and developing church ministry.

When we look back on Coe's argument in his articles today, it is quite clear that the theological education he wanted to lay stress on, either in the TTCS or in the TEF, had a continuity. Theological education is for church ministry, and church ministry has to be aware of the cultural and social situation of the church. Since cultures and societies are constantly changing, theological reflection on church ministry needs to be renewed always. It is an ongoing process of contextualizing.

---

70. Shoki Coe, "Contextualizing as the Way Toward Reform," in *Asian Christian Theology: Emerging Themes*, rev. edition, ed. Douglas J. Elwood (Philadelphia: Westminster, 1980), 48–55.
71. Shoki Coe, "Contextualizing Theology," in *Mission Trends No. 3: Third World Theology*, ed. Gerald H. Anderson and Thomas F. Stransky (New York: Paulist, 1976), 21.
72. Coe, "Contextualizing Theology," 22.
73. Coe, "Contextualizing Theology," 23.
74. Coe, "Contextualizing Theology," 24.

THE RENEWAL OF THEOLOGICAL EDUCATION
AND CHURCH MINISTRY

From Coe's theological discourses, we realize again that the church came to exist through confession, and when the church reflects its confession—its ministry, its witness, and proclamation—the church is doing its theology. No church is without theology. Churches have only the distinction between good theology and bad theology, defined by whether their theology is relevant to the living social and cultural context of the church. It seems to me that rather than being different from that in the West, Coe intended to make efforts to relate theological education to church ministry and to make both of them relevant to the living context of Taiwan.

In 2017, sixty years after the first issue of *Theology and Church* of the TTCS was published, how is the relationship between theological education and church ministry in Taiwan? Do Taiwanese churches develop contextual theologies relevant to the living cultural and social context of Taiwan? The following part of this paper will evaluate the theological education and church ministry in Taiwan with regard to what Coe said about theology and church, especially from the perspective that theological education cannot be separated from church ministry, that the church should not give up her efforts in theological study, and that theology should be "world-directed" and contextual.

CHURCH MINISTRY

Does the PCT as a whole take theological study seriously? Do the church ministries of the PCT reflect the "world-directed" theological thinking? Before the 1960s, the church ministry of the PCT was focused on evangelism, and education was taken to be the supplementary ministry. At the same time, the society of Taiwan was shifting from an agricultural one to an industrial one. The leadership of the PCT seemed to be aware of the new situation brought about by social change and started to appeal to the study on social change and the necessity of new ministries. An example of this awareness of the PCT was that the General Assembly established a new committee, that is, the Committee of the Industrial Evangelism, in 1959. However, according to the report given by the consultant invited by the PCT to assist the research on industrial mission, the PCT did not prepare itself well to participate in this new ministry. George Todd, the consultant, urged PCT theological colleges to help the churches realize the social change and its impact on the church and to understand the meaning of the gospel in this changing society.[75] In other words, PCT churches, generally speaking, did not take theological study seriously enough.

Nevertheless, things changed after the celebration of the centennial of the PCT (1965). At the end of the PKU, Presbyterian congregations were founded in most of the towns and villages, let alone the cities, in Taiwan. The PKU also pushed Presbyterians to understand more comprehensively the rapid change Taiwanese society was undergoing and to experience more deeply the lives of the people of Taiwan, namely the living context of mission in Taiwan. After the centennial celebration, the PCT launched a new mission movement, "The New Century Mission Movement" (NCMM, 1965–70). It was intended to be a movement of the renewal of the church. The TTCS became the research center of the NCMM. C. S. Song, who advocated a "theology of incarnation" in his inauguration of the principal of the TTCS,[76] introduced H. R. Weber's book, *The Salt of the Earth*, to the Taiwanese churches in the beginning of the NCMM and urged them to shift their "inward ministry mentality" to "outward ministry mentality."[77] The NCMM emphasized social involvement and mission work for farmers, fishermen, laborers, aborigines, and those who live in secluded places, namely, the people who are most influenced by rapid social change. It was obviously a "world-directed" mission movement that embraced the ecumenical understanding of "*missio Dei*." The NCMM enabled the PCT to discern even more clearly the sufferings and the hopes of the people and to identify with the people and the land than ever before. It helped the PCT to discern the mission context of Taiwan and to do mission related to its living context.

Those who pay attention to the mission of the PCT will find that the dimensions of church ministries were expanded in the 1970s and 1980s. Besides evangelism and education, social service was added. And then, social participation was included. Examples of this were three public statements issued by the PCT concerning the sufferings and the hope of the Taiwanese people in the 1970s, namely, "Statement on Our National Fate," "Our Appeal," and "A Declaration on Human Rights." The most significant contextual theology articulated in the 1970s and 1980s was called "homeland theology," emphasizing the identification

75. See Chen Nan-Jou, *The Social and Political Ethics of the Presbyterian Church in Taiwan* (Taipei: Yeong Wang, 1991), 85 (in Chinese).

76. See C. S. Song, *Towards a Theology of the Incarnation* (Tainan: Tainan Theological College, 1965).

77. *The Salt of the Earth* (The Research Center of New Century Mission Movement, 1967) (in Chinese).

with the people and the land of Taiwan as homeland, and the struggle for justice and human rights with the Taiwanese people.[78]

> In preparing to face the coming of the new century (21st century), the PCT has launched a new mission movement, the 21st Century New Taiwan Mission Movement (21st CNTM). It is a mission movement embracing the theological insights of "the Reign of God" and expecting to actualize "the Reign of God" through the mission programs in the following six dimensions, i.e. to proclaim the gospel of God's reign, to teach and to nurture the people of God, to do loving service in Christ's way, to seek to transform society, to care for the creation of God, and to reflect all these mentioned above in the context of the gospel and culture.[79] Though this mission program is based on the fivefold mission understanding of the Council for World Mission[80] and echoes the five marks of the modern theology in missiology,[81] it involves the contextual reflection from Taiwan by adding the aspect, "in the context of the gospel and culture."

It should be concluded, from what has been said above, that in terms of church ministry, the PCT is on the right path that Coe urged it to be. The PCT articulates its church ministry theologically, advocating a theology relevant to the social and cultural context of the church. The church, at least the General Assembly, which is in charge of planning the dimensions and modes of the mission program for all congregations, also renews its church ministry constantly to cope with the new situation of Taiwanese society.

THEOLOGICAL EDUCATION

Coe proposed the contextualization of theology and for theological education to respond to social change and cultural revival. Do theological workers of the PCT develop contextual theologies in Taiwan? After Coe, C. S. Song advocated the theology of incarnation, and Wang Hsien-Chih advocated the homeland theology. Afterwards, theological discussions with slightly different emphasis appeared in the PCT, such as a theology of identification proposed by Chen Nan-Jou;[82] and

---

78. See Chen Nan-Jou, ed., *A Testament to Taiwan Homeland Theology: The Essential Writings of Wang Hsien-Chih* (Taipei: Yeong Wang, 2011).

79. See https://tinyurl.com/y72lh866. Cited on November 14, 2017.

80. See Council for World Mission, *World Mission Today* (London: Council for World Mission, 1999).

81. See Andrew Walls and Cathy Ross, eds., *Mission in the 21st Century: Exploring the Five Global Missions* (Maryknoll, NY: Orbis, 2008).

82. See Chen Nan-Jou, "Contextualizing Catholicity: A Taiwanese Theology of Identification," *Asia Journal of Theology* 17, no. 2 (October 2003): 341–63.

a theology of chhut-thau-thin, or a theology of self-determination, proposed by Po Ho Huang.[83] All of these theological efforts are meant, as C. S. Song said, to confess Christian faith in one's world,[84] to identify with the sufferings and the hope of the people in Taiwan, and to struggle for self-determination in facing the future crisis of Taiwan. However, do these theological discussions influence the articulation of the church ministry of the PCT? This is worthy of further discussion. Nevertheless, we do see that the General Assembly of the PCT takes thoughts from the theology of identification as its basic theological argument for the long-term mission programs in 2006.[85]

When discussing the relationship between theological study and church ministry, Coe's opinion was that theology stands in front of the church to lead the proclamation sometimes. It is especially noteworthy to have a critical reflection in the atmosphere in Taiwan today where statements like "theology is useless" abound. What should we do to ensure that the leading theological thought can last long enough to guide and to renew the church? One special ministry can serve as an example of this reflection. The General Assembly of the PCT launched a "Reading the Bible with New Eyes" movement (RBNE) in 1998. It was a mission movement launched by the Christian Conference of Asia (CCA) and adopted and revised by the PCT. The RBNE seeks to help Taiwanese Christians read the Bible in the living context of Taiwan where people of other faiths have other scriptures, and also to learn to read the Bible from the perspective of the oppressed, the marginalized people, who are struggling for justice in Taiwanese society. The PCT would like to enhance the identification with the people of Taiwan through this new Bible reading and to encourage the church to be a sign of hope for Taiwanese people through its participation in social transformation. The theological understanding behind the RBNE is that the meaning of the Bible comes out of a process of dialogue between the reader and the text. Therefore, reading the Bible with new eyes eventually has to take the living situation and cultures in Taiwan into account and it has to be a contextual approach to the Bible. After several enablers' workshop, with the publication of materials as exemplary of Bible study, the RBNE was well received among the local congregations. However, it only lasted for a few years. The exemplary weekly or daily devotional Bible study materials still have the title of the RBNE; nevertheless, the way of interpret-

83. Po Ho Huang, *A Theology of Self-Determination* (Manila: ATESEA, 2005).

84. C. S. Song, "An Introduction of the Incarnation of the Gospel: Confessing the Faith in the World Today," *Theology and Church* 6, nos. 1 & 2 (1966): 11–29.

85. See *The Mission White Paper: Identification, Commitment, and Growth* (Taipei: General Assembly of the Presbyterian Church in Taiwan, 2006).

ing the Bible has gone back to finding the so-called "objective" meaning of the Bible. It seems to me that the RBNE today does not do contextual reflection, nor has it anything to do with "new eyes." What shall the church do to make sure that the inspiring and constructing theological thought standing in front of the ministry lead the church and, at the same time, walk side by side with the church so that the ministry will not lose its critical theological reflection in its everyday life?

What other issues does theological education in the Taiwanese social and cultural context today have to wrestle with in order to lead the church so that it can be a prophetic voice for social transformation and the hope of the people, especially of the suffering and the oppressed? The answer could be various from different viewpoints, but the issues relating to social ethics seem to be above all others. Taiwanese churches have to face the impact of globalization, and the perplexing, confusing controversies raised from biotechnological research (such as DNA and stem cell research), and the human rights of LGBTQ (lesbian, gay, bisexual, transgender, queer), and so on. Taking the issue of LGBTQ, for example, the General Assembly of the PCT appointed an ad hoc committee to do research concerning the community from the perspectives of theology, medical science, and sociology in 1996. The ad hoc committee published its report in 2004. However, there was no follow-up to this report. The theological study of the General Assembly did not provoke the congregations to reflect on the issue of LGBTQ theologically. The fifty-ninth annual meeting (2014) of the General Assembly of the PCT issued a Pastoral Letter to condemn the LGBTQ, and the following discussions in 2017 especially reflected a lack of sincerity and depth in theological reflection regarding LGBTQ among ministers and congregations. In May 2017, the supreme court, the council of grand justices of the Taiwanese government, ruled that the current same-sex marriage ban violated "the people's freedom of marriage" and "the people's right to equality," and therefore was unconstitutional. If the PCT really does theology contextually, the church has to take up LGBTQ issues from the perspective of biblical hermeneutics and pastoral care even more theologically and seriously.

Christians in Taiwan live in a multicultural and multireligious society. The church has to face the plurality of culture and religion in Taiwan seriously. Although the issues of the gospel and culture are addressed in one of the dimensions of the twenty-first CNTM of the PCT, they are not taken seriously enough, especially the issue of dialogue among religions. Both Shoki Coe and C. S. Song urged the church to discern the theological meaning of culture and religion. Nevertheless, religious dialogue and theological study on cultures and other religions have generally not received public attention in the past decades. The ecumenical mind is missing in theological education.

If the PCT today considers Coe's argument on theology and the church to be still meaningful and takes it seriously, the PCT has to renew its theological study and education constantly, especially in the fields of biblical interpretation, social ethics, and cultures and religions.

CONCLUSION

The living context is always changing. However, what makes a difference is the tempo of change. Therefore, the impact of social and cultural changes to church ministry is ongoing. Social change will not disappear. Theology, which has to be contextual, should be renewed constantly. The church ministry that has to cope with social change should also be evaluated constantly. Shoki Coe did what he had to do in his time, and now theological institutes and churches today have to face contemporary social change and the issues raised by it, articulating new theology and carrying out relevant church ministry.

PART VII

Political Witness of Faith

19.

Christian Political Witness: Shoki Coe's Involvement in the Struggle for Self-Determination

J. BEN WEI

Ng Chiong-hui, Ko Sho-ki, Huang Chang-hui, and Shoki Coe: four names for one person! Chronologically he was a Taiwanese, a Japanese, a Chinese, and an Englishman, and these names illustrate the difficulties that the Rev. Dr. Shoki Coe encountered during his lifetime.

He was born a third-generation Christian; his father and grandfather were leading ministers in the Presbyterian Church in Taiwan. Following his grandfather's vow made at his conversion that not only he himself but the firstborn of his family would go into the ministry, Coe freely chose to take the literature section of the entrance examination of the Taiwan High School, even though his favorite and best subjects were geometry and algebra.

Before making this decision, he unavoidably participated in an act of bravery. This event occurred during his fourth year at primary school. In order to represent it more vividly, allow me to quote from his *Recollections and Reflections*:

> One afternoon, when about ten of us from the Ko Gakko (Primary School for Taiwanese) were on our way home, we were waylaid by a dozen or more boys from Sho Gakko (Primary School for Japanese children). They pelted us with stones and a great deal of abuse, finally using the words "Chian ko lo." When I heard that, even though I did not then completely understand its significance, I felt a sudden rage, as if I had been hit below

the belt. So then we let them have it, blow for blow and kick for kick. We fought like animals; and yet I felt no pain, only a strange sense of release.[1]

It goes without saying that his father, a minister, could not release him without questioning what and why it had happened.

With great difficulty I began to tell of the stones and abuse hurled at us by the Japanese schoolboys, but even this seemed to bring no change in his attitude, though his tone was perhaps now just a little gentler. "Did you not remember that we are Christians, and that our Lord told us to love even our enemies?" "But father, we only started to fight back when they began shouting at us 'You cowards, you Chian ko lo!'" At that, to my great amazement, my father went suddenly silent. I looked up in alarm and saw how pale he had become.[2]

Then his father directed his mother to nurse him and said:

Alright. Calm down. Get as much rest as you can tonight, because you must go to school as usual tomorrow and face whatever punishment the school authorities decide on. Explain the first part to them as briefly as possible, but remember to tell your Form Master, Mr. Cho (a Taiwanese) that the fight only began on your side when they said, "You cowards, you Chian ko lo."[3]

Next day, after the morning assembly was dismissed, he and the other nine boys were led by the Form Master to the Headmaster's office for questioning.

I followed his (father's) advice and didn't dwell on the earlier part of what had happened. Once again, to my amazement and that of all the others, as soon as I came to say "The actual fight only started as far as our side was concerned when they shouted at us 'You cowards, you Chian ko lo,' there was suddenly a dead silence. The Headmaster and our Form Master exchanged glances, the former looking embarrassed and the latter turning quite pale. It seemed that this phrase "Chian ko lo" worked like magic to clear away difficult situations. The Headmaster turned and said to us "Alright, you can go now," not even adding "Don't do it again," or any other general warning. We were even given a week away from school to recover from our wounds.[4]

Shoki concluded this paragraph with the following comments:

1. Shoki Coe, *Recollections and Reflections*, 2nd ed. (New York: Formosan Christians for Self-Determination, 1993), 25.
2. Coe, *Recollections and Reflections*, 25–26.
3. Coe, *Recollections and Reflections*, 26.
4. Coe, *Recollections and Reflections*, 25–26

During that week my father explained what the expression meant. It was not just calling us "Chinese slaves"—no, no, far worse, we were "Slaves of Ching." That meant we were in the first place slaves of the Manchurian Chings (no Chinese would accept that the Chings, or Manchu, were real Chinese) but, more than that, as Manchuria itself had been annexed and conquered by the Japanese, we were slaves of slaves. My political innocence was rudely shattered. I understood for the first time that as a Taiwanese I was condemned to live in my own native land as a second class—even third class—citizen.[5]

This incident in his boyhood is his first awakening in the understanding of his sociopolitical surroundings. He acquired his second "enlightenment" when he completed his course at the Tokyo Imperial University and had arranged to visit his homeland, Taiwan, for a few months and then leave for England to study at Cambridge. On his way back to Taiwan by boat, he unexpectedly met his brother on the deck and there he encountered an unforgettable incident. Let us follow the detailed story as recorded in his *Recollections and Reflections*:

A day or two after our boat left Kobe, I was walking along the deck when suddenly, and completely unexpectedly, I came face to face with my brother, A-Beng, whom I hadn't seen for three or four years. He had just completed his final year of Middle School in Tai-tiong, and his class was returning from a tour of Japan (Shiu-gaku Ryo-ko) where they had all been taken by the Form Master (or possibly the Military Instructor) for a few weeks. You can well imagine that in our excitement and joy we began to talk and chatter loudly together in our mother-tongue, Taiwanese, and not in the official Koku-go (i.e. National Language, then, of course, Japanese). Soon we were in deep trouble. What was our fault then? We had spoken our mother-tongue instead of Japanese. "Ko Mei-ki (my brother's name in Japanese) come here," shouted the Form Master. I saw my brother suddenly turn pale. He went at once to his Master, who took him away. I learnt that he had been taken to the Master's cabin and was there with him alone. I couldn't get any news of him for nearly two hours, until I learned from one of his classmates that he was undergoing a "severe disciplining."[6]

Then, Coe took the following means for his brother's rescue.

I hurried to my bunk and pulled out from things the best kimono I had, a new one I had bought before leaving Tokyo. I dressed carefully as if for some very special "official" occasion (what the Japanese call Sei-so). I even took my kaku bo—my university hat—as a kind of status symbol. Thus in full glory I went off, determined to have a showdown with that master, cost

5. Coe, *Recollections and Reflections*, 27.
6. Coe, *Recollections and Reflections*, 242–43.

me what it might. I knocked at the cabin door. "Hai-re," came a shout from inside ("Enter"—a command from a superior to an inferior). I opened the door and found myself right in front of him as he sat on his heels on the floor in the formal Japanese way.

He was a little taken aback, perhaps not recognizing me dressed in so formal a fashion, or perhaps expecting it to be one of his own boys. He even began to stand up. But one glance at where my brother knelt in agony and fear—I could almost feel him trembling—and, within a second, I had instinctively changed my mind. "Please," I said to the master, "Please don't get up." I was as calm and polite as I could manage. "May I sit down?" He stretched out his hand, palm upward, indicating that I might.

Then I too sat down on my heels in the proper Japanese fashion and began to speak. "I have come," I said, "to apologize" (quite the opposite of my original intention!). "It was all my fault and not my brother's. We haven't seen each other for nearly four years; so when we suddenly met, I involuntarily began speaking to him in our own dialect (I even avoided saying "our own language") and he involuntarily responded in the same way. It was all my fault. So please forgive my brother this once—"ko shite owabi shi ma su." As I said this I knelt forward, bowing until my head touched the ground. I even repeated what I had said again—"Ko shite owabi si ma su."[7]

He continued speaking of his rescue of his brother with some observational criticism.

The Japanese male is a very strange creature. He can be as brutal as an animal, then all at once transform himself into something very human. He suddenly said to me in a completely different tone of voice, "Yo-ku wa ka ri ma si ta" (I now well understand), and turning to my brother, "Ko Mei-ki kun, mo it-te yo-I," using a form of address from teacher to student which is polite and even affectionate, "You may go now."[8]

Finally, he burst out without reservation his grievance, anguish, and conviction as follows:

Yes, I did control my "m-goan" (a Taiwanese idiomatic expression of the feeling that something is totally unacceptable) that time. I was, and am, glad that I did it for my brother's sake. But I felt the utter humiliation of it all the same. What! For talking with my own brother in my own mother tongue he was severely disciplined and I had to kneel down and bow to the ground to apologize!! No! M-goan! I refuse to accept it. A thousand times no. One's mother tongue is part and parcel of one's very existence. To try to forbid it, to take it forcibly, this is nothing less than an attempt to obliterate one's identity as a person. It is almost like treating people as things to be molded

7. Coe, *Recollections and Reflections*, 243–44.
8. Coe, *Recollections and Reflections*, 244.

into someone else's shape. At the very best it is treating others as second class human beings, second class citizens, even in their own country."[9]

After the Second World War, he managed to come back to Taiwan, despite sincere advice from a classmate from the Boys' School in Tainan that confusion reigned in Taiwan and that more than 20,000 Taiwanese were massacred by the Chinese Nationalists or had just disappeared without trace. Even so, he and his family arrived in Tainan at the end of September 1947, and on the same day he was informed that he had been appointed teacher of scripture and English at his Boys' School. And, within two years of his return, on August 22, 1949, he was ordained as a minister of the Presbyterian Church in Taiwan and appointed principal of the Tainan Theological College. Thereafter, he threw all his energy into reestablishing the Tainan Theological College and bringing into new life an institution that the Japanese colonial government had closed and allowed to fall into ruin. During his sixteen years as principal of the college, he transformed it into one of the foremost theological training centers in South East Asia.

At the same time, he displayed his ability as a leader in church affairs generally. He was in fact the only person ever to be elected twice to the office of moderator of the Presbyterian Church in Taiwan. The second occasion was the church's centenary year, 1965, when members of the Assembly clearly considered him to be essential to the planning and guidance of the celebrations and in the coordination of the involvement of overseas churches. For this reason, they broke with a long tradition and invited him to be the moderator for a second term.

During his eighteen years in Taiwan, aspects of his personal life did not go as tranquilly as his involvement in church affairs. Among other difficulties he and his family encountered, the worst was the refusal by the KMT authorities to accept his second son's birth registration unless his British wife "nationalized." But in view of the critical developments in the Chinese mainland and Taiwan Strait at that point, the British Consulate strongly advised his wife to retain her British nationality. Because of this, his marital status on his passport was always put down as "bachelor" by the authorities, and he began receiving monthly letters from the Ministry of the Interior, via the local municipal office, asking him why he was refusing to register his children as Chinese citizens. This kind of harassment did not stop until after his wife and children left Taiwan in 1959. Yet, the story did not quite end there, for during the 1966 General Assembly, a rather "notorious" minister got up to move

9. Coe, *Recollections and Reflections*, 244.

an emergency resolution, the purpose of which was to censure him for having lived with a woman without marriage and for having had four illegitimate children by her. It is needless to say that the minister was shouted down or removed, since everyone in Taiwan understood that it was an old "dirty trick" played by the KMT authorities.

The autumn breezes began to blow in 1965. Coe retired from the principal-ship of Tainan Theological College and moved to Kent, England. He was not again to live in his homeland. He accepted the invitation from the Theological Education Fund of the World Council of Churches as an acting director to take up the international task of theological education.

Late in January 1972, he called a meeting of prominent Taiwanese Christians at a retreat center in Stony Point, New York. The challenge before them was to deal with the possible aftermath of the issuance of a "Statement on Our National Fate" by our "mother church," the Presbyterian Church in Taiwan, on December 29, 1971. Because of the severe martial law system in Taiwan, one of the participants suggested that the overseas Taiwanese Christians should be organized to help promote a certain social movement to protect our church from persecution and proposed that Rev. Dr. Shoki Coe should take the initiative to set up such an organization and undertake its operation. Without any hesitation, and with everyone's support, he took on this heavy and serious "yoke." After a year's preparation, he met all the participants' expectation by holding a press conference on March 20, 1973, with the other three cofounders, Rev. Dr. Choang-seng Song, Rev. Wu-tong Huang, Dr. Chong-yi Lin, and twenty representatives from all over North America at the International Press Center, Washington, DC, to announce a new organization called "Formosan Christians for Self-Determination," which had been set up to support our "mother church" and its recently issued statement. At the same time this organization declared that we the people of Taiwan were also human beings created by God in his own image and had the right to determine our own future.

Thereafter, a monthly bulletin "Self-Determination" (chhut-thau-thin) was published. Around twenty branches were set up gradually. Several local lecture meetings were opened, and in 1975 this movement was fully prepared to respond to the KMT authorities when they confiscated stocks of our Taiwanese Romanized Bibles and New Testaments written in some of the aboriginal languages. With the support of the Taiwanese association in the United States and the World United Formosans for Independence, four mass rallies were held in Chicago, Los

Angeles, Houston, and Washington, DC, to protest against this illegal and unjustifiable act.

In conclusion, allow me again to quote Coe from his *Recollections and Reflections* where he expressed his political and theological beliefs as follows:

> I am often asked, and indeed often ask myself, why I have been, and still am, so much involved in political matters. Some even add, "When you are not only a Christian but a minister of the church." I have pondered this again and again, but always come to the same simple conclusion: I am involved because I am a Taiwanese, and because I am a Christian—and a minister at that. In other words, my political involvements are the outward expression of a twofold inner "wrestling" for the meaning of being a Taiwanese and the meaning of being a Christian. The former relates to the context into which I was born and in which I was brought up, and which has been, and still is (too much, in fact!) very determinative of my whole existence. The latter points to the text or message which has come into my life as something new and yet far older than any existence; something where the New and the Old seem to merge, in fact, into a single identity which both consoles me and challenges me, driving me on to search for a new and authentic factor in my existence which will break open the "fate" by which, it seems, I have been imprisoned. This struggle, if you like, between a concrete context and a specific text is at the root of all my political involvement. It is another example of "contextualization"!

PART VIII

Prophet from the Fourth World: Life and Legacy of Shoki Coe

20.

A Watershed Figure in Asian Theologies: The Very Rev. Dr. Hwang Chiong-Hui (Shoki Coe, C. H. Hwang) 1914–1988

JOHN ENGLAND

Many who knew Hwang Chiong-Hui, or Shoki Coe, heard him often refer to the complex issues of identity, name, and "nationality" raised for him by the heritage—and the suffering—of his family and his people, as well as by his later experiences in Asia and Europe. Born a Taiwanese, when Taiwan was part of the Japanese "empire" yet with strong Chinese traditions, and later studying in Japan and England, he had many a time pondered—and also suffered for—that identity. But he also drew on that complex identity for images both of Christian and ethnic self-hood and for words and actions that faith demands in times of revolutionary change. These would sometimes take the form of a strong denial or rejection (*m-goan*) of oppression or injustice.[1] At other times these formed the basis for his far-reaching theologies of Christian mission, of the gospel-in-context and of political responsibility.[2]

Postgraduate studies in Tokyo and Cambridge, along with years of teaching at London University and many other encounters during his years in England, would long enrich and shape Coe's worldwide ecumenical ministries later. He had been introduced to the global ecumenical movement through his attendance at the first World Conference of Christian Youth in Amsterdam, 1939, and following the war, at the second such conference held in Oslo, 1947. He would come to echo

---

1. Michael Nai-Chiu Poon, ed., *Shoki Coe, Christian Mission and Test of Discipleship*, The Princeton Lectures 1970, (Singapore: Trinity Theological College, 2012), 59.
2. Ray Wheeler, *IBMR* (April 2002): 77; Poon, ed., *Shoki Coe*, 27.

William Temple's words on the world fellowship of Christian churches, that this "is the great new fact of our era."[3] All his future ministries would be shaped by, and endeavor to embody and promulgate, that new fact across the region and the world.

Coe's own lifelong work for Christian unity and for theology in its local and global context would transform and sustain the theological and ecumenical formation of generations of church leaders around the globe. The groundwork for this was laid during the sixteen years he was the principal of the newly reopened Tainan Theological College and Seminary. During that time the college became a center of innovative and ecumenical developments in theological education that were recognized throughout the region and beyond as well as a strong center for Formosan/Taiwanese national sentiment and identity. Hwang was twice elected moderator of the Presbyterian Church in Formosa, in 1957 and 1965, and he provided leadership in new forms of joint and local mission that had then commenced and fostered action by churches on a wide range of social issues.

In 1965, when it became necessary for him because of security reasons to join his family which had left Taiwan in 1959, Coe joined the Theological Education Fund (TEF) as assistant director, and later director, notably during the TEF's Third Mandate (1970–77). It was here that he and his colleagues developed the new paradigm for *contextualizing* theology, which continues to shape all doing of theology.[4] As TEF director he provided outstanding leadership in the renewal and diversification of theological education throughout the third world and became the acknowledged mentor of generations of Asian theologians.

As a concrete expression of Christian contextualizing of the Text in its sociopolitical context, Shoki also became, in 1973, one of the four initiators of *Formosan Christians for Self-Determination*,[5] which was to have a seminal influence on Taiwan's national consciousness. He was in fact the unofficial leader of *Formosan Christians for Self-Determination* for many

3. William Temple, *The Church Looks Forward* (London: Macmillan 1944), 2.

4. Reflecting on the development of these concepts in 1978, Coe's close colleague Aharon Sapsezian recalled that long before 1972, when he and Coe were using these words, "Shoki was famous for using the phrase, 'Text and Context,' and he was pleading for contextual criticism as a necessary counterpart of textual criticism. In a sense this is the prehistory of the words 'contextuality' and 'contextualization.' The discussions in the house around these two words were that we should go beyond the older notion of 'indigenization,' in the sense that theology would take into account certain aspects of the culture which had been hitherto neglected, such as the social and economic dimensions." Aharon Sapsezian in F. Ross Kinsler, "Mission and Context: The Current Debate About Contextualization," *Evangelical Missions Quarterly* 14, no. 1 (1978): 24.

5. The first issue of the bulletin *Formosan Christians for Self-Determination* appeared in March 1973.

years. He spelled out his profound reasons for such actions in "My Political Involvement," which was demanded by his "double wrestle" with
being both Taiwanese and Christian.[6]

THEOLOGICAL PROPHET AND PIONEER

It is widely known that Coe's work and writing has been of pivotal
importance for every level of Asian theology in recent decades, not least
for his pioneering explorations in contextualizing Christian faith and
understanding. These were, however, deeply rooted in his own, and his
people's, historical experience. For the Taiwanese, this included the very
long history of its aboriginal peoples, the impact of colonization by Spain
and the Netherlands, China, and Japan, and the endurance of martial law
for almost half a century.

These were the contexts for his reflection, along with the rapid socioeconomic changes brought about by industrialization, modernization,
and urbanization. For Coe himself, there were in addition the years in
both Japan and England and the exposure to theological movements in
Taiwan, Japan, Europe, North America, and China. His passion for his
own long-suffering Taiwanese people, known to him now in many of
their local situations, had grown through these years. This was soon
enlarged and deepened by his experience with Christian communities
throughout Asia and the increasing involvement in the work of the
global ecumenical movement.

In each of these diverse cultural and political settings, Coe confessed
later that he had been forced to recognize the shaping and nurturing
power of the concrete context in which people were struggling, suffering, or creating community.[7] Then there was also the larger setting for
all peoples in Asia, of the vast social, political, and religious revolutions
taking place throughout the region. It is in this setting, and in the "living context of nation-building,"[8] of modernization and industrialization,
that the guiding principles of the gospel (the Text) are to be followed
in new patterns of unity, witness, and service, and for an authentic missionary community.[9] For this he believed a new *self-identity in context*,
and in new hope, would be discovered. "Let us once again be renewed
by that mission," he declared, "to go into . . . the new era, into the new

6. Shoki Coe, *Recollections and Reflections*, (New York: Formosan Christians for Self-Determination, 1993), 267.
7. Coe, *Recollections and Reflections*, 118.
8. Shoki Coe, "Into a New Era Together," *Theology and Church* 4, no. 1 (1964): 2.
9. Coe, "Into a New Era Together," 8.

context, seeking our new identity in Him, facing that new context with full self-identification."[10]

But along with this full commitment to understanding the contemporary context of rapid change and revolution, Coe gave as much energy to studying and restating the essential insights of the gospel—its promises, requirements, and experience of present grace. A number of his major articles deal comprehensively with the nature and calling of the church, the priesthood of all in the Body of Christ, and the unity, confession, and renewed humanity of the Spirit-led Christian community. This calling was always for Coe centered upon the life of Jesus Christ, who is Lord of all life, the good news of God's kingdom, and the vehicle of God's saving grace.[11] Yet simply because of those great truths, the Christian church and the Christian believer are inescapably committed to the world. This is because they are rooted in Jesus's life, which was and is always "world-directed" to the actual life situation of men and women. Both the church and individual Christians exist therefore in two dimensions, in unity with God and with the diverse world of peoples.

Constant social and political change across Asian countries along with church developments and political uncertainty in Taiwan would only underline these insights and callings. They would also demand an awareness "that there is no abiding place which is not subject also to the changes of time." In the church's response to God's presence—the *missio Dei*—within these changes, Coe believed we must recognize, and resist, three infections that have been inherited from Christendom: those of colonialism, denominationalism, and pietism.[12] Each of these erect barriers in Christian community and mission: in the "political disease," between colonizer and colonized; in pride and ignorance, between differing church heritages; and in faith response, between personal discipleship and political involvement.

Following his work from the late 1960s, it would soon become impossible for theologians or church historians of whatever confession or region to omit the considerations of cultural, social, and church context in their teaching or writing. In this worldwide influence his most significant writings came in the period 1962–77.

---

10. Poon, ed., *Shoki Coe*, 38.

11. See especially Shoki Coe, "The Life and Mission of the Church in the World," *Southeast Asian Journal of Theology (SEAJOT)* 6, no. 2 (1964): 11–36; "Confessing the Faith in Asia Today," in EACC's *Confessing the Faith in Asia Today* (Peterborough, UK: Epworth, 1966).

12. Coe, "The Life and Mission of the Church in the World," 11–36.

WRITINGS ON FAITH, WORLD, CHURCH, AND MINISTRY, 1962–68

We can discern here at least two major themes:

THE LIFE-OF-JESUS-WITH-OTHERS

Coe returned again and again in his teaching and writing to consider the human life of Jesus—his *way* of life, his responses to others, his patterns of friendship, and his servanthood ministry. And he would emphasize that in each of these attributes Jesus's companions were specifically included. Jesus's *human life with others* is what Coe presents as the *first* characteristic of indigenization or contextualization. This is the humanizing character and *making flesh* that is prior to any mission or any teaching of Christology. And the revolution brought about by Jesus Christ is that of "a new life, a life centered in God, open and free for all, a life in *koinonia*."[13] Now, as then, this comprehensive life of Jesus with others is the presence of God in and for the world. In referring to the life of Jesus, Coe therefore always preferred to talk of *the-life-of-Jesus-with-others*, thus highlighting both the relational or communitarian and the contextual or embodied dimensions of the gospel.[14]

It is in this world-directed "servant" life that both the ministry of the whole body and the life of the church itself find their identity and source. Ministry is firstly the worldly ministry of Christ and only secondarily the ministry of the church.[15] So the full stretch of concern and action in that life is given for ministry to the faithful community and "by entering deeply into the [revolutionary] world of men and nations in which we have been set."[16] In that life too is found the presence of God fulfilling God's mission in God's world.

The life of Jesus (with his friends) for the world is now described as the "text," which is not only indigenous to but contemporaneous with *all* places and peoples. All particular worlds and localities—urban, rural, occupational, destitute, institutional—are diverse contexts for this text. In this interaction between text and context, all genuine mission and ministry are to be found as both a personal and worldly service. Faithfulness to the text and creative relevance to the context provide the

13. Shoki Coe, "God's People in Asia Today," *SEAJOT* 5, no. 2 (1963): 37.
14. Poon, ed., *Shoki Coe.*
15. Shoki Coe, "A Rethinking of Theological Training for the Ministry in the Younger Churches Today," *SEAJOT* 4, no. 2 (1962): 10.
16. Coe, "God's People in Asia Today," 9.

larger missiological excellence, which must be continually renewed.[17] Coe would come to describe this interaction as the basis for all renewal of the church and of theological education. It is found that when this is nurtured by the disciplines of the "first-fruits" community, it "leads to a real encounter between the student and the Gospel in terms of his own forms of thought and culture and to a living dialogue between the church and its environment."[18]

THE CHURCH IN ITS WORLD

For Coe, the Christian church is a servant community directed toward the world, finding its local identity and mission in ecumenical, cultural, and social encounters with people in all their diverse forms of community. "In adopting this originally secular and political term 'ecclesia' as its name I believe," he declared, "the Church recognised, from the very beginning, that it exists between two poles or rather two Dimensions . . . a unique relationship with God on the one hand and with the world on the other."[19] Excellence in ministry and theological education—of all in the people of God—and also the catholic fullness of the church and ministry, come, therefore, through meeting and serving the changing demands of particular regions and localities where Christ is already present.

"The Gospel is directed to the 'world,' that is, to persons in society," Coe wrote in 1965. "Therefore populations and the *oikoi* [lit. 'houses'] where they live are a basic concern for the mission of the church."[20] This is because the divine movement is always outward toward others, in "a love which seeks not His own." All engagement in mission is therefore "a decisive test because it involves a moving out of the self. Crossing the frontier then becomes a theological and divine necessity."[21] This is also why Christian response amidst revolutionary ferment in Asian countries must include (indirect) advocacy for liberty and justice in the widest terms, Coe believed. And this would mean participation in the social

17. Shoki Coe, *Text and Context in Theological Education* (Tainan Presbyterian Bookroom, 1966); also *Northeast Asia Journal of Theology* 1 (1): 220; *Joint Action for Mission in Formosa—A Call for Advance into a New Era*, C.W.M.E. (1968), chaps. 1 and 9.
18. Shoki Coe, "In Search of Renewal in Theological Education," *Theological Education* 9, no. 4 (1973): 236.
19. Coe, "The Life and Mission of the Church in the World," 13.
20. Coe, "Report of Theological Education in Taiwan Today," 11.
21. Poon, ed., *Shoki Coe*, 42.

development that is directed at countering hunger and poverty, even if this would bring danger or suffering for the church.[22]

Coe therefore analyzed in a series of articles and books, and in some detail, the revolutionary changes that had come to Asian countries in particular through political independence, industrialization, and urban growth. He considered also the impacts of cultural and religious resurgence, and the rapid changes in medical, media, education, and welfare systems.[23] The inadequacies and potential of the church's response to these changes were also carefully assessed in the light of patterns of church life, ministry, and mission that have been imported to Asian contexts. He particularly advocated "world-directed" mission initiatives and forms of ministry that are ecumenical and diverse, and others that complement the ministries of those "set-apart."[24] His particular concern throughout subsequent endeavors was the development and renewal of theological education for the new ministries now required.

WRITINGS ON TEXT AND CONTEXT IN THEOLOGY AND THEOLOGICAL EDUCATION, 1966–75

(i) In this later period Coe built on earlier biblical, theological, and sociological studies to formulate a theology of contextuality and *contextualizing*, which still awaits full recognition.[25] Here he moved beyond the past-oriented processes of indigenization to the more dynamic process of contextualizing;[26] for Coe this was always a verb for the ongoing work rather than the picture of any completed "contextualization." Those who criticize Coe's radical and comprehensive practice in contextualizing—arguing that it was because of his own and his people's history—overlook the fact that this was always deeply rooted in the diverse and ongoing experiences and struggles of particular peoples and communities. For Jesus Christ as the supreme "contextualization" of the

---

22. Poon, ed., *Shoki Coe*, 55.

23. See especially *Joint Action for Mission* (1968), chaps. 2–8; also "God's People in Asia Today" (1963): 9–13; "Men in Their Oikoi—Urbanization in Taiwan," *CWME* (July 1966); Poon, ed., *Shoki Coe*, chap. 3.

24. "A Rethinking . . . ," *SEAJOT* 4, no. 2 (1962): 20–25; "The Life and Mission . . . ," *SEAJOT* 6, no. 2 (1964): 11–38; "In Search of Renewal . . . ," *Theological Education* 9, no. 4 (1973).

25. Full awareness of particular local contexts of God's world he terms contextuality, while the ongoing wrestling with God's word in such contextuality is a contextualizing theology always "on the way." TEF Staff Papers in *Ministry in Context* (1972) and *Learning in Context* (1973); Preface to *Christian Mission in Reconstruction* by C. S. Song, (1975); Preface to *The Human and the Holy*, ed. Emerito Nacpil and Douglas Elwood (1978).

26. Coe, *Recollections*, 270.

gospel is present to all women and men in their distinct cultural, religious, and sociopolitical context. And in this lies the catholicity of both God's mission and of the church's theology.

So, it is not just the determining power of social or cultural contexts that must be recognized but the nature of the church itself, which is found in such diverse settings. For the calling and faith of the one people of one God have "the essential marks of locality and particularity," he would declare,[27] being shaped by the most diverse situations and contexts. The church is both local and "in pilgrimage," called to be in one place but also called to "frontier-crossing, because it is always *on the way*." For these callings in particular "contexts," the "text" of the gospel is of course supremely important. "But to think that there might be one pattern suitable for all peoples and times is what I call the 'cathedral mentality.' God's people, as pilgrims, must be free sometimes to pitch their tents and other times to pull them up and move on; for there is no permanent abiding place between the times."[28]

(ii) Yet Coe was concerned so as to stress that in our faithful biblical studies also we find that there is "no pure text without a context (or contexts)."[29] There is always the concrete setting of a particular author and of those to whom the text is addressed, as well as historical discoveries and new truths found in the ongoing study and interpretation of the Bible. There are prophetic insights too called forth by multiple social or political revolutions that parallel the continuing changes in the life-setting and the social milieu of local Christian communities.

In any case, faith itself is both personal and world-oriented, an inward and an outward journey, for the individual and the community. In the light of Jesus's gospel of the kingdom, it is after all impossible for the faithful community to remain silent in the face of the deep suffering of particular peoples or when faced with the burning issues of the day for the human community. Mission therefore cannot be separated from "the structure of social existence in state, industry, economic life, and culture."[30]

(iii) He went on to describe a series of dynamic relationships that are involved here: within the double context of revolutionary or technological change within resurgent Asian cultures; and in the "double wrestle" between these, as one's own cultural realities, and the living text of Christ's continuing presence. This is the "textual-cum-contextual criti-

27. Shoki Coe, "God's People in Asia Today," *Southeast Asia Journal of Theology (SEAJOT)* 5, no. 2 (1963): 15.

28. *Theological Education* 11 no. 1 (Autumn 1974): 9.

29. *Recollections*, 119.

30. Poon, ed., *Shoki Coe*, 31.

cism" model that he modeled in his *Joint Action for Mission* in Taiwan (1968).[31] The necessary relationship between such a "criticism" and the conduct of missions was often spelled out, notably in his lectures at Princeton.[32]

Coe therefore believed that contextualization includes indigenization, but that it is more dynamic and features openness to change as a key factor, thus going beyond mere indigenization. The full sociological mosaic defines and conditions the proclamation of the gospel and response to it. "Contextualization has to do with how we assess the peculiarity of third world contexts. . . . [It] takes into account the process of secularity, technology and the struggle for human justice."[33] Here the gospel provides us with not only the source for all critique of society and culture but also alternative models that are brought by the reign of God.

He would go on to write that this approach presumed "a genuine encounter between God's Word and His world. It seeks to change the socio-economic plight by 'rootedness in . . . (the) given historical moment' and by leading the populace out of their plight. . . . [This] assumes that God is doing something redemptive in the target culture—that he is fashioning deliverance from the socio-economic bondage in which the multitudes of the third world find themselves."[34]

(iv) The steps necessary for such contextualizing, Coe affirmed, would include, along with the critical study of the text, both a *de*-contextualization and a *re*-contextualization of the context. The forces of colonialism and imperialism, of pietism and denominationalism, have again and again imposed false and destructive "contexts." So, this first requires a criticism and ranking of both texts and contexts where these have been corrupted or imposed from other histories.[35] Then there must be a critique of resulting institutional forms, along with a readiness to reshape

31. Poon, ed., *Shoki Coe*, 35; Wheeler, "The Legacy of Shoki Coe," 79.

32. See "Text and Context in Missions," in Poon, ed., *Shoki Coe*, 21–38; "In search of Renewal . . . ," *Theological Education* 9, no. 4 (1973): 239.

33. *Your Kingdom Come*, World Conference on Mission and Evangelism, n.d., 18.

34. Writing of Julio de Santa Ana's response to Shoki Coe, Richard W. Engle recounts that De Santa Ana says, "The contextualization of theological reflection means opting for a particular social context, that which is low, at the base of the social pyramid. Such an option 'means opposing oppression rather than confirming the powerful in oppressing other social sectors.' The contextualizer's task, then, is to enter the culture, discern what God is doing, and work with God to bring about the change which God is (supposedly) fashioning." "Contextualization in Missions: A Biblical and Theological Appraisal," in *Grace Theological Journal* (February 1981): 87.

35. "Text and Context in Theological Education," *Theological Education and Ministry*. Tainan Presbyterian Bookroom (1967), also *Northeast Asia Journal of Theology* 1, no. 1 (1967): 227; "God's People in Asia Today" (1963): 14; EACC's *Confessing the Faith in Asia Today* (Peterborough, UK: Epworth, 1966), 76.

these according to central gospel measures, and within those most serious contexts that are strategic for the *missio Dei*. This will also require of the Christian community repentance, a renewed identity, and a willingness to "go outside the camp" to the new context. It also may mean that new forms of church are to be found precisely in suffering with Jesus and his people.[36]

As for the praxis necessary for recontextualization, this is simultaneously responsive to God's contextualization in Jesus and to changing historical situations. In equipping women and men for ministry it comes through a threefold process of people-formation, which reclaims both their actual life experience and the heart of the gospel. This process is *Christian/spiritual* (that is *human* as in the life of Jesus), *theological* (the living truth as known in Jesus), and *ministerial* (equipping each in the people of God—the body of Christ—for particular and strategic contexts.[37] In this way Coe maintained throughout his teaching the recovery of the genuine and concrete context along with the centrality of the-life-of-Jesus-with-others as both the hermeneutic measure of scripture and history and also the source of all liberation and larger hope.

CONCLUSION

One of Coe's later statements would summarize much of his teaching on the relationship of indigenization to contextualization and of these to both Christian formation and the reform of the church and of theological education. There he highlighted again the "'double wrestle'" necessary with both text and context; the "extra-ordinary praxis" of self-emptying involved in theological formation; and the necessity for all theology to be *in loco* and *viatorum* [being pilgrim], as the path to having catholicity.[38]

But he also warns there of the danger of fossilized or alternatively "chameleon" theology, which may come from an extreme contextualization. True contextuality comes rather from a "conscientization of the contexts in the particular historical moment," which is assessed in the light of participation in the *missio Dei*. And this requires not only words but actions, for the gospel is the word incarnate, embodied at

36. Coe, *Recollections*, 275.
37. Coe, "Text and Context . . ." (1967): 232, 239; "In Search of Renewal . . . ," *Theological Education* 9, no. 4 (1973): 131.
38. Coe, *Recollections*, 267–75.

whatever cost "for the poor and oppressed, for the prisoners and for the neglected."[39]

Shoki Coe's life, teachings, and writing were surely such an embodiment of the gospel, which he knew as God's reign over all of one's human experience and of the particular human worlds. It is impossible today to work theologically or educationally without drawing on some part of Coe's writings on text and context, and much writing and teaching in Asia and further afield demonstrates this. But yet it remains true that in many parts of the region (and of the world) the process and resources he presents have yet to be fully applied in a *double wrestle* with both the text of "Jesus's-life-with-others" and with the concrete particularities of daily life and struggle and joy. Perhaps it is time for us to rededicate ourselves anew to those endeavors.

39. Coe, *Recollections*, 274.

21.

Shoki Coe: A Giant in His Time

YEOW CHOO LAK

INTRODUCTION

If I am not wrong, there are very few of Shoki Coe's colleagues in the World Council of Churches (WCC) who are alive today, and fortunately I am one of them. As such, this paper tends to be deliberately a bit "personal," since I wish to share with you the "spirit" of Coe's theological thinking. In particular, it is my privilege to share a conversation that very few people are acquainted with. I am using this exchange of views not only to preserve a conversation few people are aware of but also to set the stage for a discussion on, for example, how and why many African, Asian, Latin American, and Pacific Island theologians use English to formulate their theological thinking.

I would like to reiterate that my paper takes a "personal" trajectory, that is, a general overview of Coe's contextualizing theology that "enriched" the personal conversations I have had with him. Let me make an analogy.

D. T. Niles used to say how he asked Karl Barth, "How many Hindus do you know?" "Very few," replied Karl Barth. "Then, how can you justify your Christocentric theology which marginalizes millions of Hindus, Buddhists, etc.?" retorted Niles.

In Coe's case, it was the injustice seen in the Taiwanese being regarded as "slaves of the Manchurian Chings and then slaves of the Japanese," the infamous *Chian ko lo!*

It is quite customary in a *Festschrift* first for the contributors to say a few words about themselves so that the readers know something about them and where they come from, followed by how the writers rubbed shoulders with the scholar honored in the *Festschrift*. Again, such papers generally end with a special reference to how the honored scholar's unique contribution in doing theology fares in the current contexts. This is the pattern I am using in my paper.

I begin with my faith journey as Coe's junior colleague in three stages that crossed Coe's path. For example, Coe left Westminster College, Cambridge, in the early 1940s. I went to Cambridge University in 1961. These early events play a pivotal role in coloring our ministerial style and substance and especially our theological perspectives.

It seemed providentially appropriate and proper that my years of study should be tempered with practical experiences, especially to learn what it means to do theology contextually in poverty-ridden Burma, now known as Myanmar, and in a jungle setting in Sarawak and Sabah, East Malaysia. The tumultuous political events of the 1970s and 1980s in Asia challenged pastors and theological educators there to try and make sense of *doing contextual theology in a landscape of conflicts and violence.* In this setting, to repeat, Coe's work on contextualizing theology made much sense to me and challenged me to do contextual theology in Burma, in the jungles in East Malaysia, and also in concrete jungles dictated by corrupt and oppressive military regimes in South Korea, the Philippines, and Indonesia.

The next stage of my faith journey saw me dialoguing with Western theologians from various theological persuasions when I was serving in the Standing Commission on Faith and Order in the WCC (1983–1996). It was not easy to convince them that just as in the West the proponents of so-called classical theology were into doing contextual theology, theologians in Asia, Africa, Latin America, and the Pacific Islands were doing contextual theology in their own way. For many theologians from the West, it was difficult to affirm that liberation theology and minjung theology, to cite two examples, were classical theology in Latin America and South Korea respectively.

I sincerely believe Coe's work did much to make contextualizing theology acceptable in the halls of learning worldwide.

The beginning of the 1980s was almost the end of Coe's exciting contribution to theological education on the world stage. It was my privilege to have been in the company of an aged-to-perfection Coe at a time when I was starting my faith journey in theological education in South East Asia.

I was twenty-nine years old when I returned to Singapore in March of 1969 after twelve continuous years of learning in Singapore, England, and America (1957–1969). It was twelve years later that I got to know

Coe in person, when I was serving as executive director of the Association for Theological Education in South East Asia (ATESEA), dean of the South East Asia Graduate School of Theology (SEAGST), and editor of the *Asia Journal of Theology* (1981–2002).

PART I

During one of the early encounters with Coe and Kosuke Koyama, the place of language in theological construction appeared prominently. When Singapore was a British colony, almost all Chinese, Malay, and Indian parents sent their children to schools using English as a medium of instruction. Knowledge of the English language was a union membership card to a steady job. Additionally, the British colonial masters discouraged the use of our mother tongue. For example, anyone found using Chinese or Malay or Tamil in class was fined five cents (an amount good enough to purchase a bowl of warm soup noodles during recess). In time, all of us got used to thinking and expressing our thoughts in English.

Not accidentally, when Singapore was a British colony, the British colonial masters arrogantly termed our mother tongue "vernacular." And the term "vernacular" was defined as:

a) using a language or dialect native to a region or country rather than a literary, cultured, or foreign language.

b) of, relating to, or being a nonstandard language or dialect of a place, region, or country.

c) of, relating to, or being the normal spoken form of a language.

This implied that in the British colony of Singapore, English was the "literary, cultured, or foreign language." Chinese, Malay, and Tamil (our mother tongues) were the "dialects native to a region or country," . . . "the substandard languages of a place, region, or country."

Coe shared his experience of this encounter in the following words: "When Taiwan was under Japanese Occupation, the same thing happened. We were forced to learn our colonial master's language. More than that, we were severely punished for using our mother tongue."

He went on to narrate a painful experience:

Fresh from graduating from Tokyo Imperial University [analogous to a Singaporean graduating from Oxford or Cambridge], in the ship on the way back to Taiwan, I saw my brother. Naturally, we both talked in Taiwanese. Unfortunately, we were caught doing just that—talking in Taiwanese.

My brother was working as a crew member on that ship. Guilty of talking in Taiwanese meant a serious punishment for him. Somehow, I needed to get both of us out of that spot of trouble.

Fully dressed in my Tokyo Imperial University academic regalia, I went to the Captain's quarters to submit our sincere apologies. I believe the Captain was a bit confused, if not amused, to see a Taiwanese fully dressed in his Tokyo Imperial University academic regalia kneeling before him asking to be pardoned.

In normal circumstances, any ordinary Japanese would pay much respect to a graduate from Tokyo Imperial University. That a Taiwanese fully dressed in his Tokyo Imperial University academic regalia would be kneeling to a Captain of a ship is unthinkable, yet because "I'm a Taiwanese, I am automatically inferior to the Japanese Captain."

Years later, Coe was to explain how *Chian ko lo!* got him into a fight. One day after school, a group of Japanese students hurled stones and insults at Coe, who bravely fought back. Coe was pardoned by both his father and the school principal for fighting when they heard that Coe had fought back because his Japanese bullies had yelled *Chian ko lo!* at him.

That is the price he had to pay for fighting against *Chian ko lo* both in that fight and in the fight against the powers that be, who wanted nothing of the Taiwanese wanting to be Taiwanese.

Chian ko lo! means the Taiwanese were slaves, first of the Manchurian Chings and then of the Japanese who had conquered Manchuria. *Chian ko lo!* never fails to remind the Taiwanese of the utter humiliation, shame, and lifelong pain of being the colonized. In brief, the Taiwanese were third-class residents in Taiwan just as Singaporeans were British *subjects*, not even citizens of their own country when Singapore was a British colony. The Taiwanese had to use Japanese. Singaporeans had to use English. The colonized in Africa, Asia, the Americas, Australia, New Zealand, and the Pacific Islands all had to use their colonial masters' languages. That was the context then.

The above narration serves as a springboard into revisiting some of Coe's contribution in popularizing contextual theology that took into account local/national social, political, cultural, economic, and linguistic factors. It is still strange that the oppressed have to formulate theological thoughts in their oppressors' language.

Incidentally, the British colonial masters, too, have a name for their despised subjects. For example, when a Chinese distinguished himself, like the late Lee Kuan Yew's once-in-a-blue-moon double firsts in law from Cambridge University, with a star to boot, the British masters would despisingly call him a WOG—a Westernized Oriental Gentleman. Only a Chinese grand achiever who had famously outdone his British peers could be called a gentleman and a *Westernized* Oriental Gentleman at that! Oh, the height of arrogant colonial imperialism!

No wonder that in the 1950s when the British were singing "Rule Britannia, Britannia rules the waves," the Malayans retorted by singing "Rule Malaya, Malaya waives the rules!"

PART TWO

CONTEXTUALIZING THEOLOGY

As is well known by now, in the past years to be a theologian meant to be acquainted with what is commonly known as "classical" theology.

In the 1950s, 1960s, and 1970s, to know "classical" theology was to know Western theologians like S. Kierkegaard, T. W. Manson, Karl Barth, and others along with philosophers like Immanuel Kant, Martin Heidegger, and A. N. Whitehead.

During their graduate study in the West, scholars from third world countries would drink deeply from these wells and, upon their return to their homeland, they were expected to teach what they had imbibed from centers of learning in England and Germany, for example.

Coe changed the theological landscape by advocating contextual theology, a theology that is relevant to the contexts in Africa, Asia, Latin America, and the Pacific Islands. It can be said that contextual theology was "extending" what was previously learned from classical theology in the West to meet the challenges and needs of African, Asian, Latin American, and Pacific Island contexts. It was Asianizing or Africanizing or Latin Americanizing, or Pacific Islanderizing the theological *Sitz im leben* motif, a term that was picked up in biblical study.

In biblical study, *Sitz im leben* is a German phrase roughly understood as *setting in life*. It tries to speak of the alleged context in which a text has been crafted, and its function, aim, and purpose relevant at that time.

What then is so perspectively special, new, and exciting that contextual theology brings?

It is exciting to see the symbiotic connection, so to speak, between the text and the contexts when it comes to logically exegeting passages from the Bible in our contemporary contexts. It would be fair to say that in the past, good exegesis was done on texts with very precious little reference, if any, to third world contexts. Karl Barth and D. Bonhoeffer were giants in expounding the Christian faith in the fight against Nazism in first world contexts with very precious little reference, if any, to third world contexts. What is excitingly new in contextual theology is the call to take into account African, Asian, Latin American, and Pacific Island contexts (the oppressed) that were and are still so different in many ways to Western contexts (the oppressors). This means taking local/national customs, languages, cultures, political-social mores, and religions into serious account.

Incidentally, Albert Schweitzer, OM (1875–1965), a French-German theologian, organist, writer, humanitarian, philosopher, and physician somehow did not seem to have used his African experiences as a missionary to contextualize theology. Instead, he is better known for having challenged both the secular view of Jesus as depicted by the historical-critical methodology current at his time, and the traditional Christian perspective.

Coe was perceptive enough to affirm that "to take the context seriously does not necessarily mean, it seems to me, taking all contexts equally seriously, because all are not equally strategic for the Missio Dei in the working out of His purpose through history."[1]

Theology owes a debt of gratitude to Coe for his emphasis on the interrelationship of the word, the world, and the church when it comes to exegeting how the text and contexts come into play. Possibly, this could be a reflection of the Barthian approach to theology on how the word is understood as the word incarnated, the word as accurately recorded, and the word as faithfully proclaimed by the church.

As previously mentioned, Coe paid a heavy price for his espousal of contextual theology. The cost of discipleship is embedded in his contextualizing theology. This brings us to our current contexts, which are as difficult to handle as the contexts in Coe's time.

PART THREE

THE TEXT AND A SAMPLING OF OUR CURRENT CHALLENGING CONTEXTS

Snow leopards have a tail nearly as long as they are, up to three feet long! They use it to keep balance while negotiating steep and rocky slopes and also use it to keep their nose warm while they sleep.

The snow leopard's long tail has a purpose; so too does Coe's contex-

1. Shoki Coe, "In Search of Renewal in Theological Education," *Theological Education* 9 (Summer 1973): 241.

tualizing theology. The initial effects of Coe's influence (see other articles in this book) may have taken root slightly more than three decades ago, but the "construct" or "principle" or "philosophy" of his contextualizing theology remains useful today.

Coe's contextual theology was not written in stone. Its relevance remains with us today, though the understanding and use of the "text" today is qualitatively different from what was obtained in Coe's time. So too, today's contexts differ radically from the contexts found three or four decades ago.

A word on the text.

Coe's time saw a critical, in the positive sense, examination of texts from the Bible. That set the stage for posterity to take the next step, for example, in understanding texts in the Bible that have to do with *genocide* and *land-grabbing* as found in Numbers, Deuteronomy, Joshua, and Judges, and how churches in the West have used these texts to justify their countries' colonization.

What then are some of the current contexts that are "new"? Let me briefly mention some of them as observed from Hawai`i while reminding myself that Bible interpreters anywhere and everywhere are always facing new contexts and are being challenged by them.

Mention of our new contexts will show and challenge practitioners of contextual theology to meaningfully explore the "text-context" matrix. No attempt is made to offer definitive answers since contextual theologians are working on the issues/challenges.

There is not much reference by Coe to white privilege, understood as white people are naturally and logically regarded as superior to other races. White men's rule of five hundred years started when the Portuguese, followed by the Spanish navigators, "discovered" new lands that later came under their control. Following that, the British and other European colonizers claimed Africa, Asia, Latin America, and the Pacific Islands as extensions of their empire. The natives and natural resources of these countries were exploited to the maximum to enrich the colonizers and their countries.

Pope Nicholas V's 1452 papal bull (*Dum Diversas*) and his 1455 papal bull (*Romanus Pontifex*) gave Portugal's King Alfonso the green light to

invade, search out, capture, vanquish and subdue all Saracens and pagans whatsoever, and other enemies of Christ *wheresoever placed*, and the kingdoms, dukedoms, principalities, dominions, possessions and all movable and immovable goods whatsoever held and possessed by them and to *reduce their persons to perpetual slavery.*

Such an unchristian and disgusting doctrine played a crucial role in the enslaving and dehumanization of native peoples all over the world. *Dum Diversas* is credited by some scholars as ushering in the West African slave trade.

Fortuitously or otherwise, when the gospel was introduced to Africa, Asia, Latin America, and the Pacific Islands, the formulation of the essence of the gospel was affected by the linguistic, cultural, social, economic, and political forms of the colonizers.

Much of that has changed. Today there are attempts to formulate the text in new contexts. What then are some of the new contexts?

In America, there is a landscape of conflicts, contradictions, and violence as white supremacists begin to thrash quiet towns. Unlike the hooded Ku Klux Klan gang yesterday, today white supremacists are not hiding their faces. They boldly march the streets armed and uniformed to hurt/intimidate/cripple people. I cite one example.

Clashes in Charlottesville

White nationalists clash with counter-protestors in Charlottesville, Virginia, August 12, 2017. A planned rally by white supremacists, advertised as "Unite the Right," devolved into violent clashes that left at least one dead and about three dozen injured, and prompted Virginia Governor Terry McAuliffe to declare a state of emergency.

Another notable new feature marks our theological terrain, challenging Bible interpreters. Three or four decades ago, who would have imagined the homeless dotting urban areas in the richest country in the world?

In the annual nationwide homeless census in 2017, Hawai`i leads in having the most number of homeless people in America—fifty-one homeless in every 10,000 people, followed closely by New York (forty-five in every 10,000 people). Oregon and California have thirty-four homeless in every 10,000 people. The number goes down to twenty-nine in Washington. Incidentally, the District of Columbia has 110 homeless people out of every 10,000 individuals.

Never before seen in recent decades in America is the presence of beggars at traffic light junctions—shades of what is commonly seen in cities in poor third world countries.

In this setting, there is much killing in the streets and in schools. Examples abound, but I cite just one.

A would-be suicide attacker detonated a pipe bomb strapped to his body in the heart of Manhattan's busiest subway corridor on Monday, sending thousands of terrified commuters fleeing the smoke-choked passageways, and bringing the heart of Midtown to a standstill as hundreds of police officers converged on Times Square and the surrounding streets.

It was the third attack in New York City since September 2016, and the second in two months, coming only weeks after eight people were killed in a truck attack along a Hudson River bike path. Like the earlier two, the attack on Monday appears to have been carried out by a so-called "lone-wolf" terrorist.

This then is the landscape of conflicts, contradictions, and violence in America in a way hitherto not seen.

Then, too, is the exposure of seemingly widespread sexual harassment in society.

#MeToo spread virally as a two-word hashtag used on social media on October 2017 to denounce sexual assault and harassment, in the wake of sexual misconduct allegations against film producer and executive Harvey Weinstein. The phrase, long used in this sense by social activist Tarana Burke, was popularized by actress Alyssa Milano, who encouraged women to tweet it to publicize experiences to demonstrate the widespread nature of misogynistic behavior. Since then, millions of people have used the hashtag to come forward with their experiences, including many celebrities. (from Wikipedia)

The me-too movement has triggered a string of accusations on alleged sexual harassment, both verbal and physical, in the corridors of power, the film industry, and in workplaces.

I start by quoting a statement from Cambridge University on "safe places for everyone":

Universities must continue to change if they want to be safe places for everyone.

One year on from government guidance that finally gave universities the mandate to investigate sexual harassment claims, we look back on progress made, including the launch of the Collegiate University's "Breaking the Silence" initiative.[2]

Violence Erupts as Palestinians Protest Trump Action on Jerusalem
Palestinians in the West Bank clash with Israeli troops during a protest against President Donald Trump's recognition of Jerusalem as Israel's capital.[3]

---

2. https://www.cam.ac.uk/.
3. Nasser Shiyoukhi/AP, December 8, 2017, Richard Gonzales.

Life moves on. Our understanding of texts, contexts, concerns, and challenges changes. When it comes to biblical texts, it takes Solomon's wisdom and Job's patience to try to understand what is best for humans.

Coe did not have to wrestle with texts that are now viewed critically because they are written records of what is now generally understood as land-grabbing and genocide (crimes against humanity).

If Coe were still with us today, he would affirm that the Israeli-Palestinian conflict calls for revisiting ancient and contemporary land-grabbing and genocide as seen in Numbers, Deuteronomy, Joshua, Judges, 1 Samuel, and the 1948–2017 Jewish State, which looks like apartheid in world opinion.

The last challenge that Coe did not have to face but current contextual theologians do today is seen in the concern over the possibility of a nuclear war as expressed by Nobel Peace Prize winner Beatrice Fihn, who warns that nuclear war means "the deaths of millions may be *one tiny tantrum away* ." "We have a choice, the end of nuclear weapons or the end of us," she said on December 10, 2017.

Coe did not have to deal with the tensions over North Korea's weapons program that has risen in recent months.

The open hostility between Donald Trump and Kim Jong-un has at times descended into personal attacks this year.

Additionally, on this point, popular as well as social media have ignored some South Koreans' serious question: Why is America fighting the US–North Korea war in our backyard?

These South Koreans have voiced their concern by narrating an allegory. A and B are engaged in a battle of words, climaxing in A throwing a bomb at B who then throws the bomb at C (innocent party). In the process, millions are killed. Who is to be blamed? B for throwing the bomb at C, or A for throwing the bomb at B in the first place?

The above allegory provides a much-neglected perspective at scrutinizing the present dangerous situation facing the world, not just America, North Korea, South Korea, and Japan.

Let us begin with a given.

It is significant to know that in many parts of Asia, what is not said on many occasions is more important than what is said.

At the moment, the United States (A) and B (North Korea) are engaged in a battle of words. The allegory assumes that America preemptively throws a bomb at North Korea, which then, in retaliation, throws a bomb at innocent South Korea and Japan (C). In the process, millions are killed. Who is to be blamed? North Korea for throwing the bomb at South Korea and Japan or America for throwing the bomb at North Korea in the first place?

The Donald Trump and Kim Jong-un battle of minds (words) is not without its irony. When two braggarts lock horns, a lot of dangerous "Rocket Man" and "mentally retarded US dotard" gas is emitted. It is amusing to know that both braggarts know what can or cannot be done, and threats, boasts, and hot air notwithstanding, both love the grand-stand posturing.

In the Donald Trump and Kim Jong-un tirade, the latter's ace to trump Donald Trump is his unspoken strategy, to wit, and not said but clearly understood by both North and South Koreans is the assumption that the first one to attack is the loser. Hence, there is no way Kim Jong-un would make the first strike. Noisy gasbag, belligerent braggart Kim is leaving that to his equally noisy gasbag, belligerent braggart Trump.

So, Kim Jong-un cleverly, publicly, and frequently irritates, master-minds, tempts, lures, baits, and defies the quick-tempered Trump to do the first strike at North Korea ("begging for war"). In retaliation, North Korea will then kill thousands of Americans based in South Korea and Japan and, very unfortunately, also *kill millions of South Koreans and Japanese in the process* (the killing of innocents). North Korea gets away scot-free doing so. America is blamed for starting a war by throwing the first bomb.

The allegory seems to tell us that a military preemptive strike for Trump is not a viable option unless America wants to be blamed by the world for killing its own thousands in the American bases in South Korea and Japan and millions of North Koreans, South Koreans, and Japanese in the process.

Kim Jong-un is gleefully holding that trump card (holding thousands of Americans based in South Korea and Japan as *convenient hostages* and *easy targets*!) against Donald Trump. Why bother with mainland America when *convenient hostages* and *easy targets* are just next door? Let Trump annihilate North Korea. From its ashes it will destroy the nearby and very *convenient hostages and very easy targets.*

The allegory also silently hints at an issue that should not escape the world's attention, viz., why, where, and how does America get the right to wage its wars in far distant Asia (apart from eliminating Al Qaeda in Afghanistan), but not in its own backyard? That is a disturbing question many Asians are asking Americans.

The above-mentioned new contexts surely show the necessity to relate the text to the contexts à la mode, principle/construct/philosophy of Coe's contextualizing theology. No final answers are available at the moment since the practitioners of contextual theology are working on them. What is the next step?

I choose to believe that Coe's contextualizing theology was launched to ensure that doing theology continue to be uniquely placed to respond to our current contexts as we face new and daunting challenges. In a way, Coe's contextualizing theology not only attracted some of the brightest minds to create fine ways of doing theology but also to enabled them to give the space needed to create more life-changing and life-giving opportunities in making the text and the contexts "talk to each other," as seen in the other papers in the *Festschrift*.

Essential Writings of and about Shoki Coe

WORKS BY C. H. HWANG (SHOKI COE / NG CHIONG HUI)

"Across the Frontiers: Text and Context in Mission." In *Christian Action in the Asian Struggle*, edited by U Kyaw Than. Singapore: CCA, 1973.

"Come Creator Spirit for the Calling of the Churches Together." *Ecumenical Review* 16, no. 5 (1964).

"Confessing the Faith in Asia Today." In *EACC Confessing the Faith in Asia Today* (1966).

"Contextualizing as the Way Towards Reform." In *Asian Christian Theology: Emerging Themes*, edited by D. J. Ellwood. Philadelphia: Westminster, 1980.

"Contextualizing Theology." In *Mission Trends No. 3*, edited by Gerald Anderson. New York: Paulist, 1976.

"Conversion in the Perspective of Three Generations." *Ecumenical Review* 19, no. 3 (1967).

Foreword to *Christian Mission in Reconstruction*, by C. S. Song. Madras: Christian Literature Society, 1975.

"God's People in Asia Today." *SEAJOT* 5, no. 2 (1963).

"Into a New Era Together." *Theology and Church* 4, no. 1 (1964).

Joint Action for Mission in Formosa: A Call for Advance into a New Era. Commission on World Mission and Evangelism. New York: WCC/ Friendship Press, 1968.

"Men in Their Oikoi—Urbanization in Taiwan." *International Review of Mission* 55, no. 219 (1966).

"The Life and Mission of the Church in the World." *SEAJOT* 6, no. 2 (1964).

Preface to *The Human and the Holy: Asian Perspectives in Christian Theol-*

ogy, edited by E. P. Nacpil and D. J. Elwood. Quezon City: New Day Publishers, 1978.

Recollections and Reflections, introduced and edited by Boris Anderson. 2nd ed. New York: The Rev. Dr. Shoki Coe's Memorial Fund, 1993.

"A Rethinking of Theological Training for Ministry in the Younger Churches." *SEAJOT* 4, no. 2 (1962).

"A Report on Theological Education in Taiwan Today." *SEAJOT* 7, no. 2 (1965).

"In Search of Renewal in Theological Education." *Theological Education* 9, no. 4 (1973).

"Text and Context in Theological Education." In *Theological Education and Ministry—Reports from the North East Asia Theological Educators' Conference, Seoul, 1966.* Tainan: Presbyterian Bookroom, 1967.

"Theological Education—A World-Wide Perspective." *Theological Education* 11, no. 1 (1974).

"In Search of Renewal in Theological Education." *Theological Education* 9, no. 4 (1973).

With TEF Staff. *Learning in Context: The Search for Innovative Patterns in Theological Education.* Bromley, UK: Theological Education Fund, 1973.

With TEF Staff. *Ministry in Context: The Third Mandate Programme of the Theological Education Fund (1970–77).* Bromley, UK: Theological Education Fund, 1972.

With TEF Staff. *Your Kingdom Come.* World Conference on Mission and Evangelism, n.d.

Note: As unofficial chairman of Formosan Christians for Self-Determination, Shoki Coe contributed to their periodical *Self Determination*, from 1973.

WRITINGS ON SHOKI COE

Chang, Jonah. *Shoki Coe: An Ecumenical Life in Context.* Geneva: WCC, 2012.

England, John C. "Shoki Coe (Ng Chiong Hui / Hwang Chang-hue) 1914–1988." In *Research Guide to Asian Christian Theologies*, vol. 3, 2.2.2.1, ISPCK. Claretian. Maryknoll, NY: Orbis, 2004.

Koyama, Kosuke. "Spiritual Mentors: Christ's Homelessness." *Christian Century*, July 14–21, 1993, 702–3.

Poon, Michael Nai-Chiu, ed. *Shoki Coe: Christian Mission and Test of*

Discipleship. The Princeton Lectures 1970. Singapore: Trinity Theological College, 2012.

Shenk, Wilbert R. "Contextual Theology: The Last Frontier." In The Changing Face of Christianity, edited by Lamin Sanneh and Joel A. Carpenter. Oxford: Oxford University Press, 2015.

Wheeler, Ray. "The Legacy of Shoki Coe." *International Bulletin of Missionary Research*. April 2002.

CONTRIBUTORS

Wesley Ariarajah, Methodist minister from Sri Lanka, is currently professor emeritus of ecumenical theology at the Drew University School of Theology, New Jersey, United States, where he taught ecumenism and interfaith
relations for seventeen years. Before joining Drew, he served the World
Council of Churches for sixteen years, first as the director of the Interfaith
Dialogue Program and later as the deputy general secretary of the council.

Stephen B. Bevans, a member of the Divine Word Missionaries, is Louis
J. Luzbetak, SVD, Professor of Gospel and Culture at Catholic Theological
Union in Chicago and editor of *Mission Studies*. Bevans served as a missionary
to the Philippines until 1981. Among the various books he has authored
are *Models of Contextual Theology* and *An Introduction to Theology in Global
Perspective*.

Dhyanchand Carr, an ordained minister of the Church of South India, was
a professor of New Testament Studies and principal of the Tamilnadu Theological Seminary, Madurai, India. While serving the Christian Conference of
Asia as its secretary for Mission and Evangelism, Carr conducted workshops
on "Reading the Bible with New Eyes" in sixteen Asian countries. His latest
book is also titled *Reading the Bible with New Eyes*.

Chen Nan-Jou is former professor of the Tainan Theological College and
Seminary, and Yu-Shan Theological College and Seminary. He is the author
of several books, including *A Testament to Taiwan Homeland Theology*.

Edmund Kee-Fook Chia is originally from Malaysia and served from 1996
to 2004 as executive secretary of ecumenical and interreligious affairs for the
Federation of Asian Bishops' Conferences. He then joined the faculty of the
Catholic Theological Union in Chicago and taught there for seven years.
Since 2011, he has been teaching at the Australian Catholic University.

Enrique Dussel, a professor in the Department of Philosophy in the Metropolitan Autonomous University (UAM), Campus Iztapalapa in Mexico City,
is a renowned philosopher, historian, and theologian. Dussel is the founder
of the Movement of Latin American Liberation Philosophy. He is the author
of more than forty books in different languages, including *A History of the
Church in Latin America: Colonialism to Liberation*, and *Philosophy of Liberation*.

John C. England has worked ecumenically for theological education and action in many Asia-Pacific networks and countries since 1969. He was on the staff of the East Asia Christian Conference/Christian Conference of Asia, then at the Tao Fong Shan Ecumenical Centre, Hong Kong, and later was associate dean of the Programme for Theologies and Culture in Asia (PTCA). More recently he has been the chief editor/writer for the *Research Guide to Asian Christian Theologies.*

Dwight N. Hopkins is Alexander Campbell Professor of Theology at the Divinity School of the University of Chicago, United States, and an ordained American Baptist minister. Hopkins is well known as a constructive theologian working in the areas of contemporary models of theology, various forms of liberation theologies, and East-West dialogues. His latest works include *Teaching Global Theologies*, *The Cambridge Companion to Black Theology*, and *Being Human: Race, Culture, and Religion.*

Po Ho Huang is vice president and professor of theology at Chang Jung Christian University, Taiwan. He is a member of the editorial board of *Concilium* and *Theologies and Cultures*. His numerous works include *Embracing the Household of God, Mission from the Underside*, and *From Galilee to Tainan.*

Diego Irarrázaval, a Catholic priest and member of the Congregation of Holy Cross, is a resource person in grassroots, theological, and pastoral programs in Peru and other places in Latin America. He is a former president of the Ecumenical Association of Third World Theologians (EATWOT) and now teaches at the Faculty of Religious Sciences and Philosophy, Universidad Católica Silva Henriquez, Chile.

Dale T. Irvin is president and professor of world Christianity at New York Theological Seminary, New York City. He is a founding editor of *The Journal of World Christianity*, serves on the editorial board of *The Living Pulpit*, and is coeditor of the Palgrave Macmillan series Christianities of the World. He is the author of several books, including *History of the World Christian Movement.*

Michael Jagessar, a member of the Caribbean diaspora who embodies multiple identities, is secretary for Intercultural Ministries, United Reformed Church, United Kingdom. He has taught ecumenical theology, interfaith studies, black and contextual theologies, and currently writes on intercultural theology and postcolonial themes.

Veli-Matti Kärkkäinen, a Finnish theologian, is professor of systematic theology at Fuller Theological Seminary, California, United States. An ordained Lutheran minister (Evangelical Lutheran Church in America), he is also an expert on Pentecostal-Charismatic theologies. Kärkkäinen has authored, among others, a five-volume systematic theology series titled *A Constructive Christian Theology for the Pluralistic World.*

Kwok Pui-lan is distinguished visiting professor of theology at Candler School of Theology, Emory University, in Atlanta, Georgia, United States, and a former president of the American Academy of Religion. She is a pioneer in Asian feminist theology and postcolonial theology. She is the author or editor of twenty books in Chinese and English, including *Postcolonial Imagination and Feminist Theology*, *Introduction to Asian Feminist Theology*, and *Discovering the Bible in the Non-Biblical World*.

Archie Chi Chung Lee is professor of Hebrew Bible at Shandong University, China. He specializes in cross-textual hermeneutics, especially Chinese text and the postexilic biblical tradition, and is the author of several books, including *A Commentary on the Book of Koheleth*, and *Interpretation of the Megilloth*.

Wati Longchar, from Nagaland in India, is a professor of theology and culture at Yushan Theological College and Seminary in Hualien, Taiwan, and is the dean of the Program for Theology and Cultures in Asia (PTCA). Longchar is known for his commitment to and contribution in the development of indigenous theology in Asia.

Jesse Mugambi is a professor of philosophy and religious studies at the University of Nairobi, with professional training in education and philosophy of religion. Mugambi has made a significant contribution to the discussion of the relationship between Christianity and the African heritage and is known for his new initiatives in third world theologies, *Theologies of Reconstruction*.

Augustine Chingwala Musopole, a native of Malawi, is former professor of philosophy and religion at Chang Jung Christian University, Tainan, Taiwan. Musopole has made significant contributions in articulating *Ubuntu Theology*.

Anh Q. Tran, SJ, is assistant professor of historical and systematic theology at Santa Clara Jesuit School of Theology, Berkeley, California, United States. His research interests include world Christianity, religious pluralism, intercultural dialogue, Asian spirituality and theology, and Christian missions in Asia. His recent publications include *Gods, Heroes, and Ancestors* and *World Christianity: Perspectives and Insights*.

Ben Wei was the general secretary, Formosan Christians for Self-Determination. He also served as the secretary general of Taiwan Nation Building Party and was a part-time lecturer (Constitution, Japanese) at Ming-chi Institute of Technology, Taiwan.

Yeow Choo Lak, a former dean of Trinity Theological College, Singapore, was the executive director of the Association for Theological Education in South East Asia. He has also served as dean of the South East Asia Graduate Theological School and as coeditor of *The Asia Journal of Theology*.

Index

Abrecht, Paul, 97
Adorno, Theodor, 56
African evangelical theology, 259
All Africa Conference of Churches, 89, 241
Ambedkar, B. R., 196n2, 204, 207
Amoris Laetitia, 135, 136
Apel, Karl-Otto, 57
Ariarajah, Wesley, 82, 110n4, 119–21
Asian feminist theology, 71
Azariah, V. S., 118

Balasuriya, Tissa, 62, 82, 154n27
Bandung Conference, 65, 149n17
Barrett, David, 87
Barth, Karl, 46n42, 98, 99, 268, 298, 339, 243, 344; Christomonism, 98
Benedict XVI, 126
Beozzo, Jose Oscar, 215
Berlin Conference on Colonial Questions, 87
Berquist, Jim, 95
Bevans, Stephen, 38, 39, 44, 126n3, 127n5, 139n30, 145
Bhabha, Homi K., 78, 187, 188n16
Bishop's Institutes for Interreligious

Affairs (BIRA), 150n18, 154, 155, 157
black theology, 234–37, 240–44, 250, 255, 256, 262, 279, 287n9
Bonhoeffer, Dietrich, 15, 343
Bosch, David, 163n11
Boulaga, F. Eboussi, 61, 256
Brent, Charles, 113, 114
Byung Mu, Ahn, 68

capitalism, 47, 56, 58, 62, 280
Chala Catherine, 224
chameleon theology, 102
Chang, Jonah, 21n1, 35n1, 95n1, 266n2–n3
Chao, T. C., 5
Cheng Ching-Yi, 118
Cheng, Patrick S., 78
Chidester, David, 79
Chi-Ho, Yun, 118
Chou, Ivy, 95
Christendom, 24, 49–56, 60, 62, 63, 83, 112, 146, 147, 159n50, 161, 162n4, 162n8, 176, 261, 330; colonial, 51, 54, 63; cult of, 50; God of, 49; imperial, 53; post-Christendom, 74, 80; Protestant, 58
Church Missionary Society, 187